KU-382-821

OXFORD UNIVERSITY
ON MONT BLANC

OXFORD UNIVERSITY ON MONT BLANC

THE LIFE OF THE CHALET DES ANGLAIS

STEPHEN GOLDING

PROFILE
EDITIONS

First published in Great Britain in 2022 by
Profile Editions,
an imprint of Profile Books Ltd
29 Cloth Fair
London
ECIA 7JQ
www.profileeditions.com

Copyright © Stephen Golding, 2022

1 3 5 7 9 10 8 6 4 2

Typeset in Dante by MacGuru Ltd
Printed and bound in Great Britain by
Clays Ltd, Elcograf S.p.A.

The moral right of the author has been asserted.

All rights reserved. Without limiting the rights under copyright reserved above,
no part of this publication may be reproduced, stored or introduced into a
retrieval system, or transmitted, in any form or by any means (electronic,
mechanical, photocopying, recording or otherwise), without the prior written
permission of both the copyright owner and the publisher of this book.

A CIP catalogue record for this book is available from the British Library.

ISBN 978 1 80081 217 8

LONDON BOROUGH OF RICHMOND UPON THAMES	
90710 000 520 576	
Askews & Holts	12-Jul-2022
378.425 GOL	
RTTE	

For my mother, Joyce, my daughters Marina and Claire and sons-in-law Charles and Ashley, who all know the Chalet.

CONTENTS

ACKNOWLEDGEMENTS

A history of a venture like the Chalet des Anglais is not achieved without the help of many. I first have to thank those who have shared their memories and allowed me to see the Chalet through their eyes. They are listed in Appendix 4 and I apologise for any inadvertent omission.

I am grateful to the archivists of three colleges for their professional support: Anna Sander (Balliol College), Jennifer Thorp (New College) and Robin Darwall-Smith (University College), and also to the staff of the Development offices of these three colleges. Others across the University who have helped are Charlotte Berry (Magdalen College), Tilly Burn (Oxford University Archives), Caroline Dalton (New College), Bethany Hamblen (Balliol College), Clare Hopkins (Trinity College), Lindsay McCormack (Lincoln College), Julian Reid (Corpus Christi College), Tessa Shaw (The Queen's College) and Ben Taylor (Magdalen College).

I record my gratitude for the use of their archives to the Master and Fellows of Balliol College, the Warden and Scholars of New College and the Master and Fellows of University College. Extracts from the Macmillan archive in the Bodleian Library are used with the kind permission of the Trustees of the Harold Macmillan Book Trust. The quotation from *A Letter of Resignation* by Hugh Whitemore is reproduced with the permission of Amber Lane Press; the quotation from *Everest: Reflections from the Top*, published by Rider, is reproduced with the permission of the Random House Group and the quotation from *Summoned by Bells* by John Betjeman, published by John Murray, copyright John Betjeman 1960, 1966, is reproduced with the permission of Hodder and Stoughton Limited through PLSclear.

Information from outside Oxford came from Ros Anderson, Dr Jeremy Burchardt (Reading University), Annick Duffoug, Francine Duffoug, Graham Hoyland, Eléonore Rinaldi Lecciso (Archives de la

Commune de Montreux), Gianluca Loschi (Gertrude Bell Archive), Sarah Lowry, Fabrice Martin, Sir Richard Mynors, Sarah Scrope (Chilton Estate), Pascale Simond (Musée de Montreux), Michael and Susan Stillwell, and especially from our friends on the Prarion, Simone Orset-Hottegindre and her son Yves Hottegindre, and the Boucher family: Hugues, the late Nelleriek, Philippe, Lila, Ernst and Frank. Amanda Brookfield, Lexie Elliott and Reggie Oliver were generous in sharing the background to their writing.

I owe a great deal for encouragement and advice from past and present leaders of Chalet parties: Prof Jonathan Barnes, Rev David Burgess, Dr Mark Byford, Rev Christopher Dent, Dr Keith Dorrington, Rev Douglas Dupree, Dr Edward Forman, Prof Jim Hankinson, Sir Anthony and Lady Kenny, Rev Bruce Kinsey, Sir Jeremy Lever, the late Harvey McGregor, QC, Prof Iain McLean, Dr Jack Matthews, Prof Dominic O'Brien, Dr William Poole, Prof Alan Ryan, Dr Ben Smith, Dr Tom Smith, Prof Adam Swift, the late Rev Bill Sykes, Dr Nicola Trott, Rev Stephen Tucker and Dr Allen Warren.

I am indebted to two previous Masters of University College, Lord Butler and Sir Ivor Crewe, for their personal encouragement. Lord Butler and his wife Jill were both chaletites in their undergraduate days and returned in parties I led and I later had the privilege of introducing Sir Ivor to the Chalet. I am especially grateful to Drs Leslie Mitchell and Allen Warren for the guidance of the professional historian, and to Peter Gillman for that of the professional writer. All three read and commented on the manuscript, as did Keith Dorrington, Sir David Edward and the Rev Stephen Tucker. This book is the better for all of them. I am grateful to Peter Jones and his team at Profile Editions for their expertise in turning this book into a reality.

I have a particular debt to my friend and colleague Keith Dorrington for having first invited me to the Chalet, for sharing the leadership of our parties and for stimulating me to write this book. During its composition he has supplied warm encouragement, wise counsel and stringent criticism as the occasion demanded. If it is possible for a book to have a godparent, this one's is undoubtedly Keith.

Memories of the Chalet are many, individual and usually strongly held. If readers fail to find a fondly remembered event in this book I hope that I have at least provided a context which enhances their memories. Any errors are of course mine alone.

A JOURNEY

THE YEAR IS 1910 and you, a student at the University of Oxford, find yourself at the top of the steps from the dusty and noisy platforms of the Gare de Lyon in Paris, looking uncertainly into the Buffet. Open less than a decade but already famous, the Buffet reflects a Belle Époque glow of gold leaf, crystal chandeliers and seemingly the paintings of an entire generation of French landscape artists. Is this gilded, muralled place really for you, weary as you are and somewhat stained from the steam train and ferry from London and then the long walk across Paris in the August heat? However, you have been told that a good dinner is the best way to prepare yourself for the overnight train journey and, as this is your first experience of European travel, you are anxious to prove yourself equal to the challenge. After all, some of your precious French francs have been saved by walking across the city from the Gare du Nord. So, with a deep breath and shoulders squared, you push open the glass doors and enter. The *maître d'*, no doubt observing your crumpled appearance but perhaps indulgent to youth, finds you a secluded table in a corner of the end room. There is something incongruous, you feel, about having a luggage rack above the seat but this is still a railway buffet, for all its grandeur. Only after glancing up do you realise that Eugène Burnand's painting of your destination, Mont Blanc, looks down on you from its gilded surround, appearing in its superiority both to encourage your aspirations and at the same time mock their inadequacy.

For the purpose of this story you are likely in 1910 to be a young man of around twenty years, from a comfortable background, possessed of some intelligence, certainly well read, and very probably of more than average good looks. There is excitement in your journey; you are after all abroad alone and treading in the steps of those who took the Grand Tour. But there is also anxiety: you are very much aware that you have been selected to join one of the most exclusive activities available to students at the University of Oxford. Will you be equal to the select company on the mountain? Will the books that accompany you be thought well chosen? Not least, will you conduct yourself sufficiently well to avoid disapproval and win the cherished goal of future invitations?

A good dinner over and with a certain *bonhomie* – the wine was definitely welcome – you descend the steps once more into the infinitely less glamorous noise, steam and smuts of trains preparing for their journeys and the bustle of fellow travellers with their children and baggage. Finding your platform, you discover that the nearest carriages are already fully occupied, so it is a long walk along the train with your bag. Thankfully you find an empty compartment near the front where, with the aid of a few clothes pillowed into reasonable support, you are able to settle into a corner. It is not highly comfortable on the narrow bench, nor especially clean, but youth, dinner and the motion of the train soon combine to bring you the sleep of the innocent. France passes you unheeded in the night until the early morning stop at Ambérieu rouses you sufficiently to raise the blind a little and let the dawn light into the compartment. After this you doze intermittently as the train rattles on through hill country.

Just after six the train stops for twenty minutes at the tiny station of Bellegarde and you take the chance to stretch and get coffee. Roused by this, you realise as you journey on that now it is worth paying attention to your surroundings. As the long, low back of the Jura falls away behind you there are occasional glimpses of the city of Geneva through the trees. A little later your line skirts the base of Mont Salève, its nearly vertical faces striped with bands of dark pine clinging precipitously to the rock. Otherwise this is farming country, a wide rolling valley dotted with houses of sepia plaster beneath upper storeys of sun-blackened wood. Cattle wander calmly across the meadows and sometimes the clanking of their bells can be heard above the rattle of the carriages.

The train reaches Annemasse at eight and an hour's stop allows breakfast in the buffet, offering a chance to study the land ahead. The mountains remain distant but seem to rise in an extraordinary pattern. No foothills are seen but rock appears to rise vertically from the valley floor as if pushed up in a sudden upheaval of the earth's crust. For the first time snow-capped peaks are visible above the pine-clad ridges.

After breakfast the train travels on towards this wall of rock and ice, then takes a swing to the left around the isolated pyramid of Le Môle, entering a wide arena surrounded by the high walls. The train seems destined to chug straight into the rock but at the last moment a swerve to the right takes it through a short tunnel to emerge in a narrow river gorge. Here the walls crowd in, impossibly steep and dotted with vertical waterfalls. The track is joined in the gorge by a river of curiously opalescent silver-grey, its colour reflecting minerals brought down from the hills. After half an hour within these rock walls the gorge expands into a rolling valley and at last you can identify the clean glacial summit of Mont Blanc itself, towering over the other peaks. The unimposing halt at Sallanches, a facility so primitive it would be otherwise unwelcome, allows more time to absorb the scene.

As you journey on Mont Blanc appears to retreat from you as the closer peaks come to dominate the view. The train eventually comes to a halt and you alight at the terminus of Le Fayet beneath a hill of dark pinewood which now obscures the calm white mass of the mountain. The morning is hot and although this is not the end of travelling it is good to be rid of your compartment and the constant steam and smuts. Before taking coffee at the Hôtel Terminus Mont Blanc you ensure that the porter knows to take your bag across the square to the bureau of the Tramway du Mont Blanc (TMB).

The TMB rack railway has been open barely a year and spares you the bone-shaking ordeal of a mountain mule cart. It takes you past a few houses before gathering speed and turning upward into woodland on the side of the hill. The journey is pleasantly cool and it is only a short ride to the Alpine town of Saint-Gervais-les-Bains, clinging to the steep side of a river valley, but it offers new sights; a break in the trees allows a view across the valley to an imposing skyline of cliffs, the Aravis. These were behind you as you travelled into Le Fayet. After getting down at the TMB halt in Saint Gervais a few minutes' walk brings you to the Hôtel du Mont Blanc in the town centre. Here, having been so advised, you are properly polite and attentive to M. Chambel, the *propriétaire*, over a light lunch. He provides a room for you to change into walking clothes and arranges to send your bag up later by mule. This leaves you unencumbered to start the long walk up the hill of the Prarion behind the town.

As a first-time visitor you would usually be met by your host but a regretful message warned you that this might be unlikely and no one was waiting at the Hôtel. No matter: you have been given clear instructions and a good hand-drawn map. The first instruction is to call into the Post Office to collect letters for the group already on the mountain. Then, behind the Post Office a steep flight of stone steps takes you rapidly upwards past an imposing medieval tower and climbs through the houses of the town until the slope steepens and the path starts to zig-zag up the side of the hill. After half an hour you have climbed high enough to look back over the wide plain around Le Fayet, backed by the Aravis ridge. In the foreground a long, wooded slope runs upwards and to the left to the exposed cone of Mont Joly. To the north the skyline is dominated by a huge mass of rock like a giant face turned to the sky, the Aiguille de Varens.

The path continues to climb between small chalets and tiny fields of vegetables with occasional cows with their clanking bells. It is not cool in the afternoon sun on these west-facing slopes and you remove your jacket and loosen your clothes. Refreshment appears after an hour's walking when a small stream crosses the path, after which the chalets begin to thin out and you enter thick pinewood. At first it is welcome to exchange the exposed Alpine meadow for the shade, only to discover how sultry the air is under the trees. You continue to trudge upwards in the afternoon stillness, the sweat of effort making you the target for a particularly persistent breed of fly that lives hereabout. This and the frequent need to check the track against your map – this is not an environment in which you want to get lost – begin to make the outing wearying.

After another hour's trudge you find a small clearing around the farmstead of Le Plancert. Here the farmer's wife offers a jug of cool milk, the accompanying smile suggesting she knows well where you are from and where you are bound. The milk is welcome but fatigue and irritation with the height you have climbed make you less appreciative of the welcome than you should be. Instead you sit quietly while you drink the milk. The clearing allows you once more to look across the valley to where, from this height, the summit of Mont Joly has begun to look more like a sister peak. As you start upwards again you encounter the crossing you were warned to look for and take the turning which rises steeply to your left and enters the shade of the trees again to continue the upward trudge.

At last, when you have become convinced that this walk is unending, your ears pick up what they have been straining to hear, the sound of rapidly running water. A few moments later you take a turning on the left, knowing that this signals the end of your climb.

The path now offers a welcome level stretch and fords a busy stream. Another short rise brings you to a second stream and a wooden gate of unexpectedly English character, and now through the trees above you can see the gable end of a mountain chalet. Going through the gate and climbing out of the trees, you find yourself in a clearing behind the building. The back of the house is quiet as you approach and you walk around the side to where, on a wide lawn, a dozen people are sitting reading. There, '*M. le Patron*', slim and dapper, rises from his wicker chair and welcomes you with a patrician smile: Francis Fortescue Urquhart, history don of Balliol College, Oxford, and known universally as 'Sligger'.

¤

In *Brideshead Revisited* Evelyn Waugh allowed himself possibly the most benign comment he ever made in the direction of Francis Urquhart. As we shall see, Waugh had little regard for Urquhart and his activities in the French Alps. He could not, however, bring himself to ignore them. In *Brideshead Revisited* the young Charles Ryder, who has lived well and spent lavishly during his first year at Oxford, is forced to throw himself on the hospitality of his father in London for the summer vacation. The elder Ryder, more than a little disenchanted with this intrusion into his ordered routine, dominates the dinner conversation by describing the alternatives his son could have chosen. He ends petulantly with: 'In my day we used to go on what were called reading parties, always in mountainous areas. Why? Why … should Alpine scenery be thought conducive to study?'[1]

Evelyn Waugh put his finger on the key questions relating to the Alpine reading parties. Why was the practice so common in the Victorian and Edwardian eras? Why did privileged young men living a comfortable life in colleges respond so readily to spending their vacation in a remote environment? Why is it that for many this experience came to be the dominant memory of their university life? And, for the purpose of this book, how is it that the Chalet des Anglais reading parties have persisted into modern university life as a survivor of this practice, and what does this say about life in a collegiate university like Oxford?

Francis Urquhart was still an undergraduate at Balliol College when in 1891 he opened his family home on the slopes of Mont Blanc to friends at college. Reading parties were already well known to him; the practice was widespread in Victorian times and he had attended reading parties in Britain since his arrival at Balliol. These provided the model for his summer parties but he also brought to them experience of the French Alps that had been one of the formative elements of his childhood. Family circumstances had dictated that he was brought up in the Alps and this had given him a strong appreciation of French country life. It was natural to want friends to share this.

There was a paradox in Urquhart's approach, in that while he maintained that one of the functions of the Chalet was to get people away from the rarefied intellectual atmosphere of Oxford, his parties created a peculiarly intense extension of that same university life. Students in the Oxford colleges of his time lived a highly structured existence and life at the Chalet reflected this, so that the summer reading parties on Mont Blanc and the networking that flowed from them ultimately became Sligger's major achievement. When he died in 1934 he made what he thought was sound provision for the parties to continue. In the event, in the eight decades since his death, the Chalet des Anglais parties have survived through contingencies he could not have foreseen but because of commitment and determination of which he could only have approved. In its time the Chalet has been through two world wars, destruction by fire, the collapse of Sligger's plans for continuity, neglect of the fabric and frequent risk of insolvency. In the meantime all the Edwardian reading parties have disappeared, leaving the Chalet des Anglais an almost unique opportunity for students at Oxford.

This story deserves to be told for greater reason than its survival over more than 120 years. The attractions of life at the Chalet are evident from the writings of past members of the parties and from the testimony of those still living. The impact upon them was remarkable and what they have to say reveals how significant it was to their lives. An eccentric combination of primitive living conditions, healthy enjoyment of the mountains and a serious approach to study was a formative experience; for those lucky enough to be invited it often stands out from the rest of their time at Oxford. Frequently this was not due to differences from life in college but because it more eloquently expressed the nature of their academic life. In this way it reflects the vision of the University itself, which sees scholarship as integral to a way of life.

In 1936, two years after Urquhart's death, his colleague Cyril Bailey published a memoir of Sligger's life. Naturally the reading parties and life at the Chalet were prominent in his account. However, Bailey's objective was to pay tribute to a much-loved colleague; his approach was laudatory and uncritical. More than eighty years later it is possible for us to take a more considered view of the reading parties and their significance.

The Chalet parties have been inevitably linked to the changing social circumstances during twelve decades. This relates particularly to the University of Oxford but also to the world of education more generally. For this reason, enquiry into their history leads inexorably to consideration of educational strategies, the rationale of collegiate universities, relationships between environment and study and, in the early years at least, issues such as male bonding and the University's approach to a predominantly male society.

Collegiate universities like Oxford have evolved a model of close relationship between student and tutor through the medium of teaching in small groups or individual tutorials. In this system learning is seen as a shared exercise between tutor and student. In college life, the phrase *in loco parentis* is more than a platitude; the style of teaching implies a degree of intimacy between tutor and student that in Sligger's time was similar to family life. Sligger himself attached particular value to a close relationship with his students. At Balliol his ability to mix with students on their own level became well known, largely through the medium of his evening salons, but it was at the Chalet where his approach expressed itself most intensely. Despite all the changes that university life has undergone in the twentieth century, it remains the case that the reading parties provide a detailed study of how student–teacher relationships can operate.

While life in an Oxford college today may retain aspects of an underlying ethos which Sligger would have recognised, the character of that life has necessarily changed during the decades of the Chalet's existence. Not least among the stimulants to change has been the effect of two world wars and the social reform that followed. In the Edwardian period Oxford students had a life defined by their class and supported by servants; today's undergraduates are intellectually free social networkers with wider aspirations but usually less money.

Edwardian college society was almost exclusively male and arguably repressed; today's students are emotionally and sexually liberated. Admission to the University of Sligger's time was influenced by class or family connections; now the principle of equality is rigorously applied, ensuring that the college community embraces a wide social spectrum.

This collegiate approach to learning is perceived to be under threat on grounds of exclusivity. Modern educational policies, which put an emphasis on output and measurables, call into question a form of teaching that appears expensive and time-consuming. It may also be thought too permissive in allowing the student a driving role – by implication possibly inefficient – in their own educational development. A further threat is a rising level of student debt which militates against expensive 'extras' such as foreign travel. These are arguments in which issues of cost are easy to define, those of value considerably more difficult. When change occurs in social institutions there are losses as well as gains and it is advisable to recognise the elements which may be lost through being undervalued. The Chalet reading parties offer an insight into formative factors within college life and so contribute to this debate.

Accident has played a significant role in the story of the Chalet; several times since Urquhart's death there have been moments when it could easily have been lost. On each occasion there was on hand someone who shared Sligger's vision – or at least a version of it – and was prepared to take on the significant effort of maintaining the reading parties. These men and women were not necessarily mountaineers or given to outdoor pursuits and all were busy tutors, often with a family life and sometimes with significant commitments in public life. However, one thing was shared by all of them; they perceived the value of this irreplaceable institution. They showed considerable dedication to the cause of its survival, often in the face of daunting challenges.

Their success has been remarkable, and to a degree that might not be expected. In popular perception Oxford dons are not always associated with practical skills like dealing with failing water supplies, leaking roofs or invasion by wild animals, especially on a mountain several hours away from any modern services. Their commitment tells us something about being an academic charged with the intellectual development of the young. The history of these men and women and what they achieved is no less interesting than that of the reading parties themselves and no less deserving of being recorded. In this sense the life of the Chalet des Anglais bears out Benjamin Disraeli's assertion that biography is the most meaningful form of history.

This history, therefore, has two principal objectives. One is to tell the extraordinary story of the reading parties and the people involved in them. The other is to serve as an enquiry into the impact the Chalet has had on the lives of those who experienced it. Among the most interesting features of this unique institution are questions on the influence of the reading parties and why they survived through dramatic changes in society. These issues reflect on how a collegiate university like Oxford approaches its responsibility of influencing the lives of young people at a key stage in their development. Why, indeed, has Alpine scenery proved so conducive to study?

Chapter One

THE FRUITS OF ECCENTRICITY: THE URQUHART FAMILY AND THE ORIGIN OF THE CHALET

IN JULY 1865 Francis Urquhart's father David wrote to his friend and political supporter Major Robert Poore, from Saint Gervais:

> We are building, and expect to have completed a fortnight hence, a chalet on Mont Prarion, at about 6,000 feet above the sea, and reckon on being able to remain there till the middle or the end of October. This plan was adopted on the ground of health, and only after we had concluded from divers attempts at resuming work that neither of us was in a state to return to England even for next summer.
>
> This plan is based on the observations we both made during our excursion of last summer, on the effect produced upon us by high altitudes.
>
> Thus confirmed in my conclusions, I finally resolved to build the chalet on Mont Prarion. We had spent six months looking for a position which combined all the requisites, and this was not only the sole spot that did so, but the only one which afforded any. Having fixed on 6,000 feet as the level, we looked elsewhere in vain at that height for anything save abrupt peaks and bare exposures. We required a region around us available for short excursions, protection from storms and wind, some level ground, wood, water and a southern exposure. All this we have found combined in this one spot, whilst at the same time we are in immediate communication with the diligence road and telegraphic line to Geneva, and the intersection of the roads to Germany, Italy, and France, overlook the valleys of Chamonix and Sallanches, and in five minutes can reach the

crest, whence there is the grandest and closest view of Mont Blanc.[1]

¤

We owe the existence of the Chalet des Anglais to what can fairly be called an accident of personality. Judged even by the Victorian era of self-styled movers and shakers, Francis' father David Urquhart has to be regarded as eccentric. Initially a promising diplomat, somewhere around 1835 he crossed the narrow line between originality and maverick behaviour and became increasingly a *bête noire* of the British political establishment, with the result that he was obliged to live abroad. Had he been of more compliant personality he would have remained in England and the Chalet would not have been built.[2]

David Urquhart was born in 1805 to a younger son of the Clan Urquhart at the family estate of Braelangwell on the Black Isle peninsula in Scotland. His family could trace its origins back to the fourteenth century. In a pattern that was sadly to be repeated with his own youngest son, David lost his father when he was six and his schooling and the moulding of his personality came exclusively under his mother's direction. Margaret Urquhart decided that her son's education had to be predominantly European, firstly at the college of Sorèze in France, then in Geneva and finally under a private tutor in Spain before going to Oxford. The well-connected daughter of a wealthy Scottish merchant, she introduced David to leading thinkers of the day, including the philosopher Jeremy Bentham, and also to Herbert Taylor, Private Secretary to the Royal Family. These influences are clearly reflected in Urquhart's later concerns with international justice and social conditions, and also in the ability to use connections to further his initiatives.[2]

David's university education at St John's College, Oxford, was curtailed when in 1827 he volunteered for the British support in the Greek war of independence. Once involved, however, he started to swing progressively to the side of the Turks and began what was to be a lifelong habit of circulating his views in independent letters, pamphlets and reports. He obtained a place on the British delegation to Constantinople which was charged with settling the Greek boundary and, through the agency of Herbert Taylor, he attracted the personal support of King William IV. Reward came in 1833 when

Lord Palmerston, then Foreign Secretary, appointed him to investigate possibilities for trade in the Middle East. A distinguished career in British diplomacy seemed a foregone conclusion.[2]

Unfortunately, in a way that has afflicted some enthusiastic junior officials over the ages, Urquhart made the mistake of overestimating his own position. While in Constantinople he adopted Turkish dress, a gesture that was bound to raise hackles in the British diplomatic service. His Turkish sympathies extended to antagonism to the Russian threat to the Turkish Empire and he made his major political blunder in 1836: probably carried away by his own advice to the tribesmen of the Circassian coast that Britain would support them against the Russian embargo on Black Sea trading, he persuaded a British ship to flout the embargo. He was no doubt hoping that he could force the UK government to side with the Turks when the Russians seized the ship, as they duly did. The outcome was not at all what Urquhart had hoped for: faced with public outrage at home and Russian claims that the trader was spying, Lord Melbourne's administration was forced to accept the status quo. At the Foreign Office Palmerston was furious and dismissed Urquhart from the service, accusing him of breach of official secrecy.[2,3]

Although Urquhart maintained that he had acted with the covert knowledge of his ambassador and by implication of Palmerston himself, rightly or wrongly he was made to take the blame for this affair. Thereafter his life was marked by increasing antagonism to Foreign Office policy in the Middle East, and to Palmerston in particular, his feelings for whom developed to the level of paranoia. He became convinced that the Foreign Secretary and possibly the entire government were in the pay of the Czar and devoted considerable effort to investigating this. He had also become involved in the development of working men's clubs and now persuaded these to set up foreign affairs committees – pressure groups – to scour the speeches and writings of Palmerston for evidence of foreign bias.[4]

Although David Urquhart had consigned himself to a political wilderness, he was not without influence as the leading Turcophile writer of his time. He played a major role in stimulating the foreign affairs committees and his position among members was regarded as messianic. One supporter who helped with national coordination of these efforts was Major Robert Poore,[5] subsequently a veteran of the Crimea and his neighbour on the Prarion. Urquhart also continued to travel and to publish extensively, including founding new journals and producing several influential books on Middle Eastern and Islamic life. He became increasingly preoccupied with international law despite having in effect been sidelined when Britain and France eventually went to war with Russia in the Crimea in 1853.[2]

Urquhart's social conscience also extended to hygiene. He may have been the anonymous author of a pamphlet which appeared when he was in his twenties and which castigated lack of cleanliness in the English, and he now became a leading UK proponent of the Turkish bath. In his 1850 two-volume work *The Pillars of Hercules* he waxed long and lyrical (his writing was characteristically discursive) on the bath and the relationship between cleanliness and virtue, and between clean bodies and minds.[6] True to the Victorian manner, this writing contains an undercurrent of sensuality without becoming explicit. He also propounded the Turkish bath as a means of treating disease, to the extent that Sir John Fife, Senior Surgeon to the New-castle Infirmary, collated all Urquhart's writings on the subject and had them published in a separate volume.[7] The range of conditions for which benefits are claimed is quite remarkable.

Neatly combining two arenas of his activity, David Urquhart used the foreign affairs committees as a medium for promoting the Turkish bath throughout the UK and achieved remarkable progress.[8] The first Turkish bath in England was set up in 1857 by the foreign affairs committee in Manchester with Urquhart's support.[9] A dozen establishments had appeared in London by 1862 when The London and Provincial Turkish Bath Company opened the Hammam at 76 Jermyn Street, which became the leading bath of its day.[10] Urquhart was a director of the company but, no doubt characteristically, clashed with the other directors over entrance fees, which he saw as threatening the social equality he held to be inherent in the Turkish bath (the London Hammam survived until destroyed by bombing in 1941).[11]

In 1854, at the age of forty-nine, David Urquhart had married a woman twenty years his junior. Harriet Angelina Fortescue, of Dromiskin, County Louth, was the third child and only daughter of an Irish MP who came from a junior branch of the Earls Fortescue, created in 1798.[12] It was the perfect union for such a man; Harriet Urquhart was typical of the Victorian mould of wife who was completely and uncritically committed to her husband's aims. She not only supported him by providing a stable family home but joined in publishing his views, writing under the pseudonym 'Caritas', and she was to continue his work when he died after twenty-three years of marriage.[2] It is testimony to Harriet's skills in family diplomacy that she succeeded in combining loyalty to her brother Chichester Fortescue, a member of Palmerston's administration and subsequently 1st Baron Carlingford, with that to a husband whose activities were embarrassing to the British government.

The Urquharts moved into a house in Rickmansworth, converted to accommodate the essential Turkish bath.[13] David Urquhart junior was born in 1855, followed by William two years later. Unfortunately William died in a fit as an infant, having been taken into the Turkish bath to soothe teething pain. His death subjected the Urquharts to gossip about negligence, not just locally but from no less than Karl Marx, who was a contributor to one of David Urquhart's journals.[14] Public pressure made an inquest necessary but this concluded that the Urquharts had no case to answer.[15] With medical hindsight it seems likely that the child died from hyperthermia precipitated by the temperature of the hot room; infants have less ability to compensate for high ambient temperatures than do adults. The Urquharts' first daughter, Margaret (Maisie), was born in 1858 and then Harriet junior in 1862. By this time Harriet Urquhart may well have felt she had completed her family but in the event the surprise of a late pregnancy lay in store for her.

Both David and Harriet Urquhart spared themselves nothing in their crusades and travelling and both frequently suffered from nervous exhaustion or similar conditions. In 1864 they decided to live abroad, stating that this was for the sake of their health.[16] Then, as now, political activists who claimed retreat for personal reasons laid themselves open to the charge of employing a euphemism. Reading between the lines of their biographers' accounts and taking into account their attacks on the British establishment, the health in question may have been as much political as it was physical.

The Urquharts moved first to Geneva. David Urquhart knew it from his youth and the city offered a traditional focus for intellectual malcontents.[16] Later they were to divide their winter residence between Montreux and Nice but for the first year they restored their health by regular outings from the city, usually in the direction of the Alps. The mountains were sufficiently close to make excursions by horse or mule cart practicable and enjoyable. The family discovered the pleasures of mountain walking.[17]

This was the time when Alpine exploration was entering its golden age. The Alps had first been revealed to the educated world in 1741 when a young English aristocrat, William Windham of Felbrigg Hall, Norfolk, made an excursion into the secluded valley around Chamonix while studying in Geneva. Windham published his observations privately in a pamphlet that was the first to use the term 'alp' (originally meaning mountain meadow) to describe what he saw as high meadows of snow.[18] Mont Blanc was first climbed in 1786 and thereafter the pursuit of Alpinism rapidly took root. British pioneer climbers published their experiences, and poets such as Shelley and Wordsworth[19] and artists like Turner and Ruskin added to the level of interest.[20] Offered a new source of income, the Alpine villages expanded to accommodate visitors; farms became pensions, pensions became hotels and the hotels became luxury hotels. Roads were built, followed by railways. By 1863 Thomas Cook, then a fledgling travel company, was able to run its first tour to Geneva and Mont Blanc.[21]

Mountain walking provided David Urquhart with yet another bee in his bonnet. He became convinced that the brain was designed to work better at high altitude.[22] This opinion was based on changes he perceived in his own and his companions' endurance, quality of conversation and speed of thought. Studiously ignoring all other possible explanations he resolved to build a summer home around 6,000 feet above sea level, his observations having suggested that this was the level at which benefit began. David Urquhart may have been on dubious ground physiologically but, in fairness, others have since found the Chalet highly conducive to thought. I myself, in common with others, feel that some of my best writing has taken place at the Chalet; there is of course a variety of possible reasons, not least isolation from the distractions of the modern world.

In 1860 the prominent London lawyer and pioneer Alpinist Alfred Wills had published an account of building his own mountain chalet, *Nid d'Aigle* (The Eagle's Nest), in the romantic rocky amphitheatre of the Cirque des Fonds, high above the Alpine village of Sixt.[23] It is likely David Urquhart will have known the book and he may also have known Wills from his legal work. In the same period John Ruskin, whose writing had contributed to growing interest in the Alps, tried to buy a plot of land above Bonneville in order to build a chalet. However, Ruskin's plans fell foul of the local Commune: sceptical that anyone could simply be interested in mountain life, the dignitaries of Bonneville became convinced he must have found something valuable such as gold and blocked his purchase.[24] David Urquhart was subsequently to trumpet that he had succeeded where Ruskin had failed.[25]

It has to be granted to David Urquhart that he successfully identified one of the few sites suitable for his purpose in the two wooded hills above the town of Saint Gervais. On the Prarion he located a small plateau just where the woodland was beginning to thin out at an altitude of 1,685 metres (5,530 feet). Water was provided by small streams draining the water meadow beneath the summit of the Prarion, a mule track to Saint Gervais passed close by, and the plateau had an imposing western outlook across the valley of the Bon Nant river to the cliffs of the Aravis range in the west and the double peak of the Aiguille de Varens to the north. At the col of the Prarion above the Chalet the view opens out into the magnificent western prospect of Mont Blanc, though the summit itself is hidden from view this close to the mountain. David Urquhart boasted that this spectacle could be attained in five minutes. Modern visitors find this claim to be hyperbole; the Chalet is beautifully placed but the view of the massif has to be earned by a stiff uphill walk, an ascent of 200 metres.

No plans of the original Chalet have survived but its design can be deduced from photographs and letters (Fig. 1). It was a two-storey structure, strengthened by concrete seatings and spine walls of stone on the ground floor but otherwise composed of wood, including a shingle roof. On the left of the ground floor at the front a sizeable salon was entered through the inevitable Turkish bath, behind which was the kitchen. Behind the salon was a room which served variously as dining room or overflow bedroom. Upstairs four simple bedrooms with dormer windows were built into the roof. Later a wooden lean-to extension was added at the rear, housing two further bedrooms, the kitchen was extended in a similar way, and a single-storey dining room, accessed through the front porch, was added on the right, providing a wide balcony for the front bedroom. The extensions were heated by stoves which vented through the roof; this was subsequently to prove significant to the Chalet's story.

The Chalet was fronted by an extensive and well-groomed lawn, at the far end of which a small stream came over a rocky waterfall and flowed away downhill. A spring behind the kitchen gave the family their main water supply. At the rear was a wooden shed which may have been put up for the use of the builders but served variously as a woodstore or as a stable when mules were used for transport. To the east the ground rose sharply above the Chalet to a line of projecting rocks. This land was kept clear and a pathway ran around the upper boundary beneath the rocks. To the west, where the ground fell away, David Urquhart laid out terraces where he grew fruit and vegetables, including redcurrants, strawberries and raspberries, delighted that he succeeded with these despite the locals having told him confidently he would not.[26] In time the Chalet became almost self-sufficient in vegetables.[27]

An endearing piece of Chalet folklore is that Harriet Urquhart was responsible for planting the lupins which now flourish around the Chalet and over the surrounding hillsides.[28] It is certainly true that this side of the mountain has an unusually high density of these plants but *Lupinus polyphyllus*, introduced to Europe from North America, is common in the Alps. However, the extraordinary concentration around the Chalet may indicate that Harriet gave nature a helping hand. In the same way, the British visitor today may feel that the high abundance of cow parsley, *Anthriscus sylvestris*, and the rosebay willowherb, *Chamerion angustifolium*, give the Chalet's surroundings a homely English touch but in fact both are to be found generally in Savoie.

David and Harriet gave their new home the title of 'Chalet des Mélèzes', after the larches which grew all round. This wood is excellent building material with the ability to withstand the extremes of Alpine summers and winters. Renovations in recent years have confirmed that mélèze timbers can last over a century without special treatment. For this reason the trees are protected today and their harvesting is controlled by the Commune.

It was French local custom which came in time to name the building 'Chalet des Anglais' after its inhabitants. There are several examples of this in the area. Many years later Francis Urquhart was to buy another chalet at Mont Forchet, an hour's walk away. Today both this and Alfred Wills' 'Eagle's Nest' continue to be known by their neighbours as 'Chalet des Anglais'.

A couple of years after moving into the Chalet David Urquhart designed and built another, this time for his friend Major Robert Poore. They had met in 1862 when Robert Poore visited the Hammam; Poore became a director of the Hammam and one of

Urquhart's strongest supporters in the foreign affairs committees.[29] The Poore Chalet (Fig. 5) was built 200 yards away, between his own chalet and the track to Saint Gervais, and took the name of 'Chalet du Rocher' from the rocks projecting from the ground around it. The accommodation in this chalet was rather more extensive than in David Urquhart's, running to eight bedrooms in addition to the two reception rooms. The original Chalet du Rocher survives today and retains the elements of Middle Eastern design which David Urquhart incorporated, including Turkish arcading throughout the wood panelling and of course the Turkish bath. Robert Poore and his family used the Chalet du Rocher frequently during the rest of David Urquhart's life and until 1888, when the barrister and liberal politician John Wynford Philipps (subsequently 1st Baron St Davids of Roch) acquired it as a wedding present for his wife, the heiress Leonora Gerstenberg.[30,31]

Walkers who today consult the *Institut Géographique National* map of this area may find it confusing that the Chalet du Rocher bears the title 'Chalet des Anglais' and the Chalet des Anglais that of 'les Mélèzes'.[32] Given that one is a title created by local parlance only, it is perhaps unwise to expect too much accuracy in these small matters, even though the true Chalet des Anglais remains well known as such among the local inhabitants.

The Urquharts fell into an annual pattern of spending as much of the year at the Chalet as the weather would allow. It is indicative of the interest that David Urquhart's political views still attracted that the Chalet became a focus for visits from supporters. Contemporary accounts record the appearance of stout clerics emerging breathless and perspiring from the wood, to the great amusement of the children.[26] David Urquhart was also a demanding host: he required all his visitors to undergo a Turkish bath before entering the Chalet and the intensity with which he expounded his convictions could be wearing. An anecdote of the time tells of one visitor meeting a colleague in the town who remarked on their dejected appearance: were they ill? 'No,' came the resigned reply, 'I have visited M. Urquhart.'[26]

The Urquharts were accustomed to having domestic servants and obtained a cook and maids from the local town of Saint Gervais. Some of these slept in the Chalet and others travelled up by mule each day. There was also a need for maintenance, transport and help with the garden. The towns of Saint Gervais and Chamonix had grown steadily as interest in Alpinism had increased and both ran offices of mountain guides who found working for chalet owners a good way of supplementing their income. David Urquhart acquired the support of such a mountain guide, Jean-François Martin of Saint Gervais,[33] and later this work was taken over by his son Anselme.[34] Such an arrangement had the dual benefit that when the family needed a guide for an extended walk there was someone ready at hand. These *gardiens* also provided transport for supplies and luggage by mules and would act as a local agent for the family when away, dealing with bills and other business. Over the years the *gardiens'* families maintained their relationships with these employers, their daughters becoming cooks and maids for the Chalet.

Six years after the birth of her last daughter Harriet found herself pregnant again. She stayed at the Chalet as long as was practicable but transferred to Geneva just a few weeks before her last son was born on 1 September 1868. In a tribute to her brother he was named Francis, this being the name of Chichester Fortescue's wife. This may have contributed to the particularly close relationship that existed between nephew and uncle, which was later to result in Francis adopting the middle name of Fortescue at Lord Carlingford's request. This relationship was also to produce a benefit that would change Francis' life for ever.

Harriet, in the style typical of an upper-class Victorian wife, was eager to return to the Chalet as soon as possible to carry on supporting her husband and she was clearly not prepared to be encumbered by breast-feeding. A wet nurse being out of the question due to the isolation of the Chalet, the baby was fed on cow's milk, which in those circumstances would have been unpasteurised and carry the risk of tuberculosis.[35] In the event, Francis survived the risk and grew into an active and energetic child, albeit always slight in stature.

David Urquhart's health in the face of his exertions continued to cause concern and in late 1876 he was advised to spend the winter in Egypt.[36] Predictably, rather than regard this as the rest cure he needed, he saw opportunities of exploiting a base in the Middle East for further evangelising and started a tiring round of visits and meetings with Turkish officials. The six-month stay over, the family started the return journey but David grew weaker and could travel no further than Naples, where he died on 18 May 1877.[36] Harriet, who was then fifty-two, would spend the twelve years remaining to her in promoting her husband's causes, dividing her time between the Chalet and their home in Montreux.

Francis was eight when his father died, and he passed the rest of his childhood in the atmosphere of his mother's devotion to her late husband's work. Harriet now made a decision which would have a profound effect on Francis' life. In 1869 David Urquhart had drawn up a petition to Pope Pius IX in response to the Pope's initiatives on social reform.[37] In Rome the petition gained support from key members of the Curia and in February 1870 David was granted an audience with the Pope which resulted in a paper of twelve propositions for maintaining the balance of power between Europe and Russia.[38] David had come to feel that only the Catholic Church had the universal authority to promote his views on peace and on his death Harriet returned the compliment by being received into the Catholic Church.[39] Her conversion appears to have been total and wholehearted: she established in the Chalet a home altar dedicated to David's memory and had Mass said there for him weekly.[40]

It was natural that her youngest son would follow Harriet into her new faith. Whether or not Francis was then old enough to understand the significance, he became a staunch Catholic and this was to mould his character for the rest of his life. It was further strengthened by a resolutely Catholic education. His mother decided on Jesuit schooling and in 1879 he went to Hodder Place, the preparatory school of Stonyhurst College in Lancashire, and then to Beaumont College in Windsor two years later. At the age of eighteen he returned to Stonyhurst for preparation for entry to Oxford. While his letters home are marked by a boy's loneliness and homesickness they also reveal that he took his studies and religious environment very seriously and he was in fact to retain an affection for his schools which in later years translated into friendship with the masters and financial generosity. He was well regarded by his teachers and one of his Beaumont teachers noted an open-air healthiness about him and attributed this (possibly overlooking the effect of being brought up on a French mountainside) to the family history of the Hammam, saying that his appearance 'suggested the idea that he had just come out of a Turkish Bath – very fit'.[41]

The years leading up to Francis' admission to Balliol College in 1890 (Fig. 6) were a time of change for the family. His mother died in 1889 and his elder brother David became head of the family, inheriting the Chalet and becoming responsible for Francis' education.[42] His sister Maisie married William Tyrrell, a diplomat at the Foreign Office;[43] this was to give Francis one of his most enduring family connections. His mother's death also brought Francis closer to his uncle Chichester Fortescue, by then Lord Carlingford (Fig. 7). The relationship had always been close – Francis was his godson – but now the Carlingfords' house of Chewton Priory in the Mendips became a regular retreat for him (Fig. 8). The Benedictine foundation of Downside was close to Chewton and Francis developed friendships with the monks and became interested in their school. In later years Downside was to become a spiritual home where he made frequent visits and at one point he considered retiring into the community there.

It might be thought surprising that Francis could obtain admission to an Oxford college. In 1867 the Roman Catholic Church had imposed a ban on Catholics attending secular or mixed universities[44] and at Oxford graduation was dependent on subscription to the Thirty-Nine Articles of the Church of England. Despite growing support for the admission of Catholics, not least from John Henry Newman in Birmingham and in Oxford from the Newman Society, this was to remain the formal position until 1895, when the Vatican finally abolished the ban. However, gradual relaxation in admissions occurred in the years before the end of the ban and a small number of Catholics were regularly admitted, no doubt under special or individual conditions which the University felt able to accept.[45] In Francis' case the public position of his uncle, a Christ Church alumnus and by then a Privy Councillor, would have been more than enough.

Francis entered Balliol College with the intention of reading Classics but after a term he decided to change to History. This was a particularly apt choice in Balliol at the time. The college was still under the leadership of the legendary Benjamin Jowett, who had become Master in 1870. James Strachan-Davidson and Arthur Lionel Smith, both future Masters of Balliol and both strong supporters of Francis, were in charge of Roman and Modern History respectively. Under their guidance Francis established a reputation as one of the best undergraduates of his time and in 1894 he graduated with a first-class degree in the Modern History School (at this time in Oxford 'Modern' referred to everything after about AD 300). He enquired of Jowett the possibility of staying on in a Fellowship but received the brusque reply 'Out of the question'.[46] Despite this, however, when in the year following his graduation the number of undergraduates in History expanded and the tutorial staff were under pressure, Jowett's successor Edward Caird invited him back to Balliol to help out. This initially temporary position led in 1896 to a Fellowship, the first to be awarded to a Catholic in Oxford since the Reformation. Later Francis would become Junior Dean and then Dean. All this, however, was in the future. During his undergraduate days Francis established himself as a strong contributor to the life of the college, becoming engaged in rowing, tennis, hockey, the debating societies and – most significant of all – the syndrome of the vacation reading party.

By Francis' time the practice of using the vacation for reading parties had existed for around fifty years. At Balliol Jowett, then a tutor, had in the late 1840s hit upon the idea of sharing his summer vacation with a small number of selected undergraduates and as Master he continued parties until shortly before his death.[47] Jowett was under the impression that he was the founder of the practice but in fact by the time Jowett ran his first party Arthur Hugh Clough, his undergraduate contemporary at Balliol and by then a tutor at Oriel College, was publishing his pastoral poem *The Bothie of Toper-na-fuosich* which tells the story of a similar party in Scotland.[48]

These reading parties tended to follow a standard model. A site was chosen that was secluded from the pressures of town, usually somewhere coastal or otherwise scenic, where exercise and fresh air could be taken, most commonly in the form of strenuous walking. These were essentially residential house groups in which tutors and students combined in the atmosphere of a holiday. Study was pre-dominantly private reading, with the understanding that it would lead to discussion and debate. The parties also aspired to gracious living in which events like afternoon tea and dinner were social obligations. Most importantly, they constituted a forum in which the relationship between tutors and students could be closer than was possible in college.

In the Balliol of Francis' time several options were available. The Easter vacation offered the greatest possibilities, usually at a range of venues in Wales. There was also a regular fixture in Minehead at New Year in an institution known as Mr Babb's;[49] this was traditionally presided over by William Hardie, tutor in Classics. Francis regularly participated during both vacations and his fellow undergraduate and friend Frank Fletcher recorded that it was at one of the Minehead parties that

Francis was given his famous nickname of 'Sligger'.[50] This was said to be derived from 'sleek', reflecting his somewhat dapper appearance, and is an example of the university slang of the time, breakfast becoming 'brekker' and lectures 'lecker', of which 'rugger' remains in use.

Francis' own response was ambivalent. He regarded the title as somewhat 'unmusical' but accepted that it was conventional to use nicknames and took the view that this one could be considered as good as any other.[51] He never referred to himself by it and it remained his practice to sign all but the most formal letters with his initials only. In the event, to everyone else he became and remained Sligger, in both private and public life. As the writer Anthony Powell was to comment, he became either 'Sligger' or 'Urquhart', but 'not "Sligger Urquhart", as is now sometimes altogether incorrectly rendered'.[52]

At the end of his first year at Balliol, in 1891, Sligger held a summer party for six guests at the Chalet, presumably with the permission of his brother David, who was the owner. The Chalet had not been used often in the years before this due to their mother's failing health and David's interests elsewhere.[53] Thirteen years older than Sligger, David Urquhart junior was married and working for a firm of consulting engineers in London. Having less time to indulge in France David had sometimes let the Chalet out; one such occupant was Douglas Freshfield, the famous mountaineer and author.[54] One wonders whether, if Francis had not found a new use for the Chalet, David might have sold it as being of little use to the family. In the event it was spared this by Francis' initiative.

Whether the Chalet party of 1891 was the result of Sligger's experience of vacation reading parties in the UK, or of the wish to share his family's Alpine home with friends, or a combination of both, is not possible to say. However, the party which assembled on 3 August did lead to a new lease of life for the Chalet. It is worth examining Sligger's choice of guests in detail because they illustrate his personal tastes and approach towards the Chalet in a way that was to become the pattern for the future.

There were four undergraduate contemporaries from Balliol: Claud Russell was subsequently to have a distinguished career in the diplomatic service, Henry Petty-Fitzmaurice (Lord Kerry) was the future 6th Marquess of Lansdowne, and Gerard Craig Sellar would have a career in the Colonial Service before inheriting a family estate in Scotland.[55] The fourth, Cyril Bailey, would become a Fellow of

Balliol and Sligger's future biographer. Cyril and Sligger had become firm friends in their first term at Balliol and when Sligger heard that Cyril would be climbing in Switzerland during the summer he invited him to join the party.[56] This was the first of Cyril's fifteen summer visits to the Chalet and his enthusiasm for climbing tempted Sligger to undertake one of his first mountain ascents; they climbed together to the Aiguille du Goûter, a peak of 3,863 metres on the western flank of Mont Blanc and an eighteen-hour excursion from the Chalet.[57]

The party was joined by the older Herbert Trench, who was Modern History Fellow of All Souls College and newly appointed to the Board of Education.[58] Recently married, Trench was accompanied by his wife Lilian and their visit to the Chalet was part of their honeymoon. Sixty-seven years later Herbert would be followed at the Chalet by his grandson Robin and so becomes the first example of attendance at the Chalet by different generations of the same family.[59]

Sligger began a visitors' book, which was signed by all members of the party. They also posed for a group photograph (Fig. 9), beginning another Chalet tradition which has survived down the years. The 1891 party is not described in the book as a reading party, nor are any activities listed in this first diary entry, although later correspondence tells of an excursion across the Bossons glacier and an attempt to climb Le Buet, a peak beyond Chamonix.[60] There was also a visit to Chamonix to meet Claud's parents Lord and Lady Russell. However, whether with the benefit of hindsight or not, Cyril Bailey was later in no doubt that 1891 was the beginning of the tradition of the Chalet reading parties.

So the first party model revealed a mixture of backgrounds and colleges: a few close friends, one of whom was an aristocrat, two were academics and two were to be prominent in public life, together with a spouse or friend. And all of them, to judge from their photograph, were good-looking people. The choice of guests in 1891 illustrates Sligger's ability to perceive future promise in undergraduates, his taste for handsome companions, and his inclination towards those in public life and especially the upper classes (which later commentators would ascribe to snobbishness). The 1891 party was a perfect model for the approach Sligger would use for his parties over the next four decades. Whether he was aware of it at the time or not, he had founded the institution which would outlive him as the outstanding contribution of his life.

CHAPTER TWO

THE READING PARTIES: LIFE AT
THE EDWARDIAN CHALET

CYRIL BAILEY'S MARRIAGE at the age of forty may have come as a surprise to some of his colleagues.[1] Cyril, the son of a barrister who
had been Stowell Law Fellow at University College, entered Balliol
in 1890 and joined Sligger's first Chalet party at the end of his first
year. In 1894 he graduated with a first-class honours degree in Greats
(i.e. Classics: *Literae Humaniores*) and after a brief spell as a tutor at
Exeter College he returned to Balliol in 1902 as a Classics Fellow. A
keen mountaineer and subsequently a member of the Alpine Club,
he became one of Sligger's most enthusiastic supporters at the Chalet
and was there regularly before the First World War. He seemed to
all appearances to have settled into the life of a bachelor don when
in 1912 he married Gemma Creighton, the youngest daughter of a
former Bishop of London.[1]

The Baileys undertook a cultural tour of Europe for their honeymoon. Sligger was typically warm towards the wives of colleagues
and as his gift he gave them the Chalet for the month of June before
the 1912 parties started.[1] This was all new experience for Gemma and
her letters home are full of the excitement of her discovery.

When they arrived in Saint Gervais they were met by Anselme
Martin, Sligger's *gardien* at the Chalet. Lunch in the village was followed by a leisurely ascent by the usual path.[2] Cyril was startled to
discover that they were there at a season unfamiliar to the reading
parties; the meadows of the lower walk were ablaze with gentians,
primroses, poppies and cornflower which were usually over by July.
Higher up the snows had lingered late and the trees were beginning
to bud, the white beneath them pierced by crocuses and *Soldanella*,
the Alpine snowbell. Despite the snow the walk was hot and they
took advantage of what icy streams were exposed. At the Chalet the

lawn had a coating of snow and there was a large drift behind the house.[2]

Anselme Martin had engaged a resident cook, Madame Paget, and arranged for one of his teenage daughters to deliver supplies and post every few days.[2] The elderly Mme Paget proved to be a motherly woman, full of solicitude for the young couple and especially for the new wife. She had experience of working as a cook in England and took all responsibility for the household off Gemma's shoulders, leaving her free to enjoy the Chalet and its surroundings.[3]

The Baileys' arrival was followed by a night of snowstorm and they woke the next day to find themselves in a world of white, the Chalet surrounded by huge drifts. Despite this they managed to get out for what Cyril termed 'a trudge' every day. In view of the weather they took over the smaller of the salons, where Mme Paget kept the fire burning permanently. Indeed Cyril reported to his mother that their cook/housekeeper kept the house 'beautifully warm' for them despite the unseasonable conditions.[2]

In her letters home Gemma reserved her highest praise for Mme Paget's skill and economy in the kitchen and expressed amazement at what could be created from simple means.[3] Main meals were largely vegetarian, avoiding dullness by the variety of ways in which they were prepared. Breakfast started with porridge, followed by 'eggs done in all sorts of beautiful ways & delicious coffee and honey'. Lunch consisted of two vegetable dishes but a meat dish sometimes made an appearance at dinner, along with vegetable soup and dessert. Cheese supplemented most meals and Gemma enjoyed especially a 'dessert of soaked bread, fried and dusted with sugar'; this was clearly her first encounter with French toast. A bishop's daughter, she dutifully reported that she felt she was seeing an existence that was simple and good, and a long way away from privileged life in England, and also that this way of life would be good for Cyril.[3] Sligger would no doubt have approved very warmly of the sentiment.

¤

If Sligger had any idea in 1891 that he had established a new pattern of reading parties, the following year he might have wondered if it stood any chance of survival. Unknown to anyone a molten lake had built up inside the Tête Rousse glacier. This popular walking destination is a horizontal shelf of ice high on the west face of Mont Blanc, at the base of the Aiguille du Goûter, and at an altitude of 3,167 metres. During the night of 11 June 1892 the lake burst through the front wall of the glacier, discharging an estimated 300,000 cubic metres of water and ice down the cliff into the valley of the Bionnassay glacier 500 metres below.[4]

By the time it hit the lower glacier the flood had picked up tremendous power and behaved like an avalanche, dragging up the rocks of the moraine and surrounding trees. It is thought that when it reached the lower end of the Bionnassay glacier it had doubled in volume. In its path lay the sleeping villages of Bionnassay and Bionnay. Bionnassay was saved by its elevated position above the river where the curve of the valley directed the flood onto the opposite side but below the village the narrowing valley channelled the full force onto Bionnay. The wooden houses were no protection and the village was swept away, only a handful of buildings on the outskirts surviving.

From Bionnay the flood discharged onto the Bon Nant river and turned along its course towards the town of Saint Gervais. Most of the town sits high on the eastern slope of this steep valley and only the lower part around the old Roman bridge was lost. However, beyond the town the river funnels into a gorge before reaching the flatter area around Le Fayet. In this gorge was the popular spa centre of the Le Fayet Thermal Baths, which received the concentrated power of the flood. The main building was lifted bodily and carried several hundred yards before disintegrating.[4] After this the flood dissipated over the plain around the town of Le Fayet, depositing debris and rocks, some of which were the size of a haystack. The force was so severe that a tidal bore was seen in the Arve river at Bonneville, 50 kilometres downstream.[4]

Given the timing of the event and its speed, no moves could be made to protect lives or property. One relative mercy was that the Thermal Baths, which could accommodate 400, were only a quarter full that night.[4] However, the death toll was finally estimated at around 200. Any thought of putting together a Chalet party in 1892 was impractical, with the people of Le Fayet, the railway terminus, rebuilding their homes and lives.

To add to that disaster, in August that year Lewis Nettleship, Classics Tutor at Balliol, made an attempt to climb Mont Blanc from Chamonix with the help of two guides. They were prevented by worsening weather from reaching the Vallot refuge 400 metres below the summit and were obliged to bivouac in the snow. The next morning the storm was still blowing but Nettleship, against the advice of his guides, insisted on trying to descend and shortly afterwards died of exposure.[5] The year 1892 was not a good one for members of Balliol to contemplate outings in the Haute-Savoie.

Sligger ran a party again in 1893 and in doing so established a pattern that was continue throughout his life, barring the interruption of the First World War. After *la Catastrophe* of Tête Rousse the 1893 party was small and partly exploratory, consisting of four Balliol undergraduates, including Cyril Bailey, and one from Lincoln College. The single more mature member was Edwin 'Jimmy' Palmer, the son of the Archdeacon of Oxford, who was already a Fellow of Balliol and subsequently to be the College chaplain and then Bishop of Bombay.[6]

The 1893 members arrived together as a group on 30 June and how long they stayed is not recorded. The following year, however, the year of Sligger's graduation, the Chalet was open from late June to the beginning of September and a total of sixteen members came at different dates throughout the summer; this change was the final factor completing the pattern for the subsequent years. The 1894 party (Fig. 10) was almost completely composed of Balliol undergraduates, possibly as celebration of Sligger's recent graduation. The sole addition was because William Dugdale brought his younger brother Edwin who was admitted to Balliol in 1895: whether introducing him to Sligger played any part in his admission is not known but in the future Sligger would sometimes use invitations to the Chalet to sound out promising candidates for college entry.

Today it is still easy to appreciate the excitement with which these young men must have seen the Chalet for the first time. Many of them would be undertaking their first trip abroad, with all its new experiences. When after the long train journey and the arduous walk up from Saint Gervais of around two hours the Chalet finally emerged through the forest it did so with a real sense of magic. Today the route of approach has changed but similar emotions are still seen in those who arrive for the first time.

One thing that emerges from the accounts left by Sligger's guests is the warmth of the welcome that he provided. For first-time visitors this would mean meeting them in Saint Gervais if he was free and sharing the long climb up to the Chalet during which he took the trouble to get to know his companion better. If he was not free he would usually get someone else to do this. His photograph albums make it clear that arrivals and departures were treated as special events. For people he knew to have problems there would be an extra welcoming gesture, such as a bowl of flowers in their room.[7]

For many the setting must have seemed idyllic. The Chalet nestled on its little plateau, secluded on three sides by the larch forest, the wide lawn providing good space for relaxation and games. Like a hillside amphitheatre the west side was open, looking out over the valley to where the cliffs of the Aravis range and the massive bulk of the Aiguille de Varens dominated the horizon. At night the lights of the town of Sallanches could be seen, twinkling in the valley below. A walk up to the col of the Prarion provided the wide west view of the Mont Blanc massif and a view down into the Chamonix valley.

The original Chalet had a romantic atmosphere with small, cosy rooms of darkened wood. It was cool in the mornings, before the sun had risen over the bulk of Mont Blanc, then warmed progressively during the morning in the clear light of the Alpine air until the building and the lawn were bathed in sunlight throughout the afternoon. As the light lengthened it lit the salon with a warm glow until the sun setting over the Aravis ridge provided evening skies that were often of staggering beauty. Admittedly, visitors could not expect this weather every day: this is mountain country and subject to the rapid changes that mountain weather undergoes but none of it was without a strong sense of romance. On a wet day the Chalet, because of its altitude, might be completely enveloped in cloud, isolating the party from the rest of the world. Sometimes after an unusually cold night the party might wake to a sprinkling of snow on the lawn. Particularly striking were the storms: Alpine storms are frequently short but very fierce and to experience thunder and lightning concentrated by the surrounding mountains and the drumming of rain on the Chalet was to feel the power of the elements at their most impressive.

Until 1894 and while Sligger was still an undergraduate, the early parties can be seen as a gathering of friends supplemented by mature visitors. Sligger's education had made him three years older than most of his fellow students when he entered Balliol and those few years probably gave him an advantage. As the Chalet tradition took shape, however, Sligger became and remained '*M. le Patron*', a concept to which he gave a modest welcome. Those who were invited were under no doubt that they were his guests and that he would go out of his way to make their visit memorable. At the same time, there was never any doubt that the duty of consideration to a generous host was also expected of them; those who presumed too far on his hospitality or were inclined to be disruptive usually waited in vain for another invitation.

At some time during these early years Sligger's guests came to be known, and to know themselves, as 'chaletites'. This title began with the passage of the years to reflect a select club whose members had in common the experience of life on the Prarion. It should perhaps be noted that Sligger only ever used the word as 'Chalet-ites'; loss of the hyphen is something that a succeeding generation has adopted.

Among the mature guests it became the norm for Sligger to invite a priest or someone from a Catholic school. In the early years this was most commonly the Abbé Félix Klein from the Catholic Institute in Paris, present for seven years between 1897 and 1921. Chaletites came to regard this as a regular feature and some of the priests, the Abbé Klein especially, became popular with the undergraduates. When a priest was present Sligger would hear Mass most mornings but the rest of the party did not usually attend.[8]

No doubt Sligger's personal vision of a Chalet party evolved during these early years but his approach seems from the very beginning to have been based on a firm routine and to have included a degree of discipline. Reveille was at eight, when water for washing was brought to the bedrooms. Sligger often did this himself, rousing the inmates with cheerful badinage. Some of them – the most hardy, at any rate – would then join him in braving the cold of the garden waterfall for a morning shower. Breakfast was served and over by nine, when reading was expected to start (Fig. 11). The salon was arranged so that members each had a table on which to arrange their books. Sligger put a high value on study at the Chalet and expected that reading would proceed in silence, being quite capable of dampening down the enthusiasm of anyone tempted to talk. A mid-morning break for coffee or hot chocolate was taken and then reading resumed until lunch. The period after lunch was free for a short walk or games on the lawn, after which the party gathered for a limited tea – Sligger was adamant that this should never constitute a meal – after which reading resumed until dinner. The evening meal and the time after it were reserved for conversation, in the French style.

The meals would have been a new experience for many, as they were largely vegetarian, comprising salads and pulses alongside more substantial vegetable dishes given variety by different methods of preparation or dressing. Water was served at lunch and *vin ordinaire* provided only at dinner. Sligger expected appetites to be restrained (for example no one was expected to take more than a single bread roll) and those with more robust stomachs sometimes found the regime too spartan for them compared to home or college. Most, however, seemed to have enjoyed the fare and found it part of the charm of the party.

Sligger's approach to reading at the Chalet was that it was an opportunity to use quiet and protected time to explore new areas. He did not regard this as an extension of his college teaching despite always being willing to answer questions on any historical points, or to advise on reading material. It is clear that in his own reading he aimed to adopt the same pattern he expected of his guests, in other words to extend his knowledge, which he habitually referred to as 'The Pleasure of Learning'. Above all, he put a high value on talking with the party on a wide range of topics. This was why he tended to look down on any undergraduate's inclination to play cards in the evening, feeling that this limited conversation. He was, in fact, concerned that the Chalet party might reproduce the atmosphere in college and what members thought and talked about there, and did what he could to prevent this.

In one respect the chaletites would have found comparison with life in England familiar; they were supported by servants, as many of them were at home and as they were in college. Sligger provided a cook and maids and also employed Jean-François Martin, his father's chalet *gardien*, or caretaker.[9] It was usually the role of the *gardien* to arrange the hire of the other domestic staff, typically before the season began so that the Chalet could be ready for its visitors. In the early years there were visits of a woman to wash linen, the *blanchisseuse*, who was provided with a laundry hut below the waterfall at the end of the lawn. Jean-François died a few years after the parties began and the work was taken over by his son Anselme, who was also responsible for getting supplies and luggage up to the Chalet by mule cart or sledge (Fig. 13). In time several of Anselme's daughters came to serve on the domestic staff at the Chalet.[10] The biologist Julian Huxley (Chalet 1908 & 1910) remembered that 'each morning a stocky French maid would climb those three thousand feet with eggs and milk and the day's letters, and go down in the evening to sleep'.[11]

Good personal conduct and consideration of their peers was required of all members. Tidiness was encouraged; a jacket was to be worn at lunch, and a tie at dinner. The efforts of the servants were to be appreciated and chaletites were expected to do what they could to help them. Out on the hillside they were expected to greet the local people with warmth and politeness. A contemporary remarked that at the Chalet Sligger simply asked his guests to do what came naturally to him.

No doubt Sligger sometimes had his challenges in maintaining decorum among these healthy and energetic young men. Over the years he wrote and eventually published *The Perfect Chalet-ite*, a guide to good behaviour at the Chalet (Appendix 1). This lays down his expectations for travelling and arrival, work and games, use of the Turkish bath and conduct on the mountain. Those who went further qualified for the title 'Pluperfect Chalet-ite'. Today Sligger's rules read as something of a period piece, social conditions having changed radically since then, and in many ways it represents an Edwardian guide to basic etiquette. Cyril Bailey was emphatic that in his approach to the summer parties at the Chalet Sligger simply applied his own values and then extended them into his life as a tutor at Balliol.

For future diplomat Sir Hughe Knatchbull-Hugessen (Chalet 1905–7) the Chalet became a household word to Balliol men of several generations and above all a tribute to Sligger. He called it an ideal spot for quiet and concentrated work but noted the continual distractions of the locality: the view across the valley to Aravis, the col of the Prarion above the Chalet with its seasonal pansies, gentians and other wild flowers. He recorded that a ban on mountain-climbing was understandable but was frequently broken under the leadership of Cyril Bailey, an accomplished member of the Alpine Club. With Cyril Hughe climbed the Aiguille du Midi (3,842 m) and the Aiguille de Bionnassay (4,052 m), both ascents for the serious climber.[12]

Cricket usually dominated the afternoons and was played on the lawn with tennis balls, a home-made bat and walking sticks as wickets. The rules were constrained by circumstances: a hit to the Chalet scored four (strict rules applied about closing the shutters: getting repairs done on the mountain was difficult and remains so), past the Chalet five, and over the roof six. The high incidence of the

Classics among chaletites frequently found expression in Chalet life. Opposing teams would take names such as 'Philosophers v. Historians' or 'Catholics v. Protestants', and the stream at the far end of the lawn was christened the Jaxartes and that which passed the Chalet du Rocher the Oxus, the intervening ground being known, by a shift of geographical logic, as Mesopotamia.

It might be thought futile to have introduced golf, given the topography of the mountainside, but in fact several reasonably level areas alongside the uphill walk on the Prarion were used at different times. Playing was not without its challenges in view of the common streams and potholes in the ground, not to mention the overriding risk of lost balls among the mountain undergrowth. One can only admire the determination of chaletites to attempt to play under these conditions.

A more modern innovation was Chalet tennis, in fact a gentler version of squash, in which players hit against the side of the Chalet and the direction of shot was hidden from the opponent by the sloping roof of one of the Chalet's lean-to extensions. Of all Chalet games this has proved the most durable but in fact its greatest development came later when a significant event changed the circumstances of the Chalet considerably.[13]

It is easy to detect in Sligger's approach what he had absorbed from reading parties in the UK but at the Chalet they had a different emphasis due to the location and the style of living. This was an essentially French way of life and was one of the aspects that Sligger wanted to introduce to his guests in addition to leading them to appreciate the pleasures of dedicated study, the Alps and European culture. The historian A. J. P. Taylor, sent from Oriel College for a term's teaching from Sligger, was impressed with his ability to think from a European context in a way that differed greatly from the teaching of the time: 'Three years with him would have been intolerable. One term did wonders for me. Sligger did not have much historical knowledge in the conventional sense. But he knew nineteenth-century Europe at first hand.'[14]

Sligger was emphatic that the Chalet, despite being surrounded by some of the best climbs in Europe, was a base for walking rather than climbing. He might have been influenced by the tragedies of people like Lewis Nettleship but it is just as likely that once again he was expressing his own tastes, and that the effort involved in climbing would simply intrude on what he saw as the primary functions of the Chalet. That said, party members noted on occasion that he had appreciable skill as a mountain man and he was tolerant that Cyril Bailey occasionally involved members of the parties in his climbing excursions.

The short afternoon breaks on reading days naturally limited members to the locality of the Chalet for their walks. However, there were plenty of opportunities for afternoon strolls on the slopes of the Prarion, either in the shade of the forest or above the tree line in the clear Alpine air. Twenty minutes' uphill walk would bring them to the col of the Prarion and reward them with the imposing western view of the Mont Blanc massif. Those who wanted to be more energetic could climb the Prarion itself and enjoy a panoramic view of the surrounding peaks and the Chamonix and Contamines-Montjoie valleys.

Sometimes one or two would go down to Saint Gervais for post or provisions and this practice started another durable tradition: challenges were set for speed of the descent and ascent. Records in Sligger's time were said to be close to fifteen minutes for the descent and fifty-five for the ascent and suggest an impressive level of fitness; as anyone who has done the walk will know, the ascent is around 1,000 metres and can take more than two hours to walk. Sligger took part himself and is said to have often held the record. Julian Huxley was allowed to bring his brother Trevor to the 1910 party and recalled that Trevor's long legs easily beat the rest of that party, getting down to the village in under thirty minutes.[11] These Edwardian claims might be thought to be exaggeration were it not for the fact that they have been equalled or beaten by successive generations. Today the tradition survives as a means of obtaining breakfast pastries from Saint Gervais, and hence is now known as the 'croissant run'.

Several times during the season the walks would be longer and take in a local peak such as Mont Joly (2,525 m) or the Aiguille de Varens (2,544 m). These would involve crossing the valley and another ascent on the other side, with a final trudge back up to the Chalet at the end of the day. Care and skill were required; the Aiguille de Varens in particular needed rope work for its final pinnacle. Sometimes members would go further afield and spend a night in a mountain refuge, as they did when climbing Le Buet (3,096 m) beyond Chamonix.

The western side of Mont Blanc also offers good walking

opportunities from the Chalet. Here the start was to go down from the Prarion to the Col de Voza below and then begin the long pull up the mountain to Mont Lachat (2,113 m), or across the gorge of the Bionnassay valley to Col de Tricot (2,120 m) and the ridges that run up the western flank of the mountain to the Aiguille de Bionnassay, a peak accessible only to climbers. One walk that Sligger always recommended was the ascent to the Tête Rousse glacier at the base of the Aiguille du Goûter, one of the traditional setting-off points for attempts on the Mont Blanc summit. Tête Rousse was above the snow line and, although within the skills of careful walkers, was a tiring ascent to 3,167 metres. It did, however, offer the inducement of a refuge (Fig. 15) which served soup, which could be enjoyed after the climb while appreciating stunning views back over the area around the Chalet, distant and tiny when seen from this height (Fig. 83).

Summer walking in the Alps is often very hot and on longer walks advantage was taken to cool down in the mountain lakes or rivers, the tradition being that the party bathed nude; this was less surprising and more commonly accepted among university men in those days than it would be today (stretches of the river in Oxford were reserved for naked swimming). Indeed, on some days the swim itself became the objective of the walk, especially at the watersmeet above the Nant Borrant refuge in the Bon Nant valley or Lac Vert in the woods above Passy on the northern side of the valley beyond Le Fayet.

One excursion which the parties traditionally undertook is surprising in view of its length and technical demands and especially in view of Sligger's professed avoidance of climbing. This was a route around the central mass of Mont Blanc and usually took several days, requiring the group to cross onto the Italian side of the mountain. This walk happened in most of the years before the First World War and required a mountain guide. The usual route was for the group to descend into the Bon Nant valley and walk up to the Nant Borrant refuge, where sometimes the night would be spent in order to make an early start the following day. The route then continued to climb to the headwall of the valley, where the path crossed over the Col du Bonhomme (2,329 m) or the Col des Fours (2,665 m).

On this stretch there were two desolate lakes surrounded by bleak cliffs, the Lacs Jovet, another of the traditional bathing sites. After the col the route descended into the next valley and then rose again to the Italian border at Col de la Seigne (2,516 m). From this col

the group would descend the long valley alongside the Miage and
Brenva glaciers to Courmayeur (1,226 m), a distance of some 15 kilometres. Here the second night would be spent; from Nant Borrant to
Courmayeur was usually about ten hours' walking. The next phase
was the steepest (Fig. 14), climbing up the ridges on the south side
of the Mont Blanc massif to reach the Col du Géant (3,356 m) where
another night would be passed in the Abrazzi Hut.

Edward Cadogan, younger son of the 5th Earl Cadogan and subsequently a politician, was a member of the 1901 party and reported
that Sligger led 'immense excursions, involving more physical than
mental exercise. One lasted four days and took us over the Col de la
Seine [sic] to Courmayeur in Italy, where much the most impressive
view of the massif of Mont Blanc is provided. The following day we
climbed the Col de Géant, 11,000 feet in a little over five hours. The
view from the cabane where we spent the night is I suppose one of
the great views of the world.'[15]

This demanding climb must have been an education to some chaletites but in fact a dangerous part of the journey was yet to come:
the long walk – usually starting at dawn – over the vast ice field of
the Géant glacier, descending on the Mer de Glace, France's longest
glacier, where negotiating the crevasses and towering seracs could
prove challenging. A break would be taken at the mountaineers'
centre at Montenvers and the group would descend finally to Chamonix and then travel along the valley back to the Prarion. Sometimes
this Mont Blanc circuit would be done in reverse.

Sligger's chaletites had one advantage in that they would have
been very fit: some form of active sport took up most afternoons
for the Edwardian undergraduate. Furthermore, transport was
limited and they would habitually walk or run to all their activities
in Oxford. Nonetheless, the Géant walk was a daunting expedition
which required a range of skills. Today the difficult parts would be
graded as 'scrambling', i.e. on the verge of climbing, with complicated or exposed sections and significant risk. These would generally
be undertaken only by accomplished mountain walkers. Sligger's
chaletites were the more remarkable because many of them must
have been mountain novices. They usually had the benefit of a skilled
mountain guide, who from 1905 onwards was the Chalet's faithful
gardien, Anselme Martin. One wonders how many of the party were
near the end of their endurance by the end: the final walk up to the

Chalet from Chamonix is longer than their usual ascent on the Saint Gervais side and might for many have felt like the final straw.

Sligger himself was present about half the years this walk was done and did it for the last time in 1919 when he was fifty-one. It was on expeditions like this that Sligger's skills and understanding of the mountains became evident; he was rigorous in ensuring that the members who took part had a chance to acclimatise and acquire their mountain legs on previous walks, and in marshalling the group to a slow, steady pace and frequent stops. He also ensured that everyone was properly equipped; his instructions to those invited to the Chalet included the requirement of a pair of boots capable of having nails put into the soles. Ropes were used but even so the members were poorly equipped in comparison with modern mountaineers and one wonders that no injury or fatality ever happened. The novelist L. P. Hartley (Chalet 1920) recalled that on one of these walks one man slipped 'and sent Sligger off like a comet' to rescue him.[16]

When Sligger stopped taking part in this excursion he continued to recommend it to chaletites. When Robert Boothby, Charles Mathew and Peter Rodd undertook it in 1922 he went so far as to provide the cash for their trip. Unfortunately this characteristic piece of generosity did not survive the discovery of a casino in Courmayeur, after which the party were on short rations. Boothby said the morning view from the hut where they slept (presumably the Abrazzi) was magnificent but they took serious risks over the crevasses on the Mer de Glace and in Chamonix, enjoying his first decent meal and bath in several days, he decided that in future all his mountain viewing would be done from the valley.[17]

Throughout all these activities Sligger insisted that the members of the party should acquire an understanding of their surroundings. In contrast to the atmosphere at the Chalet he discouraged much conversation on walks, regarding it more important that walkers should learn from what they were seeing. He expected them to learn the names of the leading features of the Alps and to leave with some knowledge of Alpine plants and animals such as the mountain marmot and the chamois. Above all he wanted them to be open to the influence of the mountains, which he referred to as '*la paix de la grande nature*'. As Cyril Bailey commented, one did not feel so much like a tourist as a temporary Savoyard.[18]

A good example of Sligger's French sympathies is provided by his feelings about Chamonix, of which *The Perfect Chalet-ite* enjoins members to be 'properly contemptuous'. Since the opening up of the Alps in the eighteenth century this town had expanded under the influence of English tourism. The peasant farmers were not slow to capitalise on an unexpected source of income: their homes became pensions from which grew hotels adapted to English tastes and practices[19] and Chamonix acquired its English church. The first luxury hotel, the Hôtel de l'Union, was founded in 1816[20] and others followed rapidly, the period of the early Chalet parties seeing Chamonix' greatest expansion. By 1896, when the mountaineer Edward Whymper published his first guide to Chamonix[21] he could list fifteen such hotels. His second edition of 1910[22] included twenty-eight, some of which, such as the Majestic or the Palais, offered luxury to match the best anywhere in the world. At the Hôtel de Londres et d'Angleterre, whose title is said to have been suggested by William Windham to his host in 1741[23] and which Murray's 1842 guide claimed offered more comfort than was to be found in England,[24] Queen Victoria's doctor John Forbes found that he could have an English meal, entirely surrounded by English guests.[25] Sligger had no tolerance for this insularity; the Chalet's link with the outside world was the very French Saint Gervais and it is easy to see that someone whose formative years were passed in that environment would indeed feel contempt for what had happened in Chamonix. Nor was he alone in these sentiments: when Alfred Wills was trying to buy the land for 'The Eagle's Nest' at Sixt he discovered that some of those opposed to the purchase were asking why their valley should be 'over-run by foreigners like that of Chamonix'.[26] These circumstances probably only increased the determination of Sligger – an Oxford don and, one might therefore think, an archetypically British type – to Gallicise his parties.

It could be expected that these efforts of an English academic in France would attract a reputation but the extent to which they did so is surprising. By the time the 1907 edition was published Baedeker's *Switzerland and the adjacent portions of Italy, Savoy and Tyrol* – the standard guide for anyone travelling in the area – had modified its entry for Le Fayet-Saint Gervais to include specific reference to the Chalet.[27] Its description of the walk from Le Fayet to Les Houches over Col de la Forclaz contained the advice: 'A longer but more interesting route (6–7 hrs) is from Saint Gervais via the Chalet des Anglais, the (2½ hrs) Pavillon du Prarion … with a splendid view, and the Col de

Voza.' It is remarkable that a student retreat buried in a hillside forest should appear as a recognised landmark in an international touring guide. Whether walkers were expected to call in and whether Sligger would have welcomed this are unknown, though neither appears very likely: in *The Perfect Chalet-ite* he referred to the influx of tourists as the 'Invasion'.[28]

Until 1896 Sligger used the Chalet with the permission of the owner, his elder brother David, who dealt with the costs such as paying for the services of Jean-François and Anselme Martin.[9] However, the members of Sligger's parties were expected to pay their own expenses and contribute to running costs. In 1893 Sligger's fellow student Arthur Cunliffe owed sixteen shillings at the end of the party and sent it to him with a youthful poem in which he described his experiences of Nature in the mountains. Sligger thought enough of the poem to transcribe it into the diary. The following year Jimmy Palmer provided another poem on writing paper from the Hôtel du Mont Blanc in Saint Gervais, presumably on leaving the party. Later generations have been moved to copy their example, usually in the same humorous vein and not without merit.

Sligger's elder brother David, married and working for a London firm of consulting engineers, had less opportunity to use the Chalet than university terms allowed his brother. However, his affection for it remained: in 1893 while writing to Sligger to ask for money for Jean-François Martin he added, 'I hope you are enjoying yourself. I do wish I could see the dear old place again.'[9] In fact there is no record that David ever visited the Chalet again, although their sisters Maisie and Harriet continued to do so.

By 1896 it must have been clear to the family that of all of them Francis had the leading call on the Chalet and the most viable use for it and in July that year he paid David 7,500 francs for the purchase.[29] In UK terms this was around £300 (around £32,000 today). It is indicative of Sligger's sense of propriety that until 1896 he had signed the Chalet diary as a guest but he never did so after the sale: the Chalet and the diary were now his. At this point the diary entries also begin to expand and to describe the parties' activities and walks.

Modern chaletites may be familiar with the suggestion that David sold the Chalet independently and Sligger then bought it back, a story which has been repeated in the notes of parties after the Second World War. This claim originates from a statement made by Cyril Bailey in the *Memoir*[30] but the deed of sale in the Balliol College Archives makes it clear that the transaction was between the two brothers.[29]

Then in 1898 an event occurred which would change Sligger's life for ever and would be highly significant to the Chalet's future: his uncle Chichester Fortescue died, leaving Sligger his chief beneficiary.[31] Lord Carlingford was childless and was the sole remaining member of the senior generation, having survived his wife, Frances Waldegrave, his elder brother Thomas and his sister Harriet, Sligger's mother. At his death his house at Chewton Priory reverted to the Waldegrave family but there was still a considerable estate comprising land in Ireland and England valued at nearly £42,000 (around £4 million today). Chichester had enjoyed a special relationship with his sister Harriet and her youngest son, which he referred to warmly in his will. He left small legacies to other family members but gave Sligger the bulk of his estate on condition that Francis should adopt the name Fortescue in tribute to his mother's family. This he did, thereafter signing himself 'F.F.U.' in all but his most formal letters.

After 1898, therefore, Sligger was a wealthy man and having acquired the Chalet from his brother David he now had the means to support it without concerns. He could have chosen to live in considerable style but being of modest tastes he inclined instead to good works, often anonymously.[32] He was a strong supporter of the development of the Catholic Chaplaincy in Oxford,[33] and possibly assisted the purchase of The Old Palace in St Aldate's which gave the Chaplaincy a permanent home.[34] He also declined any salary from Balliol for the rest of his life. It appears that he subsequently disposed of the Carlingford lands as and when he needed, because he held no land at his death and left an English estate of £15,139 (around £900,000 at today's values).[35] This did not include his French property, in which he had also invested, as we shall see.

One aspect of the freedom which wealth gave Sligger was the opportunity to travel. Although he frequently kept up attendance at reading parties in the UK, from this time on his vacations were occupied by visits to the cultural centres of Europe. In a typical year he would spend part of the Easter vacation in France or Italy, often in Rome. In the summer he would usually leave the Chalet in late August and travel back to Oxford through France, Italy or Germany. Catholic countries inevitably dominated his programme and although he acquired favourites – Chartres in particular – he took in new places throughout his travelling. It became his practice to invite a few favourite students to accompany him on these trips, and he probably paid their expenses; sometimes he did this during the other vacations. By this means he aimed to deepen their understanding of European art, culture and architecture in the way which informed his own approach to History. For example he told his students that History should always be read with the aid of a map and that to visit somewhere offered authentic experience.[36]

A significant call on Sligger's wealth came only a few years later. On the morning of 18 September 1906 Humphrey Paul, a History undergraduate from New College, sat down at the Hôtel du Mont Blanc in Saint Gervais to write what may have been one of the most difficult letters any undergraduate ever wrote to a college tutor: he had to tell Sligger that in the night his Chalet had been destroyed by fire.[37] Wisely, he wrote factually and in detail, sending a telegram in advance of the letter and also notifying William Tyrrell at the Foreign Office in London.

Sligger had left the Chalet at the end of July to undertake a world tour. A party of around twelve, including Cyril Bailey, had spent August there but most had departed by the end of the month, leaving only a handful for the next few weeks. There was nothing unusual in this: it was common for Sligger to leave the Chalet to a group at the end of the season, as the closing down could be reliably left in the hands of Anselme Martin.

The residual party was a characteristic cross-section of Sligger's invitees. Apart from Humphrey Paul the only other two undergraduates were Alan Lidderdale, a Balliol student of Cyril Bailey's, and Frederick Bewsher, from Merton College. Bewsher's tutor Heathcote Garrod was also there with another of his students, John Leofric Stocks, a Philosophy graduate from Corpus Christi College. Garrod and Stocks were sharing a ground-floor room in the rear annexe and Bewsher was in the small room beside them (Sligger's own bedroom). The snow had come early and the two maids had come down from their room upstairs and taken the adjacent room behind the salon which had been vacated a week before. Humphrey Paul and Alan Lidderdale were the only ones sleeping upstairs in the two rooms at the far end of the Chalet. Humphrey Paul wrote that the fire seemed to have started in the early hours of the morning:

On Friday it turned very cold, and Garrod, who has not been very well and said he was used to a fire, wanted one in his bedroom (the double room next to your little room in the annexe), which he shared with Stocks. The stove and chimney seemed all right, and drew perfectly when the fire was lit; and as snow came on Saturday they had a fire in that room each of the four successive nights. Last night, Monday, I shut up and went to bed about 10.30, Lidderdale following some minutes later. I was suddenly woken in the night by Clementine crying 'le feu' and by a crackling of wood. Lidderdale woke the same time, I had time to get great-coat and boots in my hand and get down the staircase (it would have been impossible to get up again). We got as much furniture and books from the drawing-room as we had time. This was not much, as the rooms above soon caught. Of course it was hopeless to put the fire out, there being no hose and very little water (constant, but slow) and half the place in a blaze by the time I got out.

Garrod seems to have woken first and seen the roof above him smoking. He rushed upstairs, waking Clementine with his shouts, to the room at the top of the stairs on the right, where he found the floor alight in two places, which he put out. When he got down, he found the whole annexe in a blaze. The whole roof of his room must have been on fire when he woke. No one was hurt. I didn't get my watch, but the fire seems to have been discovered between 3 and 3.30 am. When we had done all we could, I fetched Anselm [*sic*]: but he found nothing to do except get the embers down. When I left (about 10 o'clock), they were smouldering a little. I waited two hours for the gendarmes, who made a report. The insurance agent has telephoned to his superior at Bonneville, who will be here tomorrow morning. Lidderdale went up to the chalet again after he had got breakfast here (I met him as I was coming down) but found nothing to do. Anselm's [*sic*] brother-in-law has been in charge since the gendarmes left, and Anselm [*sic*] himself is now going up, and will stay the night. I don't think I can do anything more today. I am telegraphing to you, and also writing Mr Tyrrell to telegraph any instructions; I shall wait as long as there is anything to do, which I fear is little (except to get the insurance money paid all right).[37]

It appears that the roof of the annexe had been set alight by the flue of the stove. The party obviously had no hope of saving a wooden building which had been desiccated by fifty years of hot summers and freezing winters and which had limited access to water. Commendably, they were able to save from the salon some of Sligger's more precious books, including the Chalet diary, and some furniture but apart from that they were reduced to watching the Chalet and their own belongings turned to ash. Anselme Martin took the view that the flue of the stove may have been inadvertently left in the winter position inside the roof but this hardly mattered when the party and the maids had been lucky to get out with their lives. No attempt was made to explore Anselme's idea, principally for fear of invalidating any insurance.

An endearing legend that has grown up around the Chalet fire is that it was due to the future Archbishop of Canterbury William Temple, then a tutor at Queen's College, smoking in bed.[38] While this makes a good story, it is untrue: William Temple had been at the Chalet with Richard Tawney, the historian and political thinker, but they had both left the week before the fire, after which their room was taken over by the maids. Had they still been at the Chalet it might have been possible to argue that Humphrey Paul's account was an attempt at a cover-up. As it was, the maids had come down to use the ground-floor room vacated by Temple and Tawney and this may have saved their lives.

Humphrey Paul wrote that he did not think he could bear to look at anyone who had been at the Chalet and in fact he never went there again, as he left Oxford the following year. However, when the news reached Sligger in Hong Kong he was remarkably phlegmatic and there is no evidence that he was inclined to 'kill the messenger'. No doubt his reaction was in part influenced by his devout faith but the view he expressed to friends is illustrative of how he saw the reading parties. He said that the Chalet was really an institution rather than a building and therefore was not capable of being burned. He said that he would inspect the remains on his way back through Europe and would then explore the insurance and rebuilding.[39] The Chalet du Rocher was available and he decided to rent it and to continue the summer parties during the rebuilding.

We do not know the detail of what was destroyed in the fire. The existence of some of David Urquhart's papers in the Archives at

Balliol College indicates that at least some of his work had been transferred there but to what extent his papers and pamphlets had been
cleared out is unknown. The only artwork that appears to survive
from the Old Chalet is a fine watercolour (Fig. 43); this may have been
rescued from the burning building or brought in after the rebuilding.
It appears probable that much material relating to the work of David
and Harriet Urquhart was lost that night.

The Chalet du Rocher was available because the Wynford Philipps
family had used it with decreasing frequency as John Wynford
Philipps' career in public life had grown more demanding.[40] This
allowed Sligger to continue the summer reading parties through the
next three years while the new building proceeded. We do not know
how much what quickly became known as the Old Chalet had been
insured for but thanks to Chichester Fortescue's legacy Sligger had
the resources to rebuild exactly as he wished. The Old Chalet had
been built as a summer home and rarely accommodated more than
eight people; to judge from the number of visitors recorded over the
years there must have been times when every available room was
pressed into service. Now Sligger set about creating a building suitable for his reading parties.

The Old Chalet had a central core of four ground-floor rooms
with dormer bedrooms above. The New Chalet was of three storeys
and covered a considerably greater area (Appendix 2). It had less the
character of a family chalet and more that of one of the larger mountain refuges or a small Alpine hotel (Fig. 16). On the ground floor the
original layout was closely followed but this time the front entrance
opened directly into a large salon on the left side of the building.
Behind it was a smaller salon, which could be used as an additional
bedroom, as previously. The Turkish bath led off the salon to the
right of the entrance; unlike his father, Sligger did not insist that
guests entered the house only after bathing. A scullery occupied the
space behind the Turkish bath and a new feature was a rear entrance
and lobby between the petit salon and the scullery, from which the
stairs to the first floor ascended. The dining room, as previously,
was to the right of the Turkish bath but much bigger and incorporated into the main building and, together with an enlarged kitchen
behind, added significantly to the building's footprint and space for
bedrooms above.

Bedrooms for guests were on the first floor. There were four double rooms across the front, opening onto a balcony which with its south-facing aspect proved valuable for drying clothes. At the back were three single rooms, separated by a roomy landing with storage cupboards. The balcony extended around the western end, providing cover for two west-facing porches on the ground floor. It also connected the western bedrooms at the front and rear, which may have been why Sligger himself always preferred to use the secluded rear room at the east end, at the far end of the first-floor corridor. From one point of view this was a surprising choice, as the western elevation gave the best mountain views to be had from the Chalet while the eastern rooms looked into the slope of the hill. Perhaps it was a feature of Sligger's character that he provided his maids with a better outlook from the loft than the one he had himself. On the other hand his room was quiet and was heated by the kitchen below.

The loft provided a large central open area with rooms for the staff at the east and west ends. A remarkably modern feature – indeed revolutionary for its time in the mountains – was a projecting tower in stone at the rear which housed ground- and first-floor water closets. Another surprising feature, given the history of the Old Chalet, was the provision of open fireplaces in the petit salon, scullery and dining room. The main salon was equipped with a sealed wood-burning stove and the kitchen had an open range, again heated by wood. The Turkish bath had a wooden floor with sunken tiled areas for the braziers and a cold sluicing area.

In view of the size of the Chalet, there was more building in stone, this time going up two storeys to the floor of the loft. The work was carried out by two local craftsmen, M. Besia and M. Bouchard,[41,42] and the cost of the rebuild was several times that of the purchase price for the Old Chalet.[43] Mélèze timber was used for the structural elements such as the beams and uprights, the rooms being clad in Douglas fir. The mélèze showed its quality as building material: the ground-floor beams were laid on the soil of the mountainside without protection and lasted a hundred years before they needed replacement. Fixtures and fittings were provided from local suppliers and from Oxford, including fine blankets of wool which can still be seen in the Chalet today. Sligger seems not to have stinted on the provision of the New Chalet in any measure.

The New Chalet opened in July 1909. While Sligger had created a building to serve his aims, he never lost his affection for the Chalet of his childhood. His comment was that the New Chalet left him feeling like the ancient Jews who looked at the New Temple and wept for the thought of the Old but that it would improve as the wood darkened.[44] That said, he had created a building that was eminently fit for his purpose, as parties over the last century have demonstrated. Overall the New Chalet offered comfortable accommodation for more than a dozen people, excluding the staff. Later generations, less used to privileged living and servants and more willing to share living space, have found that parties of around twenty can be accommodated without discomfort. Over a century later Sligger's building still serves faithfully the purpose which dictated its design.

In keeping with this new provision, numbers in the parties began to rise from 1909 and also to split into two groups, one visiting in July, the other in August. Generally from this time there were a dozen or more undergraduates in each of these groups.

In 1912 Sligger employed a local builder and carpenter to create a small chapel at the rear of the Chalet (Fig. 18). This was built between the main building and the wooden stable and was a small stone box, around three metres wide and four metres long, with a gabled roof with wide eaves. Internally it was panelled in pine with a wooden altar and altar rail (Fig. 19). Sligger bought reproduction Della Robbia ceramics to decorate it: a depiction of the Gloria for above the altar, a small holy water stoup and two large rondels to set in the front wall. A set of vestments was acquired and Sligger would take Mass regularly with his visitor priests. On Sundays the local population would also join in.[44]

Perhaps it was the fire of 1906 and the need to find another house for the parties which in 1913 prompted Sligger to extend his property with the purchase of a second chalet, at Mont Forchet. This lies on the southern side of the Prarion, about an hour's walk from the Chalet des Anglais and a little above the Motivon halt on the TMB track from Saint Gervais to Nid d'Aigle on the west side of Mont Blanc. It is one of just two chalets occupying a small south-facing escarpment.

The Mont Forchet chalet was bought from Miss Alice le Geyl for the sum of £303.[45] Sligger seems to have had business with Miss le Geyl before 1913: the Mont Forchet chalet appears in his photograph albums well before this and in 1908 Miss le Geyl received a bill for spices in both their names (as 'M. Urquoi'.[46] The way in which the traders of Saint Gervais addressed him was subject to charming phonetic variations: 'Eurguard' is another example).[47] However, nothing else is known about their relationship. This later purchase may, perhaps, have given rise to Cyril Bailey's impression that Sligger's brother David sold the Chalet des Anglais and Sligger was obliged to buy it back.[30]

The Mont Forchet chalet was a simple affair of a stone-built ground floor and wooden first floor and comparable to the first Chalet des Anglais. Sligger's motivation in buying a second chalet is unknown but it may have been an investment or due to a wish to provide another venue for friends visiting the Haute-Savoie. It is possible that he wanted to replace the facility that his family had lost: his sister Harriet was often to use it with her lifelong friend Gertrude Robinson, their father's biographer. It is not beyond the bounds of possibility that he bought it to relieve Miss le Geyl of financial problems. The Mont Forchet chalet seems never to have been used for overflow of the reading parties and became known as the 'Honeymoon Chalet' because it was frequently offered to chaletites and friends for this purpose: the idea may have been prompted by the Baileys' honeymoon at Mélèzes the year before the purchase. Among those to benefit from this arrangement were barrister and politician Walter Monckton and his wife Polly just before the First World War[48] and future Prime Minister Harold and Dorothy Macmillan after the war.[49] This apart, it never seems to have figured large in Sligger's affections like the Chalet des Anglais and very little has been recorded to tell its story until it was sold in 1959. It survived largely in its original form until 2016, when it underwent extensive rebuilding and modernisation.

In keeping with local practice, the Honeymoon Chalet also became known to its surrounding community as the 'Chalet des Anglais'. As we have noted earlier, this was also the colloquial name attached to Alfred Wills' chalet of 'The Eagle's Nest' above the village of Sixt. Both have continued to hold the title into modern times.

In May 1914 the Chalet's *gardien* Anselme Martin died suddenly at the age of fifty-three. Sligger inserted a touching tribute in the diary, referring to '… the excellent, capable and faithful Anselme Martin, to whom the Chalet and its inhabitants have owed so much for many years'. Anselme's widow Noémie, fourteen years his junior, was left pregnant with their ninth child and only son, who was born three months after his father's death and baptised Anselme.[10] Sadly the boy died the following spring, leaving Noémie with eight daughters to provide for, five of them under the age of fifteen. However, Noémie Martin was a strong mountain woman who was able to bring up her large family single-handedly. The family connection with the Chalet was not lost on Anselme's death, as three of the daughters were to join Sligger's domestic staff after the First World War. The Martin family chalet was at Mont Paccard, just above the town of Saint Gervais, and Noémie Martin made her last ascent to the Chalet des Anglais in 1970 at the age of ninety-five in the company of two of her daughters, her grandson and his wife, and three of her great-grandchildren.

By the time Sligger reached middle age the Chalet had become an established institution moulded around the personality of 'M. *le Patron*' and it was a major component in his relationship with students. He had financial independence, a fine new building which was well suited to his purpose, a standing in the community in France, and he could rely on loyal support from local firms and families. All of this was directed towards his objective of bringing to young men an understanding of the value of study, of the character of the French, and of the Alps and life in the mountains. It was a heady mixture and one which could not fail to make an impact on his chaletites and the guests he increasingly invited to join them. Just how intense and far-reaching the effects could be is described in the next chapter.

CHAPTER THREE

EDUCATION AND RELATIONSHIPS: THE CHALET IN FRIENDSHIP AND NETWORKING

IT IS A MATTER OF DEBATE why the mother of future Prime Minister Harold Macmillan removed him from Eton College in 1909. Helen Macmillan, known as Nellie, was an American of powerful Nonconformist views who had a morbid fear both of Roman Catholicism and of the relationships which can develop in a male public school. Ostensibly the move was made for his health but it may be relevant that in 1906 a scandal had erupted in the college over abuse of boys and also that while there Harold's elder brother Daniel had developed a suspiciously close friendship with the bisexual John Maynard Keynes.[1] It is probable that Nellie's action was intended more to ward off potential problems with her good-looking younger son than that he had committed any misdemeanour.

At home in London she engaged as private tutor Ronald Knox, a Balliol graduate who was preparing for the priesthood (and happened to be a close friend of Sligger), only to dismiss him a year later when friendship between the two became too close for her comfort.[2] However, she could not prevent the friendship resuming when Harold went up to Balliol in 1912, by which time Knox was chaplain at Trinity College next door. In fact, as Knox inclined progressively to Catholicism (he was to enter the Catholic Church in 1917), Harold toyed with converting.[3] Nellie would have been horrified had she known.

The young Harold Macmillan perfectly fitted Sligger's preferred model of chaletite. A pupil of Cyril Bailey, he was studious (he was to achieve a First in Honour Moderations), handsome and engaged in university activities such as the Union.[4] Moreover, his elder brother Daniel, also at Balliol, had been at the Chalet in 1905 and 1907. In 1913 Harold was 'tried out' at an Easter reading party at Porlock and must have impressed because he duly received an invitation for France for that summer. This was an exciting development: he knew that parties usually comprised the intellectual cream of the college and it was to be his first trip abroad alone.[5]

Harold had attracted Sligger's attention in his first term and had adapted to the intensely male atmosphere which dominated the college.[6] He began to write Sligger letters which would characteristically open 'My dearest Slig' and close 'Your ever-loving Harold'.[7] Through the agency of Ronald Knox at Trinity he also became close to one of Knox's protégés, Guy Lawrence, but his closest friendship in Balliol was with his contemporary Humphrey Sumner.[8] His comments in a letter to Sligger are typical of the uninhibited expression shown by students of this time: 'Humphrey ... I have begun to worship more every day – but I am so frightened that he is beginning to find me out as a weak and shallow thing, and that he will forget or despise me.'[9]

At the Chalet for the month of July in 1913, Harold joined what was in many respects a golden year of chaletites (Fig. 20): Evelyn Cardew, later adviser to the Siamese government; future diplomat Victor Mallet; future lawyer and politician Walter Monckton; Gilbert Talbot from Corpus Christi College, who appeared destined for a career in politics but who was to die in the First World War; Sligger's nephew Frank Tyrrell, future Olympic oarsman Arthur Wiggins from New College; and Sligger's especial protégé, the Roman Catholic Stephen Hewett. On 14 July they had a visit from the son and daughter of Prime Minister Herbert Asquith, Cys (Cyril) and Violet, who were staying at the Chalet du Rocher, probably as Sligger's guests.

Harold took part in demanding walks during his stay, most especially to the glacier at Tête Rousse, which he described with excitement in letters to his mother.[10] However, his main enthusiasm was for the company around him. The diary records an intimate community; Harold is shown in one photograph (Fig. 21) resting his head across Sligger's thigh.[11] After his return to England he wrote:

> What a jolly time we had! I *am* grateful to you, Slig, ever so much
> I want to say which I can't because I'm English ... but it really
> was Heaven. I believe Heaven will be rather like your reading
> parties ... The party we had was so well made that I believe you
> to be a sort of matrimonial agency. Gilbert I thought so much
> nicer than before – you get to know him and he's awfully good.

Arthur Wigg I was especially glad to get to know as I had hardly spoken to him before, and he's very good-looking and has such jolly eyes! (which is such a good thing) and Victor I hope enjoyed it and wasn't *too* much ragged. I don't think he saw it and he was *twice* as nice I'm sure when he left than when he came. And Stephen annoys me (which is good for me) because I don't believe he's ever committed a decent sin to speak of (you're different as the admitted Superman) and your nephew I think expanded largely in the course of a walk; and Walter's a dandy.[12]

Harold never lost his enthusiasm for the Chalet. An invitation for 1914 followed[13] and he had his bags packed ready when an attack of appendicitis in early July meant he had to cancel his plans. His doctor hoped to have his recovery sufficiently advanced to benefit from the air at the Chalet[14] but by then the outbreak of the First World War had brought to an end his time at Balliol. As he remarked, he had been 'sent down by the Kaiser'.[15]

Harold Macmillan's friendships and the way he expressed them were typical of his generation in the Edwardian University. They were affectionate to a degree that might raise eyebrows today; this persisted until he met his future wife Lady Dorothy Cavendish, when these male-orientated sympathies underwent a complete sea change.[16] In short, he passed through a protracted and arguably juvenile homosocial phase which fuelled his affections, a characteristic he shared with his contemporaries. For him, as for them, one of its chief features was that the friendships which resulted were to be intense and lifelong, not least that with Sligger himself.

¤

The Edwardian undergraduate existed in a world very different from that of today's student. It was self-contained, privileged, and dominated by socialising and sport as well as study.[17] It was also almost exclusively male. Contact with the few women's colleges was discouraged and both men and women were locked into their colleges at night. These circumstances moulded their attitudes to each other and in order to understand their relationships and how the reading parties fitted into their lives it is necessary to view the Edwardian student from the context of Sligger's time rather than ours.

In their college students had rooms serviced by a 'scout', a man-servant shared with other undergraduates.[17] Their scout provided morning water for shaving and a cooked breakfast could be taken in their rooms. Chapel, which was a daily event, might follow. Meals could be taken communally in Hall but could also be brought to rooms by the scout and widespread entertaining was the norm. Lectures were usually held in the morning to leave the afternoon free for sport and students were expected to uphold the standing of their college by taking part in competitive sports almost every day. Transport was limited and their usual means of moving about was to walk, run or cycle. The amount of physical exercise which they managed to pack into each term explains why the two-hour mountain walk up from Saint Gervais and the other walks from the Chalet may not have been so daunting as might appear today.

Although some lectures were given the University prided itself on the tutorial system of teaching, as it continues to do. Students studied privately to produce an essay which was read to their tutor at weekly tutorials. It was a dominant feature of college life that tutors and students lived in close proximity, an expression of the University's self-perceived role *in loco parentis*. College rooms were organised on individual staircases, in effect dividing the wings of quadrangles into separate houses in which a tutor's room was surrounded by under-graduates'. Within each college a small number of the University's students were attached to individual tutors for teaching and mentoring in their subject. Each college was therefore a multidisciplinary body in which social life and sport were the unifying factors. Each college aimed to provide its students with a rich communal experience, an approach which was regarded as sound preparation for the public life that so many of them would lead after graduation.

Sligger was generally not regarded as a skilled lecturer except in areas of personal interest or experience, when he could be more illuminating.[18] Like many of that time, and indeed since, he regarded tutorials with 'his' students as the main thrust of his teaching. The future actor Raymond Massey (Balliol 1919) found him a good tutor, offering an easy-going but witty exploration of the political philosophy of Modern History.[19] Sligger's students discovered that he was not inclined to criticise their essays stringently, nor to impose his own view; instead he sought to widen their vision by offering his own perspective, drawing on his large collection of books, many of which he annotated with comments. He was generous in lending this material out and also in making gifts of books that he thought should accompany students through their life.[20,21] It is interesting to speculate how much of Lord Carlingford's fortune was spent in this way.

In general Sligger was less concerned with how well his students performed in their degree than how they prepared for their future lives, which for him meant an emphasis on good taste and civic duty.[21] This was partly influenced by his own background: he embodied the Edwardian principles of diligence and loyalty to institution and country.[22] His view of History, especially European History, was wider than that of many of his contemporaries, for whom the subject was usually dominated by England and the British Empire.[23] He gave practical expression to this by inviting selected students to accompany him on the cultural tours of Europe with which he occupied his vacations. The future author and baronet Lawrence Evelyn Jones (Balliol 1904) was '... deeply impressed by him ... he seemed to get under the skin of the men for whom the Middle Ages were modern times and to take his pupil with him'.[24]

Sligger's outstanding feature was his degree of empathy with students; he was one of those people for whom difference in age is of no importance. Some who try this approach, of being 'one of the boys', suffer a loss of authority. In Sligger's case his natural dignity and culture seem to have protected him, especially when he became Dean and was responsible for student discipline. For the writer Cyril Connolly (Chalet 1923–7), Sligger was 'a Dean who you can pinch, put your arms round his neck and call Sligger with no self-consciousness at all'.[25] Undergraduates came to know that it was acceptable to call at his rooms above the back gate of the college at any time. If he was working he would simply direct the visitor to his books or photograph albums and then invite him to talk when he had completed the task in hand.[26]

This ability to treat everyone as equal was the root of his popularity. Paul Rowntree Clifford (Balliol 1932) was surprised in his first term to find the elderly Sligger knocking at his door: Paul's old headmaster was coming to lunch and would he like to join them? Paul was struck that an elderly man, who at that stage clearly had difficulty with his breathing, should have climbed three flights of stairs to deliver an invitation when he could easily have sent a note by one of the college porters.[27] In fact Sligger always preferred his first contact with a student to be a social event like lunch or tea (he once remarked that there were insufficient meals in the day for this).[28] As Walter Crocker (Balliol 1926) remembered, 'Examinations and results and academic committees and all the fussing repelled him. He entertained well and did his entertaining on the principle that a dinner party can stand a sprinkling of success, but not more than a sprinkling. Good company was what mattered.'[29]

It is unsurprising that Sligger's approach found a ready response in his students. Their accounts of their time in Oxford are scattered with tributes to him, such as the 'immediate friendliness' with which Philip Mason (Chalet 1925) was welcomed,[21] or, from Herbert Scheftel (Chalet 1929), 'this wonderful human being, gentle, learned and understanding'.[30] For Percy Wykes (Balliol 1926), he had a 'happy interest in other people'.[31] Lawrence Jones described him as 'this friendly man, with a touch of the friar alike in his looks and his ubiquity'.[24]

Future politician Robert Boothby (Chalet 1922) at Magdalen College felt that the reasons Sligger's influence extended so far across Oxford were simple: 'He genuinely liked the young, he was the kindest man I have ever known, and he was always out to help.'[32] Liberal Party leader Jo Grimond (Chalet 1933 & 1935) remembered him as 'a type of don now rare and much missed', who 'lived not for promotion nor by writing articles or books' but who 'spread through the college a feeling of goodwill'.[33] However, these comments imply that Sligger took his own scholarship less than completely seriously, which was not the case: Quintin Hogg (later Lord Hailsham, Chalet 1927–31) perceptively summed up Sligger as a combination of serious scholarship and informal social habits.[34]

Within the college this relationship with students was most intensely expressed in evening 'salons' in his rooms above the back gate of Balliol; these became famous throughout Oxford. The salons were held after dinner, generally from around 9 p.m. until about midnight.[26] Although Sligger welcomed visitors at any time, attendance at an evening salon was by invitation. Those from other colleges who arrived after Balliol was locked for the night could call at his window and he would throw down a key to the back gate. Soft drinks – usually lemonade – were served and the main objective of this gathering was gentle conversation. This practice would find its most concentrated expression at the Chalet.

The salons were not confined to Balliol members and sometimes up to half might come from other colleges. Philip Mason recorded that, while Sligger liked men of a certain background, notably Etonians and Wykehamists, he tried to include some with other backgrounds.[26] Future art historian Kenneth Clark (Chalet 1924) recalled: 'Into this room drifted every evening a very mixed assortment of undergraduates – earnest young scholars, minor royalty, priests, budding poets and a few lonely nonentities ... of course there was no drink, which kept out the more spirited undergraduates, but it was a reservoir of kindness and tolerance and I went there most gratefully.'[35] He described Sligger as *'like the perfect hostess'* [my italics]. Less positively, George 'Dadie' Rylands, who often visited from King's College in Cambridge, found the Dean 'a prim maiden aunt who won popularity among the undergraduates because he encouraged them to be men of the world rather than scholars'.[36]

Evenings would frequently end with one or two favoured students staying on into the small hours. Harold Nicolson (Chalet 1906), the future author and husband of Vita Sackville-West, is typical: Sligger invited him to lunch shortly after his arrival at Balliol in 1904. Nicolson was initially suspicious of the motivation of this senior member of the college but soon found himself demonstrating his skill at the piano in Sligger's rooms until the early hours of the morning.[37]

This was an environment in which friendships were readily made and consolidated. The philosopher Isaiah Berlin attributed to the salons the long-lasting friendship between Sligger's Balliol colleagues Roger Mynors and Humphrey Sumner (later to be Warden of All Souls College), Richard Pares (subsequently Professor of History at Edinburgh), Tom Boase (from Magdalen College where he was later President and also University Vice-Chancellor), Christopher Cox (a Balliol undergraduate and later Fellow of New College) and John Maud (from New College and subsequently Master of University College).[38]

When it came to choosing members for the summer reading parties, therefore, Sligger had experience to draw on. His evening salons allowed him to identify those who were good company and who he felt would benefit. In fact, his ability to select men of promise and future achievement was remarkable. Admittedly, the constituency he drew from was selective, especially in the Balliol of the time which was widely regarded as the leading college for preparation for public life, but analysis of the careers of those who went to the Chalet shows such a strong correlation with success that it can only indicate an unerring skill. Setting aside those who were to die in the First World War, the register of chaletites up to Sligger's death reads like a roll-call of politicians, civil servants, judges, diplomats, academics and headteachers, high-ranking churchmen and senior army officers.

A characteristic example of Sligger's ability to choose men of promise was the Australian Frederick Septimus Kelly (Chalet 1902). A student of the piano, Kelly wanted to study with a pupil of Chopin's but instead his parents insisted on him entering Balliol as Nettleship Musical Scholar in 1898. He rowed for Balliol and the University and later in the 1908 Olympic Games and, although highly skilled at sport, after leaving Balliol he decided to concentrate on composition. He entered war service in 1914 in the Royal Naval Division and in 1915 produced a notable *Elegy for String Orchestra* in memory of his naval colleague the poet Rupert Brooke, who died of septicaemia before seeing action. Kelly received the Distinguished Service Cross for service at Gallipoli but was ultimately to die in the Battle of the Somme.[39] He joins the list of gifted musicians of that generation who were lost in action.

In the same way that Sligger's salons were not limited to Balliol members, when it came to the Chalet he chose from across Oxford and sometimes beyond. Before the First World War, apart from wives and visitors, around a quarter of the chaletites came from other colleges. A significant number were from New College, closely followed by Christ Church, Magdalen and Trinity. There was also a small number from the other Oxford colleges and occasional guests from other universities. Between the wars the proportion rose to around 40 per cent with a similar distribution across the colleges.

Sligger could be expected to know the Balliol students well but he appears to have been equally skilled in assessing those from outside Balliol. For example, the three members of University College who were at the Chalet before 1914 and who survived the First World War subsequently comprised a specialist in art history of the Middle East, James Wilkinson; a deputy Secretary-General of the League of Nations, Francis Walters; and a leading barrister, Clive Burt. From Trinity College came the private secretary to three monarchs, Sir Alan Lascelles (Chalet 1907–8). The inter-war period would boast three future heads of Oxford colleges from outside Balliol: William Hayter (Chalet 1926–9) and Lord Redcliffe-Maud (Chalet 1924–5) from New

College, and A. L. P. Norrington (Chalet 1921) from Trinity College. Balliol itself provided three more: Tom Boase (Chalet 1920–32), John Sparrow (Chalet 1926 & 1929) and Humphrey Sumner (Chalet 1919–29). From Magdalen College David Lindsay, Lord Balniel (Chalet 1921 & 1923) would go on lead a series of arts institutions, culminating in chairmanship of the National Trust.

So what did a student need to qualify for an invitation to the Chalet? The membership is testimony to Sligger's ability to select achievers but they also reflected his personal tastes. First and foremost they had to be studious. Sligger always did what he could to help the floundering student and many recorded their gratitude to him but such cases do not figure prominently in the Chalet lists. He had no time for those who failed to take work seriously, and especially not for those who regarded their time at Oxford as an opportunity for high living. Harold Macmillan remembered 'In Aubrey Herbert's time the inspired summer reading parties managed to gain four Firsts from the eight Balliol men present.'[5]

A sporting interest could also be considered an advantage but here Sligger was more inclined to be inclusive. Undoubtedly he liked to have around him a few who would not find the environment of the Alps too demanding and in any case most undergraduates then were highly fit but he also liked to use the Chalet to introduce some to the mountains and outdoor life.

Predominantly, it was a distinct advantage to be good-looking; the photographs in the Chalet diaries and his personal albums make it clear that his selection usually fell on the more handsome examples of the undergraduate body and he became well known for this.[40] It was also commented on locally in France, the chaletites becoming known as '*les beaux jeunes hommes de M. Urquhart*'. Sligger's comment was that they might be αγαθοί (*agathoi*), an expression which in Homer's writing would suggest they were brave and well-born. While he might also have been reflecting the University's prevailing taste for Hellenism he may have meant no more than that as men they had qualities which could be admired.

However, the desideratum of good looks was not overriding; if he felt he was dealing with someone of particular value their looks became irrelevant. For example, the writer Cyril Connolly (Chalet 1923–7), to whom Sligger devoted considerable effort during and after his undergraduate time, would not have fallen within a conventional view of handsome (Fig. 23).[41] Conversely, Beverley Nichols (Balliol 1917) might have been thought to have been an ideal chaletite – intelligent, handsome, stylish and popular across Oxford. Nichols had a false start at Balliol before the war; after it Sligger encouraged his return and tried to promote him but became frustrated when Beverley's attraction to the Union took precedence over his work.[41] No invitation to the Chalet was forthcoming; it is clear that where the Chalet was concerned good looks did not outweigh scholarship.

In Walter Crocker's view, Sligger had an inherent respect for scholarship and intelligence, undoubtedly combined with a preference for good-looking students and with an inclination to the governing classes. Yet he possessed 'too much Christianity and (especially) too much good breeding to be a snob'.[42] Crocker believed he frequently helped the impoverished student but always secretly. Crocker was never invited to the Chalet and later commented, 'perhaps I was a little rough-hewn for that'.[42]

As the Chalet became an institution and attracted attention it was inevitable, given the claustrophobic nature of the University community, that Sligger's practices would raise questions about his motivation. Gatherings of young people in a secluded place, the reading parties raised suspicions of nefarious activity; they still do today among less informed colleagues. Sligger's close contact with his students did not meet the approval of all his colleagues and those inclined to be critical were only encouraged by his practice of taking selected students on cultural tours of Europe.

Maurice Bowra, at New College first and later Wadham College, was a vocal critic. There were some similarities between the two men: Bowra also ran salons and UK reading parties and was certainly open to the homoerotic tendencies of his time,[43] but his approach was essentially hedonistic to Sligger's ascetic.[44] Bowra was inclined to be scornful of the restraint in Sligger's entertaining, dismissing him as 'a nice old nurse'.[45] He was delighted when Cyril Connolly told him that at the Chalet he had written obscene comments on the back of Sligger's Catholic pictures;[44] this was subsequently checked by Dr Leslie Mitchell from University College (Chalet 1970–76) and found to be untrue.[46] No doubt the students of the time played up the factional division, as students will, and the truth of the relationship between the two men is more complex. They sometimes shared British reading parties[43] and Sligger's photograph album shows them having tea together on the lawn at Balliol. When Bowra published his reminiscences thirty years after Sligger died he was inclined to be generous to Sligger's memory.[47]

John Betjeman's autobiographical poem *Summoned by Bells* provides an eloquent description of Sligger and his circle in the late 1920s when Betjeman was at Magdalen:

What time magnolia's bursting into bloom,
By Balliol's brain-grey wall,
See clever satyr sprawl,
And well-bred faun,
Round 'Sligger' in his deck-chair on the lawn.[48]

The description is of Sligger on home ground in Balliol but many chaletites would also have recognised the atmosphere around Sligger at the Chalet. As always Betjeman reveals his sensitivity to the underlying emotion and his skill in creating a world of meaning in a few words. By describing 'clever satyr' he combines the intellectual and aesthetic with a priapic sensuality. That the fauns were 'well-bred' acknowledges the aristocratic and privileged among Sligger's circle but ties it to an earthiness and sense of wildness. Both expressions invoke an aura of youthful beauty beyond the natural. Finally, the word 'sprawl' invests the circle around Sligger with something intimate and perhaps louche: one thinks back to the photograph of the young Harold Macmillan lying affectionately across Sligger's thigh (Fig. 21).

These, then, were the men who provided Sligger with his chaletites. He gathered around himself attractive students who, in the manner of their time, were attuned to close emotional ties between men. At the Chalet the environment and activities only intensified the intimacy, as the diaries and photographs make clear. The question has to be asked – because it was asked in his own time and has been raised by commentators since – to what extent this may have been a function of Sligger's own sexuality.[49,50]

Evelyn Waugh is famously claimed to have sung under Sligger's window 'The Dean of Balliol sleeps with men' to the tune of 'Here we go gathering nuts in May'.[51] Setting aside for the present the fact that Waugh has to be regarded as a hostile witness, suspicions were definitely fostered by the exclusive nature of the reading parties and by Sligger's proximity to young men. These perceptions may have acted against him when the Mastership of Balliol came up for election in 1924 when he was the senior Fellow.[52] In fact it is more likely that the college, an Anglican institution, would never have elected a devout Roman Catholic as Master at that time.

Today the question of Sligger's orientation would be of little relevance. At the time, however, active homosexuality was a criminal offence, resulting potentially in dismissal and imprisonment but certainly social disgrace. While the University, in common with the rest of British society, turned a blind eye to covert relationships between men, the famous trial of Oscar Wilde in 1895 (presided over by Sligger's fellow chalet-owner Alfred Wills)[53] had shown that there was no tolerance for overt homosexuality. This would remain the position in Britain until the law changed in 1967.

Consideration of Sligger's sexuality is today significant only for what it might say about his relationships and whether it influenced life at the Chalet. To modern eyes there appears some justification for Evelyn Waugh's claim. Sligger enjoyed the company of attractive young men and he had his favourites; Volume 2 of his photographs consists largely of portraits and might justifiably be entitled 'Good-looking young men I have known'. Pictures of students swimming naked during the reading parties (Fig. 22) were preserved openly in his photograph albums and sometimes labelled '*Naiads*', which would raise eyebrows today. However, at that time nude swimming was the norm in many public schools. The family association with the Turkish bath may also have been relevant: David Urquhart's Hammam was a place where Victorian men enjoyed male company away from female influence at home but which also provided an environment for gay men to meet. Even up to a few years before he died Sligger was in the habit of sharing a Turkish bath with past students when they visited. His father's influence may have been more fundamental: David Urquhart encouraged nudism and in later life Sligger recalled that when he was a boy his father had taken him across Europe by train totally naked, covering him with a copy of *The Times* if other passengers objected.[54]

It is facile to assume that all unmarried Edwardian dons were covert or latent homosexuals. In any serious enquiry about Sligger there are two apparent witnesses for the 'prosecution', as it would have been regarded in his time, Rupert Hart-Davis and Evelyn Waugh.

In 1978 Rupert Hart-Davis published his correspondence with George Lyttelton, his old teacher at Eton, in which he described Sligger as 'a purring old doctored tom-cat, who gave lemonade-parties at which he stroked the knees of rugger-blues – ugh! I've never seen a more completely homosexual man.'[55] Definitive though this sounds, there is a great deal that is wrong about Hart-Davis' comments. He arrived at Balliol in the autumn of 1926, found university life uncongenial and left in January 1927, so his experience was limited. Anthony Powell, who entered Balliol three years before Hart-Davis, reported that the evening salons had come to an end well before his time, so Hart-Davis cannot have seen them.[56] Sligger's sports interests were cricket and rowing; his photograph albums show plenty of these but none of rugby. Moreover, Hart-Davis, who was never a member of Sligger's circle, nor a chaletite, was writing thirty years after the event and trying to impress on Lyttelton a point about the dons of his time. He overlooks the fact that he contradicts himself in another letter, where he said there was 'never a whisper' about Sligger.[57] Overall he appears merely to have seized on Sligger as a convenient model for the bachelor don of popular legend.

Evelyn Waugh's motivation is more dubious. Arriving at Hertford College a term late and out of step with his contemporaries, Waugh was highly sensitive to feelings of exclusion. He was never a member of Sligger's circle despite having close friends at Balliol, some of whom were frequent chaletites, another exclusion which may well have rankled. Sligger attached high value to scholarship, whereas Waugh was too fond of the high life to perform well in his studies. For his model Waugh inclined to Maurice Bowra and was no doubt influenced by Bowra's views of Sligger.

But Waugh had a more powerful reason to dislike Sligger. He joined the Hypocrites, one of the University's more riotous drinking clubs with strong homosexual leanings. Tellingly, although he published his youthful diaries, he destroyed the Oxford volumes but it is now believed he had several homosexual attachments while at Oxford.[58] One of these was with Balliol student Richard Pares. Pares was a product of Winchester: quiet, boyish, good-looking and gifted with a fine mind that would win him the Chair of History at Edinburgh. He was, moreover, a favoured student of Sligger's and a frequent chaletite, going there every year. It is not known if Waugh's relationship with Pares became physical but in a letter to

Nancy Mitford thirty years later Evelyn Waugh described him as 'my first homosexual love'.[59] When Waugh tried to enlist Pares in the Hypocrites Sligger saw danger coming and intervened; the friendship between Pares and Waugh foundered.[51] In later life and happily married, Pares was content to acknowledge the relationship and remained on good terms with Waugh. The latter's feelings, however, are not difficult to interpret: the theft of a lover, or even a potential one, is not to be borne and Waugh's campaign against Sligger became a long-running feud in which he never lost an opportunity to make a slighting reference. It was only after Waugh converted to Catholicism and twenty-five years had passed since Sligger's death that he felt able to describe Sligger more dispassionately when recalling his part in supporting the Catholic Church in Oxford and the career of Ronald Knox.[60]

Commentators have claimed to see Sligger in some of the less attractive of Waugh's fictional characters but the most powerful barb came in 1924 in the form of a silent film that Waugh made. In *The Scarlet Woman* (see Interlude) he showed an effeminate Roman Catholic Dean of Balliol plotting to seduce the Prince of Wales. The reference to Sligger was explicit, as the student newspaper *Isis* made clear in its review. The film was shown in Oxford and may well have done significant harm to Sligger's standing.

The two main claims for Sligger's homosexuality, therefore, are suspect. When one turns to witnesses who knew him well, no claims are found that he was homosexual.[24,40] Gay men of the time were necessarily committed to a secret life but friendships with Sligger were so close and so numerous that it is highly likely that if he had been actively gay some contemporary would have revealed the fact. This is borne out by living conditions at the Chalet, which are claustrophobic to a degree that precludes secrecy. Given the overheated psychological atmosphere of the Edwardian University it is unthinkable that any physical relationships would not have become common knowledge. It is also probable that competitive colleagues would have been ready to expose anything which appeared hypocritical in a man whose intense religious faith expressed itself in ways which were regarded as austere and monkish. The fact that no one ever did has to be regarded as significant.

Overall there is no evidence to suggest Sligger was anything other than a celibate bachelor don with close friendships with his undergraduates, and in that respect he can be regarded as typical of his time. He may well have enjoyed the homosocial environment in which he lived but in this respect also he was a product of his era and upbringing. It is possible that he had, and enjoyed, a voyeuristic or homoerotic streak, but if so he would not have been dissimilar to many of his Oxford contemporaries.

Sligger's students therefore came into the orbit of a don who strongly enjoyed the company of young men and saw nothing wrong in close friendship with them, and who did not expect these friendships to end when they left university. The Chalet offered a much more fruitful environment than colleges for pursuing this approach. As Julian Huxley (Chalet 1908 & 1910) put it, 'At the Chalet the mixing process continued, with excellent results – many new friendships were made on those airy heights, with their superb view of Mont Blanc.'[61] It was this aspect of relationships at the Chalet which allowed Harold Macmillan to describe Sligger as a 'matrimonial agency'.[12]

To understand student relationships around Sligger one needs to look with the eyes of their time rather than ours. In their inward-looking, intimate and male community they treated each other in a way that today would be considered unconventional. It was common for heterosexual men to walk about arm-in-arm and to regularly use words like 'beautiful', 'dear' and 'love' in their interactions, which today would be unusual but which for them simply reflected their constricted male society and its intimacy. For example, nude swimming was common on stretches of the river in Oxford, as it was in the lakes around the Chalet. Today this is a specialist activity for naturist clubs but then it was natural for men when together. Sligger's photograph albums record the bathers, both in France and in Oxford; clearly at the time nothing was thought wrong in taking photographs and displaying them openly. As the writer Max Hastings commented in relation to Winston Churchill, their generation had a lack of embarrassment about nakedness 'characteristic of English public schoolboys, soldiers, and patricians accustomed to regard servants as mere extensions of the furniture'.[62] When it came to behaviour at the Chalet itself, however, *The Perfect Chalet-ite* is positively daunting in demanding decency at all times. The meaning is clear: out on the mountain men could be naturally male with each other but at the Chalet, where maids slept in the loft, normal Edwardian etiquette prevailed.

These young men had a radically different background to that of their peers today. Brought up in well-to-do families, their fathers tended to be distant and their unsupervised female contact was likely to be limited to mothers, sisters and nannies. Otherwise their contact was with their own sex, especially as they were almost exclusively the products of public schools. In popular imagination the English public schools have long been regarded as rife with sodomy, but even superficial examination reveals this to be caricature. No doubt many gay boys discovered their sexuality at school but there is no reason to believe that the incidence of homosexuality then was different from now. Instead, the majority of boys going through puberty – which for their generation occurred later than it does today – had to find what exploration of sexual emotion they could within their own environment. This might have extended to sex with another boy and sexual predation by older boys on younger ones certainly occurred but it need not have been widespread. As E. M. Forster commented, the public schools were guilty of sending out into the world boys 'with well-developed bodies, fairly developed minds, and under-developed hearts'.[63] For many of them, any real emotional exploration had to wait until university and they were well primed for the environment they found there.

In the middle of the nineteenth century Benjamin Jowett, Master of Balliol, had led major reform in the University's approach to classical arts, replacing slavish attachment to grammar with understanding of classical culture, especially that of the Greeks.[64] Jowett's hope was that what came to be known as 'Hellenism' would provide the model for a stable Victorian society.[65] These Greek concepts embodied admiration of bodily perfection and heroic nudity as demonstrated by *kouroi* statues, and pursuit of physical fitness and nude athleticism as in the Olympic Games. They also included idealistic male friendships, for example that between Achilles and Patroclus, and the principle of old men mentoring younger ones.

These ideas could not have fallen on more fertile ground than Victorian Oxford. The college environment, tutorials and sport were all given new meaning by Hellenism. Tutorials could be seen to reflect Plato and his concepts of group debate and mentoring, with an undercurrent of intimate friendship that was not necessarily sexual. The reading party also could be viewed as a Socratic or Platonic concept and concurred with the mood of the time. However, Hellenism also removed negative associations from close relationship between men. Gay writers such as Walter Pater and John Addington Symonds – both students of Jowett's – felt free to expound the concept of ideal love between men and to destroy the social myth that homosexuality meant effeminacy.[66] When Symonds arrived at Balliol in 1858 he found himself in a world where 'perfervid friendships between undergraduates, and to a lesser extent between undergraduates and dons, were commonplace if not quite unremarkable'.[67] Hellenism gave gay men a cloak under which their orientation found acceptability and for heterosexual students it meant that affection between men could have positive associations. And, as the young typically incline to challenging behaviour, it offered both an avenue for flouting social conventions. Forbidden pleasures, after all, usually arouse a frisson of excitement, especially in young men. Hellenism simply opened the gates to an enhanced level of homoeroticism in Victorian Oxford.

The effect was to polarise the perception students had of themselves into two camps. In one intellectualism was associated with homosexuality, either real or affected (the 'Aesthetes'); in the other heterosexuality was held to equate to brawn and prowess on the sports field (the 'Hearties').[68] This is a generalisation and like all such is dangerous, even if it was the dominant perception among undergraduates in Sligger's time. The ideal of sport among the Hearties had its Hellenistic and homoerotic elements and it would be illogical for homosexuality to have been exclusive to Aesthetes, for many of whom a gay persona was in any case only a passing affectation.[69]

In essence the cult of the Aesthetes was unchanged from the time of the young Oscar Wilde and the Aesthetic Movement, which W. S. Gilbert parodied in the 1881 Savoy Opera *Patience*. As John Betjeman observed, the Aesthetes, in 'cream or strawberry-pink flannel', spent most of their time in cafés and sherry parties and 'never found out … where the college playing fields were or which was the college barge'.[70] Admittedly, this was all changing by the later years of Sligger's life. The Irish poet Louis MacNeice, who arrived at Merton College in 1926, found that 'the master decadents had gone and their acolytes were soon to follow'.[71] It was still possible to attend parties with students in powder, perfume and velvets but MacNeice, who 'was not, and could not pretend to be, homosexual', was relieved to discover that it was possible to pursue his studies less flamboyantly. He was inclined to attribute the change to the General Strike of that year, but a more powerful factor is probably the long shadow cast by the First World War, which had destroyed the certainties of the Edwardian era.

Into this heady atmosphere came young men who were by modern standards of very limited sexual maturity.[69] They were projected into a homoerotic environment at an age when they were still struggling with their own sexual development and it is unsurprising if they adopted behaviour which for many was foreign to their later lives. Close friendships of openly romantic character thrived and constituted one of the norms of student behaviour. Kissing and hugging was common, and sharing a bed; it is unlikely that for many this ever extended beyond embrace or masturbation but even there the boundaries are vague.[72] It need not be assumed that then, any more than now, intense friendship automatically involved physical intimacy even if it did for some. In any case, most of those who showed what would be regarded today as actively gay behaviour subsequently left this phase behind them and became happily married men. For these reasons care has to be exercised in defining a gay 'affair' between Edwardian students.

In 1975 the author Noel Blakiston published the youthful 1920s correspondence between himself and Cyril Connolly under the title *A Romantic Friendship*.[73] Cyril had befriended Noel at Eton, where Cyril had shown homoerotic leanings (when he left the headmaster warned him off further contact with boys there)[74] and their friendship continued into Noel's time at Cambridge while Cyril was at Oxford under Sligger's tutelage. Their letters are liberally distributed with terms of endearment and pleas for closer contact and the overall feeling is of an unsatisfied longing. There are coy references to Margaret Kennedy's *The Constant Nymph*, a rather innocuous story of Bohemian life that occupied for that generation the place that D. H. Lawrence and *Lady Chatterley's Lover* would for a later one.

While continuing to pursue Noel, if largely in writing, Cyril also conceived an infatuation with another Etonian, Robert (Bobbie) Longden, by then a Magdalen College undergraduate and another of Sligger's protégés.[75] In December 1922 Sligger took both Cyril and Bobbie on a tour of Rome and Sicily. At this point Cyril's feelings were so confused that he was capable of writing to both Noel and Bobbie to explain his feelings for the other; one wonders what they each thought of this. Sligger met Noel Blakiston in 1924 and approved of Noel's looks and intelligence, regarding him as a good influence on Cyril. Characteristically, he also developed his own friendship with Noel and maintained this after both men had left university. Cyril angled successfully for Noel to get an invitation to the Minehead reading party in January 1925, only to be dejected when Noel turned it down. However, Sligger restored the equilibrium by inviting both to the Chalet that year (Fig. 23).

Despite open expressions of desire,[76] it is doubtful if Cyril's attachments ever amounted to physical sex. Viewed from the later perspective of their married lives it is easy to appreciate that Noel Blakiston's title 'A Romantic Friendship' sums up exactly what it was. This is shown evocatively in a letter of 1963 included in the book, in which Cyril says that their friendship was so perfect that it could only have moved onto a further plane if they had lived together like some of their contemporaries but that this was impossible because *'we weren't homosexual'* [my italics]. It is a perfect expression of the yearning, 'what might have been' quality which invested so many of these Edwardian relationships.

Sligger was both sensitive to and tolerant of these youthful entanglements, although to what extent he approved of them is unclear. In 1923, when Cyril's infatuation with Bobbie Longden was at its height, he gave them attic rooms at the Chalet to use as bedroom and sitting room.[77] Bobbie chose to leave the party early and Cyril became despondent, possibly on account of missed opportunity for sex. Sligger spent that evening with him, gently exploring his thoughts, and they ended in prayer – although given his feelings at the time, it must have been difficult for Cyril to know whether his aspirations were at all suitable for prayer.

In the circumstances it should be emphasised that there was nothing misogynistic about Sligger. Women had been welcome at the Chalet since the parties began, as Herbert Trench and his wife had demonstrated in the very first year. Visitors included Sligger's sisters Harriet and Maisie, the latter coming with her husband William Tyrrell, and there were other female guests. He was genuinely pleased for colleagues who married and was welcoming to their wives, as in the cases of Gemma Bailey and Dorothy Macmillan. He also used his French properties to support their relationships: the Honeymoon Chalet at Mont Forchet acquired its name through regularly being offered to colleagues and friends for this purpose.

That Sligger's friendships were genuine and not merely the result of passing attraction is shown by their lasting nature. He was a natural networker with strong motivation to advance the lives of those around him. It was understandable to do this at Balliol, as this was the *raison d'être* of his employment, but once someone gained admission to his circle they rarely left it except by misdemeanour. The commitment and effort he put into those he had chosen for the special favour of an invitation to the Chalet were remarkable. Lawrence Jones (Balliol 1904) was a member of Sligger's circle but was prevented from seeing the Chalet by the cost of travel: as a result he felt his knowledge of Sligger was incomplete.[24]

Harold Macmillan made it to the Chalet only once, in 1913, but he never lost his affection for it, nor allowed his friendship with Sligger to fail until the latter's death. Over the twenty-four years of their acquaintance Harold wrote to Sligger on average ten times a year and met him as often as he could. Throughout this period there is hardly an aspect of his life that he did not share with Sligger, and it is notable that he wrote as a friend and not as a past student to a mentor.

Memories of the Chalet sustained Harold throughout the First World War. He wrote frequently and, knowing that Sligger would have been receiving letters from other chaletites, regularly asked for news of them. Just before the Battle of the Somme he wrote, 'Too violently sleepy to write. But I can dream of the Chalet and forget this horrible trench,'[78] and later, during the battle, 'How lovely old days have been and what a help to us now ...'[79] As the war proceeded news came of the deaths of friends and when facing this he still took consolation from his memory of the Chalet: when he was wounded a second time in the Battle of the Somme and invalided out of action to a nursing home in England he wrote, 'You know, Slig, that the happiest times I've ever known have been with you – at the Chalet and in Italy.'[80]

For much of this time Harold's feelings retained a male-orientated view. He expressed mystification when Cys Asquith chose to marry in 1918[81] and later he referred to the marriage of Geoffrey Madan (Chalet 1914) as 'this sinister disease' and looked back again to the days of their company in Sligger's circle; being in the Rocky Mountains had made him dream again of the Chalet.[82] However, when he met Dorothy Cavendish, daughter of the Duke of Devonshire, in Canada he described her to Sligger as 'the most perfect thing God ever made' and himself as 'the happiest man in the world'.[16] Sligger, who had seen this all before, would have been pleased for him but possibly would also have allowed himself a wry smile.

Harold and Dorothy married in 1920 and the following year Sligger provided them with the Honeymoon Chalet at Motivon. Photographs show them in relaxed and sunny mood there (Fig. 25) and the visit inevitably stirred Harold's memories of the past, especially when Humphrey Sumner paid them a visit. 'The most glorious time imaginable' was his comment to Sligger when he wrote in thanks.[83]

Harold Macmillan continued to share with Sligger his personal life, his work in the family publishing firm and his burgeoning political career; in reply Sligger often took the opportunity to recommend those who were looking for work.[84] Harold's letters remain sprinkled with profound nostalgia, often as a diversion from the pressure of his work. It was a particular pleasure to receive letters addressed from the Chalet[85] and as late as 1931 he was wondering about possibly visiting there once more.[86] When Sligger died in 1934 Harold's letters were returned to him by Cyril Bailey and he preserved them in a bundle labelled in his own handwriting. They make it clear that the friendship was very real and shared on both sides. Macmillan would go on to a distinguished career in politics, a successful time in office as Prime Minister, and later would be a long-standing and much-loved Chancellor of the University. Sligger, with his ability to detect the promise in young men, would not have been at all surprised.

Similarly, James Lees-Milne, Harold Nicolson's biographer, claims that it took Sligger just two weeks to perceive the talent dormant in Nicolson (Chalet 1906), treating him with affection and respect and encouraging his qualities.[87] Nicolson himself left a powerful tribute: 'He imposed nothing while suggesting everything. He suggested to young men that they would grow out of their affectations and attain to their own realities. He taught them that their failings and even their vices were important and that they must surely possess inside themselves an inner core of energy and righteousness. He inspired confidence in the young.'[88] As with Macmillan, Sligger maintained a lifelong correspondence with Nicolson.

Sligger's predilection for people in public life inevitably attracted accusations of snobbishness, which he did little to counter. Indeed, he was inclined to boast of his personal contacts with the British Cabinet.[89] His sister's marriage to William Tyrrell gave him access to the Foreign Office and the Tyrrells' contact with the Chalet was strengthened when their two young sons Francis and Hugo started visiting in 1900. However, Sligger's association with Whitehall was stronger. Herbert Asquith, Prime Minister from 1908, was a support-ive Balliol graduate, having held a Fellowship there before going into politics.[90] The Prime Minister's second son, also Herbert, was at the Chalet in 1901 and his fourth son, 'Cys', who subsequently became a Law Lord, in 1910. Then in July 1913 Cys paid a day visit with his sister Violet; they were staying at the Chalet du Rocher (Fig. 24), probably as Sligger's guests. Violet had known Sligger since 1906, having been introduced to him by another chaletite, her friend Archie Gordon (Chalet 1904), son of the Earl of Aberdeen (Violet's intended mar-riage to Archie was forestalled by his death from a motoring accident in 1909).[91]

Herbert Asquith was in the habit of relaxing from the demands of office with breaks at Easton Grey, his sister-in-law's house near Malm-esbury. In the spring of 1914 he recorded that he had spent a weekend there with a nice 'Papist don from Oxford' with whom he discussed Cicero and Western manuscripts of the Gospels.[92] It seems very likely that Sligger was getting his thanks for supporting the younger Asquiths. The connection was to strengthen further still when in 1915 Violet married another chaletite, Maurice Bonham-Carter (Chalet 1900), who had become her father's Private Secretary.[93] Later members of the Asquith family at the Chalet were Herbert's grandsons Michael in 1936 and Julian (2nd Earl of Oxford and Asquith) in 1937. Future Liberal Party leader Jo Grimond (Chalet 1933 & 1935) also joined the family when he married the daughter of Maurice and Violet.

Whatever satisfaction Sligger derived from these contacts, he was prepared to use them to further the lives of those who attracted his support. When Cyril Connolly was having difficulty finding work Sligger used his contacts to find him a private tutor's post as a base from which to develop his career in publishing.[94] Few of those in Sligger's network can have doubted that maintaining contact was desirable, though the terms in which their letters were couched make it plain that their reasons went beyond self-interest.

The Sikh student H. S. Malik from Rawalpindi was one such; when Malik found himself in Oxford at the start of the First World War he was keen to serve the war effort but Indian students were at that time barred from active service. Exploiting his contact with the wife of the French Military Attaché in London, Sligger secured Malik a position in the French Red Cross as an ambulance driver.[95] Later, when Sligger heard that Malik was interested in enlisting in the French Air Force, he went to work again and secured an interview with General Sir David Henderson, head of the Royal Flying Corps. Sligger is said to have told the General roundly that it was scandalous that a British subject who wished to serve should be disregarded.[96] As a result, Malik became the first turbaned fighter pilot in the service, an event which promoted a rethink of official attitudes to uniform.[96] After the war Malik would go on to a distinguished career in Indian diplomacy and international relations.

It is probable that Michael Dugdale got his place at Balliol in 1923 through Sligger's contacts: his father Edgar had been a student of Sligger's in 1895 and his mother Blanche was the niece and biographer of past Prime Minister Arthur Balfour.[97] She appears in Sligger's photograph albums from 1912. Her role in setting up the League of Nations Union no doubt appealed to Sligger, and another of his students, Theobald Mathew (Chalet 1924), joined the League Secretariat. Blanche spent a few days at the Chalet in 1923 although without Michael, and was there again in 1926. Michael's cousin Patrick Balfour was at the Chalet in 1923; of the large number of the Balfour family who went to Balliol, only Patrick seems to have been at the Chalet as an undergraduate.[97]

Sligger also used the Chalet as a means of enhancing European connections. The diplomat Sir Hughe Knatchbull-Hugessen (Chalet 1905–7) recalled that one summer Sligger took him to a villa near Saint Gervais to have lunch with Émile Ollivier, the last Prime Minister of Napoleon III (Fig. 26). This was a visit that Sligger made each year.[98] Ollivier was using retirement to produce his multi-volume work *L'Empire Libéral*, essentially an apologia for the Second Empire,[99] and it is likely that he and Sligger would have exchanged views on history.

It was one of the visitors to the Chalet who prompted Sligger to make his only ascent of Mont Blanc. In August 1900 the redoubtable Gertrude Bell arrived the same day as the ill-fated Roger Casement. At .this point Gertrude Bell was exploring a new interest in Alpine climbing.[100] She was a friend of the Tyrrells and probably visited at their suggestion, although Sligger would also have known of her as the first woman to be awarded first-class honours in History at Oxford. She had already acquired the interest in the Middle East which was to dominate her life and, as Sligger always promoted his father's work whenever he could, it is intriguing to speculate whether their meeting had any influence on her future work.

Roger Casement had no Oxford connection but had established a reputation in the Colonial Service and was probably also invited at the instigation of William Tyrrell, then Permanent Under-Secretary for Foreign Affairs.[101] This was well before Roger Casement had embraced the Irish sympathies that were to lead him to collaboration with Germany in the First World War and ultimately to execution for treason.

Gertrude Bell described the Chalet as 'a most fascinating little place' and was amused by the arrangements for the Turkish bath.[102] Of Roger Casement, she wrote to her stepmother that he was 'one learned in Central Africa, who tells us shocking tales of fetish and juju'.[102] Sligger she regarded as 'a dear'.[103] A further guest on the party was Count Gebhard Blücher, great-great-grandson of the commander of the Prussian forces at the Battle of Waterloo and another friend of the Tyrrells.

On 19 August 1900 Sligger, Gertrude Bell, Roger Casement, William Tyrrell and Margaret Stanley, another friend of the Tyrrells, made a leisurely climb to Tête Rousse (3,167 metres), taking most of the day and lunching on the ridge at Les Rognes.[104] The intention was for the party to return, leaving Gertrude to make the summit ascent that night with two guides, Schwartzen and Fuhrer, but at this point Sligger had a change of heart and announced his intention of accompanying her. This required the hasty acquisition of suitable clothing from the *patron* of the refuge, to the great amusement of William Tyrrell, who was well acquainted with his brother-in-law's professed aversion to mountaineering.[104]

Sligger and Gertrude left for the summit at 2 a.m. the next morning. They made steady progress, reaching the Aiguille du Goûter (3,863 m) at 4 a.m. and the Dôme du Goûter (4,304 m) at 5 a.m. By 6 a.m. they had arrived at Joseph Vallot's observatory (4,362 m) where Vallot invited them in for breakfast. Gertrude reported that the scientist and his assistants had blackened their faces with lamp black, presumably as protection against the sun at this altitude.[104]

They parted from Vallot at 7 a.m. and by 8.25 a.m. were on the summit (4,810 m), where Gertrude used Sligger's camera to record his achievement (Fig. 27) and they briefly admired Jules Janssen's discarded observatory, which was steadily sinking into the ice.[104] The weather was ominous so they stayed on the top for only twenty-five minutes before returning as rapidly as they could to Vallot. Here he demonstrated his scientific equipment and Gertrude would have liked to have stayed longer but it had begun to snow and a gathering electrical storm was causing sparks to erupt from their ice-axes and Vallot's instruments. They left as soon as possible, descending rapidly by the Grands Mulets route to Chamonix. It was an arduous descent through thick snow and at one point three of them were sliding downhill on their backs. Fortunately Schwartzen showed his skill and arrested their slide.[104] They reached Chamonix by 1 p.m., a considerable achievement in such weather, and lunched at the Hôtel Couttet. There Sligger's departure brought to an end Gertrude Bell's brief association with the Chalet des Anglais; the Tyrrells invited her again in 1904[105] but by then her widening interests, especially in the Middle East, were taking her life's trajectory in a different direction.

So strong has become Sligger's reputation for these relationships that inevitably some legends have crept in. One is an alleged friendship with the poet Rupert Brooke. It was said that Sligger had a portrait of Brooke on the wall of his college room[26] and it has been claimed that Brooke visited the Chalet in 1913 with Cys and Violet Asquith while Harold Macmillan was there.[4] This is clearly wrong: there is no signature for Rupert Brooke in the diary with the Asquiths' and in any case Brooke – a Cambridge man – was in the United States when this party took place.[106] In fact this is a simple case of mistaken identity: Joshua Rupert Ingham Brooke – also known as Rupert – entered Balliol a year before Harold Macmillan. Like Macmillan, he found his university career cut short by the war but he was mentioned in dispatches and later went into farming.[107] Macmillan's own memoir, *Winds of Change*, appears curiously ambiguous on the subject;[108] musing in a Belgravia nursing home after being invalided out of action in 1916, Macmillan appears to refer to Rupert Brooke as among the war dead, which would have been correct for the poet, who died in 1915, but also refers to him having visited with Sligger in 1916.[109] Writing fifty years after the event, and after Joshua Rupert had also died, Macmillan too may have confused the two men.

It is not beyond the bounds of possibility that Sligger had on his wall a photograph of the poet; once called 'the handsomest young man in England',[110] it would certainly have been in character. But there appears to be no definite evidence of a friendship although at Rugby School Brooke had had a youthful attachment to Michael Sadler,[111] who entered Balliol in 1908 and was one of Sligger's chaletites the following year. However, Sligger's connection with the Balliol Brooke, who studied History, is not in question and is recorded in Sligger's photograph albums.

Another friendship which might be considered equally apocryphal is that with the Everest pioneer George Mallory. In fact, this was a real association and is recorded in Sligger's albums, although it is only recently that the full extent of it has been recognised.[112] Mallory visited Oxford in May 1911 and Sligger took him rowing on the Thames. A similar visit took place during the Easter vacation of 1913: one of Sligger's photographs shows a wistful Mallory sitting in the bay window of Sligger's room at Balliol (a more accurate term might be posing: Mallory's photographs often suggest that he was strongly camera-conscious, perhaps as a result of his contacts with the Bloomsbury Group and the nude modelling he did for the artist Duncan Grant in 1912).[113] In June 1915 Sligger spent a weekend with George and his wife Ruth at their home near Charterhouse School, where George was then teaching.

After leaving Cambridge in 1910, George Mallory had been appointed to Charterhouse to teach History and to prepare boys for Oxbridge entrance.[114] Sligger, as History Tutor at Balliol, was a natural contact in Oxford, and furthermore one of George's new colleagues at Charterhouse, Frank Fletcher (Chalet 1894 & 1896), was a friend of Sligger's from undergraduate days and was keen that his best pupils should be admitted to Balliol.[115] Sligger's contact with George therefore appears to have arisen through academic objectives, not their shared love of mountains.

The biography of George Mallory by his son-in-law David Robertson confirms that after climbing in Snowdonia during Easter 1911, George went on to stay with Sligger at Balliol.[116] George had been captain of rowing at Magdalene in Cambridge and it is understandable that Sligger should have introduced him to the Oxford rowing scene. The biography by George's friend David Pye reports that around 1913, possibly after the Easter visit, George seriously considered a suggestion from Sligger that he should apply for a college position, but he decided against it. George described his Oxford visit as 'a very good time'.[117]

Their continuing contact is confirmed by David Robertson, who reports quoting letters from Sligger in the Mallory family collection.[112] This is consistent with Sligger's instruction to Cyril Bailey to return correspondence to their author after his death; in this case the letters would have gone to Ruth Mallory because George died on Everest in 1924, ten years before Sligger's own death. That their contact continued up to George's death is confirmed by a signed portrait photograph which George sent Sligger from a series taken in New York during George's 1923 lecture tour.[112]

So did Sligger ever invite Mallory to visit the Chalet? He would not have allowed such a visit to take place without Mallory's signature in the Chalet diary, and there is none. Moreover Sligger regarded the Chalet as a base for walking, not climbing, and although Mallory was on Mont Blanc during their friendship he usually climbed from Chamonix where climbing was more advanced than on the Saint Gervais side. Overall it is probable that Sligger would have tried to strengthen their friendship with an invitation to the Chalet – it would have been characteristic of him – and it is equally probable that Mallory would have declined on the grounds that his vacations were occupied with more strenuous activity further east in the Alps.

There is an additional tenuous link between George Mallory and the Chalet: the Chalet library contains a number of mountaineering books owned and signed by George's early climbing partner Cottie Sanders (later Lady Mary O'Malley and the novelist Ann Bridge).[112] These cannot have reached the Chalet through George's friendship because some of them date from after his death in 1924. Lady Mary and her husband retired to Oxford and their son, who predeceased them, had been at Balliol, so although the provenance of the books is unknown it seems likely to have been an Oxford connection.[118]

The atmosphere which surrounded Sligger at the Chalet was summed up perceptively by his friend the Abbé Félix Klein, who observed Sligger closely during the parties before the First World War. Klein wrote [my translation]: 'There was no service that he did not offer his students, equally prepared to plot the schedule of their excursions and their travel, to ensure their material well-being, to advise in their reading and in their studies, to guide them in their excursions and in their moral life. There was nothing more touching than their confidence. To "Slig" they could ask anything, as to a teacher or to a father, I would almost say as to a mother: the choice of a book to consult, or that of equipment for ascents, the exchange of the pound to francs or the English translation of a text in French, Greek, Latin. Twenty times interrupted in his own work, he always welcomed them with the same calm and the same patience. His intellect responded to all the questions, his kindness to all queries. The young people had the air of finding this completely natural and not even noticing it. But when they were on the point of leaving I read in their eyes and in their handshake, in spite of the imperturbable reserve of young British men, a recognition and an affection of which the sincerity and the depth would certainly not have escaped the sensitive soul of Urquhart.'[119]

The lasting friendships which the Chalet provided were very much in tune with how Sligger saw his role as a college tutor. This role found its most intense expression at the Chalet and his attachment to those who had been there was especially close, perhaps not surprisingly, as they were there by his own selection, and all remembered their time there with affection. The Chalet, despite its French and European context, must have appeared to him and to the chaletites as representing the essence of Edwardian college life, with its atmosphere of a summer house party. In common with so many of their social class they may have thought this life to be immutable. It is doubtful if many of them, even Sligger himself with his profound European sensitivities, could have foreseen how much this was to change with the murder of the Austrian Archduke Franz Ferdinand in Sarajevo on 28 June 1914.

CHAPTER FOUR

BETWEEN THE WARS: THE END OF THE OLD ORDER

STEPHEN HEWETT WAS PREDESTINED to appeal to Sligger: a friendly, studious high achiever, modest and shy, good-looking, and a devout Catholic.[1] He was born in 1893 in India where his father worked in the telegraph service. When his father retired to Exeter, Stephen was sent to the Benedictine establishment of Downside, where his dedication to study rapidly gained him the approval of the monks. He also showed skill in cricket and hockey and, having a good baritone voice, appeared in a production of *The Gondoliers* by Gilbert and Sullivan.

Stephen's teachers found him reticent about his own abilities but with a capacity that was never in doubt. They also saw that his immersion in literature, combined with Downside's location on the northern slopes of the Mendips, gave him an abiding love of the outdoors and sensitivity to pastoral or visionary writing with a strong sense of *genius loci*. He took to writing poetry, some of which was published.

While at Downside Stephen became friendly with Sligger's nephew Frank (Francis) Tyrrell. Sligger himself was a frequent visitor; he continued to visit Chewton Priory after the death of his uncle Lord Carlingford and the school is only six miles away. Applying to Balliol was the obvious outcome: Stephen won an Exhibition when he was sixteen and the following year obtained a Scholarship, entering Balliol with Frank to study Classics in 1911. That Christmas Sligger took them both on a trip to Rome. Subsequently Stephen was successful in three other scholarship examinations and he excelled in hockey, joining the University team, and also became a committed member of the Bach Choir. Principally, however, his tutors noted that studying the classics came to mould his personality. It was felt he would be a natural teacher, or possibly a priest. Downside might well have been pleased to get him back.

His character emerges most clearly in the letters he wrote from the Front during the First World War, a selection of which Sligger published.[2] Typically for a young man, they reflect thoughts of home combined with the camaraderie of army life. But at a deeper level he does not shy away from the risks or the cruelty of war: he accepted this as a test he had to face. He reported the death of friends dispassionately, though not callously, as a sacrifice that had to be made. His mind was also large enough to find sympathy for the young Germans dying in the same way.[2] Above all his letters reflect a calm faith that those who came through the conflict would be stronger, wiser and kinder human beings as a result.

Such a man was an obvious candidate for the Chalet and in 1912, at the end of his first year at Balliol, he was there for the month of July. He took part in the most exacting of the walks, including the ascent to Tête Rousse at 3,200 metres and the long walk to the natural swimming pool at Nant Borrant. Invitations to the 1913 and 1914 parties duly followed. In 1913 he once more walked extensively, largely in the company of Harold Macmillan and Frank Tyrrell (Fig. 20). Photographs from these parties show a slight, tidily dressed young man with a modest smile. There are also shots of him hard at work over his books during the study periods.

The summer of 1914 at the Chalet was warm and calm. There was a small party under the leadership of Cyril and Gemma Bailey as Sligger was busy in the UK. Most of the members had departed by the last week in July and Stephen was one of just four staying on to the end of the season. Despite the Chalet's isolation, they cannot have been immune to the European news. On 28 June the heir to the Austro-Hungarian Empire, the Archduke Franz Ferdinand, had been assassinated in Sarajevo and the tenuous balance of power that had built up in Europe over the previous century began to unravel. On 28 July Austria-Hungary declared war on Serbia, precipitating the mobilisation of Russia and Germany and then of France and Britain.

Stephen Hewett left the Chalet on 1 August 1914, two days before Germany declared war on France. His journey home across a France gripped by mobilisation was long and arduous.[1] He saw the preparations for war, the men leaving and the women crying at their doors. For a time he and a friend were isolated in Paris with little money and little apparent chance of getting home. Characteristically he saw this as a test of character; later he wrote, 'Now that it is all over I feel that I would not have missed it for anything. I know it has done me the world of good, to learn what hunger and poverty is, and to have seen the spirit with which the French people are going to war. Indeed I cannot resist the temptation of quoting from a sermon about the 17th century ancestors of Downside: "Then, when the weary vigil is over, and the light breaks over the sea, one by one, and two by two, they will come back again to set their foot on England's shore, better men and stronger, since long schooled by bitter adversity."'[1]

Stephen returned to Balliol for the Michaelmas term of 1914. In December he obtained his commission as a Second Lieutenant in the Royal Warwickshire Regiment. Although he was enthusiastic to see action, the whole of 1915 was spent becoming frustrated by continual exercises in the UK: only later did he discover that he had been kept back because he had been found to be a good trainer.[1] He was finally posted to France in February 1916. Five months later he was dead, gunned down in the mud of the Somme. He was just twenty-three and his body was never recovered.

¤

Little could happen at the Chalet with France embroiled in war and Balliol occupied only by those either too young to enlist or unfit for service. Most of the younger dons had joined up and others entered war service in other ways, such as work for the government. Sligger, then the college's domestic bursar, felt that he had to remain at the college but fretted at the inactivity. He wrote prodigiously to those in the trenches, often sending books to entertain them, and would travel to see those who were on leave even if it was only for an hour or two.[3] In fact he was later to find employment through his friend the Abbé Félix Klein from the Catholic Institute in Paris. Klein's Archbishop had drafted him as chaplain to the American Hospital at Neuilly-sur-Seine, a suburb of Paris, and Sligger worked there as a hospital orderly during his vacations.[4] In 1916, during a month's stay in France, he paid a day visit to the Chalet, presumably to check its war-time state. Otherwise only Félix Klein used it, taking parties of French friends in 1917 and 1918.

The war meant that Sligger had to face more than the loss of the golden protégé Stephen Hewett. Of the Balliol members who went into war service nearly 200 died,[5] more than a fifth. Twenty-eight of these were chaletites who Sligger would have known well and whose fortunes he would have followed closely. Worst of all, he had to endure the death of his two nephews Frank and Hugo, the sons of his sister Maisie and William Tyrrell. Frank died in January 1915 from bullet wounds[6] and Stephen Hewett wrote a memorial poem expressing the wish that he might prove worthy of his friend's sacrifice. Hugo died in naval action in February 1918.[7] Sligger was close to Maisie's family and had loved both boys, treating them as surrogate sons. They had been at the Chalet, both with their parents and alone, and Frank had been a member of the 1913 reading party with Harold Macmillan and Stephen Hewett. Frank had in fact been named after Sligger and it is more than likely that had they lived one of the boys, probably Frank, would have inherited the Chalet.

Nor were the Wynford Philipps family, his neighbours on the Prarion, spared their own tragedy. Lady St Davids died from complications of surgery early in the war and later both their sons were killed in action.[8] In 1916 Lord St Davids remarried and decided that the Chalet du Rocher, which had been his wedding gift to Leonora, should be returned to the Poore family for a token sum.[9]

The Balliol that reassembled after the war differed markedly from its pre-war character. Those who had their time at college interrupted needed to return and there were others whose education had been delayed by the war. Before 1914 Balliol College had held a total of around 200 students. The immediate post-war intake was 150 and late entries in Trinity term brought that year's admissions alone to 233, obliging the college to acquire separate accommodation in Beaumont Street and later in Holywell Manor.[10]

Undergraduates had changed in character as well as numbers. Students who had war experience took their education and self-advancement more seriously and most family finances no longer supported an indulgent lifestyle. Future Reader in English J. I. M. Stewart (also a crime writer under the name Michael Innes) found that books bought at home in Edinburgh could be read quickly and sold at profit in Oxford; the income funded his journeys home.[11] For the novelist Angus Wilson, entry to Merton College became possible only when he inherited his deceased mother's capital.[12] The Edwardian creed of loyalty to state and institution had also been severely dented by experience in the trenches: what Noel Annan, Vice-Chancellor of London University, called 'the age of Almamatricide' had begun.[13]

Sligger's response to these changes appears to have been to carry on as he always had. No doubt he was strengthened by his firm faith but there is a sense that he may have felt that the values for which he stood had become more important since the war, rather than less. By the end of the war he was Dean and therefore in a strong position to influence the undergraduates. However, by 1919 he was fifty-one and his college duties would have eaten into both time and energy. The major casualty appears to have been his evening salons, which came to an end shortly after the war. It is also possible that his students found them less attractive in the post-war mood of greater pragmatism.

Sligger continued his participation in UK reading parties and also his practice of taking favourite students on cultural tours in Europe. During the Christmas vacation of 1922 he took a party of Etonian freshmen with him through Rome, Naples and Sicily (Fig. 28). These were Cyril Connolly, Denis Dannreuther and Roger Mynors from Balliol and Cyril's especial friend Bobbie Longden, who had entered Magdalen College.[14] Cyril, a particular protégé, became a regular at the Chalet (1923–7), as did Bobbie Longden (Chalet 1923–7, 1931, 1936 & 1938) and Roger Mynors (Chalet 1924–37), who was to have a highly significant part in the Chalet's story.

The remaining man, Denis Dannreuther, was typical of Sligger's taste: good-looking, studious – he was subsequently a Fellow of All Souls – and connected with Whitehall.[15] His father Sigmund had been knighted for leading work in Ordnance in the war and his uncle Tristan had recently become Assistant Director of Naval Intelligence.[16] (Denis' grandfather Edward Dannreuther, a professor at the Royal College of Music, had been a close friend of Richard Wagner and named his first four children after Wagnerian characters.)[17] However, despite his suitability Denis never went to the Chalet; his health was often poor (he was to die at the early age of thirty-five)[15] and Sligger may have felt the mountain environment too demanding for him. A member of the Dannreuther family finally made it to the Chalet fifty years later, when David, the son of Denis' cousin, became a member of a University College party in 1973 (and, one might conclude, luckily, because David's maternal grandfather was one of only six survivors of HMS *Invincible* at the Battle of Jutland in 1916).[18] The Dannreuthers would become another family who could claim multi-generational attendance at the Chalet when David's niece Sophie joined a New College party in 2010. Sligger might well have approved.

Life at the Chalet seems similarly not to have changed. Sligger was still in a financial position to maintain Edwardian practices and to engage servants; the parties began again in the summer of 1919 with a season of nineteen members, split into July and August groups as had become the norm before the war. Of these, only ten were Balliol undergraduates and others came from Christ Church, Magdalen, Trinity and University colleges. In fact in the inter-war period Sligger tended to involve students from other colleges more than he had before the war. Sligger's colleague Humphrey Sumner joined the 1919 July group and the Abbé Klein was there once more. This mixture of senior and junior guests would not have been out of place before the war.

The usual walks were undertaken and Sligger continued to take part, although as the years passed his participation in the longer walks became intermittent. The 1919 party, when he was fifty-one, was the last time he led the three-day excursion into Italy and over the Col du Géant to the Mer de Glace (Figs 29 & 30), although later he sometimes did just the first stage. It may be that Sligger's decreasing participation allowed the parties greater scope, because individual members began to roam farther afield: destinations such as Mont Tondu or the Grand Charmoz, which involve real climbing, begin to appear in the diaries.

The composition of the inter-war parties shows that Sligger had lost nothing of his skill in detecting promise in the young. To take only those who subsequently became politicians, names which would become familiar to a later generation, include Robert Boothby (Chalet 1922), Richard Crossman (Chalet 1928), Quintin Hogg (Lord Hailsham, Chalet 1927–31) and Douglas Jay (Chalet 1929–30). Among those who would achieve academic success were future heads of Oxford colleges: Tom Boase (Chalet 1920–32), William Hayter (Chalet 1926–9), John Maud (Chalet 1924–5), John Sparrow (Chalet 1926 & 1929) and Humphrey Sumner (Chalet 1919–29). Visits of Catholic priests during this period were represented by Dom Charles Pontifex (Chalet 1921–31) and Dom David Knowles (Chalet 1925–9), both of Downside.

Son of the Attorney General and subsequently a Lord Chancellor, Quintin Hogg ticked most of Sligger's boxes for invitation. An undergraduate at Christ Church, he was introduced to Sligger by his elder half-brother, Edward Marjoribanks,[19] and, having been inducted into mountain walking by his father, he found the Chalet a good base for a growing interest in climbing. Despite this divergence from the

Chalet's usual practice, Sligger obviously approved because Quintin was there four times between 1927 and 1931 and Sligger was prepared to indulge his interest by providing the services of a guide.[20] Like his fellow politician Harold Macmillan before him, Quintin Hogg regarded his time at the Chalet as one of the happiest of his life[20] and was sustained during the later war by memories of his time there. He achieved membership of the Alpine Club and was to recall his days at the Chalet as the decisive stage in his climbing career.[20] His verdict on Sligger: 'he was one of the most agreeable men I have ever met: a Roman Catholic by religion and a saint'.[21]

One notable feature of the parties after the war is that they often included people who were there repeatedly. These included favourites such as Cyril Connolly, Quintin Hogg and Bobbie Longden but for the first time a number of colleagues made a regular appearance. Before the war only the loyal Cyril Bailey had really done this, but now Tom Boase, Alan Ker (Chalet 1925–37), Roger Mynors and Richard Pares (Chalet 1922–36) were there together for many years. One senses that Sligger may have been thinking of the time when the parties must be handed over and may have been trying out potential successors. One invitee who may have shown some reluctance was Christopher Cox, who had been at Balliol studying with Cyril Bailey but was a Fellow of New College by the time he made a single day's visit to the Chalet in 1928, his only visit during Sligger's lifetime. Sligger was clearly fond of Christopher, as there was an extensive and friendly correspondence between them, and he certainly saw Christopher as a potential successor; in view of Christopher's poor contact with the Chalet before Sligger's death, this was to prove to be evidence of Sligger's long-sightedness.

Perhaps there were also differences in students' expectations after the First World War. The author L. P. Hartley, who was there in 1920, felt that the lower portions of glaciers were the ugliest things he had ever seen and complained that he was missing his bath.[22] Generous as ever, Sligger fixed up a bucket and hose to give him the benefit of a shower. The Canadian and future constitutional expert Eugene Forsey also felt out of place there. Having by his own admission regarded Sligger as 'a very saintly looking man' and admired him to the point of reverence, Eugene was overjoyed to receive one of the prized invitations to the Chalet in 1927. However, 'the visit fell flat. I had no idea what to say or do. I did not even know whether I was expected to contribute to the expenses, and was too shy to ask'.[23] Clearly, this was one young man Sligger failed to draw out in the usual way.

Sligger was faced with a challenge in the immediate post-war period: Anselme Martin had died in 1914 and the Chalet needed a new *gardien*. At this point one of the great characters of the Chalet's story enters the picture. Sligger turned to the Broisat family in Saint Gervais[24] and his first choice, Lubin Broisat, was a gardener and mountain guide. However, the Chalet work soon passed to Lubin's second son, Louis (Fig. 31).[25] Aged just nineteen when he was taken on by Sligger, Louis was to work for the Chalet for the next fifty years, albeit not without a degree of strain on both sides. He had been trained by the *Compagnie des Guides* at Saint Gervais but, being of independent spirit and disinclined to take direction, he eventually parted company with that association and the Chalet became his main preoccupation. However, his guiding skills, like those of Anselme Martin before the war, proved useful to the parties as their excursions became more extensive. He successfully guided groups to the summit of Mont Blanc in 1923, 1926 and 1927.[26] Louis' brothers Léon and Alphonse were also employed by Sligger in this way.

Links with the Martin family were not lost on Anselme's death. His daughter Sara came in as maid until she married in 1920, when her place was taken by her sister Julia, who was to marry Louis Broisat's younger brother Victor; Julia continued until 1931, becoming the cook. Later still their sister Berthe (Fig. 32) was employed. Louis' sister Lea also joined the staff in 1928. The staff were in the habit of signing their names on the rack of the kitchen dresser. Many have now faded but enough remain to give some idea of the Chalet staff during this period.

It would not be unfair to regard Louis Broisat as the Chalet's lovable rogue. Although he was devoted to Sligger and the Chalet, it was not long before everyone noticed that he had his own way of working and was not very biddable. Things got done, but only when Louis was ready for them. Generally taciturn and inclined to be secretive, he could be eloquent with a few words: when people commented that it was a pity that the Chalet du Rocher had to be fitted with a roof of corrugated iron, Louis' laconic comment was: 'You don't need to take care of beauty in the mountains.'[9]

Louis was responsible for bringing up luggage from Saint Gervais, where the Hôtel du Mont Blanc remained the Chalet's contact point. He also transported any who needed help with the walk and soon became well known to the chaletites, as did his mule Lulu, who he had named after his grandmother: whether out of affection or satire is unknown. At the Chalet Lulu was stabled in the wooden shed behind the chapel and Louis sometimes slept there with her. At other times, when the chalets were empty, he used a room in one of them, often the Chalet du Rocher which was cosier in cold weather.[27]

Louis' approach to billing for his services was to wait until the end of the season and then send Sligger a request for a global sum representing maintenance, transport of food and guests, purchases and other tasks. He was also responsible for hiring staff for the Chalet and agreeing wages, and his duties included the Honeymoon Chalet at Mont Forchet. Sligger occasionally became irritated by Louis' inability or reluctance to account for individual tasks and wondered whether he should get independent advice.[28] On the whole he was prepared to accept that the cost of doing anything in an isolated place was high (this is still very true today) and that Louis' fidelity was beyond price. It is pertinent that Sligger was content to put some of the Chalet's other financial transactions in Louis' hands, and as time went on there was a general acceptance that Louis' approach, idiosyncratic though it might be, was more informed and more practical than that of some of those he worked for.

Sligger continued to allow other people to use the Chalet as he had before the war: in June 1924 Hughe Knatchbull-Hugessen (Chalet 1905–7), now at the British Embassy in Paris, was at the Chalet with his wife. In July Sligger's colleague Roy Ridley, Fellow in English,[29] and his wife led a party of seven students. That year Sligger also extended Chalet contacts; in the company of Roger Mynors, Richard Pares and future civil servant Christopher Eastwood from Trinity College he walked to 'The Eagle's Nest' above the village of Sixt, the chalet that had been established by pioneer Alpinist Alfred Wills. Here they were 'hospitably entertained' by Wills' daughter, Mrs Norton.

Between the wars the Chalet du Rocher became little used. Major Robert Poore died in 1918 and his wife's health had been poor for some time. The chalet was inherited by his son, Robert Montagu Poore, a famous cricketer who served in the 7th Hussars, achieving the rank of Brigadier General.[30] General Poore and his wife Flora Douglas-Hamilton had no children and used their chalet infrequently, so that it was usually left closed. Sligger seems to have pressed for its more frequent use and Roy Ridley rented it sometimes. Robert Montagu Poore's sister Nina married the Duke of Hamilton and had a family of seven; with his inclination to aristocrats, Sligger tried repeatedly but unsuccessfully to get their sons to come to the Chalet.[9]

There was, however, a new development in relationships on the mountain which was to be highly significant for the parties. Sligger was close to the Orset family, who rented and farmed the *alpage* at Bellevue on the slopes between Mont Blanc and Col de Voza, where there was a small summer refuge, or *pavillon* in the local terminology.[31] When Sligger bought the Chalet des Anglais from his brother David in 1896 Phillipe Orset had acted as the local agent, or *mandataire*.[32] Around the time of Sligger's purchase, the owners of the Bellevue *pavillon* began its replacement with a sizeable Alpine hotel and the business of this hotel increased in 1909 when the Tramway du Mont Blanc (TMB) line was extended from Col de Voza to Nid d'Aigle and a halt was provided at the hotel.

In 1928 Philippe Orset's son François and his wife Hortense purchased the Bellevue hotel from its owners and under the French system of shared inheritance, or *partage*, it passed later to François' sons, Gabriel and Paul (twins), Edmond, Léon and Georges.[31] Later Léon bought his fifth from Paul and Edmond and Georges' daughter. Gabriel never sold his share (in early 1990, long after Gabriel's death, his daughters Simone Orset-Hottegindre and Françoise Orset-Legoux were to exchange Gabriel's fifth with Léon's daughter for some pieces of land:[33] this was how *partage* was frequently managed by members of families).

During the period of the early reading parties there had also been a small refuge, or *buvette*, on the Prarion above the Chalet but it had fallen out of use since the turn of the century.[34] In 1928 Francois Orset's son Gabriel rented this small square building of seven rooms from the Saint Gervais Commune and reopened it (Fig. 40). Like many members of the local families, several of Francois' sons belonged to the Saint Gervais *Compagnie des Guides* but this was also the time of developing interest in winter ski sports and the slopes around the Prarion, being relatively clear of trees, offered skiers good opportunities. Gabriel Orset kept the Prarion *pavillon* open for the first time throughout the 1928–9 winter and began the local ski centre around what would become the Hôtel du Prarion. He became

1

2

3

1 David Urquhart's chalet of 1865. 2 David Urquhart at the time of his marriage. From Robinson, G. (1920). *David Urquhart: Victorian Knight Errant.* Blackwell, Oxford, p. 121. 3 Harriet Urquhart. From Bishop, M.C. (1897). *Memoir of Mrs Urquhart.* Kegan Paul, Trench, Trübner & Co, London, frontispiece.

4

5

4 The view of Mont Blanc from the col of the Prarion: not quite attained in David Urquhart's 'five minutes'. **5** The Chalet du Rocher.

6 Francis Urquhart as an undergraduate. **7** Chichester Fortescue (Lord Carlingford), Sligger's uncle and benefactor. **8** Sligger and the family at Chewton Priory, with his sisters Harriet (behind) and Maisie (seated with her son Hugo) and Maisie's husband William Tyrrell.

9

10

9 The first party of 1891: at rear (left to right): Sligger, Lord Kerry, Craig Sellar; seated: Claud Russell, Lilian and Herbert Trench. **10** Sligger and the faithful Cyril Bailey (front) with members of the 1894 party: rear (from left) Gilbert Russell, Arthur Pickard-Cambridge, Henry Tollinton, Arthur Latter, Amyas Waterhouse; (middle) Roland Farrer, Sligger, Clarence Marten.

11

12

11 Morning reading in 1906. **12** Chalet golf on the mountainside.

13 The 'excellent, capable and faithful' Anselme Martin (left) bringing up Sligger's nephews Hugo and Francis Tyrrell. **14** Anselme Martin (right) guiding (from left to right) A. Villiers, Humphrey Paul and Thomas Balston on the ascent to Col du Géant. **15** Outing to the Tête Rousse refuge: (from left) Henry Bowlby, Greville Irby (Lord Boston) and George Clark.

16

17

16 The New Chalet of 1909, ready to 'improve as the wood darkens'. **17** Chalet tennis, made possible by the New Chalet's storeroom.

18 The chapel of 1912, with the Abbé Klein. 19 The interior of the chapel. 20 The 1913 party: (rear, from left) Gilbert Talbot, Walter Monckton, Evelyn Cardew, Victor Mallet, Frank Tyrrell; (front, from left) Harold Macmillan, Arthur Wiggins, Stephen Hewett. 21 Chalet familiarity: Harold Macmillan relaxes across Sligger's thigh, with Victor Mallet (right) and Stephen Hewett behind.

22 Traditional swimming at Lac Vert. **23** Cyril Connolly (left) and Bobbie Longden, together at the Chalet at last. **24** Violet and Cys Asquith at the Chalet du Rocher.

25

26

25 Harold and Dorothy Macmillan at the 'Honeymoon Chalet' at Mont Forchet.
26 A visit to Émile Ollivier (second from right) at Saint Gervais.

27

28

27 On the summit of Mont Blanc: Sligger (left) with guides Schwartzen and Fuhrer, photographed by Gertrude Bell. Janssen's abandoned observatory is in the background. **28** Cultural tours: chaletites in Rome, (from front) Roger Mynors, Cyril Connolly, Bobbie Longden, Denis Dannreuther.

29

30

29 At the Col du Bonhomme on the way to Italy. **30** Crossing seracs on the Géant glacier.

31 Louis Broisat, guide, *gardien*, handyman: loyal, if wayward. **32** Martin daughters as maids in the 1920s: Julia (left) and Berthe (see also Fig 61). **33** A party in 1927: (rear, from left) Frederick Murthwait, Humphrey Sumner, Richard Pares, Bobbie Longden, Donald Armour; (front, from left) James Woodroffe (standing), Dom Charles Pontifex, David Farrer, Lennox Alexander.

34 One of Sligger's last parties: (rear, from left) Paul Willert, Tom Boase, Richard Crossman; (front, from left) John Tilney, Fr David Knowles, Sligger, 'Budgie' Firth, John Witt. **35** Sligger's final summer at the Chalet, 1931, with Quintin Hogg. **36** Alan Ker proving that the Chalet can be a base for climbing.

37 Christopher Cox on the south-west porch, a favourite position. **38** Staff in the 1930s: the maid Yvonne Masse (left) and cook Angèle Bayetto. **39** Louis Broisat with his mule 'Lulu' and 'The Boy' Raymond.

40

41

40 The inter-war Hôtel du Prarion of Gabriel Orset. **41** The last pre-war party of 1938: (rear, from left) John Spalding, David Cox, Thomas Harley, Arnold Curtis, Aidan White, John Compton; (middle, from left) Lawrence Pumphrey, Frank Lepper; (front, from left) Ian Grant, Peter Ollard, D. A. Cameron.

recognised as a *guide-skieur* of the French Alpine Club,[34] as did his brother Léon at Bellevue. Léon in particular had a highly success-ful career, receiving many distinctions and decorations.[35] In the early 1920s Sligger used both Gabriel and Léon as alternatives to Louis Broisat when needing guides for party members, describing Léon in the diary as 'much commended'.

In 1931 and again in 1935 Gabriel Orset was able to undertake extensions to the Prarion building, tripling its size and adding a *salle à manger* extension.[34] Two of the Orset sons therefore had a hotel on the mountainside in the area well known to Sligger's walkers. Their brother Georges was also instrumental in the development of refuges at Nid d'Aigle, Tête Rousse, Goûter and Vallot before his death at the early age of thirty-six. Later Léon purchased another refuge at Tré la Tête.[36]

Sligger was ambivalent about the developments, regarding what he called the 'Invasion' of tourists as having started when the Prarion *pavillon* was first built in the 1880s.[37] However, it is clear that this did not affect his friendship with the Orset family and it is to be assumed that his chaletites, in their excursions through Bellevue on the walk to Tête Rousse, or through Tré la Tête on their Italian walk, were not slow to take advantage of the facilities and keep the association alive. It is also very likely that they found that Gabriel Orset's Prarion *pavillon* provided welcome refreshment while returning to the Chalet after a day on the mountain. If so, they began a tradition which continues to this day and which was to have important implications after the Second World War.

A personal change which happened in 1928 was that Sligger became the 25th Chief of the clan of Urquhart.[38] The chiefship had been held by a distant cousin, the Rev Edward William Urquhart. Edward's only son predeceased him and when Edward himself died in 1916 the title passed to Sligger's elder brother David as the closest male relative, and then on David's death to Sligger. Sligger was con-scious of his family history and his bookplate reproduced one of the clan mottos: '*Per Actum Intentio*' ('the intention is judged by the act': no doubt with its echoes of the teaching of the New Testament and of his father's friend Jeremy Bentham this held personal resonances for him). Yet he seems not to have set any great store by the chiefship and in any case the clan's hard times over the two previous centuries had reduced the Braelangwell estate to a disused church on the south shore of the Cromarty Firth. After Sligger's death the title would lie idle until it was claimed twenty-five years later by an American descendant of the family.[38]

As he turned sixty, Sligger began to be short of breath in the mountains and necessarily had to curtail some of his walks. As the chronic chest disease which was to be his final illness worsened, he found sleeping at altitude difficult and in 1931 made the decision that he had to leave the Chalet for the last time. He is said to have told the *patron* of the Hôtel du Mont Blanc in Saint Gervais that it was the bitterest parting of his life and that dying would not be nearly so bad.[39]

His devotion to the Chalet was not diminished and he turned his mind to its future. There were two issues to consider: the ownership and the future direction of parties. On the former point he had already made a decision. In 1929 he had written to Roger Mynors (Fig. 28) to say that he was 'wondering what to do with it – the "old problem" ... Best solution seems to leave it to you ... less likely to find it a white elephant than anyone else – there will be no condition attached and you can get rid of it if it does turn out to be a white elephant.'[40] He said that he would need to make a separate French will but that his English will would contain £100 per annum to ease the financial burden of supporting the Chalet. This French will was made two months later and left both French chalets to Roger.[41] However, a change of heart was to come before Sligger died.

It might be thought that among the candidates for ownership, Cyril Bailey was the leading choice as a colleague and the most enthusiastic chaletite before the war, as well as being Sligger's chosen biographer. However, Cyril was Sligger's close contemporary in age, had married in 1912 and had visited the Chalet only once in the inter-war years. Of the others Sligger once considered as possible successors,[39] only Humphrey Sumner, Roger Mynors and John Fulton still held positions at Balliol. Humphrey Sumner had not kept up his Chalet visits since 1921 and at this point John Fulton had not visited the Chalet. Among Sligger's most frequent guests, Tom Boase and Bobbie Longden had moved to Hertford College and Christ Church respectively, and Richard Pares had left Balliol for a Fellowship at New College. Alan Ker, another contender, was a New College member who was destined for a Fellowship at Brasenose College.

Roger Mynors was a Classics don and, like Sligger, a studious bachelor, modest and aesthetic. Born in 1903, he represented a younger generation and would, it could be assumed, take the Chalet parties forward into the future. It has to be said that some in Roger Mynors' circle found Sligger's decision inexplicable on the basis that Roger was preoccupied with work and had limited interest in the Chalet, although this is a harsh view of a man who had been at the Chalet annually since 1924 and is arguably made with the benefit of hindsight.[42] In 1929 Sligger could have had no way of knowing that the future would be very different from what he imagined. It is also possible that, with his taste for upper-class contacts, he was influenced by the fact that Roger and his twin brother Humphrey were joint heirs to a country estate through a distant cousin.

Sligger's idea was that Roger Mynors would own the Chalet and administer its funds and that a group of colleagues would between them sustain full seasons.[39] This was a policy that depended to a large extent on Roger's ability to coordinate the team. Although Sligger could not visit the Chalet again after 1931, he still retained influence over the parties and in 1932 he made what was to prove his most significant invitation; he wrote to Christopher Cox at New College to say that he wanted Cox to join the summer season.[43] This is surprising as Christopher had left Balliol and at this point had paid only a single day's visit to the Chalet. Even with Sligger's encouragement Christopher was undecided about taking on the role but it would turn out to be another example of Sligger's ability to judge character.

Sligger's correspondence with Christopher Cox shows how well he understood his man. He emphasised the traditions of the reading parties and Christopher's suitability as a leader. This approach fell on fertile ground. Christopher had strong empathy with history and tradition; for example his lifelong habit was to refer to himself as a Victorian because he had been born in 1899.[44] The warmth of Sligger's letters to Christopher amounts to a form of grooming and the ground he prepared so carefully bore fruit when Christopher finally agreed to lead groups at the Chalet.

In 1932 Sligger travelled to Saint Gervais to be close to the parties under the leadership of Roger Mynors, Tom Boase and Richard Pares. As late as 22 August Tom Boase was reporting that Christopher Cox was still not definitely engaged[45] but Christopher finally agreed to come for three weeks in September. Sligger, by then back in the UK and visiting Downside, arranged for Tom Boase to stay on to show him the ropes.[46] He reinforced Christopher's decision by writing during the September party to say that he had had a good report of the season, drawing Christopher into exchanges over practicalities such as the Chalet's water supply and enquiries about Chalet cricket and costs.[47] Involving Christopher in his thoughts on the future, he wrote, 'I cannot tell you how glad I am that Vol III of the Chalet History has begun so well this year. I really think it ought to go on all right now.'[47] He listed those he saw as helping Roger Mynors: the 'four shepherds of this year' plus Humphrey Sumner, Bobbie Longden, John Fulton and Alan Ker, 'all old chaletites and all are capable of carrying a good start … so I think that between you the future should be safe'.

That winter Sligger went to Rome with his sister Harriet but suffered an attack of pneumonia which left him significantly weakened. After this his life was constrained to a series of nursing homes but he continued to play an active role in the organisation of the parties. The 1933 season proved problematic, as Richard Pares had conflicting family and work commitments, Tom Boase was considering a trip to Palestine, and Roger Mynors appeared to be slow in making a decision.[48] Sligger wrote again to Christopher, this time suggesting a New College party, although admitting that he personally preferred 'judicious mixtures'.[48] A few weeks later he wrote again to press Christopher to recruit the others to put pressure on Roger Mynors.[49] He added that he was asking Louis Broisat to recruit the season's servants and that his doctor had advised him to spend the summer in Switzerland. But he still hoped that an improvement would allow him to reach altitude once more. In a later letter he asked to be remembered to the staff.[50]

In the event, a season was put together for 1933 without Roger Mynors: Tom Boase led a small July party which included Jo Grimond, future leader of the Liberal Party, Alan Ker brought a Brasenose College party and Christopher again took the September slot.[51] Sligger was slightly critical of Christopher's choices, remarking that his party looked 'terribly homogeneous – all Greats men!', repeating his preference: 'I believe in mixtures – even of colleges – it prevents the Chalet being just a *réchauffée* of term.'[52] His view may have been prompted by the inclusion of Christopher's friends the philosopher Isaiah Berlin and the barrister and legal philosopher Herbert Hart, but such invitations would not have been far from his own practice. By September he had relented and wrote to say: 'I enjoy the thought that the Chalet still goes on giving a healthy life and pleasure to the young and "middle aged"!'[50]

By the April of 1934 Sligger had to accept that he was no longer fit to travel and Roger Mynors took over the organisation of the parties.[53] In May Sligger returned to Oxford from a Bournemouth nursing home and was admitted to the Osler Chest Pavilion at Headington, later being transferred to the Acland Nursing Home on Banbury Road. He improved sufficiently to be allowed back into Balliol for the summer and was given ground-floor rooms in the Master's Lodgings, where he enjoyed visits from the many friends conscious of the shadows drawing around him. He undertook the private printing of *The Perfect Chalet-ite* and, with the help of Roger Mynors, decided on the disposal of his library. As the summer was warm he was able to spend much of it in a wheelchair in the Fellows' garden, where he received his visitors. He wrote to Christopher Cox to say he was glad that Christopher would be taking another party.[54] His last letter to Christopher, it ends not with his usual 'As Ever' but with 'Addio'.

It was at this point, knowing that limited time remained to him, that he seems to have had doubts about leaving the Chalet to Roger Mynors. An extensive correspondence with his lawyers from the middle of July centres on whether the Chalet could be left to Balliol under French law and whether the succession costs would be less.[55] By late August the legal advice was that it appeared best to continue leaving the Chalet to Roger Mynors with endowment to Balliol to deal with costs.[56] But at the end of the month Sligger took advice in France about setting up a non-profit-making French company.[57] These moves may have been prompted by Roger's reluctance to involve himself in the 1933 parties.

However, it may simply have been too late for a decision, whatever he would have chosen to do. At the end of August his condition worsened and he went back into the Acland Home where he spent most of the time dozing between visitors. A frequent one was his confessor and on 17 September Sligger surprised the priest by asking for the Last Sacrament. Father Bellanti had to admit that he had come unprepared and that the Elements were back at the church, whereupon Sligger good-humouredly told him to go and fetch them. He received the Sacrament later that day, as he wanted. What was in his mind can never be known but he died quietly in the early hours of the following morning, the 18th. It was the anniversary, almost to the hour, of the fire that destroyed the Old Chalet in 1906. Had it remained a significant date for him through all the years?

Sligger's Requiem Mass took place in St Aloysius' Church on 21 September and he was buried in Wolvercote Cemetery (although, oddly, not in the Catholic section). Around his gravestone were inscribed in Latin the opening words of Psalm 121: 'I will lift up my eyes to the hills, from whence cometh my help.' The same day a Requiem was held in the chapel at the Chalet by the Abbé Nord, previous Curé of Saint Gervais.[58] Gabriel Orset's daughter Simone remembers being taken by her parents 'in honour of M. Urquhart'.[59] A Memorial Service was conducted at Balliol on 9 October by Sligger's old friend Jimmy Palmer, Bishop of Bombay, and on the first Sunday of Michaelmas term the Master paid a touching tribute in chapel during which he described Sligger as a man who had found peace at the heart of himself and whose perpetual sense of youth had enabled him to be the same to people of all ages.[60]

Tributes in France were principally directed to his sister Harriet, who was well known locally from her frequent visits to the Mont Forchet chalet with Gertrude Robinson. Supplier Gabriel Perroud wrote recalling the long association they had enjoyed with the family and saying that Sligger would be a great loss to Saint Gervais because he made the countryside known in England for all the years he brought out his friends.[61] The unidentified author of a notice in *Le Petit Dauphinois* clearly knew him well, writing of the way he revealed the beauty of their region to his students.[62] These notices implied that his loss would be keenly felt in France by those he had supported charitably. As far afield as Melbourne, Sligger's ex-student Theobald Mathew (Chalet 1924) published a touching tribute which concluded: 'Balliol without Urquhart will seem an incomplete place to his many friends but the memory of his personality and friendship will live in their hearts forever, and no man could desire a better form of immortality.'[63]

Colleagues at Balliol mounted a memorial appeal to support students who might not be able to afford to attend the Chalet. This was administered by Roger Mynors and Humphrey Sumner and by 1935 had gathered £1,570 from 370 contributors.[64] That year Humphrey Sumner wrote to Christopher Cox to thank him for a contribution, although adding pointedly that Balliol undergraduates would have first call on funds.[64]

Death came close to the Chalet in other ways in 1934. Christopher Cox led the September party and invited his brother David to the Chalet for the first time. Fourteen years younger than Christopher, David was an undergraduate at Hertford College and, unlike his brother, was a keen member of the University Mountaineering Club. He found the academic atmosphere at the Chalet stifling, later describing it as 'absolute agony', but on 12 September he hired a guide and escaped to climb the Aiguille de l'M above the Mer de Glace.[65] A late descent prevented him from reaching the tent where he had hoped to make contact with two fellow students from Oxford, John Hoyland and Paul Wand.

Then nineteen, John Hoyland, son of the Warden of the Quaker college in Birmingham, was a medical student at St Peter's Hall (later St Peter's College) and was already regarded by members of the Alpine Club as one of the most promising British climbers since George Mallory.[66] He was a cousin of Everest pioneer Howard Somervell, a member of the 1924 expedition on which George Mallory died.[67] Another cousin, Donald Somervell, had been at the Chalet in 1910 and 1911 despite being a chemistry undergraduate at Magdalen College. Donald went on to become Attorney General in Stanley Baldwin's administration of 1935 and finally Baron Somervell of Harrow;[68] he is yet another example of Sligger's ability to identify men of promise, even when studying a different subject at a different college.

John Hoyland had been born in India and the Himalayas had sealed his attraction to mountains.[67] His mother died when he was young and he was brought up by grandparents in Sheffield, beginning to climb in Cumbria and North Wales. He was partly motivated by admiration for Howard Somervell's achievements (possibly also in his choice of career; Howard went on to become a famous medical missionary). At Bootham School in York John had made his mark in athletics, cricket, rugby and football: small, muscular and determined, he could be argumentative but was also intensely loyal.[67] A prize essay from Bootham shows a mature grasp of both the enjoyment and frustrations of climbing and also his sensitivity to the beauty of landscape.

David Cox and John Hoyland were an established climbing partnership. Both were members of the University Mountaineering Club and early in 1934 they had achieved an ascent of the east buttress of Clogwyn Du'r Arddu in Snowdonia, one of the most challenging of British climbs.[67] In Oxford, by way of further challenge, they had surreptitiously carried off the bronze weathervane from the dome of the

Indian Institute.[65] It may have been David Cox who wrote the letter later published by John's father, which described John as: '... quite the most brilliant climber I have come across – he used to lead up the most astounding places in Wales, and yet he always seemed to do it most safely and securely – and so modestly. And he was, of course, a most charming companion and friend.'[67] It was natural that the two of them should plan to meet up during their first Alpine excursion.

In fact if David Cox had made it to the rendezvous tent he would have found it empty. John Hoyland and Paul Wand had arrived in Chamonix in August. Paul was an undergraduate at Balliol and a pupil of Sligger's colleague Humphrey Sumner.[69] An accomplished rower, he was the only child of the Archbishop of Brisbane and was passionate about art. He had found the Oxford intellectual atmosphere congenial and after graduation was intending to write in partnership with his father. John and Paul had travelled to Chamonix with the intention of climbing on the north side of Mont Blanc. On Plan d'Aiguille they established the camp where David Cox had hoped to meet them but their plans were frustrated by bad weather. When it cleared they were able to climb the Aiguille du Grépon (3,482 m) but were benighted on their descent and forced to spend the night on an icy floor of a stone hut. Three days later they successfully climbed the Aiguille again, John leading. This is a difficult climb and John was only the second Englishman to achieve it without a guide.[67]

John and Paul then made a fateful decision to move to the Italian side of Mont Blanc in the hope of better weather.[67] They left their camp at Plan d'Aiguille, crossed the vast Géant glacier and climbed to the Torino Hut on the Col du Géant, an historic border crossing for accomplished climbers. The guides at the hut noted that they had taken longer than expected to make the ascent and were heavily loaded with equipment; it was felt that this probably reflected inexperience but in fact John elected to carry a lot to improve his fitness.[67]

On 18 September, the day that Sligger died, Alpine Club member Frank Smythe was asked to mount a search, as it was realised that the two Oxford students were missing.[70] The search party learned that they had last been seen on 23 August leaving the Gamba Hut above Courmayeur, from where they intended to climb the Innominata Ridge, a difficult route across the steep southern face of Mont Blanc. This was within their capabilities under normal conditions but bad weather had set in and they never returned to the hut. The searchers found one of their ice axes near the ridge and this led them to their bodies on the surface of the Frêney glacier below.

Although death is now more common on Mont Blanc, reflecting the greater number of people on the mountain, at the time the loss of two promising young climbers sent shockwaves through the mountaineering community, especially in Oxford. Archbishop Wand lost his only child and because of duties in Australia was obliged to send a representative to his son's funeral.[65] John's death added to the tragic story of his father's first marriage; John's mother died a month after giving birth to her third son, who himself survived only two months.[67] Their remaining son, Denys, entered Balliol the year after his brother John died on Mont Blanc but was lost in action in 1944, thirteen years before his father's death.[69] However, John Somervell Hoyland's second marriage had a happier outcome and produced another four children. One of his grandsons, Graham Hoyland, became an author, mountaineer and film director and was a moving force behind the 1999 Everest expedition which located George Mallory's body.[71]

David Cox would go on to become tutor in Modern History at University College and a celebrated mountaineer and President of the Alpine Club despite contracting poliomyelitis in 1958.[72] He returned to the Chalet just once more in the final pre-war party of 1938, when Donald Somervell, now Sir Donald and a member of the Privy Council, paid a return visit. Once again David could not share with his brother Christopher, who was certainly no climber, his passion for the reading parties and he used the Chalet as his climbing base, though his attempts that year were frustrated by poor weather. He never went to the Chalet again and it is probable that, like many serious climbers, he simply found the situation there too tame. As we shall see, when after the Second World War he found himself well placed to combine with Christopher in a Chalet partnership, he let the opportunity pass. Had Sligger been alive he might have repeated placidly his assertion that the Chalet was not a base for climbers.

When Sligger died, Christopher Cox, of all those who had maintained his tradition since 1931, was the only one actually at the Chalet. There would inevitably have been extra poignancy to being there when learning of Sligger's death back in Oxford. In a letter to Roger Mynors, Christopher wrote that he was sitting in the shade of the veranda (Fig. 37) with only the sound of the stream and popping of lupin pods for company and had 'never been less ready to leave the Chalet and feel I should like to abandon Oxford and stay here happily until the snow comes. It has been a quite delightful three weeks.'[73] In a later letter he wrote, 'I would give next year's salary to be here another three weeks instead of leaving tomorrow.'[74]

It appears to have been Christopher Cox who notified the Poore family of Sligger's death. In reply General Poore said that he was considering selling the Chalet du Rocher and, on the basis of past association, would give first refusal to any of Sligger's friends who were interested. This was not a practical proposition and in the event this chalet was to remain in the Poore family until well after the Second World War.[75]

Those left with commitment to the Chalet were certainly in no position to respond to Poore's suggestion. Sligger's will had left the bulk of his estate of around £15,000 to the Balliol College Endowment Fund.[76] Roger Mynors had received the two French chalets by a separate will and it is notable that the small legacy for maintenance which Sligger had mooted in 1929 had not materialised. This situation left Roger Mynors responsible for the costs of the chalets and parties, although over the next few years Balliol did in fact make a contribution to the overheads.[77]

Sligger's vision for the parties after his death began to fall into place in 1935. A season from early July to late September was led successively by Richard Pares, Alan Ker and Roger Mynors, Christopher Cox taking the September slot as before. Roger Mynors introduced his younger brother David, wondering if it was right to put a keen rowing freshman into a party that largely consisted of Greats men.[78] Christopher Cox bought along Frank Lepper, a New College student he was keen to interest in the Chalet. The following year Roger Mynors was faced with a challenge in that it appeared that none of his colleagues could help and so he ran a short season of six weeks.[79] Despite this he told Christopher Cox that the season had been a great success and encouraged Christopher to go again the following year, having like Sligger concluded that the Chalet needed 'a succession of *patrons*'. The 1937 season was again a full one, Roger sharing it with Tom Boase, Alan Ker and Christopher Cox, despite Christopher having moved from New College to become Director of Education in the Sudan.

These pre-war parties were notable in that for the first time

Balliol members found themselves in the minority. This is not surprising given that the majority of the leaders were not at Balliol and
would have wanted to invite undergraduates with whom they were
familiar. There was also an increasing number of visitors, some from
the Honeymoon Chalet where they were guests of Roger Mynors.
Others who had been at the Chalet in undergraduate days came
back for a visit.[79] In 1938 Christopher Cox's party was visited by New
College alumni William Hayter (Chalet 1926), Patrick Reilly (Chalet
1934) and Edward Bradby, all in the diplomatic service, and by Attorney General Sir Donald Somervell (Chalet 1910–11) with Vyvyan Holt
from the Civil Administration in Iraq. Both Hayter and Reilly would
prove to have post-war roles in the Chalet's fortunes. The Curé of
Saint Gervais usually visited each year to conduct a Requiem Mass
on the anniversary of Sligger's death.[80]

Family links were also maintained: in 1936 Roger Mynors invited
his student Thomas Sadler, son of Michael (Chalet 1909–10), and the
1937 party was joined by Frederick Temple, grandson of Archbishop
Frederick Temple (Balliol 1838), whose father had been at Balliol in
1898 and whose uncle William, another future Archbishop, had been
at the Chalet in 1906. In 1936 Michael Asquith, a grandson of Prime
Minister Herbert Asquith, followed his father's Chalet visit of 1901
and those of his uncle Cyril in 1910 and aunt Violet in 1913. The 1938
party was joined by Michael's cousin Julian, 2nd Earl of Oxford and
Asquith, who was studying with Cyril Bailey and who had inherited
the title at the age of twelve when his grandfather Herbert Asquith
died, his father Raymond, the Prime Minister's eldest son, having died
in the First World War.

In 1937 Christopher's student Frank Lepper embarked on the excavation of a *piscine* in a hollow bowl on the hillside through which
flowed the stream which fed the garden waterfall. At first it was only
knee deep but the following year he successfully enlarged it for swimming. Louis Broisat is said to have reported that an elderly member
of the Orset family, Michel, claimed that David Urquhart had kept
fish there but this story seems unlikely, as there are no references to
Sligger's parents ever keeping fish at the Chalet.[81]

These parties tended to widen the scope of the walks. In 1935
Christopher Cox took a group by train to the Argentière glacier
beyond Chamonix and the party also explored the lower slopes of
the Aravis ridge. In 1937 a party did Sligger's traditional Italian walk,

though in the reverse direction; the following year this walk was extended by a visit to Aosta by train. In 1938 Louis Broisat guided two attempts on Mont Blanc, the second for Christopher Cox's brother David: unfortunately both were defeated by that season's heavy snowfalls. However, Léon Orset, brought in as guide to Frank Lepper and others, had more success in getting his group to the Col Infranchissable on the Dômes de Miage (3,340 m), the first time this had been achieved by a Chalet party.

Sligger's absence and then death allowed Louis Broisat more licence in dealing with those who continued the parties. While he had kept in touch by letter when Sligger was alive, taking his instructions from his *patron*, after Sligger's death Christopher Cox and the others found him frustrating, ignoring some requests for work but going out of his way to do alternative jobs to perfection. He may well have regarded Sligger's lieutenants as *arrivistes*, given that he had had strong personal loyalty to Sligger. He had also developed an increasing appetite for wine and frequently arrived 'in liquor'.[79]

The kitchen staff had changed, presumably after Julia Martin's marriage to Victor Broisat, and the new team became a focus for the unmarried Broisat brothers. The maid Yvonne Masse (Fig. 38) was a very attractive woman and Christopher Cox wrote to Roger Mynors that there seemed to be a lot of male life in the kitchen and that Louis' brother Alphonse was likely to turn up after an evening drinking at the *Pavillon*, looking for a bed for the night.[74] On the final day of the 1935 party the members were brought running to the kitchen by screams from Hélène, another maid, because Louis had led his mule into the kitchen to 'entertain' her.[82] The Chalet also appeared to have become home to one of the Broisats' dogs, which slept in the scullery.[74] The party leaders seemed to have no way of dealing with these challenges: Cox's comment to Roger Mynors, 'Louis has somehow evaded the call that came to him to serve as *réserviste* ... his fatal charm is as disarming as ever (our new arrival had to wait 44 hours for his luggage!)' says it all.[83]

There were also surprising variations in Louis' bills. Roger Mynors was inclined to take the same circumspect approach as Sligger had done, commenting to Christopher Cox that he had no doubt that Louis had an 'understanding' with suppliers but that he doubted that they were seriously dishonest.[84] He thought the best approach was to appear to take an interest in the prices to prevent them overdoing it. Like Christopher, he found Louis too likeable: one evening Louis had called on Roger's guests at Mont Forchet 'rather bottled' and ended up sitting on the floor, as Roger said, 'like calling on an Oxford dean when slightly buffy, to establish an alibi'.[84] Louis had also hired a boy, Raymond (Fig. 39), who in Roger's view was 'not *méchant* but *un peu bizarre* as Madame puts it' (the 'Madame' here was Gabriel Orset's wife Julie at the Hôtel du Prarion, who was proving increasingly helpful to these parties).[79] Raymond developed a teenage crush on the maid Yvonne, prompting frequent '*crises*', which the parties were spared when she left in 1935.[85]

Christopher Cox's letters show that his mind was turning towards the future care of the Chalet and that he was steadily moving into a leading role.[74] He was concerned about the chapel where the walls were beginning to bow outwards and the roof was showing signs of imminent collapse. His conclusion was that the construction had not been of good quality. It appeared that the New College architect had visited to advise: one wonders whether Roger Mynors found this at all intrusive. Christopher also felt able to share with Roger his reservations about some of the staff, because he commented that Yvonne's replacement Hélène was 'alpha minus' to Yvonne's 'alpha'.[74] Yvonne Masse and the cook Angèle Bayetto (Fig. 38), who happened to be Julie Dion-Orset's aunt,[86] were clearly a good team, because Christopher reported that 'Madame Bayetto went off a lot after Yvonne's departure'.[74] Madame Bayetto had been replaced by a Madame Ducroz and Roger Mynors must have taken Christopher's comments to heart because the following year Louis wrote to confirm that Madame Ducroz would indeed be continuing.[87]

Christopher was also aware that Roger bore the costs of the Chalet. Party members paid their own living expenses but there had been French inheritance tax to pay on both the chalets. There were annual French property taxes too, and Louis Broisat still to be paid. Christopher offered a contribution but Roger nobly declined on the basis that this was not what Sligger had intended.[78] Roger Mynors had of course inherited the costs of the seasons, along with those of both of his chalets, and he regularly reimbursed the other leaders for their expenses.[82,88] He may have compensated for this by renting out the chalet at Mont Forchet: Louis Broisat regularly relayed requests from people who wanted to use it.[89]

A vivid record of the last pre-war party of 1938 (Fig. 41) has been left by Aidan White, who won a scholarship to study Classics at New College in 1935. Christopher Cox led the final September group and was assisted by Frank Lepper, who had moved to a lectureship at Corpus Christi College. Frank wrote to Aidan White to say that the Balliol fund was not being fully used and suggested that this would allow an upgrade from the usual third-class rail travel to second class.[90] At that time Cook's offered a 40 per cent reduction for students and this reduced the price of a second-class return ticket to 7 pounds, 5 shillings and 7 pence (£7.28p), a third-class one being 4 pounds and 13 shillings (£4.65p). Aidan accepted the improved option and Frank sent him a cheque for the larger sum, commenting that if his companions opted for third-class travel Aidan was welcome to keep the difference.[91]

Aidan travelled out with two contemporaries, John Compton and John Spalding. Sligger had given his students detailed advice on travel and for these pre-war parties Christopher produced a typed set of notes on the journey and what to expect at the Chalet.[90] These were the precursor of the notes in use today but, consisting of one page only, were decidedly terse compared with the six or seven closely typed pages a chaletite is likely to receive now. Christopher followed Sligger's example in recommending an evening meal at the Gare de Lyon but commented that the famous Buffet (now the *Train Bleu* restaurant) with its landscape art was 'garish'.

The three students travelled by the night train as usual: at that time it was necessary to change at Aix-les-Bains at 5 a.m. and they narrowly avoided going on to Turin when they woke to find the train standing at the station in Aix.[92] Aidan wrote home to say that the notes had not exaggerated in describing the walk up from Saint Gervais as 'very, very long', though he did say that the Chalet was worth it; later in the party he was disinclined to visit Saint Gervais on the grounds that the ascent was 'an ordeal beyond description'.[93] However, he did manage it at least once, in the company of Christopher's brother David who was making his second visit to the Chalet. Noting that Aidan wore nailed boots, David concluded that Aidan was, like himself, a mountaineer; Aidan's denials were dismissed by David as mere modesty.[94]

Being misunderstood seems to have been a liability for Aidan. Having a little French he had succeeded in buying a few forgotten items while passing through Saint Gervais. Christopher was impressed that Aidan knew the French for cotton wool (by a fluke, as it happened) and concluded that they had a fluent French-speaker in their midst.[93] The Saint Gervais Curé was to visit later in the party in order to conduct the annual memorial Mass for Sligger and Christopher detailed Aidan to be interpreter, causing Aidan to express to his father the heartfelt wish that the priest would not arrive. Later, on an afternoon walk they came upon a 'peasant at a water trough' and Christopher instructed Aidan to ask directions; on this occasion Aidan's lack of skill avoided exposure when the man turned out to be stone deaf.[93] Aidan's letters reveal a real fear of being shown up but when dealing with Christopher Cox it is difficult to know precisely how much he understood and whether his comments were merely a manifestation of his sense of humour.

Certainly Aidan had no fear of being close to Christopher. He described him as a 'very likeable person, rather stout, and full of jokes'.[93] Christopher had been given an expensive Zeiss camera about which, Aidan said, he appeared not 'to know the first thing'. (Christopher's problems with photographic equipment were to continue into the 1970s, as we will see.) He had recently stood down from his position as Director of Education in the Sudan, so all the party took to calling him 'The Director'.

Christopher took the opportunity to explore Aidan's academic progress while they walked and discovered that he was having difficulty getting input from his Philosophy tutor, who happened to be Isaiah Berlin.[93] At the time Christopher was inclined to make excuses for his colleague but after the party he wrote to Aidan to recommend a renewed approach to Berlin and also being open with his other tutors about any difficulties.[95]

The members were required to pay a daily charge to cover food and the pay of the servants. This worked out at around 7 shillings (35p) a day.[90] A cost of around 7 pounds for the party, excluding excursions and personal cash, plus travel costs of a similar amount, needs to be seen in the context that in 1938 a man working in manufacturing or similar industry might take home less than 4 pounds a week, as Harold Macmillan as Chancellor of the Exchequer confirmed in Parliament.[96] Louis Broisat charged 8 shillings (40p) for bringing up the luggage, which could be shared if several people travelled together.[90] As foreign exchange was not always easy, Christopher Cox tended to take francs to cover the entire party and to ask members to pay in sterling back in Oxford.[90]

Aidan White's reports home confirm that the party still con-
formed to Sligger's model of work between breakfast and lunch and
between tea and dinner and he thought it 'clever to put people who
are required to work so far away from civilization'.[92] He found that
the cook and maid spoke not a word of English but served them well.
Post was brought up from the village by a boy called Gilbert, who
had replaced the Yvonne-smitten Raymond. However, Louis' services
remained variable and in his first letter home Aidan reported that he
and the others were still waiting for their rucksacks.[92] In fact Christopher Cox had resorted to warning of this complication in his notes for
the chaletites.[90] To reassure them he said that the Chalet had a large
store of discarded clothing, including pyjamas, which they could use
pending arrival of their own. As the daily charge included washing,
we must assume that the services of the *blanchisseuse* were still available and that the Chalet's stock was in an acceptable state. Aidan White
was able to tell his father that they had spent an amusing time fitting
themselves out after a wet walk up and that he had acquired 'a pair
of old grey trousers, some brown brogue shoes, and a check shirt'.[92]

The diary for 1938 ends with the group photograph in front of
the Chalet (Fig. 41), a happy collection of young men in tweed jackets
and slacks which would not have been out of place in any of Sligger's
early parties. By the end of that party, though, it must have been
clear to everyone that a European war was once again a serious risk,
if not a certainty. The rise of Adolf Hitler in Germany and his expan-
sionist policy held too many signs of impending danger, even though
other Western governments had been taking a conciliatory stance.
Some of the 1938 group had walked to Courmayeur but had faced
extra checks at the Italian border and had seen the next valley full
of military forces. Incredible as it appears in retrospect, in 1939 Louis
Broisat wrote to Roger Mynors about preparations for the year's
season.[97] Nothing was to come of this, as it was overtaken by the
steadily worsening situation across Europe and Britain's declaration
of war in September. However, for the Chalet, quite apart from the
effects that a further world war would have on its fortunes, unforeseen events would occur which would ensure that Sligger's plans for
its future would unravel and that the Chalet would sink into a period
of silence. At this point the story of the Chalet des Anglais very nearly
came to a complete end.

SLIGGER AND THE CHALET IN FICTION

A student author at the Chalet

WHEN GIDEON SAW THE CHALET he loved it instantly. It was like something out of literature, old, dusty, full of venerable smells and shafts of late afternoon sunlight slanting through the windows. Like a living thing, it creaked and shifted around him as it warmed in the day and cooled in the evening. Backed by a larch forest, it stood secluded on a small plateau on the mountainside, looking out over a wide valley to a skyline of peaks which were lit in ever-changing colours as sun passed over and sank behind them into sunsets of spell-binding grandeur. He felt as if he had strayed into a Victorian romance.

Knowing their friend well, the others had reserved a single bedroom for him at the rear of the building where he could spread the books he had brought and retire into his own thoughts. However Gideon found a new enjoyment in sharing the communal life of the Chalet. In the evenings he found he preferred to be with the others around the wood stove in the large sitting room. When they walked out on to the hillside the others chattered but he was usually silent, open to the calm of Nature around him. He soaked up the atmosphere, the dappled light in the forest trails, the long trails over the high pastures, the scrambles over rocks. He made the ascent to the shelf-like glacier at Tête Rousse and sat outside the refuge, nursing his cup of soup and contemplating the world laid out below him, tiny and distant like a relief map. He climbed to a glacial lake where, under the awe-inspiring backdrop of the Mont Blanc massif, he swam in the stinging, exhilarating cold of the water. Bathed in the clear warm sunlight, it was all transcendently beautiful. He felt a new peace and confidence settling into himself. He saw for the first time what his father had pursued and began to understand why.

There was another discovery. The Chalet was full of words. The gifts of successive students over more than a hundred years had given it an eclectic library into which Gideon sank his eyes and mind, the books he had travelled with forgotten. There was Alexis de Tocqueville, writing history as if it were a novel; Chekhov putting a whole world into a short story; Vachell, cosy and complacent; Maurois' thoughts on Shelley. He felt that Disraeli might have been unfairly criticised as he turned the pages of his work. He discovered Simenon's Maigret. He let his choice range over the books, exploring the words of those who wrote on philosophy, religion, politics.

Early one morning late in his stay Gideon kicked off his sleeping bag and slipped quietly into his clothes. He crept cautiously down the stairs, anxious not to disturb the softly breathing bodies in the surrounding rooms. Around him timbers creaked intermittently as if the Chalet itself was also stirring in preparation for the new day. Downstairs the big sitting room was still fragrant with the smell of last night's wood fire. Freshening himself with a splash of cold water at the kitchen sink, Gideon laced on his walking boots and left the house. The air was cool and still as he climbed the jeep track, the crunching of his boots on the gravel the only disturbance in the morning silence.

After twenty minutes' confident stride uphill his long legs brought him to the crest of the slope above the Chalet. Before him the grey mass of Mont Blanc hid the brilliance of the dawn in the east, as it would for several hours yet, and the light that came around it was soft and gentle, creating no shadows. Ahead of him lay the small hotel on its own horizon below the massif. There the staff would be busy with morning patisserie and coffee, hot and flavoursome, but this morning Gideon was not interested in creature comfort or human company. Turning to his left, he started to make his way up through the trees that covered the slopes of the Prarion, the branches soaking his clothes with their morning dew as he passed.

Half an hour of effort brought Gideon out of the trees and onto the open slope leading to the grassy summit of the Prarion, where he could sit comfortably on the peak and take in the view. Around him stretched the panorama of the high mountains. In the east the contours of Mont Blanc were etched by the strengthening morning light. To the west of him this light was beginning to paint in pastel shades the unrelenting cliffs of the Aravis and the double peak of Varens. Below him the morning mist was rising from the long, curving valley where the chalets and houses of the villages were about to wake to the new day.

Sitting isolated on this peak as if he was the only wakeful creature in the world, Gideon allowed his mind to roam over the experiences of the last week: the strenuous days on the hillsides, the deep satisfaction of exploring the written word in morning study, the camaraderie of a shared life he had at last learned to appreciate, and above all the magic of the location, its surroundings, and the peace and tranquillity that seemed to reflect the calm, massive confidence of Nature itself. This morning the concerns of the life he had left to come here – his real life, the one in the world outside this place – seemed strangely distant from this dawn reverie: the battle to balance work for his degree with the ever-present creative urge waiting to draw his mind into another world, the practical need to address the empty bank account, even the warm nights back in Oxford with his body comfortably entwined with Rosalind's and where, he knew, he was sinking into a love for her that was enduring.

He looked up at the far peaks. His father had loved these mountains but they had taken his life from him at an unfairly early age. He had planned and anticipated his visits and come back from his annual excursions tanned and happy. He had done so, Gideon realised, because this was part of his nature. His father had wanted to wander alone over the high passes and he had seized his opportunities with both hands precisely because he had wanted it. Dead when he was barely forty, he had lived a life that was as full as he wanted it to be.

'So what have I done?' Gideon quietly asked the watching peaks.

They looked back, silent with the patience of millennia, as if inviting his answer. Gideon knew what it was: all his life he had turned in on his own mind. All his effort had been internalised and he had fought to create a world personal and controllable within his own head. Words of the Indian mountaineer Hari Pal Singh Ahluwalia that he had read in the Chalet came to him:

In climbing to the summit you are overwhelmed by a deep sense of joy and thankfulness which lasts a lifetime, and the experience changes you completely. The man who has been to the mountains is never the same again; he becomes conscious of his smallness and loneliness in the universe.

That other summit – the summit of the mind – is no less formidable and no easier to climb. The mind has its mountains and cliffs, fearful, sheer, unfathomed. The physical act of climbing a mountain has a kinship with the ascent of that inward, spiritual, mountain.[1]

When you climb a mountain it is difficult to see, in the early stages, where you are going or how far you have travelled. There comes a point high up in the journey when you are able to look back and see the track you took and how it has brought you to this point. From his seat on top of the Prarion Gideon looked down the path his life had taken. He saw how the worlds contained in literature had allowed him to escape from his pain and loss. He saw that he had immersed himself in their narrative but insulated himself from their emotions. He saw that the protective carapace in which his mother had wrapped herself was no different to what he had done to himself, and that she had done it because she had to. He saw that his father had not loved him the less because he had loved the mountains too.

Burrowing into these thoughts came an idea, tiny and quiet but still persistent, like a worm in the ground beneath him: something that was not yet grown but might develop, given care and nurturing. Knowing that he had to surrender to it, Gideon pulled his rucksack round onto his chest and fumbled inside for the pencil and notebook that he always carried. Turning onto his stomach in the grass, he listened for a few moments to the great silence of the world around him, and then began to write.

(From *That Other Summit* by the author)[2]

¤

In view of the powerful character of both Sligger and the Chalet, it was inevitable that writers would draw inspiration from them. This chapter introduces examples of fiction that either reflect Sligger or the Chalet and enlarge our appreciation of both. These fictional references occupy a niche in the extensive literature which has been stimulated by the life of the University and activities of dons, including such classics as *The Adventures of Mr Verdant Green* (Cuthbert Bede, 1853),[3] *The Comedy of Age* (Desmond Coke, 1906),[4] *Zuleika Dobson* (Max Beerbohm, 1911)[5] and *Sinister Street* (Compton Mackenzie, 1913).[6] In our own time this genre has extended to Colin Dexter's series of Inspector Morse novels and the fantasy novels of Philip Pullman.

Oxford aesthetes of Sligger's time had a strong tendency to see themselves in terms of romantic fiction. In this way, Cyril Connolly's generation often interpreted their environment in terms of Proust's novel *À la recherche du temps perdu*, a concept in which Maurice Bowra became equated with Swann, and Lady Ottoline Morrell at Garsington with the autocratic hostess Mme Verdurin. In this scheme Sligger was interpreted, not entirely to his advantage, as Françoise, the narrator's loyal but stubborn maid, who had a strong sense of tradition and duty.[7]

Reading parties have also had such a strong character that it is not surprising that they have provided inspiration. For example, Fenella Gentleman's 2018 novel *The Reading Party*[8] examines a UK party when women members were introduced for the first time. This is based on her own experience of reading parties in Cornwall organised by Wadham College.

Although Sligger has been claimed to be the model for several figures in literature, most authors do not usually base a character completely on one individual but draw from many to build personalities which are composite. As we shall see, this applies to several figures in whom commentators have detected elements of Sligger's personality. In fact some of these characters come so close to Sligger that there cannot be any doubt about him being the model. Other examples imply that he and the Chalet were regarded as inseparable; this is hardly surprising when it was such a large part of his life. It also has to be a measure of the reputation of both that some writers have created a reflection without close personal experience of either.

An example of how an author draws on their experience is given in Michael Sadleir's 1915 novel *Hyssop*.[9] Michael Sadleir, né Sadler, the son of the Master of University College, entered Balliol in 1908 and went to the Chalet in 1909 and 1910. He subsequently became an author, publisher and bibliographer, his most famous work being *Fanny by Gaslight*, a novel of 1940 based on prostitution in Victorian London.[10] Publication caused something of a storm and prompted Michael to change the spelling of his surname to prevent embarrassment to his father, also Michael.

Hyssop, an early work, is a story of unfulfilled undergraduate love and clearly draws on Sadleir's own time at Balliol. Its protagonist, Philip Murray, is obliged by his father's pursuit of European art to live in Switzerland until the death of his father at an early age. As a result he becomes multilingual and a keen Alpinist; there are clear echoes here both of Sligger and of his father. Michael Sadleir was a student of A. L. Smith's in Modern History at Balliol but he obviously knew Sligger. Philip Murray finds his own tutor daunting but makes the acquaintance of another don, Trafford, who is known by a nickname, 'Trips', and who keeps open house in the evenings in his rooms: these are lined, like Sligger's, with the photographs of past students. Trafford is described as being good at putting people at their ease, as was Sligger, but there are otherwise no further points of direct comparison. Later Philip Murray and one of his fellow students make a summer trip to Aosta in Italy, taking in some Alpine climbing. In one excursion he climbs to the Col du Géant and his description of the view into Italy is so clearly described that it is difficult to believe that Michael Sadleir was not writing from experience. Similarly, there is strong suggestion of personal knowledge when Philip Murray opines that Courmayeur is 'a hole' on the grounds that 'it is neither Italy nor Switzerland because it tries to be both'. It is very probable that Sadleir took part in the traditional three-day outing from the Chalet, though the walk in question did not take place during his 1909 party and the diary entry for 1910 is uncharacteristically silent on that year's walks.

If *Hyssop* draws on Sligger and the Alps in a general way, there are other references which are or are claimed to be more specific. Several sources postulate that Sligger was the inspiration behind Walter Pater's novella *Emerald Uthwart* of 1892.[11,12] This is an elegy told from standing over the grave of a young man long since dead at the age of twenty-six. Pater, who had been a pupil of Benjamin Jowett and who taught Classics at Brasenose College, had contacts with the Aesthetic Movement and was a leading light in Hellenism and the recognition of male relationships. A lifelong bachelor, he cultivated a taste for young men; one of his more public liaisons had involved a Balliol undergraduate, Walter Hardinge, and had resulted in Hardinge being sent down temporarily by Jowett to distance him from Pater.[13]

By the time of Sligger's arrival at Balliol in 1890, Walter Pater was at the end of his career as a tutor – he was to die in 1894 – but at this period of his life he had become attracted to young men of Catholic and Anglo-Catholic belief.[14] The date of publication indicates that there would have been time to know Sligger at Balliol and the points of comparison between his protagonist and Sligger are so numerous that it appears that Pater both knew the young Sligger and found him inspiring.

In Pater's retrospective through Emerald Uthwart's life we learn that he had been the youngest of four sons and had spent little of his life in Britain, being sent to school abroad. There he adapted to a school life which was monastic and he acquired a love of Latin and Greek and was accomplished at cricket. A place at Oxford followed; thus far there are strong points of similarity with Sligger's early life. There is also obvious parallel between the names of Urquhart and Uthwart; Pater tells us that the latter were an old-established family. Moreover, Emerald had a nickname, always being shortened to 'Aldy'. Pater describes him as slim, trim and bashful. Further description comes from the surgeon conducting Emerald's post-mortem examination, who notes that the body looks younger than its twenty-six years and has a fine brow capped by abundance of fair hair. Once again the comparison with Sligger is strong.

If Pater was indeed inspired by a late affection for Sligger his aim cannot have been to create any forward vision of Sligger's life. The Emerald Uthwart of fiction leaves Oxford to fight abroad in the company of a close friend from Oxford, with the aura of a romantic friendship as is characteristic of Pater's work. Emerald is wounded in battle and recovers only to undergo court-martial with his friend on dubious grounds. Both are sentenced to death and Emerald is forced to watch the execution of his friend before his own sentence is commuted to dishonourable discharge. He travels back to Britain but weakness and grief cause his wound to fester and lead to his death. He survives just long enough to learn that re-examination of the trial has resulted in his exoneration.

Pater's story is marked throughout by the yearning sense of lost youth and beauty that inhabits much of the writing of this period, as for example in the poems in A. E. Housman's *A Shropshire Lad*,[15] published two years after Pater's death. Strong parallels between Sligger and Emerald suggest that Pater may have been drawn to both the physical and intellectual character of the young Sligger. Otherwise he had a message of his own to promote and Sligger provided only a basis for the idealised young man who was the vehicle for Pater's expression.

Another claim made for representing Sligger is the character of Sillery in *A Question of Upbringing* by Anthony Powell, published in 1951.[16] Powell entered Balliol in 1923 to study Modern History and was taught by Sligger's colleagues Charles Stone and Kenneth Bell but was also tutored briefly ('not very effectively') by Sligger. He described their relationship as good but claimed that he could never call himself 'a Sliggerite' and implies that he turned down an invitation to the Chalet on the grounds of its spartan conditions.[17]

A Question of Upbringing is the first part of Anthony Powell's *A Dance to the Music of Time*[18] and tells of the college life of one Nicholas Jenkins. The tutor Sillery (usually greeted as 'Sillers') is described as easy in his relationships with undergraduates and Nicholas Jenkins meets him first at a tea party in Sillery's room, where students are encouraged to call in. There are echoes of Sligger's evening salons; these had come to an end before Powell's arrival at Balliol but his comment makes it clear that he was aware of their reputation.[17]

In fact, Anthony Powell denied that Sligger was the model for Sillery, pointing out differences between the two men and saying that if he had wanted to offer his own projection of an important personality like Sligger he could have done so.[17] However, writers are good at assembling characters from diverse sources, not always consciously, and there are sufficient points of similarity with Sligger to indicate that some of his character crept in. The informal tea party aside, Sillery is described as disliking being called 'Sir', avoiding strong drink and having little aptitude for formal teaching. We are also told he was fond of cultivating contacts with people in public life, as was Sligger. However, unlike the dapper Sligger, Sillery is untidy and bears a florid moustache; this feature may have come from Anthony Powell's tutor Kenneth Bell, who affected a military appearance. Moreover, where Sligger was genuinely interested in students' personalities and their conversation, Sillery is a power-seeking gossiper who controls conversation, 'never taking his tea without intrigue'. Those who have studied the University of this time might take the view that this more likely reflects Maurice Bowra. Whether Anthony Powell allowed some of Sligger's personality to creep into his writing or not, he does not provide any new insights to Sligger or his activities.

If there is doubt about Anthony Powell's sources, in Beverley Nichols' 1922 novel *Patchwork* the references to the Sligger character are so strong as to be almost biographical.[19] Nichols, who entered Balliol to study with Sligger in 1917, drew heavily on his own experiences at Oxford to such an extent that his novel is considered to be autobiographical; in his introductory note Nichols rejects the traditional author's disclaimer that his characters are fictional and says that at Oxford he did many of the things which his protagonist does.

Patchwork is the story of Raymond Sheldon, son of a privileged family, who enters Balliol after service in the First World War. Beverley Nichols' account is probably an accurate description of the war-weary students who took up their places after the war because Nichols' own time at Oxford was interrupted by war service and he was well placed to compare the shift in mood. Raymond Sheldon's response is to throw himself into an attempt to stimulate Oxford to return to its pre-war values. He becomes editor of the *Isis* magazine, then starts a new journal, *The Oxford Mercury*, then a new political club and finally becomes involved in the Union; he becomes Secretary but is narrowly defeated in the election for President. There is much in this that is almost a direct account of Nichols' own time at Oxford.

Raymond Sheldon is a student of the Dean of Balliol, as was Beverley Nichols. The Dean in question is called John Fortescue and is known to everyone by his nickname, 'Tugly'. Nichols describes him as about fifty but looking ageless, with the air of a cherubic faun; he dislikes being called 'Sir' and provides a social centre for students. His room, which overlooks the Martyrs' Memorial in St Giles, is decorated with photographs of past students and other young men; for all of this description to pass for Sligger one has only to substitute the names. Raymond Sheldon's work suffers due to his many commitments and Tugly makes efforts to support him, which is precisely what Sligger had to do for Beverley Nichols.[20] In fact Nichols was faced with being sent down from the University for poor performance but Sligger defended him successfully.[21]

If this portrays an affectionate view of Sligger, Nichols' contemporary Evelyn Waugh provides the counterpoise. As we have seen (Chapter 3), Evelyn Waugh's antagonism to Sligger amounted almost to obsession. When he came to publish *Brideshead Revisited*[22] in 1945, eleven years after Sligger's death, Sligger was clearly in his mind when he included a slighting reference to Alpine reading parties in an exchange between Charles Ryder and his father: putting the words into the mouth of the latter also created a link between Sligger and the unattractive personality of the father in the book.

Sligger has been said to be also the inspiration for the snobbish and controlling *Brideshead Revisited* don, Samgrass.[16] However, Evelyn Waugh's friend and biographer Christopher Sykes claimed that Samgrass was modelled on Maurice Bowra.[23] This distressed Bowra, who was a frequent guest of Waugh's, and Sykes reports that Bowra covered his feelings with a pretence of enthusiasm for the portrayal, which in turn upset Evelyn Waugh.

It has to be allowed, though, that the character of Samgrass has a quieter and more subliminal persistence than was typical of Maurice Bowra. In the way that Samgrass approaches other characters in the book, there could well be echoes of how Evelyn Waugh remembered Sligger's interference in his relationship with Richard Pares. As with many other authors, Waugh may have drawn on traits from several acquaintances when putting this character together.

In view of Evelyn Waugh's insistence that Sligger was homosexual, it would be surprising if the flamboyantly gay character of Anthony Blanche did not reflect some of Waugh's attitudes to Sligger. However, in *Brideshead Revisited* Blanche is a fellow student rather than a don and there is evidence that Evelyn Waugh intended to portray his contemporaries Brian Howard and Harold Acton.[24]

Evelyn Waugh's real and vicious attack on Sligger came in a forty-minute silent film he made shortly after leaving Oxford in 1924. *The Scarlet Woman: An Ecclesiastical Melodrama*[25] tells the story of an attempt by the Catholic Church to return England to Catholicism by converting Edward, Prince of Wales, through his attachment to an effeminate Dean of Balliol. If the plan succeeds, a second St Bartholomew's Day massacre of Protestants is proposed. The film was put together by Waugh and the author and actor Terence Greenidge, who like Waugh was an undergraduate at Hertford College. They also recruited Greenidge's brother John and future film producer John Sutro.[26] Evelyn Waugh wrote the screenplay and the film was shot in Oxford and London, Terence Greenidge directing.

The Scarlet Woman can be regarded as a hymn to the Hypocrites. The Greenidge brothers and John Sutro had all been members with Evelyn Waugh and the film has a strong alcoholic and homoerotic undercurrent. The actors were drawn from their circle of friends at Oxford and included William Lygon, the future Earl Beauchamp.[26] The only female member of the cast was Elsa Lanchester, future film actress and long-suffering wife of the actor Charles Laughton; Evelyn Waugh was to boast that he gave Elsa her first film role. Evelyn's elder brother Alec was brought in to play the mother of a cardinal and Evelyn himself played the gay Balliol Dean.

The film was intended for private viewing and was shown in 1925 by the Oxford University Dramatic Society, receiving an enthusiastic review in *Isis* magazine.[26] It was later shown to the Newman Society and although its creators seem to have had a sentimental attachment to it there were few further screenings until 1964, when Waugh featured it in *A Little Learning*, his first volume of autobiography, where he made clear that Sligger was the target.[26] Through Terence Greenidge, the Royal Shakespeare Company hosted a viewing and an abridged version was later shown by the BBC, after which appearances became more common. Again through Terence Greenidge it was taken up by the late Professor Charles Linck of the East Texas State University and screened in the United States.[26]

The subversive plot is hatched between Cardinal Montefiasco (a name presumably derived from the Italian for Mont Blanc, Monte Bianco) and the Pope, who is romantically attached to the Cardinal's mother. The Dean of Balliol is described as England's leading Catholic layman and the reference to Sligger is obvious, as Waugh confirmed in *A Little Learning*.[27] At the start of the film the Prince of Wales is shown in a fawning relationship with the Dean and when King George V is informed he insists that steps are taken to separate them. In view of the way that Sligger had intervened in Waugh's own attachment to Richard Pares, it is possible that Waugh was getting his own back by reversing the roles. The story also happens to be ironically prophetic in that six years later William Lygon's father, the (unknown to his family) bisexual 7th Earl Beauchamp, was advised by Privy Councillors to go abroad to avoid a scandalous trial; this was allegedly at the insistence of the King.[28] William Lygon's younger brother Hugh was also gay and is believed to have been both one of Waugh's lovers at Oxford and the model for Lord Sebastian Flyte in *Brideshead Revisited*.[29] The Earl himself may have been the model for Sebastian's father Lord Marchmain, who spent much of his life outside England (although a heterosexual character in the book). If so, William Lygon may have been the basis for Sebastian's starchy elder brother Bridie, although Evelyn Waugh was no doubt following the writer's traditional method of picking and choosing when assembling his characters.

In the film the British establishment responds to the Prince's friendship by recruiting Beatrice, an impoverished and drug-abusing cabaret singer, to seduce the Prince. Prince Edward takes the bait but an emotional tug of war with the Dean ensues, which Beatrice appears to lose when the Cardinal threatens to disclose her character to the King. However, Beatrice confesses to the King herself and pre-empts the intended massacre. With the aid of a Buckingham Palace footman Smeaton Welks, who we learn had been sent down from Oxford and holds a grudge, the Dean and the plotters are called to a meeting at the Palace to discuss resurgent Catholicism, whereupon Welks poisons them. The film never makes clear who is the Scarlet Woman of the title; logically this should have been Beatrice but Waugh might have intended the ambiguity that this could be the Dean or the Cardinal.

The interest generated by this piece of juvenilia appears surprising today considering the contrast between the talents engaged in it and the storyline. This rarely rises above secondary-school standard and the film's forty minutes feel longer, especially as the quality of acting is frequently no more than high camp. Terence Greenidge maintained that it had been written as a skit on the work of D. W. Griffith, whose direction of *The Birth of a Nation* in 1915 had revolutionised filming techniques.[26] However, as Evelyn Waugh wrote the story, it has to be assumed he had points of his own to make.

In portraying the Prince of Wales Waugh and his colleagues would have been aware of the real Prince Edward's taste for socialising and liaisons in contrast to the rigid court of his parents but it was a step further to imply that he might be susceptible to homosexuals. They could have been on more dangerous ground still if they had any inkling that the King's deceased elder brother Albert Victor had been linked in gossip with gay brothels in London.[30] Perhaps though one should look no further for motivation than the louche attitudes which the Hypocrites encouraged.

Whether *The Scarlet Woman* was intended as farce or satire, it is the portrayal of Sligger that concerns us here. In this film Waugh drives home his claim that Sligger was a manipulative and controlling homosexual. It should be remembered that at the time this was an accusation of criminal activity and potentially highly damaging to Sligger's standing. It is unthinkable that Sligger did not know about the film, especially after the *Isis* review, and while we do not know what he thought of it he took no action at the time; perhaps he thought it best simply to ignore it as the sort of thing that fuelled the attitudes prevailing in the Hypocrites. Later, however, he was to be one of those driving the moves which closed the Hypocrites down.[31]

As we have seen (Chapter 3), one of Sligger's most loyal and committed friends was Harold Macmillan. A reflection of how Harold Macmillan saw Sligger and the Chalet appears in Hugh Whitemore's play of 1997, *A Letter of Resignation*.[32] The play is based on Macmillan's response to the Profumo Affair of 1963, in which John Profumo, a minister in Macmillan's administration, was sexually involved with the model Christine Keeler, who was thought through another sexual liaison to be a security risk.[33] As portrayed by Hugh Whitemore it was a situation which Macmillan found profoundly distasteful, the more painfully so because it revived memories of Dorothy Macmillan's adultery with Conservative MP Robert Boothby.[34] The setting is perhaps more poignant when one recalls that this scandal was one of a number affecting the late stages of Macmillan's administration and that within a few months he had resigned as Prime Minister.

Late in the play Macmillan reminisces with his Private Secretary, looking back to the Edwardian era as a golden age. The speech Hugh Whitemore puts into his mouth is characteristic of Macmillan's youthful feelings and, although it panders to Macmillan's penchant for affecting a tired Edwardianism, it could easily have come straight from one of his undergraduate letters:

> I was at Balliol. It was the happiest time of my life. Sligger Urquhart was Junior Dean. A wonderful man, Sligger Urquhart. The first Catholic don at Oxford since the Reformation. Not an outstanding scholar but a man of the greatest kindness and generosity of spirit. He had a chalet near Mont Blanc, and group of us went there for a summer holiday, a reading party. We talked, we climbed, we read, we argued. I remember waking up one morning and looking out at the mountains and the clear, cloudless sky and thinking: I am now, at this moment, perfectly happy. Within a few months, war was declared and that golden age was gone forever.[32]

Set in that apparently golden age when Harold Macmillan was at Balliol is another of the more perceptive representations of Sligger, if not so accurately of the Chalet. This occurs in the 1921 novel *A City in the Foreground* by Gerard Hopkins,[35] nephew of the poet Gerard Manley Hopkins. Like his uncle, Hopkins was a Balliol man, arriving at the college in 1910 to study *Literae Humaniores* ('Greats'). He became a member of Sligger's circle and his book indicates close study of Sligger. He never went to the Chalet, so any knowledge of it had to be acquired at second hand. The novel was published after Hopkins had served in the First World War in the Royal Warwickshire Regiment with Sligger's favourite Stephen Hewett. He survived the battles of the Somme, Arras, Passchendaele and Cambrai but was taken prisoner in 1918.

The central character in *A City in the Foreground* is Hugh Kenyon, an orphan brought up by an aunt and uncle of cloying Edwardian conventionality from whom admission to Knox College in Oxford in 1913 offers welcome escape. At Knox he meets Duncan Creighton, a don famous for easy relationships with undergraduates and who holds evening salons. Creighton is known universally by a nickname, 'Camel'. Hugh Kenyon describes him as small and good-looking, with a smile of peculiar sweetness and an air of hospitable dignity. He came, says Kenyon, from a family 'not aristocratic but landed'. Camel deprecated drink and noise at his evening gatherings, in which the typical member was a good-looking aesthete. In Kenyon's words 'he liked to collect around himself young men who moved easily in life, with the gift of adding ornament …' In Hopkins' book the walls of Camel's room are decorated with the names of members of the circle. As in Beverley Nichols' *Patchwork*, all that is required for this to correspond to Sligger is to substitute the names. As for the fictional name of the tutor Creighton, this was the maiden name of the wife of Balliol's Classics tutor, Cyril Bailey, and 'Knox College' is a short step from the Catholic Sligger to his friend the priest Ronald Knox.

When we first come across Creighton he is in trouble with the college for aiding the late return of a drunken student. This would have been an unlikely position for the Dean of Balliol, even one who favoured close relationship with undergraduates. Hugh Kenyon's introduction to an evening salon includes a debagging, an event improbable in a don's room even by the standards of the time. Neither of these two incidents really rings true for Creighton's character as it emerges from the novel, any more than it would have done for Sligger. It is possible that Hopkins tried to achieve distance from his model by introducing elements distinct from Sligger's own personality.

A City in the Foreground otherwise reveals a sensitive study of Sligger. Hopkins describes a taste for social networking that did not exclude snobbishness. He notes that Camel preferred to facilitate rather than lead friendships and refers to an aura of friendliness that could be interpreted as grace, strengthening the implication by later finding the Catholic Church as an analogy for the permanence of Camel's friendship. He has no doubt that admission to this community gave Hugh Kenyon a lifelong relationship with Camel, as so many did with Sligger, and notes that this extended to wives after friends married. Hugh Kenyon's thoughts fall to questioning whether Camel had no life outside his circle of friends and whether this fuelled his determination not to let them go. He comes to feel this was part of a conspiracy to keep Camel young, in return for which Camel always played the considerate host.

Hopkins' description of Camel makes it clear that he drew from personal observation of Sligger. When it came to Camel's reading parties he was on thinner ice, never having experienced them. When Hugh Kenyon meets Camel he is recruiting members for a summer reading party, extending his invitations to students outside Knox College in the same way that Sligger did outside Balliol. In Camel's case the party is at a cottage in Surrey. Hopkins may well have been a member of the UK parties such as those at Minehead and may have these in mind but instead he chose as his model Sligger's summer parties. Presumably he recognised the limitation of his experience and felt on firmer ground setting his story in the Home Counties but his attempt to combine his setting with what he had learned about the Chalet holds an amusing level of incongruity to anyone familiar with it.

Camel's cottage is described as approached by a steep rise through a larch wood, its white walls becoming visible above the walker through the pines. It is overshadowed by a local peak 'like Fujiyama', from where it is possible to climb to clear ground and look down on the larches. This description is familiar to any chaletite but these are not exactly features for which Surrey is notable. Further, in a passage which could have come straight from *The Perfect Chalet-ite*, Hugh Kenyon arrives in the locality and leaves his luggage at the local hotel while being met by Camel for several miles' walk to the cottage.

Their reading party follows a mixture of reading, long walks, eating, sleeping and tennis. It includes members who, like Sligger, spend the rest of the summer touring European centres, one of whom arrives from visiting Cologne Cathedral; this only needed to be Chartres to have fitted Sligger perfectly. Sligger's connections in Whitehall are represented by a civil service visitor. The party have the services of a housekeeper, as did the Chalet des Anglais, and members sun themselves on the veranda in deckchairs and indulge in comfortable conversation. A comment from one of the party members that the setting is perfect apart from the absence of mountains (apparently ignoring the presence of 'Fujiyama') may be a moment of intentional irony. Tellingly, Hugh Kenyon departs wondering if he had lived up to the exercise, a sentiment shared by many of Sligger's chaletites.

Hugh Kenyon finally takes his leave of Camel and Knox College on the outbreak of war. Camel remarks sadly that he is too old to be of use; Sligger seems not to have taken such a view and was to use his time supporting the war-time college and spending his vacations helping in a field hospital in France. At their parting Camel is portrayed as 'immobile, symbolic, staring with unseeing eyes on the quiet trees and long shadows, at the empty windows and the grey walls reddened by the level beams of the early August sun'. This is a poignant passage; when he wrote it after the war Hopkins would have been aware of the loss of Sligger's two nephews and Stephen Hewett and he may have had some insight into Sligger's personal feelings. But the impression of futility is not characteristic of Sligger nor his view during the war. In 1917 Sligger sent Tom Boase, who was on active service, a copy of the newly published *Weather Calendar*, a collection of writings for every day of the year, inscribing it, 'To Tom Boase, a soldier in Flanders or Picardy, from FFU, just a civilian in Oxford. Nov 23, 1917, a very gentle, autumn day with a friendly sun and a peaceful feeling in the air.'[36]

Hopkins' epilogue takes the form of a letter of 1918 to another of the Camel circle, its last thought questioning whether the group can survive the war and the loss of so many friends. One leaves Hopkins' book feeling that although he never experienced the Chalet he understood Sligger and his values very well.

If Gerard Hopkins' views of the Chalet suffered from being reported at second hand, a better example of how this limitation may be overcome is Amanda Brookfield's short story 'Lost and Found' of 2013.[37] Amanda Brookfield entered University College in 1979 to study English. She was never at the Chalet but wrote this short story as a birthday gift for Dr Leslie Mitchell, who was, at the suggestion of Rajiva Wijesinha (Chalet 1973, 1974 & 1976).

Amanda Brookfield was conscious of her lack of experience of the

Chalet des Anglais and indeed could be said to have distanced herself from it by describing access from Lyons airport rather than Geneva, and by the chalet being accessible by minibus: a chalet reading party rather than Sligger's Chalet Reading Party. However, she successfully based her story on facets of Chalet life which will be more than familiar to anyone who has been there.

'Lost and Found' centres on Lawrence, a world-weary don at the end of his career and mourning the recent death of his wife. Obliged by his head of house to complete his twentieth annual visit to the chalet before retiring, Lawrence finds himself questioning the meaning of everything; it is only by monumental effort that he succeeds in pulling together a party. After this he hands over the party's minibus and airport transfer to Harry, one of the students, and takes a back seat, finding the students' familiarity distasteful and avoiding interaction where possible.

Amanda Brookfield's description of the chalet may be a generic example rather than the Chalet des Anglais, which she did not see, but her description will satisfy any experienced chaletite: wood floors with rugs, plain furnishings, a wood-burning stove, large kitchen, the Alps visible through long windows. Drinking too much at dinner and finding conversation too painful, Lawrence goes to bed early and leaves the group to their apparent frivolity.

The story is resolved by a crisis. Lawrence is woken by one of the party: Harry has gone missing during the night. Instructing the group to call the mountain rescue service, Lawrence goes out to search in the morning fog, eventually finding the young man lying on the edge of an escarpment. In love with one of the party, Harry had been rejected during the evening and had gone out contemplating suicide. Lawrence's initially lame attempts to rouse him suddenly receive a boost when, in his desperate state, Harry mumbles something about Lawrence's bereavement and sympathy for his tutor. As they sit together in shared loss, they see the morning mists clear and the mountains appear in all their glory. Each has turned a corner and has a new journey stretching ahead.

Amanda Brookfield's story is notable for reminding us of two aspects of the reading parties which many would regard as key. The close proximity of senior and junior members is a fact of life there and cannot be ignored, whether its effect is positive or negative: most chaletites and their leaders would consider it positive but this is not always the case. Secondly, human beings in distress can benefit from being taken out of their normal life and into a different environment; for many this is particularly true of mountains, which have a way of putting human feelings into perspective. In Lawrence's case the environment was familiar to him after twenty years but he was privileged to see it afresh through the distress of another human being. Those who, like Lawrence and the equally fictitious Gideon at the beginning of this chapter, have seen dawn from the top of the Prarion may well understand the impact on their feelings and on their lives.

If the reflections of Gerard Hopkins and Amanda Brookfield were created from a distance, those who know the Chalet will find its atmosphere evocatively, even hauntingly, recalled in 'The Babe of the Abyss', a ghost story by the writer, actor and director Reggie Oliver.[38] This is so powerful that it could only reflect personal experience. Reggie Oliver, who studied Classics at University College, was a member of the 1973 and 1974 parties under the leadership of Tony Firth. While there he did several demanding walks, including Le Buet and Tête Rousse, but seems to have been sparing in his choices, possibly because of the amount of material in the Chalet for any aspiring author; during the 1973 party he conceived with fellow chaletite Michael Brand a musical based on Max Beerbohm's *Zuleika Dobson*, which ran at the Oxford Playhouse the following year and initiated a series of musicals by Michael.

'The Babe of the Abyss' was published in 2005 in Reggie Oliver's second collection of short stories, *The Complete Symphonies of Adolf Hitler*. He reports that the idea of the Chalet being haunted came from being told by Tony Firth that he had once spent a night there before the arrival of a party and had been alarmed by the noises.[39] Tony Firth was not alone in feeling this: others have had the same experience with exactly the same awareness of how alive a wooden building can seem. Another distinguished and phlegmatic party leader once told me that he had slept alone there only once and would never repeat the experience.[40]

Reggie Oliver's story is set just before the Second World War and centres on a legacy to the fictitious St Matthew's College from a previous Fellow, the gift being dependent on also accepting the deceased Fellow's chalet in the French Alps. This idea was stimulated by a later event which reveals the long gestation of the story. In 1994 the writer Sir Harold Acton died. He had previously indicated a wish to leave his Italian villa to Oxford but felt that the University had dragged its feet over the offer.[41]

Harold Acton was the son of a British art dealer and an American banking heiress. The family fortune had enabled his father to purchase the Villa La Pietra on the hills outside Florence, which was the family home for most of Harold's life. At Eton Harold had been introduced to romantic friendships in a group which included Cyril Connolly, Brian Howard, Evelyn Waugh and Cecil Beaton. Admitted to Christ Church in 1922, he has been said to be the model for the openly homosexual Anthony Blanche in *Brideshead Revisited*, although Evelyn Waugh claimed that Blanche's character was only partly based on Harold and that Brian Howard was also a model.[24]

When Harold's intended gift to Oxford was rejected, he left the Villa La Pietra to New York University, stipulating that it should be used for educational purposes.[42] He was never one of Sligger's chaletites, but it is probable that he had experience of reading parties in the UK. It is also likely that, as an undergraduate reading Modern Greats and more significantly as a Roman Catholic, he knew Sligger and had in mind the Alpine parties when proposing his gift. Today the Villa La Pietra is used by New York University for courses in the Arts and Social Sciences, although not for reading parties in the sense in which the Chalet des Anglais continues them.[42]

In 'The Babe of the Abyss' the Dean of St Matthew's College, Cordery, is informed of the bequest by the Master, Lord Arlington, with the summary instruction that he should represent the college at the funeral and then investigate the chalet, which had been out of use for some years. The donor, Dr Simeon Ray, had taught Ancient History but had been dismissed from the college under a cloud and had been living an apparently poverty-stricken and reclusive existence in Oxford. Despite this, he had settled on the college a large sum on condition that his Alpine chalet should return to its previous use by undergraduates.

Sligger died surrounded by the affection of his colleagues and the Chalet was left to Roger Mynors, not to the college. Apart from this the identification with Sligger is powerful: the teaching of History, a sizeable legacy to Balliol, and the wish to see the Chalet parties continue. Cordery tells us that Ray was not particularly scholarly but concerned with the education of young men in the widest sense. He also had boyish features and curly hair, possessed a personal affinity with undergraduates, who were welcome to drop into his rooms for a sherry in the evening, and preferred the company of good-looking men and aristocrats. Moreover, he had a nickname, Panter, derived from the dictum of Heraclitus *Panta Rhei* ('a state of flux').

Cordery was well placed to understand the importance of Panter's gift because he had been at the Chalet during Panter's last summer party there, which had resulted in his dismissal. The Chalet was approached by train to St Genièvre Les Eaux, which stands for Saint-Gervais-les-Bains, and Cordery was met by Panter, taking the Tramway du Mont Blanc to the 'Col du Prarion' (actually Col de Voza) and then walking to the Chalet des Pines (rather than larches). In Reggie Oliver's story the local peak is Mont Saint Genièvre.

That party followed the traditional mould and Panter was in a sunny mood which was enhanced by the company of an outstandingly good-looking young aristocrat, Lord Felbrigg, son of the Marquis of Attleborough. This mood was disturbed when another student, Stanley Seddon, arrived and brought with him a destabilising influence, especially on the relationship between Panter and Felbrigg. The atmosphere was further troubled when one night the group in the salon heard what sounded like the feet of an infant on the upper floor, although this was found to be empty when investigated. Later Cordery stayed alone at the chalet during a walking day but was repeatedly disturbed by the sound of a child's laugh with a malicious ring in it. Shortly afterwards Felbrigg returned from his walk in an agitated state, followed by two other members of the party who reported that they had watched from a distance some form of struggle between Panter and Felbrigg.

A strained evening was followed by the discovery the next morning that Felbrigg had gone down to the village to post a letter. He returned for lunch but then announced that he would walk alone to one of the glaciers. When he failed to return, a search party found his body at the bottom of a crevasse; it was thought that he had jumped in rather than fallen. On returning to Oxford the party had learned that Felbrigg's father, the Marquis of Attleborough, had received the letter from his son and as a result had threatened the college with legal action unless Panter Ray was removed. The college complied.

Making his visit to inspect the chalet for St Matthew's, Cordery finds it essentially unaltered despite years of disuse. The rooms are peaceful, smelling of pine and old books, but he is surprised to find it oppressive. Caught there by bad weather, he waits and dozes in an armchair but, as the weather fails to clear, he decides to stay the night and makes up a bed in Panter's room. In the early hours he is woken by the sound of a child's feet on the landing, coming closer to his room. When he opens his eyes it is to see the huge and grossly misshapen face of a child at the foot of his bed. This disappears but leaves Cordery watching out the night in terror.

At dawn he goes to investigate sounds in the salon and is amazed to find Seddon there. Seddon claims to be a psychiatrist and also the rightful new owner of the chalet. Shocked into openness, Cordery tells him of the experience in the night but Seddon is not at all put out. It was, he explains, the Babe of the Abyss, a demon he himself had located in a medieval grimoire and had tried to call up by performing its rite. He launches into a long Jungian explanation of the need for each individual to wake the evil within themselves. Inexplicably infuriated by this monologue, Cordery beats him to death, hearing as he does so the gurgling laugh of a child in his mind. The story ends with Cordery back home and looking aggressively at his own children while in his head he hears the approach of the Babe once more.

Reggie Oliver sums up the character and atmosphere of the Chalet to a remarkable degree. His work also shows very clearly how professional writers gather material from a wide range of sources and mould it to their purpose. There is much that could have come from the study of material at the Chalet, such as Sligger's fondness for handsome young men, and aristocrats, and his legacy to Balliol. The altercation between Panter and Felbrigg clearly draws on suspicions of Sligger's orientation. However, Panter's dismissal appears to reflect more the famous legal case involving Oscar Wilde, brought by the Marquess of Queensberry, father of Wilde's lover Lord Alfred Douglas.[43]

The chaletite reading this story will find many familiar facets, such as details of the locality, the atmosphere in the building and the fact that it was closed up for years. The story also demonstrates how Reggie Oliver has assembled disparate elements from the background of the Chalet and its surroundings. One detail suffices to demonstrate his thorough research: Lord Felbrigg is the young aristocrat who commits suicide. Felbrigg Hall was the family seat of the William Windham who in 1741 made the excursion into the Chamonix valley from which interest in the Alps grew (Chapter 1). There is an additional, though coincidental, resonance for readers from University College: William Windham's son, destined to become a noted parliamentarian, was a member of the college. Reggie Oliver's story is well worth reading by any chaletite for all its references, though anyone with a vivid imagination may prefer to read it away from the Chalet and its dark nights (this did not prevent me from adding it to the Chalet library for those with stronger minds).

No doubt the Chalet will continue to exert its effect on writers. At the time of writing the author Lexie Elliott is using the Chalet as a setting for her fourth novel, reflecting her experiences of a party in 2000. She says, 'I was particularly captivated by the idea of using the setting of a chalet party for several reasons: firstly, thrillers work particularly well in a closed environment, where a group of people are thrust together for a period of time without any easy escape route. Secondly, a chalet party allows for people of different age groups, social background and academic strata (dons, post-docs, post-grads, undergrads, etc.) to be forced into each other's company, from which, as a writer, one can see various interesting possibilities for friction! And the last reason, which is perhaps the most important, is that setting has always been very important to my writing; the setting can almost become a character in its own right. The stark contrast between the chalet in daylight – a thoroughly wholesome scene of fresh air, sunshine and stunning views – and at night, when one naturally becomes much more aware of the isolation, the darkness and every single creak and groan of the building, seemed to me to be the perfect setting to exploit for a novel in the psychological thriller genre.'[44]

All these works of fiction show the ability of writers to absorb material from individuals and circumstances around them in order to create an effective story. Looking through their eyes enhances our view of Sligger and his reading parties and helps us to understand the strength of the Chalet's appeal. After the Second World War this appeal was to lead to a remarkable renewal of the parties and their survival into a second century in a way that Sligger himself could never have foreseen.

CHAPTER FIVE

RENAISSANCE: UNIVERSITY COLLEGE, NEW COLLEGE AND THE RETURN OF THE PARTIES

ROGER MYNORS MUST HAVE BEEN SURPRISED to receive in July 1945 a letter from a Meredith Starr.[1] Since 1939 he would have assumed that his two properties in France had fallen into disuse during the war, but now Meredith Starr wrote with the startling news that the Chalet had not been idle during this time.

Starr, a homeopath and occultist, was born Herbert Close in 1890, later adopting the pen name he used when writing for the *Occult Review*. He had a varied freelance career, moving from one ideology to the next as and when his interest faltered. In 1917 he was endeavouring to found an artists' colony in Cornwall with his first wife when he made the acquaintance of the writer D. H. Lawrence, who had set up home with his wife Frieda at the Cornish village of Zennor. Lawrence described Starr as 'rather dreadful' and reported – with perhaps a degree of exaggeration – that the Starrs lived on nettle leaves and meditated naked at the bottom of mineshafts.[2] Later Meredith Starr played a leading role in bringing to the UK the Indian Zoroastrian guru Meher Baba and went on to provide relaxation courses in Devon.[3] He subsequently embraced Subud, an Indonesian form of spiritualism, which he used for lifestyle classes in Cyprus after the war.[4]

Whatever the inspirations guiding Meredith Starr's life, they did not extend to making a sound choice of summer holiday for 1940. France and England had been at war with Germany for seven months when Starr and his second wife arrived in Sospel near Monte Carlo in the Alpes-Maritimes, intending to take an extended holiday on the Riviera.[1] On 10 May German forces invaded the Netherlands and France, evading the French defences of the Maginot Line by crossing the poorly defended Ardennes Forest. By 20 May the north of France had been isolated, cutting off the return of the British Expeditionary Force to the UK from the south. On 10 June Italy declared war and invaded the south-east of France. The French government capitulated on 25 June and Meredith Starr and his wife found themselves in an occupied country.

The Italian forces converted an army barracks in Sospel into a camp where the Starrs were interned with other foreign nationals.[5] Later in the war it became policy to move expatriates away from coastal areas and in 1943 the Starrs were transferred to Saint Gervais under the system of *résidence assignée*.[1] Once there they appear to have slipped the net of their residency restrictions because they came to hide at Motivon, almost certainly in the Honeymoon Chalet, because by then they had acquired the help of Louis Broisat. In September 1943 Italy surrendered to the Allies and the area came under German occupation. The Starrs continued to hide at Motivon during the winter until the German presence on that side of the mountain intensified and Louis brought them to the Chalet des Anglais for more effective concealment.[1]

Meredith Starr wrote that they spent most days out on the mountain and usually only slept at the Chalet.[1] Despite keeping the house locked they had the misfortune to be burgled three times by the Communist Resistance, the *FTP* (*Francs-Tireurs et Partisans*), and lost most of their belongings. The *FTP* also robbed the Chalet of a large number of blankets and broke into the chapel, taking one of Sligger's Della Robbia reliefs; Louis Broisat was kept busy with repairs to the damage. Because of these intrusions the Starrs moved to the other side of Saint Gervais in June 1944, and were able to start their journey home across a liberated France in September that year.

Meredith Starr made it clear to Roger Mynors that he was writing at Louis' request, ostensibly to thank Mynors for their safety during the war but also to emphasise that Louis had done what he could to protect the property as far as his own personal safety allowed; to make any complaint would have been very dangerous. Louis was presumably taking the opportunity of these grateful British refugees to ensure that his standing with his employer remained good for work after the war.

¤

Meredith Starr's is not the only evidence we have that the Chalet, although devoid of student parties, was occupied during the war but it is the best documented. Louis' niece Francine Duffoug reported that Louis was active in helping people to escape capture by the Germans and it appears that both of Sligger's chalets were put to this use; Louis' sister Lea once took food to a Jewish refugee.[6] Usually, however, Louis would appear at Lea's house in Saint Gervais and announce that he needed food for a certain number of people.[6] Nothing else was ever said but the family would know that the people had moved on when Louis merely said that food was no longer needed.

The story of two Canadian airmen being hidden in the Chalet has entered post-war Chalet lore and is recalled by those who were there in the early post-war years but no confirmation has been found. The Chalet was, however, perfectly placed for this, being isolated but with its own water supply and within practical reach of the town. It seems that the Savoie people were well-inclined to help those who needed to escape German detection. Mountain people traditionally have such sympathies: Simone Hottegindre discovered only years later that her father Gabriel Orset had supplied the Maquis with food.[7] The Germans had established a Gestapo base at the Richemond Hotel in Chamonix,[8] so extreme care was needed, but as a mountain handyman Louis could move about with some freedom. This is presumably how he became aware of Meredith Starr and his wife when they came to Saint Gervais. The family also believed that Louis became adept at listening for news of forthcoming raids and moving people around as necessary.[6] The Swiss and Italian borders were both less than a day's walk away and as an experienced mountain guide Louis knew the locality better than the occupying forces did. The Chalet du Rocher might also have been used but this chalet, as it was not hidden among trees like the Chalet des Anglais, had the disadvantage of being clearly visible from the route between Saint Gervais and the Prarion.

Just how important were the actions of Louis Broisat and others like him during the war is unknown and never likely to be known. Absolute secrecy was essential if the local population was not to suffer reprisals which could be terrible: at Glières above Annecy the Germans took horrific vengeance when a pocket of resistance held out there.[9] In any case taciturnity was second nature to Louis, who probably derived considerable private pleasure from deceiving the occupying forces and who in many ways can be regarded as naturally equipped for underground activity.

Apart from this the Chalet's story sinks into obscurity for fourteen years. Events, not just the war, had overtaken Sligger's plan to leave it in the apparently capable hands of Roger Mynors. At the outbreak of the war Mynors, like many academics, went into government work and towards the end of the war his circumstances changed dramatically: in short order he accepted the offer of the Kennedy Chair of Latin in Cambridge, he married, and with his twin brother Humphrey he inherited from a cousin the country estate of Treago at St Weonards, near Hereford.[10]

The move to Cambridge proved uncongenial. Mynors missed the life of a tutorial fellow and complained that he had little to do.[11] He buried himself instead in translation and publishing, becoming joint editor of Nelson's Medieval Classics (subsequently Oxford Medieval Texts) and making distinguished contributions to medieval scholarship which were to continue into retirement.[10] In the meantime the Mastership of Balliol came up for election in 1949. Roger's supporters were confident of his success and there is some suggestion that he had accepted the Cambridge post because it might strengthen his case. In the event, in a closely run contest the college chose David Lindsay Keir, Vice-Chancellor of Queen's University, Belfast.[12] Mynors' disappointment ran deep and, a sensitive man, he came progressively to shy away from anything to do with Balliol.

Whatever Roger Mynors' feelings about the Mastership, he was no longer the bachelor don in Balliol to whom Sligger had left the Chalet in confident hope of the future. These circumstances could not have been foreseen by Sligger in 1934. When Roger Mynors returned to Oxford in 1953 it was to the Chair of Latin at Corpus Christi College and without association with Balliol, which made it impractical to put together summer parties even if his feelings about Balliol had allowed him to.[10] In fact, apart from taking his wife Lavinia to the Chalet for a brief visit in August 1950, he was never to see it again.[11] His regard for it did not fade, however; as late as 1987 he was able to write, 'How that place does get under one's skin! I think about it as little as I can, and cannot fail to think about it constantly.'[11] In 1991, when Michael Winterbottom, who was writing a memorial tribute to Roger, visited Lavinia she was anxious that he should appreciate Roger's affection for the Chalet.[13]

So after the war Roger Mynors was left with two chalets on the Prarion for which he had no immediate use; this was compounded in 1947 when he had an approach from Dennis Poore, who had inherited the Chalet du Rocher from his uncle and fruitlessly offered Roger the purchase.[14] It should be recalled that Roger Mynors held both the Chalet des Anglais and the Honeymoon Chalet at Motivon as private possessions and he had the right to sell them, for example to support the estate at Treago. Roger probably felt some moral obligation to Sligger's intentions but in 1929 Sligger had admitted that Roger might dispose of the Chalet if it proved to be 'a white elephant' (Chapter 4). Additionally, French land taxes still had to be paid, even in wartime, and so did Louis Broisat. In fact in 1946 Roger Mynors had received an offer for the Honeymoon Chalet from the Comte de Rohan Chabot.[15] The offer was rejected but Christopher Cox was concerned that, although Roger might hesitate to sell the chalets, circumstances or family pressure might force his hand.[16]

However, the Chalet still lingered in the collective memory in Oxford. In 1947 Frank Lepper wrote from his new position at Corpus Christi College to remind Mynors that while at New College he had been a member of the pre-war parties.[17] He asked if it might be possible to use the Chalet when post-war travel improved; nothing came of this in the short term. Later, in early 1952, the director of a London travel company wrote to say that he had heard from one of Roger Mynors' colleagues at Balliol, John Bryson, that the Chalet was unlikely ever to be put to its original use.[18] His company arranged travel groups for public schools and he was keen to rent the Chalet. Roger declined but the danger signs are evident: there was clear risk of the Chalet passing into private use or even different ownership.

At this point the Chalet was rescued by one of those accidents of history that have been a feature of its life. Mynors' wife Lavinia was the daughter of the Dean of Durham Cathedral, Cyril Alington. She was a woman of strong character and in many ways the perfect partner for a retiring academic who had inherited a run-down country estate without the means to restore it; her accounts of weekends there are full of the gusto with which things like brambles were attacked.[19] More importantly from the point of view of the Chalet, she was the sister of Giles Alington, History Fellow at University College (known colloquially throughout the University as 'Univ').

Giles Alington was surprised to be offered a position at Univ in

1944 after an undistinguished time as an undergraduate at Trinity College.[20] However, his commitment to Univ rapidly confirmed that the college had acquired an asset; he was appointed Dean in 1945 and then Senior Tutor in 1948.[20] He was especially friendly and approachable to undergraduates and his rooms became a focus for them.[21,22] One was later to write, 'He came to occupy a unique position in our lives, a sort of ideal compromise between our parents and our undergraduate friends. It was as if everything we ever did became more important because we could tell Giles about it. I have never known anyone with such a fund of sympathy and generosity.'[20] There is an obvious parallel with Sligger.

Giles had accompanied Roger and Lavinia on their brief visit to the Chalet in 1950 and would have known the Chalet's *raison d'être*.[23] It is not surprising that, despite health which had been precarious since surgery in 1939, he would have perceived the Chalet as a chance to extend contact with his students. It is also probable that he heard about the reading parties from his Univ colleague David Cox, even though David was not interested in running parties himself despite the enthusiasm of his brother Christopher.

In August 1952 Giles Alington reopened the Chalet with a party of six undergraduates, one of whom, Stephan Dammann, he had taken under his wing. Stephan, a handsome Anglo-French student, had spent the war in Paris and his education had been fragmentary. Stephan's mother had appealed to Giles that her son had promise that Oxford would bring out and Giles took her at her word.[21] Stephan would attend the Chalet as Giles' companion for the next three years and would also return in the 1960s. Giles' confidence was well placed, as Stephan went on to be an outstanding teacher of History at Ampleforth College.[24] In gratitude Stephan kept a photograph of Giles on his desk for the rest of his life.[21]

Of the other members, Christopher Elrington, Tony Price and Roger Smith, like Stephan Dammann, were studying History with Giles. John Fox was studying Law and Donald Vass Philosophy, Politics and Economics. Christopher Elrington had graduated that year and was married and his wife Jean was invited along to be the party's cook, as due to limited funds there was now no question of a Madame Paget or any other servant.[25]

John Fox decided to reach the Chalet by hitch-hiking from Grenoble to Saint Gervais. This proved so easy that he arrived a day before everyone else and had to make contact with Louis Broisat in the village. Louis led him up the long walk to the Chalet, where they opened up the house, and Louis stayed the night for company.[26] So it was that John Fox, Law student at University College, became the first Oxford undergraduate to set foot in the Chalet since 1938.

The following day Louis met the other members and guided them up the hill. Roger Mynors had clearly arranged for Louis' support and Giles may have known the history of the Chalet but their brief diary entry is plaintive, saying that their walks were chiefly exploratory, as no one knew their way around; this was, after all, a group which contained not a single person who had ever experienced a Chalet party. However, rooms were opened, beds made (with, it was said, sheets so damp that they steamed), logs cut for the kitchen range, and food brought up from the town by Louis.[25] There was consternation when the chickens and rabbits supplied by the local farm were delivered live but Roger Smith, Jean Elrington recalled, proved equal to the task of dispatching them.[25]

Appreciation of Jean's cooking was no doubt helped by the traditional undergraduate appetite but those who were there recall it as one of the most memorable aspects of the party: one described her to me as 'the Jewel in the Crown'.[27] One of Jean's 1952 menus lists *hors d'oeuvres*, tomato soup, grilled steak, fruit salad in kirsch, cake, fruit and coffee, all washed down with a variety of wines and liqueurs.[25] With post-war food rationing still in force in Britain it must have seemed heaven-sent.

At this point they still used the wood-burning kitchen range from the 1930s.[25] Washing up was done in a shallow wooden sink beneath the window and difficulty in lighting the kitchen meant that it was often left until the morning. Washstands were used in the bedrooms, with a water ewer for each room. Evidence of the past visits of the *FTP* was found in obscene graffiti in the outside toilet.[25] Attempts to revive the Turkish bath failed but much Chalet tennis was played. There does not seem to have been a great deal of reading but members recall stimulating conversations with Giles around the fire in the evenings on or the lawn during the day (Fig. 45). A few days' visit from Giles' Philosophy colleague Peter Strawson with his wife Ann took their talk onto a higher plane.[25]

Although walks had to be largely exploratory, they had Sligger's accounts of parties for guidance and one day the group divided to do walks away from the Prarion. Giles led Stephan Dammann and Tony Price down to the village of Servoz, and then north across the Arve valley to climb to Lac Vert, a secluded forest lake at 1,300 metres. In the meantime Christopher Elrington, John Fox and Roger Smith went west, down to Saint Gervais and then across the Bon Nant valley to ascend Mont Joly, a climb of 1,700 metres. Both are long and tiring excursions; it was well after dark when the Lac Vert party returned. It was also raining heavily; this scenario may well be familiar to present chaletite readers.

Whatever the challenges in 1952, Giles ran a second party in August 1953. Peter Wilcox, another History undergraduate, drove out in his Jowett Javelin with Roger Smith and David Aitken, a medical student.[27] Christopher Elrington had moved on to Bedford College, London, but he and Jean were invited back, no doubt with Jean's cooking at least partly in mind. Another recent History graduate, Michael Walker, visited from his post at the *Centre d'Études Industriels* in Geneva.[28] The 1953 party was more adventurous, making a circuit of what they called 'Mt Picard' (shown by a later diary entry to have been Mont Vorassay, across the outflow from the Bionnassay glacier). They descended to Chamonix to climb the Brévent on the north side of the town and also revived one of Sligger's favourite walks, to Tête Rousse. Another Sligger tradition which Giles Alington revived was the competitive run down to Saint Gervais for provisions. Roger Smith recalled just beating David Aitken on the ascent, although the times are not recorded.[27]

The socio-economic effects of the Second World War were more profound than those of the previous war. Britain had been impoverished and there was now no chance of supporting the parties with servants apart from Louis Broisat, who Roger Mynors continued to employ. However, the post-war visitors had a few advantages over their predecessors. Firstly, the Chalet du Rocher was more likely to be occupied because Dennis Poore had agreed to rent it to a single mother from Holland with her three children. Solange Boucher-Véret, described by Jean Elrington as 'friendly and nice', had become interested in the Chalet du Rocher in 1929 during a holiday at Gabriel Orset's first ski school;[29] in fact she had broken in to explore, as it appeared disused.[30] In 1951, during an Easter ski holiday with her children she had approached the Poore family, who were making little use of it, for the purchase; they did not want to sell but allowed her summer use of it in return for looking after it and paying the French taxes.[30] Solange took it on in 1952 and while Univ were opening the chalet next door she was there scraping decades of rat droppings off the surfaces and making repairs.[30] After this she used it regularly with her two sons, Hugues and Philippe, and her daughter Florine, and became increasingly friendly with the student parties. Solange kept up the lease until 1973, when it was taken over by her elder son Hugues, who was finally able to purchase it in 1981. It remains in the hands of his family to this day.

Secondly, the Prarion Hotel had developed in a way that would become highly significant to post-war parties. The hotel had remained closed during the war but Gabriel Orset's daughter Simone had married Max Hottegindre in 1947 and they had come to the hotel to take over the management from Simone's father.[31] Jean Elrington found Simone Hottegindre extremely helpful and willing to supply bread and eggs (Jean had discovered that these never survived the journey from Saint Gervais in undergraduate hands). She also noted that Max supplied the Bouchers with food by jeep, and wondered about asking him to do the same for them.[25]

These moves were being watched from Oxford. Christopher Cox, of all those who Sligger had seen as potential successors, retained the strongest commitment to Sligger's tradition and was keeping a close eye on events. In 1945, hearing of Roger Mynors' marriage, he had commented that the Chalet 'was about to get a mistress' and openly wondered if this spelled the end of reading parties.[32] He may well have felt that Univ was muscling in on sacred territory. Possibly he discussed it with his brother David, who had been a Fellow of Univ since 1939, but we know from the pre-war experience that David found the Chalet unsuitable for his mountaineering interests.

However, Christopher Cox was in an anomalous position. After being Director of Education in the Sudan he had been recruited in 1939 to a new position of educational adviser to the Colonial Office.[33] He had been knighted in 1950 for his contribution to international relations and was to continue in this role throughout changes in the Colonial Service until 1970. In view of his international standing New College had taken the unusual step of providing him with rooms as if he were an active Fellow and his practice, when he was not travelling abroad, became to spend the week in Whitehall and weekends in New College. However, he was insufficiently involved in the college to put together parties and any development based on his alma mater, Balliol, was blocked by Roger Mynors' sensitivity. If Christopher was to intervene in the Chalet he needed a different approach.

He turned instead to the next generation, as Sligger had done before him. His former student Frank Lepper (Fig. 48), with whom he had shared pre-war parties, was now Dean at Corpus Christi College. The bond between them was no doubt strengthened by Frank having taken over Christopher's teaching at New College when Christopher left for the Sudan in 1937 and Christopher saw Frank Lepper as a natural successor. In letters which echo Sligger's treatment of himself he began to encourage Frank to take a leading role; in one he stated openly, 'you are really its guardian angel'.[34] Christopher may well have been behind the fruitless approach which Frank Lepper had made to Roger Mynors in 1947 and it is probable that in 1954 he encouraged Frank to renew the appeal, this time successfully; Mynors was by then Frank's colleague at Corpus Christi. Univ's party in early August 1954 was followed by a second one under Frank's leadership.

Giles Alington's party that year included Stephan Dammann, Roger Smith, Peter Wilcox and the Elringtons as before; among the group was another of his students, Tony Firth, who was to have a distinguished association with the Chalet. They also had a visit from one of Sligger's favourite chaletites, Tom Boase, now President of Magdalen College; it was felt that the presence of this golden age chaletite would require some moderation of their behaviour but Tom Boase proved charming and gave them a sense of the Chalet's history with his stories of the pre-war days.[25]

The Lepper party was different and introduced a new element to Chalet parties. The core of it was two families: Frank brought his wife Elizabeth and their two children Patrick (13) and Veronica (11). A friend from their New College days, Charles Stanley-Baker, did the same with his wife Helen and their two children Richard (11) and Penny (8). This began a pattern in which post-war parties were to differ from those before the war but also reduced the number of junior members: of a party of eleven only three were undergraduates. Christopher Cox joined them for a week as a guest.

In 1954 Christopher Cox, as his letters make clear, was quick to see that friendship with the Hottegindres at the Prarion Hotel and the Bouchers at the Chalet du Rocher was key to the future of Chalet parties. He would have known Gabriel Orset's hotel from his time as a pre-war chaletite and will have seen the support which Max and Simone Hottegindre were prepared to give the Chalet. He began to cultivate these relationships and what started for him as a matter of policy was to mature into warm and enduring friendship on both sides.

The 1954 Lepper party proved energetic, recording the walk around 'Mt Pickard' [sic] again and the ascent to Tête Rousse. They also undertook one limb of Sligger's traditional circuit of Mont Blanc to the Col du Bonhomme but were disappointed to find that the refuge had been destroyed by the German forces during the war and they had to retrace their steps. Frank and Elizabeth Lepper also broached the issue of asking Max Hottegindre for help in getting supplies with his jeep.[35]

These post-war parties had to manage without the support of servants and for the parties' guidance Jean Elrington began a handbook of survival on the mountain.[36] Handwritten in an Automobile Association notebook, this was a practical counterpart to *The Perfect Chalet-ite*. She wrote with an eye to the needs of living but also with an engagingly light-hearted touch on aspects of Chalet life which would not have been familiar. Thus advice on where to shop and what to get, helpfully accompanied by pencil sketches of Saint Gervais, was combined with how to handle the idiosyncrasies of the kitchen range and the water system, and how to avoid being fleeced by the local farm. There are the practicalities of Chalet life: potatoes were heavy to carry and had to be peeled (and the peel disposed of) but rice and pasta were light and easily cooked without waste. The insatiable undergraduate appetite was countered by leaving some food out in the kitchen – 'or you will find that some speedy people have already eaten what you intended to give them for dinner'. Jean Elrington's notebook, which became a vehicle for communication between the Alington and Lepper parties, is a piece of card-carrying social history and one of the gems of the archives relating to post-war Chalet parties.

Jean also reported that the Chalet was in poor condition: the roof leaked in several places, mattresses were damp, the upstairs toilet bowl leaked and the floor of the downstairs one was so rotten that it could not safely be used.[36] The salon fire was unreliable, a paraffin heater little better. The middle legs tended to fall off the dining table; later generations of chaletites may recall – perhaps fondly – that this remained a problem for the next fifty years. On the other hand there were still plenty of wild raspberries, redcurrants and strawberries, the descendants of David Urquhart's garden.

With two colleges in residence in 1954 it appeared that the reading party tradition was reborn but in late August Roger Mynors agreed to a request from Rosemary Ince of the Portsmouth Pathological Service for a holiday in an Alpine chalet.[37] Dr Ince had been alerted to the Chalet by her colleague Dr John O'Brien (Chalet 1936). Roger Mynors agreed to the four doctors taking over the Chalet in September when Frank Lepper's party ended. This was another reminder that the Chalet was his property, to do with as he wished.

The 1955 season expanded: Frank Lepper ran a Corpus Christi party of seven students for two weeks before they were replaced by the Lepper and Stanley-Baker families. Eleven Univ members then took over for the last two weeks of August. Christopher Cox joined the Corpus Christi party and he and Frank Lepper arranged for Louis Broisat to make repairs to the balcony; they also took the decision to replace the wood-burning kitchen range with a Butagas stove. All of this was billed to Roger Mynors, who responded that Frank's letter had been received 'with passionate interest'.[36] He also said that more repairs could be done but only after the other calls on his income, which almost certainly meant the cost of restoring the estate at Treago.

The 1955 season was notable for extensive walks and included going round the north side of Mont Blanc to the old climbers' centre of Montenvers and also across the Bon Nant valley to Mont Joly. The Lepper party took a two-day walk which took in Nant Borrant and then climbed through the Tré la Tête glacier to the Dômes de Miage (3,673 m), a series of snow peaks on the south-western flank of Mont Blanc. The Lepper party also renovated the bathing pool, or *piscine*, which Frank had created in 1937. The season now extended from the middle of July to early September and, with larger parties under the leadership of two dons, the future must have appeared secure.

Sadly, it was not to be. Giles Alington died in February 1956 after a short battle with cancer.[38] Frank Lepper took no party that year and instead the Chalet was loaned to Hugh Keen, Secretary to the University Chest, who had shared undergraduate days at Balliol with Roger Mynors.[39] Hugh took his wife Catherine and their daughter with two of her friends, and was joined later by his son Maurice, subsequently a Balliol Fellow,[39] with his friend Tom Bingham, later a judge.[40] The threat to the continuity of reading parties was again clear and Christopher Cox secured himself an invitation with the excuse of advising these Chalet novices. However, a typically convoluted thirty-six-page report he sent to Frank Lepper reveals that he was also protecting the interests of would-be party leaders.[41] He wrote to Frank rather than Roger Mynors and indeed he expressed the view that if they made any changes to the Chalet Mynors would probably never know.

Christopher's letter tells how he arrived late in the second day of the Keens' stay but, eager to renew friendship with the Hottegindres, dined with Max and Simone before going down to the Chalet. Conversation flowed, together with Pernod and wine, and by the time he came to leave, somewhat unsteadily, night was falling and mist was rising from the valley. Only Christopher Cox could have decided in these circumstances to avoid the track and to try to reach the Chalet by an old path through the bushes. Predictably, he mistook his landmarks in the dark and was soon lost, tried to retrace his steps and failed, located a stream he believed led to the Chalet and fell, losing one of his bags, his walking pole and his spectacles. He wondered if he blew his whistle loudly it might be heard by Solange Boucher-Véret at the Chalet du Rocher, if she slept with her window open; this strategy collapsed when he found that the whistle was in the bag which he had lost. His challenges were not helped when his torch battery went flat.

Meanwhile at the Chalet another small drama was unfolding.[41] Hugh Keen had located Jean Elrington's Chalet notebook and, taken in by her sense of humour, had become alarmed by her warning, 'when going to bed it is advisable to make your room impregnable. People seem to hang around the verandas and there are ghosts in the roof.'[36] As the only man there at that point he went to secure the shutters but was alarmed in the dark to make out a figure in the bushes. As it happened, this turned out to be only the younger Boucher son, Philippe, who was netting moths. However, as soon as Hugh returned to his wife and the girls, who were using the petit salon for warmth, they were alarmed by heavy beating on the locked front door. Going through the salon, they found the lawn empty and on returning to the petit salon were the more alarmed to find a ghostly white face at the window; Christopher Cox had finally navigated his way through the night.

In another example of sensitivity, Hugh raised the fact that the Chalet had few chamber pots for night use.[41] Christopher was obliged to point out as gently as he could the difference between the carefully nurtured girls of Hugh's party and the male undergraduates, for whom the balcony provided an alternative and indeed an opportunity for a little male competitiveness ('high cockalorum' in his words). He did, however, add that they were required to use 'due precautions', referring to Dr Johnson's experience with 'effluvia' from the houses in Edinburgh Old Town.[42] Hugh was shocked but Catherine seems to have taken it in her stride. In his next visit to the town Christopher made the party the gift of a number of buckets, wondering as he did so if they would have any future use.[41]

Catherine Keen's later guests included her cousin James Cummins, a farmer. He and Tom Bingham made the ascent of Mont Blanc, initiating the post-war practice of using the Chalet as a base for summit attempts. Also visiting was a friend of Catherine's who signed herself Marie de Boucherville Baissac.[41] This was actually Mary Herbert, who had been an agent in the Special Operations Executive (SOE) in the Second World War.[43] Mary brought her daughter Claudine, who had been called after Mary's war-time codename. After the war Mary Herbert had married the French agent Claude de Baissac, legitimising the daughter they had during the war, although they do not appear to have had a life together after this.[43]

In writing to thank Roger Mynors, Hugh Keen said that Mary Herbert claimed to know the Colonel Starr who had been hidden in the Chalet during the war.[44] This is surprising, as the Meredith Starr who wrote to Roger Mynors in 1945 was a civilian and his story of being interned at Sospel rings true. It is very unlikely that an SOE agent would need to concoct such a story and Mary Herbert was probably thinking of her SOE colleague Colonel George Starr, who was active around Toulouse and unconnected with the Chalet.[45] Hugh Keen may have mentioned that someone called Starr had hidden in the Chalet and they may have simply assumed that the two men were the same. This is another story which shows how murky the Chalet's history was during the war years.

In view of the fact that Meredith Starr was a pseudonym adopted by the occultist Herbert Close, it might be questioned whether the Chalet's Meredith Starr was the 'real' one. However, this was confirmed by scrutiny of the will of Meredith Starr, obtained from the probate service. The will was written in Cyprus in 1955 when Starr/ Close was running relaxation courses there and his signature matches that on the Chalet letter.

A new leader emerged for the Univ parties in 1957. Giles Alington's protégé Tony Firth, a student member in 1954, had been appointed History Fellow in Giles' place and it was said that Giles instructed him from his deathbed that he would be taking on responsibility for the Chalet.[22,46] As it was, the Chalet was to become a major part of Tony's life for the next twenty years.

Tony Firth was a kind and considerate man who, like Giles before him, welcomed undergraduates in his rooms, although in his case the attraction was often a game of bridge and then a visit to one of the local pubs.[47,48,49] One former undergraduate described him as 'relaxed, witty, encouraging and entertaining in equal measure'.[50] He was regarded as a 'brilliant conversationalist' and always available for discussion on any subject, seeing himself as primarily a pastoral don. Robert Bateman (Chalet 1959–62) (Fig. 46) said of him, 'His friendship was warm and unconditional, he asked little of others and gave freely,' and felt that Tony's continuing friendship had made the biggest impact outside his own family.[47] Robert's brother Christopher agreed, commenting that it was one of the best friendships of his life. For another contemporary his 'engaging, self-deprecating manner disguised an organised and decisive personality'.[51] Some felt that he was slightly old-fashioned and would have fitted well into *Brideshead Revisited*.[52] Tony did, however, have his demons: a homosexual and possibly in conflict with his Roman Catholic faith,[51] he had a necessarily closeted existence which he kept very private. In fact very few of those he befriended knew anything about his orientation until much later, if then.[47,48]

Within a couple of years Tony Firth had established a pattern for the Univ parties, which rarely contained fewer than ten members and often more than fifteen. He made an effective leader, caring of the chaletites and 'very much in charge … although he was a friend to everyone and never showed any overt sign of exercising responsibility'.[22,47] There were no disagreements about duties and no cross words. Robert Bateman said, 'It was rather as though there was an invisible conductor.'[47] For Mark Savage (Chalet 1969–75), Tony was 'pivotal', being 'a very good raconteur of witty stories about a wide variety of individuals that did much to add to the general hilarity of the Chalet'.[53] He would often accompany new arrivals on the two-hour walk up from Saint Gervais and Roger Potter (Chalet 1966) found he was perceptive in striking a balance between realism and false hope when encouraging them in the climb.[50]

Tony Firth took responsibility for most aspects of the party, including the grocery order in Saint Gervais. Meals were simple and cheap, with porridge (a slow-release food excellent for walkers) in the morning and a limited lunch; members felt that they ate 'sparingly but well'.[21] Dinner was the main meal and often hysterically full of laughter, fuelled by the company and a liberal amount of rough red wine.[22,53] Members recall that the wine was supplied by barrel which was either brought up by Louis Broisat on his mule or delivered to the Prarion Hotel, to be collected at the end of a walking day and rolled down the hill from the hotel – a task not made any easier by the 'seven glasses of Pastis there by way of aperitif on the way home from some trek across the massif'.[53] Kevin Garnett (Chalet 1972–4) remembers the party 'being told off by Tony Firth like a group of naughty schoolchildren because in the first half of the stay we had drunk almost all the barrel of wine, which was supposed to last the whole trip'.[54]

While Tony Firth liked his chaletites to enjoy themselves, he was also serious about Chalet life, in particular the reading.[22,55] He was enthusiastic and competitive in Chalet tennis[56] but no games were played in the mornings and the walks were an integral part.[22,47] David Miers (Chalet 1958 & 1960) found that 'one was soon initiated into the agreeable routines and practices of chalet life, and the ethos was such that no time was wasted. Everyone was encouraged to have a plan. This was not a holiday but a "Reading Party". Play hard and work hard. No lounging about doing nothing.'[49] Those who did not volunteer for the walks were expected to settle down to some work instead. Perhaps prompted by Sligger's comments about card games being the enemy of conversation, Tony discouraged bridge, despite this being his favourite pastime in Oxford.[57] Another way in which he followed Sligger was to take round the morning washing water himself; he disapproved of chaletites looking untidy.[57]

Walks were aided by Tony's knowledge of the locality and tended to be extensive (Fig. 49). They were undertaken by a few members rather than the whole group, who were able to roam further afield because Tony usually had a car. Excursions across the Grand Balcon to the Mer de Glace begin to appear in the diaries, as do longer ones to climb Le Buet beyond Chamonix.[21] Montagne de la Côte (La Jonction), the route by which Balmat and Paccard first ascended Mont Blanc, appears in the diaries and was to remain a challenging walk for future parties. Pointe Percée, a difficult peak on the Aravis ridge, was essayed by the more courageous; Tony Firth's diary entry records that Louis Broisat claimed, 'evidently untruthfully', that this was '*très facile pour les enfants*'.[21] A regular favourite was the walk down across the Arve valley to climb the Aiguillette les Houches, which faces the Prarion from the north. A notable event in 1963 was a visit from Giles Alington's protégé Stephan Dammann, who led Michael Hand and Marcus Miller in an ascent of Mont Tondu (3,196 m) on the south-west flank of Mont Blanc. Thomas Cullen (Chalet 1962–72 variously) recalls the effort required for Sligger's circuit around Mont Blanc: when the party arrived at the Italian refuge a French walker expressed surprise that he had not seen them at the earlier refuges the two previous nights. On hearing that the group had walked from Saint Gervais that day he swept off his hat, saying, '*Mes compliments, messieurs!*'[58]

Tony Firth often drove out to the Chalet, sometimes accompanied by members of the party. His driving was famously erratic, as his attention was distracted by 'frequent observations on the French, their driving prowess and their signposting'.[59] Hugh Davies Jones felt he was lucky to arrive unscathed.[59] He and Tony stopped for a night at Soissons where they discovered that the hotel had only one free bedroom. During the night they were plagued by mosquitoes, causing Tony to remark, in his characteristic use of double negatives, that it was 'not improbable that the non-availability of hotel rooms may have been because of the Mosquito Conference in Soissons'.[59]

An outing which became a regular feature of Tony Firth's parties was a car journey with a selected few to Annecy, where an alcoholic lunch was taken at the Auberge de Savoie (Fig. 50).[22] After this the group resorted to naval battles on the lake in pedalos; on at least one occasion the Battle of Salamis of 480 BC was re-enacted, after a fashion.[53,54] As the group was likely to get wet the battle was often followed by a swim, which had to be in a section screened by a small island because swimming in the lake was forbidden. The return journey after this outing could be hazardous; Tony Firth's wayward driving did not improve under the influence of the meal and arrival in Saint Gervais was usually well after mountain transport had closed, so the group usually fortified themselves for the walk up with another dose of spirits.[53,54] After this the climb could be more than usually demanding, Tony needing all his skill in encouraging them in the ascent.[50] Jeremy Lever, who joined Tony Firth in leading the Chalet parties in 1966, was inclined to view the outings to Annecy as a lapse from the usual standard of Univ reading parties.[46]

Chaletites noted that Univ parties under Tony Firth also tended to be scholastic and to comprise more Arts undergraduates than scientists, and that he had a tendency to invite repeatedly those he liked: examples include Thomas Atthill (Chalet 1961–4 & 1967), Thomas Cullen, who was there over the summers of a decade, and the Bateman brothers Christopher, Robert and Nigel, who between them represented the college between 1959 and 1965 (Fig. 46). Tony's own faith was reflected in a high proportion of Roman Catholics.[47] A result of this was to re-inaugurate the chapel behind the Chalet, where Tony's guest priests would celebrate Mass in the tradition of Sligger.[60] One person who attended most of Tony's parties was Colin Lowry, a Univ graduate and civil servant, who, as a skilled cook, was brought in to take charge of the kitchen.[61] There were those who noticed that the combination of Tony and Colin Lowry could give the parties a heavy drinking, heavy smoking character.[46]

For many the Chalet was unlike anything they'd been used to. After the Second World War students tended to be more adaptable to rugged living, especially those who had been through National Service.[21,22] The waterfall was used for showering and no attempt was made to renovate the Turkish bath; there was in any case no means of heating water except on the kitchen stove.[49] Jeremy Lever found the Chalet's ancient hip bath the most convenient form of washing.[22] A hose in the stream above the Chalet brought water into the kitchen and lighting was by candles or hurricane lamps.[54] Some small repair jobs were undertaken but there appears to have been a general sense that the Chalet was waiting for major work.[47,54] Mice could be a problem, waking members at night, and one year the Chalet was found to be infested with rats, even in the mattresses.[54,62]

During this period, while the party leaders were concerned with getting a new tradition under way, attention was required to the structure of the building, now five decades old. The shingled roof at the rear had continued to leak and in 1959 it was clear that it must be replaced. Roger Mynors was in no position to pay for this and he resorted to what was his most disposable asset in France, the Honeymoon Chalet at Mont Forchet. This had been used with decreasing frequency; early post-war visits revealed that it was 'like the *Mary Celeste*', with even the 1938 breakfast table and newspapers untouched.[22,63] The Honeymoon Chalet was therefore sold for £250, which just covered repairs and the installation of galvanised steel cladding to the rear side of the roof.[23] The roof at the front was left in place, as there was insufficient money to replace it and this was to result in more serious challenges later.

Access to the Chalet was still for many the long walk up from Saint Gervais, and the Hôtel du Mont Blanc in Saint Gervais continued to provide support, including a shower after a difficult overnight journey.[21] However, the installation of ski lifts over the Prarion meant that it became possible to travel up from the TMB halt at Col de Voza by *télésiège* to the escarpment above the Prarion Hotel and then walk down to the Chalet. Kevin Garnett remembers that when they undertook this trip for shopping Tony would often provide the return ticket.[54] Chalet tennis was a popular game for these Univ parties and would often take on an aggressive note, when the players gave the ball a vicious spin to make it race along the roof top and down the other side.[54] In the evenings they played the Dictionary Game (a version of the BBC radio show *Call My Bluff*), though Colin Lowry, being an experienced civil servant, tended to have the winning vocabulary.[54]

Tony Firth followed Sligger's example of writing the diary entry himself and of listing the initials of those who did the walks. His entries, however, could be famously terse: one of the ascents to Tête Rousse merely says, 'V. fine day'. A note on the party overall could be equally laconic: the 1967 party qualifies for 'Good party, good weather'. Even when a group undertook the famous cable car ascent to the Aiguille du Midi, 'By téléphérique. Good views' hardly conveys the experience of the world's longest cable car ascent and spectacular views across the huge glacier of the Vallée Blanche to the summit of Mont Blanc, together with the vista of the Alps to the east and the Matterhorn in the distance. These post-war parties were at least more prodigal with diary photographs than Sligger had been and when the Chalet received a visit from Jacques Allien, who had seen the Chalet with the Abbé Klein during the First World War, Tony copied into the diary the entire note left by M. Allien, in which he said he was delighted to find himself in the house again after five decades and wished Sligger's successors the same happiness.

The parties still used the Chalet with Roger Mynors' permission and Tony Firth was adept at managing Mynors' sensitivities. He communicated frequently with Mynors and encouraged his chaletites to do the same. Miles Tuely (Chalet 1962–5) told Roger Mynors it had been one of his most enjoyable holidays and reported his ascent of Mont Blanc.[64] Christopher Bateman (Chalet 1957–60 & 1965) wrote, 'My stays at the Chalet have been amongst my happiest holidays and I shall remember them always. My Oxford career is now over and one of my chief regrets on going down is that I have probably paid a last visit to the Chalet without having been able to thank you personally for making these visits possible.'[65] In fact this was not to be Christopher's farewell to the Chalet, as he and his two brothers returned to the Chalet with their wives when the centenary of the New Chalet was celebrated in 2009.

If the Univ parties appeared to be established under Tony Firth's leadership, it was a different story for Christopher Cox, who was discovering that Frank Lepper's view of the Chalet did not concur with the traditions Christopher had absorbed from Sligger. Frank liked a walking holiday with family and friends, with only a few undergraduates and little emphasis on study.[66] Charles Stanley-Baker's daughter Penny confirms that they prided themselves on being 'The Non-Reading Party', as indeed they labelled one of their group photographs. Christopher Cox continued to encourage Frank with long, enthusiastic letters and to join Frank's parties as a visitor but he began to look around for other possibilities. In 1958 he turned to John Buxton, the Reader in English at New College, who he had taught in the 1930s; John and his wife Marjorie organised a party of four New College undergraduates and Christopher joined them for part of their stay. They were also joined from Christ Church by Peter Jay, son of the Labour MP Douglas Jay (Chalet 1929–30), who had studied with Christopher at New College.[67] This is another example of the Chalet's intergenerational connections and the following year Douglas' younger son Martin, also at New College, joined Peter.[68]

Christopher got on well with Marjorie Buxton, whom he thought highly capable.[69] Although she found the primitive kitchen a challenge, she coped well with catering for the party:[63] Christopher commented that, as she had spent the previous two weeks sailing around the British coast, 'there's nothing she can't do with guano but I hope it won't come to that'.[69] John, who the chaletites found to be a kind father figure, was to Christopher's mind practical but inclined to become moody when tired or if things did not go well.[63,70]

The fiftieth anniversary of the New Chalet occurred in 1959 and Christopher was determined that it should be marked appropriately; Frank Lepper showed some reluctance despite Christopher's encouragement and so John and Marjorie Buxton again took a New College party of five undergraduates to follow Tony Firth's Univ party.[34] In fact, Frank relented and he and Elizabeth put together a party of seven Corpus Christi undergraduates to begin the season, following them with a group of Oxford friends which included the Colchester family of five.[66] Christopher Cox, rather in the role of guardian angel, joined both the Lepper and Buxton parties.

By 1960 Christopher seems to have accepted that Frank Lepper would never fulfil the tradition of reading parties as he saw it. He decided to take the bull by the horns and wrote to Roger Mynors from Dar es Salaam asking with considerable humility if he might lead parties himself.[71] The letter is remarkably self-effacing, especially when one knows what occurred later. Christopher wrote with considered points and tight construction, very different from his usual style, and – knowing the man he was dealing with – he emphasised the academic points that would appeal. It had taken him nearly a decade to reach this point but it was to be a turning point in the Chalet's fortunes.

Christopher Cox still remained in an unusual position in New College. His week in Whitehall and travel for the colonial work made it difficult for him to select students for parties. The next few years were therefore something of a patchwork: in 1960 he was able to combine a small number of New College members with his Whitehall colleagues Margaret Read[72] and Colin Baynes,[33] and several others involved in colonial education. The Leppers, as if relieved by his intervention, took only a family party that year.

Christopher's difficulties are reflected in numbers which were small compared to Tony Firth's parties. In 1961 he simply joined the Stanley-Baker family for a holiday there; Frank Lepper's son Patrick, who was at New College, had joined the Univ party that year and stayed on to be with them. In 1962 Frank led his last Corpus Christi party of five undergraduates, following this with a holiday with the family of Paul Odgers, a friend from New College days.[66] Frank's next and final Chalet visit was in 1965 when he took a holiday with the Stanley-Bakers once more. They had with them just one junior Corpus member, Andrew Thornhill, who was to contribute to Christopher's New College efforts; Christopher joined them for a dinner to celebrate the centenary of the Old Chalet, at which they ate *escalope de veau*, read passages from the *Memoir of Mrs Urquhart* and drank a toast to the Chalet, David, Harriet and Francis Urquhart, and to 'all chaletites, past present and future'. It is not difficult to detect Christopher's hand in this event.

The 1965 season closed, unusually, with two couples taking the Chalet, Christopher Bateman (Chalet 1957–60) and his wife Hilary with Michael and Gillian Williams. They hosted a visit from one of Sligger's favourite chaletites, Robert Baldwin (Chalet 1919–24) and his wife Sarah. Robert Baldwin, a retired teacher from Harrow School, had had his time at Balliol interrupted by the First World War and when he married in 1925 had been loaned the empty Chalet du Rocher for his honeymoon. The 1965 visit was in celebration of the couple's fortieth wedding anniversary.

In the intervening two years Christopher Cox had arranged no parties but had made visits late in the season, staying at the Prarion Hotel to work in the mornings 'for the sake of Max's wonderful lunch', and visiting the empty Chalet in the afternoons.[73] In a discursive letter of eighteen pages to Frank Lepper – it is notable that he still reported to Frank in detail – he said that he had found in his room a strange basin on a stand which he thought might be a *bidet*. His commode also contained no chamber pot so he removed one of Sligger's from the Chalet, scoured it out and christened it Ferrando, adding in the scatological mood to which he was sometimes prone, 'My word, F's not had such a lot to talk about since those far-off days in his youth when he tells me he was used by Supermac – in case you are reading to Liz, I will not go into details' ('Supermac' was the nickname by which Harold Macmillan was known while Prime Minister).

The watershed for Christopher came in 1966 when a gift allowed New College to establish Salvesen Junior Fellowships. Harold Salvesen had studied Philosophy, Politics and Economics at Univ and in 1923 was elected to a New College Fellowship to teach economics.[74] He subsequently moved into the family whaling firm, becoming chairman in 1945, and shortly before he retired in 1965 he funded junior fellowships at both Univ and New College. The New College Salvesen Fellows were required to act as a bridge between dons and students. They were therefore perfectly placed to choose suitable chaletites, as Christopher was quick to see. Indeed, he came almost to regard the reading parties as part of their job description. Allen Warren, appointed Salvesen Fellow in 1968, recalls that at dinner after his election Christopher approached him as the party were making their way to coffee saying, 'My name is Cox. Are you free to come to the Alps this summer?', in a tone which suggested that declining was not an option.[16] In fact Allen happened to be free for the last ten days of the New College party and travelled there from Corsica.[16] In taking this approach Christopher began a tradition of junior leaders that has endured for New College parties ever since.

The junior fellows recruited party members, who Christopher would meet for sherry or dinner. He was disinclined to veto any but also took soundings from colleagues and would suggest some who might also join.[16] If he was abroad a postcard might appear with some reference to the Chalet; it was his way of reminding the junior fellows that he was watching. Another task the junior fellows inherited was to ensure that Christopher was properly packed for the Chalet. His rooms were famously chaotic due to hoarding: he had kept newspapers dating back to the 1936 abdication crisis and papers choked his main room, bedroom and lobby, in time extending down the stairs from his room.[16,75] (When his documents were being archived after his death a further collection dating back thirty years was found under a pile of furniture in a cellar.)[76]

The New College parties under Christopher's leadership finally got under way in 1966 with a party of fourteen. Corpus Christi's Andrew Thornhill was brought in from the 1965 visit to help and was joined by New College junior fellows John Emmerson, Christopher Fielding (both on Guinness-funded fellowships) and Patrick Martin, the first Salvesen Fellow (Fig. 51). Andrew Thornhill would also help with the following year's party and his presence probably accounts for a small number of Corpus Christi students who made it into these parties as the last regular representatives of their college at the Chalet.[77]

In 1966 the New College party received a large number of visitors, notably the UK Ambassador in Paris, Patrick Reilly (Chalet 1934 & 1938) (Fig. 51), the politician Denis Healey, then Secretary of State for Defence, who had been a pre-war student of Cyril Bailey's at Balliol, and Martin Hollis, a New College alumnus who was at the Foreign Office. Healey is reported to have worn lederhosen, which must have been an interesting sight in view of his stature.[78] Significantly, Christopher wrote the entire diary entry for the first time and he would do so for all his parties thereafter. The following year he took the whole of July for his party and, echoing Sligger's practice, divided it into two groups. This pattern was possible because he always took his leave from Whitehall in a single block and he never varied it for the rest of his life.[16] At the age of sixty-seven he had finally achieved the aim he felt Sligger had bequeathed to him more than thirty years before. It had been a long journey but one from which he had never wavered.

Christopher Cox's junior managers found that he gave them their head and never specified how a party should run.[16] Rather, he preferred an approach that moulded parties from his pre-war experience. He was in fact deeply conscious of how much he owed the junior managers. When John Emmerson gave up management of the parties on returning to his native Australia, Christopher's letter of thanks said that his mind reeled at the thought of a New College party without the 'bursar' and that the essence of the parties was something which John had made his 'very special concern'.[79] John Emmerson showed his management skill to his successor John Woodhead-Galloway in the quiet advice, 'Never underestimate the power of declaring a crisis. Its specific nature need not be spelled out too clearly – its power lies in its timing.'[80] John Emmerson was also caring of Sir William and Lady Hayter when they visited, recruiting John Woodhead-Galloway to join them in bridge. In view of how Christopher worked with these junior fellows, it was a particularly apt move by New College that when he died in 1982 the college used his legacy to set up the Cox Junior Research Fellowship.

There are those who revel in eccentricity and even as a young man Christopher Cox had been one such.[81] The legal philosopher Herbert Hart, who had been taught by him and was a lifelong friend, said of him, 'It was as if he was continuously experimenting with his imagination and inventing *de novo* a fresh and often comic perspective from which to view the world about him.'[82] Having been born in 1899, Christopher always affected being a Victorian, a stance which fitted his character well. His letters are scattered with classical allusions which can be oblique and obscure; he often allowed new ideas to take his thinking down convoluted side-alleys. Given the bizarre nature of his handwriting, which often makes him difficult to interpret, one wonders whether the recipients of his letters always followed what he tried to convey. He also enjoyed nicknames: when Roger Mynors became Sir Roger in 1963, Christopher, also Sir, took to referring to him by his middle name of Baskerville. Solange Boucher-Véret's son Hugues became an ophthalmic surgeon and was therefore 'Dr Strabismus of Utrecht'.[83] He likened his Whitehall document case to a 'black obstetrician's bag' and called it BOB. It was only to be expected that the Chalet would appeal to such a man and that students would respond to this mercurial intellect.

This was only part of a complex personality and could conceal serious intent.[84] Christopher was also prone to episodes of depression, referring to these as 'the fumes', but developed his own prophylactics against them, including an interest in botany which led to a new inclusion in the list of British flora, *Artemisia norvegica*.[82] Friends noted the role of the Chalet: 'once he reached the Chalet the genius of the place would assert itself and relative calm would descend on him'.[82] The reading party was the high point of his year and he always had a sense of contentment when there.[85]

Christopher's parties were consciously modelled on Sligger's. Mornings were reserved for study and the afternoons were for games or walks as preferred. Dinner was the main social event and, in accordance with *The Perfect Chalet-ite*, a jacket and tie were to be worn. Walks were voluntary but if a group decided on an extensive one the day's routine would be varied accordingly.[75] Christopher took part in the games and was especially keen on umpiring Chalet cricket.[84] Shopping was done in the mornings and the shoppers had to be out by 9 a.m. to allow reading to begin.[85]

The food tended to be austere, the day starting with porridge, bread, jam and coffee.[16] Christopher prepared the porridge himself, wearing a plastic raincoat kept for the purpose (Fig. 53) and, despite using modern 'rapid' oats, insisted on stirring it for forty minutes as he had been taught by Margaret Read from the Colonial Office in 1955.[16,87] A light lunch offered lively conversation after the morning's reading. Like the Univ parties, New College had red wine delivered by barrel (Fig. 52), claimed to be French Army issue,[83] possibly in a little embroidery by Christopher. Dinner preparation was a shared task and as one member commented, 'The one thing about chalet cooking is that it does keep a large number of people amused for a long time.'[88] So too to an extent did the washing up and drying, which were frequently accompanied by singing.[62]

Dinner was always preceded by drinks and is remembered among New College's members for Christopher's wide-ranging conversation.[63,86] As Herbert Hart described it, 'sometimes he seemed to be speaking with oral footnotes, or with gigantic parentheses which threatened to engulf the main theme'.[82] Christopher always took the position at the head of the dinner table and, while he did not initiate conversation, once it was under way he plunged in with gusto. Party manager Ian Bradley (Chalet 1969–72) remembers 'wonderful and hilarious conversations' over dinner and for Miles Young (Chalet 1975–6) the way Christopher handed down Chalet lore 'in meandering but addictive monologue' could be as 'life-enhancing as a glass of champagne'.[62,83] Some found that this could inhibit the others but still appreciated the inspiration and enthusiasm he had for their experience.[88] In fact Christopher had a 'gift for friendship across the generations' and was genuinely interested in young people, being a good listener who treated their views with tolerance and regard.[16,22,83] For Allen Warren, he 'represented in personal microcosm many of the highest ideals of the liberal education to which [he] had dedicated his life'.[16]

Chalet visits gave Christopher Cox a chance to catch up on his work in Whitehall. Most years he had international trips in spring and autumn and much of his work was conducted by letters which he wrote from wherever he happened to be, apparently keeping everything in his head; his deputy in Whitehall claimed to have taken early retirement because he could not cope with Christopher's lack of normal civil service method.[33] At the Chalet he would spend the first few days getting to know people and then settle down each morning to working at a table in one of the Chalet's porches, where he laid out his stock of airmail paper; this was the signal for the party to get down to study.[16] He did this whatever the weather, and sometimes his morning coffee would be taken to him through the mist. When he read for pleasure he did so on the lawn, indicating that he was free from work and could be interrupted.[16]

Christopher Cox undoubtedly saw himself as the embodiment of Sligger's tradition and his personality dominated the New College parties even though he did not impose it.[75,85] He was always at pains to emphasise their place in the sweep of the Chalet's history and its

The Environment of the Chalet des Anglais

1 Site of the Chalet
2 Hôtel du Prarion
3 Le Prarion
4 Tête Noire
5 Nid d'Aigle
6 Tête Rousse

7 Aiguille du Goûter
8 Mont Blanc
9 Aiguille de Bionnassay
10 Pointe Inférieure
11 La Jonction
   (Montagne de la Côte)

12 Saint-Gervais-les-Bains
13 Le Fayet
14 Contamines
15 Servoz
16 To Chamonix

43

44

43 Chalet art: the Old Chalet in a Victorian watercolour by an unknown artist.
44 Chalet art: the New Chalet in a watercolour by Vivian Williams, 1958.

45

46

45 Giles Alington's 1952 party: (from left) Christopher and Jean Elrington, Giles Alington, Stephan Dammann, Roger Smith. Kindly supplied by Christopher and Jean Elrington. **46** Robert (left) and Christopher Bateman at Chalet tennis in the 1950s. Kindly supplied by Dr Christopher Bateman.

47

48

47 The Chalet as it first appears on the traditional arrival from Saint Gervais.
48 Frank (left) and Elizabeth (fourth from left) Lepper with one of their larger
Corpus Christi groups, in 1957.

49

50

49 Tony Firth as one of the boys at Col de Tricot: (from left) Michael Hand, Mark Blythe, Nick Owen, Tony Firth, Miles Tuely. **50** One of Tony Firth's Annecy lunches, with (from left) Rick Porter, Tony Firth, Colin Lowry, Mark Savage, Thomas Cullen.

51

52

53

51 Sir Patrick Reilly (centre) visiting New College's first full party of 1966, with Christopher Cox on his left and junior managers Andrew Thornhill (sixth from left), Patrick Martin (second from right), John Emmerson (third from right) and Christopher Fielding (fourth from right). **52** A great moment: New College's wine barrel arrives among the lupins with Max Jourdier (front) and Patrick Martin. **53** Morning stirrings: Sir Christopher's traditional contribution to porridge, with the famous plastic raincoat.

54

55

54 A quiet reading afternoon in the 1960s. **55** Chalet art: crayon sketch of the Chalet and woodshed by Fr Dominic Milroy, 1967.

56

57

56 The newly extended Hôtel du Prarion, 1966. **57** The view of Mont Blanc from the terrace of the hotel.

58

59

58 Friendships: Christopher Cox with Solange Boucher-Véret, a photograph he entitled 'Beauty and the Beast'. **59** Friendships: John Emmerson (jacketed) at the Hôtel du Prarion with (from left) Max Hottegindre, Georges Hottegindre, Julie Dion-Orset, Simone Orset-Hottegindre (and Max's all-important jeep).

60

61

60 Sir Christopher's hotel dinner speech in 'excruciating accent and mangled French', with Simone Orset-Hottegindre on his left and Yves Hottegindre on his right, Julie Dion-Orset (far right) and Solange Boucher-Véret (second from left).
61 Four generations of Anselme Martin's family visit in 1970: Noémie Martin (front, right) with (on her right) daughters Julia and Berthe (see Fig 32), her grandson Jacky Martin (rear, left) with his wife Mimi and in front of him their children Brigitte and Fabrice, and Thierry Broisat (rear right), grandson of Julia.

62

63

62 Louis Broisat's final visit to the Chalet in 1971. **63** An early Balliol party: Tony Kenny (standing, second from right) with Jennifer Barnes on his left and Jonathan Barnes on his right, Nancy Kenny (seated in chair) holding Charles Kenny, Catherine Barnes (front, far left), Camilla Barnes and Robert Kenny (front, far right).

64

65

64 Jeremy Lever (left) in 1969, with Nicholas Warren. **65** Carpenter Rémy Parcevaux (left) in 1976 with his son Michel, who would also work for the Chalet (see Fig 99).

66

67

66 New College's traditional kitchen music: Harvey McGregor conducts (from left) Stephen Tucker, John Sherlock and Norman Vance. **67** Changing Chalet fashions: afternoon relaxation in the 1970s very different from the dress code of *The Perfect Chalet-ite*, with (from left) Charlie Parton, Steb Fisher, Jeremy Lever. Kindly supplied by Stephen Roberts.

68

69

68 A New College afternoon in 1970: future ambassador to France Peter Westmacott prepares for dinner while James Bradby reads, resting from more risky outings. **69** Friendships: Christopher Cox with the Boucher family at the Chalet du Rocher, with (from left) Lila, Nelleriek, Frank, Hugues and Knud, taken by the young Ernst Boucher.

70

71

70 The visit of the Hottegindres to Oxford in 1974: dinner in New College, (from left) Simone Orset-Hottegindre, Christopher Cox, Max Hottegindre. **71** On the rooftops of Oxford: Simone Orset-Hottegindre with Sir William and Lady Hayter.

72

73

72 The 1978 restoration: work starts on the roof. **73** Hugues Boucher (left) formally opens the restored toilet. Edward Forman (right) introduces.

traditions. Regular readings were taken from Cyril Bailey's *Memoir* of Sligger and from the biographies of David and Harriet Urquhart.[75] In the words of one chaletite, it was all 'a sort of aspic-shrouded homage to the '20s and '30s with vivid splashes of the Edwardian and Victorian chaps'.[84] His diary entries, in handwriting much clearer than that of his letters although still not without its challenges, were meticulous in referring events back to historical precedents. After each season he would invite the year's parties to a celebration in New College, asking them to bring their best photographs, from which he would complete the diary. It is noteworthy that he always adhered to the historical name *Pavillon* for the Prarion Hotel, a practice that has persisted for New College chaletites.

However, this was a version of history seen through the prism of his own personality.[16] As Simone Hottegindre perceptively commented, his was a new episode in an old tradition.[7] Convinced that the lupins were a legacy from Harriet Urquhart, he fought annual battles against the rosebay willowherb he believed threatened them.[87] During foreign travel he acquired a collection of lurid shirts and odd hats which he took to the Chalet (Fig. 58). He also had a taste for dramatic ties, and could take up to fifteen for a single party.[16] This habit was picked up by his chaletites, who started taking their most outrageous ties for the dinners.[89] At this time the New College parties still used Sligger's table linen from 1909 and Christopher also liked to use it on his bed, claiming that it was better quality.[16] At the end of each season the linen would go down to Louis Broisat's sister Lea Pognan for laundering;[16] its safe return in Louis' hands and disputes over payment would sometimes result in friction between the parties.

Another way Christopher's eccentricity expressed itself was in copying Sligger's fondness for attaching classical names to teams in games and to the local topography, and to those members who undertook jobs. Inevitably, some members of the party found Christopher's approach affected but generally they recognised that they and the tradition they had immersed themselves in were being treated with affection.[84] As one summed it up, Christopher's Chalet 'was absurd, bordering on the precious, arch, very male, smugly elitist, camp, but it was also great fun. Its rituals were inviolable but never took themselves too seriously, a cultural trick very much of a period now possibly past.'[84]

Another practice of Sligger's which Christopher copied was to open the parties to guests. He liked to have a few senior friends with him,[16] such as New College dons like Herbert Nicholas, who was with him regularly over the decade from 1967, or colleagues from the Colonial Service like Margaret Read or Freda Gwilliam.[72,90] When in 1970 William Hayter (Chalet 1926–9) came back as Warden of New College, Christopher recorded it as the first visit of a Head of House since 1925. Hayter, who was well placed to assess Christopher's achievement, said that it was 'marvellous being back there' and that he was filled with admiration for how the party gave the impression of running itself.[91]He also said that the food was much better than in Sligger's time.

A tradition which both Christopher and Tony maintained was a dinner at the hotel during each party, usually at the end.[7] For New College this included a speech by Christopher (Fig. 60) in which he would thank the Hottegindres for their support in 'excruciating accent and mangled French'.[86] His grasp of French could be comic: once, asked to collect a *bidon* of milk at the local farm, he is said to have asked for a *bidet*,[16] but with Christopher Cox one never knows whether this might merely have been a mischievous affectation. When preparing for the dinners at the Prarion Hotel he would take a dictionary and pick at random three bizarre words such as *gribouiller* (scribble), *bégueulerie* (prudishness) and *amonceler* (build up) and then work them into his speech to impress his hosts.[87]

The hotel was the Chalet's link with the outside world, providing members with telephone and postal services. Access to the mountain had been improved by ski lifts from Col de Voza, and although some still preferred the walk up from Saint Gervais, relying on Louis Broisat for transport of their luggage,[63] Max Hottegindre's help with his jeep became increasingly important, especially after Louis' mule Lulu died in 1959. Christopher made relationships on the mountain his particular care but had in any case developed a close friendship with the Hottegindres. At the hotel he was known as 'le Chevalier Cox'[16] and Simone's mother Julie Dion-Orset described him as having '*richesse de pot*',[87] a phrase which has something of the beachcomber about it. By 1969 he was giving English lessons to the Hottegindres' third son, Yves.[92] He also maintained close friendship with Solange Boucher-Véret and when her elder son Hugues married reported his wife as 'charming',[92] a judgement which can be readily endorsed by successive generations of chaletites, who could always be certain of a warm welcome to the Chalet du Rocher from Nelleriek Boucher-Verloop and her family.

The relationship between Christopher and Tony Firth was more complex, as it could only be between two such contrasted personalities. As self-appointed guardian of tradition, Christopher suspected Tony of an iconoclastic streak; in 1958 Tony's party had demolished the external staircase to the balcony on grounds of being unsafe.[73] He was also suspicious of Tony's practice of inviting favourites to the Chalet.[16] Worse, he feared that Tony, a younger and more impulsive man, might do something precipitate such as dismissing Louis Broisat for being drunk and unreliable.[73] This was unfair to Tony, whose commitment to the Chalet was no less strong, albeit different in style. Tony's view was that dealing with Christopher Cox 'needed skills of a peculiar kind' but conceded that the world was a better place for him.[93]

In fact where Louis Broisat was concerned, there were real grounds for concern. Louis had worked for the Chalet for five decades and was no longer a young man. He had developed arthritis and was much less mobile without his mule. He also remained no more biddable and his taste for wine had become dependence, making him 'a bleary old boy'.[22] David Edward (Chalet 1957–61 & 1967), whose good grasp of French got him the job of interpreter, remembers that Louis had a thick, guttural accent and that while working he would roar apparently incomprehensible single-word orders for what he wanted.[21] By the mid-1960s Max Hottegindre described him as very '*chargé*'[94] but he continued to work for the Chalet when asked; those asking found it was advisable to leave out a bottle of wine for him but sometimes returned to the Chalet to find the wine gone and the work still not done.[92] When writing to others in Oxford about this, Christopher asked them not to mention it to Tony Firth, as he was trying to play down the problems.[94]

Max Hottegindre rather mischievously suggested to Christopher that Tony Firth was better at handling Louis because he treated him harder and with less understanding.[95] Those of a later generation who know the humour of Max's sons may suspect that this was said with a twinkle. Christopher was prepared to admit that Louis had become 'a monstrously tiresome old man' and wondered if it might be possible to pension him off but feared that Louis might be demoralised by losing the Chalet, his one remaining occupation.[92,95] Generally he was inclined to be circumspect as long as the Chalet was kept secure. Louis did in fact work on it as late as 1969, despite needing two sticks to walk with by then.[92] Christopher's fundamental kindness is shown by his treatment of Louis during this period of gradual retirement; the Cox parties would hold a collection for Louis and then visit him at his home in Les Plages, where Christopher, with infinite tact, would explain how the parties wanted him to be comfortable.[77]

The parties were not without incident. In 1960 the hotelier at Col de Voza, M. Lavigne, had an alpine eagle in a cage. One night a New College member, feeling that this was wrong, crept down to the col and left the cage open to let the bird out.[96] However, the eagle was still there the next morning. What the student did not know was that it had a broken wing and had been rescued by the hotelier.[31] That same year Simone Hottegindre provided analgesic suppositories for a member with bad toothache.[63] Being British and unfamiliar with this form of treatment, he swallowed them instead of inserting them. When he developed stomach ache, Simone found herself surrounded by worried students while trying to explain the problem on the telephone to a dentist who was hysterical with laughter and kept repeating through gasps of breath, '*il a boulotté le suppositoire!?*'[31] '*Henri a mangé le suppositoire!*' became a catchphrase for the rest of that party.[63]

There were also reminders that mountains are to be treated with caution. In 1966 Thomas Cullen and Roger Potter of Univ had difficulty on a ledge below Pointe Inférieure and were helped out with a rope by Max Hottegindre's son Yves.[50,58] In 1967 Lincoln Allison had a narrow escape when crossing a stream in the Grand Couloir.[97] A rock avalanche started from the moraine, a recognised risk in the couloir, and as rocks came bounding down the slope he had just enough time to reflect on the tragedy of meeting his death so soon after graduation. Fortunately the rocks veered away, hitting him only on the thigh and causing bruising and shock. Large quantities of rock were being released at the time because the ice was melting back in record amounts during a heatwave. He learned later that six people had died in similar circumstances that weekend.

The same year a New College member very nearly came to grief. Christopher Cox was protective of the individual's identity when he wrote the diary entry although this can be made out by a process of exclusion. One member of a small group who walked to Pointe

Moyenne de Tricot was delayed on the return by blistered feet and sent the other members ahead with his backpack.[31] Alarm was raised when he had failed to return by the end of dinner and the party appealed to Max Hottegindre for help. Max formed a search party from people at the hotel and set off at 11 p.m., having notified the mountain rescue team at Saint Gervais who sent a party up the Bionnassay valley. They eventually found the man in the early hours of the morning, wandering in the dark beside the Bionnassay glacier in T-shirt and shorts, without a torch and badly chilled.[31] Christopher wrote in the diary a stern warning about parties separating and about crossing the glaciers alone.

Fortunately no lasting harm had been done and there was a lighter sequel: a few days later Christopher had to pay a stiff bill from the Saint Gervais rescue team. Being loyal to the Hottegindres, he felt that he should offer Max a similar amount. Max at first declined but when pressed said that there was indeed something he would like: a brand-new Land Rover.[31] For once Christopher was lost for words until one of the party muttered gently, 'I think this is a joke.' Christopher was able to rebound at once: as the French President Charles de Gaulle had recently given a speech in Montreal in which he had said '*Vive le Québec libre!*', Christopher said, 'Wouldn't you like a little bit of Quebec instead?'[31] He did not forget the debt, however; the following summer he presented Max and Simone with a quart-sized pewter tankard – a quintessentially English gift – on which was engraved in French a warm tribute to the 'great friendship' which existed between the Hottegindre family and the Chalet des Anglais.[31]

In 1966 Tony Firth made the move for which he deserves the gratitude of all chaletites even if he had done nothing else for the Chalet. The lawyer Jeremy Lever had been at the Chalet as a Univ postgraduate student in 1957. In 1966 he was at All Souls College when Tony Firth invited him back to help lead the Univ parties.[98] Despite a growing practice at the Bar – he would go on to a distinguished career in European law and a knighthood – Jeremy Lever was to be involved in the Chalet for over twenty years. Later they were to be joined by David Burgess, the Univ chaplain.

Jeremy Lever was another party leader for whom intergenerational friendship was important, as Tony's chaletites soon found.[54] He also took on the role of quartermaster, though his requests for items which provided meals economically sometimes defeated the ability of his shoppers; a forehock of pork would provide meat and stock cheaply but mistranslating this into '*avant-jarette*' produced only confusion in the village.[21] Jeremy Lever also introduced a style of mountain walking which was unfamiliar to some; he preferred the slow, steady approach and in time members came to copy this.[54] Kind to chaletites and much appreciated though Jeremy Lever was as a leader, at the time it can't have been realised that he would also be the key to the Chalet's long-term future.

And in 1966 the future must have looked tenuous. The winter had been severe, with heavy snows following in the spring. The rear side of the roof had been sheathed in steel in 1959 but in 1966 Tony Firth's opening party found that rot in the main beams had allowed the front side of the roof to collapse, leaving bedrooms and salon saturated with water.[58] Immediate repairs costing £80 were made but it was clear that nothing less than complete replacement, estimated at £500, would serve. Roger Mynors was not in a position to help and the safety valve of selling the Mont Forchet chalet had been used in 1959. The position was further complicated by the fact that Harold Wilson's government had limited the currency that could be sent outside the UK; personal travellers were limited to £50 and business needs were subject to bank approval.[22] Christopher Cox appealed for help to one of his past students, Sir Patrick Reilly (Chalet 1934 & 1938), who was UK Ambassador to France, and it must have helped that Roger Mynors' brother Humphrey had until recently been a deputy governor at the Bank of England.[16] In the event, the Bank authorised a loan of £500 which was claimed to have been sent out to France in the diplomatic bag.[16] This was sufficient for repairs to the structure and a new roof sheathed in galvanised steel.[23] This left a small residue which allowed repairs to some shutters, a new stove for the salon and a replacement for Sligger's wooden kitchen sink.[23] The party members themselves knuckled down to plastering the kitchen and restoring the Turkish bath for use as a sauna, despite Christopher Cox being afraid of repeating the 1906 fire.[88]

This still left the Chalet with a debt which was equivalent to around £8,000 at today's values and it was clear that provision must be made for future maintenance.[23] An appeal to previous chaletites was suggested by Sir Patrick Reilly, who visited that year and was delighted to find the character of the Chalet unchanged from his undergraduate time.[99] Hugh Keen at the University Chest also recommended an appeal.[100] However, this was a sensitive issue: they would be appealing for funds to support a property which belonged to Roger Mynors and any approach to Balliol members was felt to be precluded by Roger's feelings.[100] In response Tony Firth started a limited appeal linked to Univ members[23] which got off the ground quickly thanks to gifts from Tom Boase, David Edward and the Bateman brothers.[101] After careful approaches, Roger Mynors agreed to lend his name to a more general appeal. He also made a donation which, together with the Univ income, was sufficient to discharge the bank loan as well as a personal loan of £200 which Jeremy Lever had made.[102]

The pressing need had been dealt with but uppermost in the minds of the leaders was the future viability of the Chalet. No cover against fire had been taken out for several years, leaving the Chalet at risk of loss. Roger Mynors paid annual overheads such as the French land taxes but a reserve was needed for inevitable repairs and replacements; increasingly these were being met out of the leaders' own pockets. Accordingly, it was decided to mount a general appeal to all previous chaletites with the aim of generating capital of more than £1,000.[102] They hoped that the sum could come from a small number of donors but Harold Macmillan wrote to plead the privations of taxation and suggested more modest contributions would be suitable.[103] This may have been a shaft at the policies of Harold Wilson's Labour government; Macmillan did in fact give generously.[104] In the event, he was proved correct, as the appeal grew slowly from small gifts, many in the form of long-term covenants. Although it may not have been apparent in 1967, this probably served the development of the Chalet better than short-term gifts might have done.

The appeal also had the aim of raising a pension for Louis Broisat, now crippled with arthritis. This was laudable but the Chalet was never in a position to support Louis in this way. Christopher Cox, who in all probability made this proposal,[95] was forced to rely on the donations he got from his parties. Louis made his last visit to the Chalet in 1971 (Fig. 62) and sadly was to die in a house fire one night early in 1973. It was widely thought that he had fallen asleep while drunk and smoking in bed. His death left Christopher Cox as the last person involved in the Chalet who could speak from experience of Sligger's time.

Meanwhile the structural challenges were accumulating. Within two years there were problems with the plumbing system, dismissed by Christopher Cox as Tony Firth's 'Heath Robinson invention', and the stove flue in the salon collapsed.[92] Repairs were needed to doors and windows to restore security; any intruder might start a fire which could be fatal to the Chalet's existence.

A nodal point in the Chalet's history had arrived. There was now a corps of leaders dedicated to its survival, the struggles of re-establishing the seasons were behind them and the summer was as full of students as it had been when Sligger was alive. On the other hand, the Chalet needed serious maintenance but was still owned by an individual who was disengaged from it. This meant that there would always be constraints on the leaders' ability to act, despite Roger Mynors' agreement to support in 1967. Further, the Chalet's founder college, Balliol, was disenfranchised and nothing could be done about this without trampling on Roger Mynors' feelings. In fact, the leaders were conscious that for nearly two decades they had managed by carefully skirting around Roger Mynors' sensitivities and expressing sympathy about the Balliol Mastership; Christopher Cox was prepared to concede that Tony Firth had the superior skill in this.[100] Although no one wanted to be harsh to Roger, it was clear to them that there was a limit on how long they could rely on this approach. Christopher Cox was also concerned that ownership of the Chalet might be caught up in unforeseen events such as Roger Mynors' sudden death.[105] It was time for a fundamental change. This came when the seeds sown in 1966 and the combined talents of the leaders took the Chalet into a new phase which would ensure, as far as anything could, its permanence for members of the University.

CHAPTER SIX

THE NEW ORDER: THE TRUST
AND THE RETURN OF BALLIOL

THERE HAS TO BE A CERTAIN IRONY, given what was to happen later, in the fact that Edward Forman was never invited to the Chalet during his undergraduate years studying French and German at New College: presumably he failed to attract the attention of Christopher Cox's lieutenants. However, Edward's appointment as Salvesen Fellow in 1975 to pursue a doctorate on Molière made him a sitting target for Christopher's policy of using the junior research fellows as his representatives on the ground.[1] An invitation followed to 'learn the ropes' in the 1975 party under Norman Vance's management.

However much learning was necessary, it did not preclude Edward making an ascent of Pointe Inférieure and then a successful ascent of Mont Blanc with David Loughman and Clive Norton. The only previous New College summit ascent had been made by James Bradby in 1972 and Christopher Cox proudly recorded their achievement in the diary, meticulously recording details of the route, the risks, especially of falling rocks in the Grand Couloir, arrangements at the refuges and the necessary equipment. With the example of 1975 before them members of the 1976 and 1977 parties under Edward's management climbed the mountain and Christopher boasted in the diary of this New College hat-trick. A further attempt in 1979 was defeated by bad weather and there were no more New College ascents of Mont Blanc in Christopher's time.

Edward Forman exemplifies the best of Christopher Cox's policy of placing the parties in the hands of junior managers. Edward's peers say that his quiet and modest leadership came naturally and that by being inclusive in his approach he allowed people to be themselves while delivering their best.[2] One describes him as well organised and 'a counterpoint to Christopher Cox', and 'better than most of us at

mountains and chalet tennis'.[3] The task included choosing people
to constitute a successful party; this was helped by the pastoral role
played by the junior research fellows in New College and decades
later Edward still finds it possible to refer fondly to 'my own chaletites' and the links that have persisted from that time.[1]

However, this period called for more than just an effective party
manager; the Chalet was running into significant structural problems.
Repairs to the balcony and roof had been made by local contractors
in 1976 but the single toilet needed flushing with a jug, the toilet floor
was dangerously rotten and there was the need to lay a new water
supply from the stream.[4] Temporary repairs to the kitchen required
completion. Worse, the 1977 party found on opening that faults in
the chimney led to smoke leaking into the Turkish bath, some of the
bedrooms and the loft. In a season of constantly poor weather the
party was saved from the cold by Kit Prins (Chalet 1969–71), a visitor
from his position at the United Nations Secretariat on Forest Matters
in Geneva, who provided funds to buy Butagas heaters. Christopher
Cox wrote in the diary that it was quite the most worrying party that
he could recall.

The Chalet had by now passed from the ownership of Roger
Mynors to that of a charitable trust and Edward's response to these
problems was to submit a practical and detailed plan for a volunteer working party at the start of the 1978 season, which he would
be managing.[5] This was strongly supported by Christopher Cox and
Arthur Cooke, recently elected Warden of New College and a trustee
and visitor to the parties Edward led. One volunteer being worth a
dozen pressed men, the trustees went further and requested that the
galvanised steel roof also be painted in bitumen, specifying an overall
budget of £500.[6]

Disclaiming any personal skills, Edward assembled his forces for
the 1978 season. Stephen Adcock, who had valuable climbing experience, was to lead a three-man roof-painting team and Anthony
Nowlan, having proved his worth in 1977 with chimney repairs, was
to direct the toilet repair. Anthony and Edward drove out in Edward's
Austin A40, taking with them a new toilet cistern, a large number
of tennis balls and, as it happened, Christopher Cox, who acquired
a camera to record their trip, only to discover later that it contained
no film.[4]

Christopher Cox took refuge at the *Pavillon* as work at the Chalet proceeded. The roof was painted, the kitchen also cleaned and painted and the external store cleared of the detritus of decades. It was unfortunate that just as the old toilet was removed one of the workers developed diarrhoea which necessitated repairing to the bushes with a spade but the new floor and flush toilet were still installed on time. This latter was celebrated, in a typical Cox gesture, by inviting Hugues Boucher to conduct a formal opening ceremony in the company of his family and Simone Hottegindre. Edward's own celebration included the visit of his fiancée Debbie at the end of the month.

The 1978 working party showed what effective party leadership could do, as Christopher Cox was quick to point out. Edward's detailed accounts and report for the trustees showed that the work had been achieved for 25 per cent less than the budgeted £500;[7] the fact that it included hospitality for the workers simply indicated his grasp of good leadership. There was one additional and modest request to the trustees; it had not been realised that after three days spreading bitumen the roof-painting trio would need a new set of clothes.[8]

Edward's departure that year for a lectureship in Bristol brought to an end his leadership of New College parties but, like others who had held the position, he maintained a warm correspondence with both Christopher Cox and Arthur Cooke. Edward and Debbie returned to the Chalet for visits in 1980 and 1981 (welcomed by Christopher Cox as the 'veteran chaletite') and Arthur Cooke's invitation for 1982 was precluded only by the demands of Edward's work in Bristol,[9] after which circumstances changed, as we shall see. In 2003 Edward and Debbie went back to introduce their family to the Chalet during a camping holiday.[1] Sadly they found it empty, this being due to my party following the Univ tradition of walking as a body. It is my regret that I failed to meet this pluperfect chaletite on ground which had become dear to us both.

¤

By the late 1960s Christopher Cox, Tony Firth and Jeremy Lever were clear in their aims for the Chalet. They wanted to preserve the building for the use of students, find funds to put it on a permanent footing, and bring back Balliol students. Their position was made simpler when Roger Mynors made it clear that when the time came for him to relinquish the Chalet, however that occurred, he wanted its original objectives adhered to as far as possible.[10]

Sir Patrick Reilly and others had suggested setting up an educational trust[11] but advice had been received that too many difficulties existed. French law, unlike British, did not recognise charitable trusts and it was not possible at that time for a British corporation to own property in France.[12] A further complication was that when property in France was transferred significant inheritance tax had to be paid. These may have been some of the problems which in 1934 had prevented Sligger from changing his intention to make the Chalet a bequest to Roger Mynors.

At this point Tony Firth's recruitment of Jeremy Lever bore its major fruit; not for nothing did Christopher Cox refer to 'Tony's clever lawyer'. Jeremy Lever's legal mind was more than equal to the challenges of French law and the solution he devised, while superficially complicated, was simple in its logic.[13] The Chalet would be owned in France by a *Société Civile Immobilière* – a non-profit-making investment company – which in turn would be owned by two British companies, each holding one share. This provision meant that there would always be two or more shareholders; if no shareholder held more than 50 per cent they were not liable for inheritance tax. The two British companies would in turn be directed by a charitable trust, the trustees also being directors of the companies. The success of this structure is evident from the fact that it survived intact for fifty years and has recently been renewed.

The moves took some time to achieve, not surprisingly in view of the number of organisations involved. First the English companies had to be set up with Roger Mynors as the shareholder. Then the French company was created with the English companies as shareholders. Following formation of the Trust the trustees received the shares in the English companies: this required approval from the Department of Education and Science, awarded under the general heading of advancement of education.[14] After this Roger Mynors transferred the Chalet into ownership by the *Société Civile* – this sequence of events ensured minimal tax and stamp duty. The legal process was handled by Macfarlanes solicitors in London under the direction of Jeremy Lever and on the French side through Maître Bucaille, a lawyer, and Maître Baillie, a notary.[15] In December 1970 Macfarlanes said that the UK arrangements could go ahead.[16] Slower progress was made in France but in March 1971 Macfarlanes were able to report that Maître Bucaille would have the French side of the transaction ready for completion before permission from the French Ministry of Finance expired on 1 April.[15]

The English companies were set up as the Chalet des Mélèzes Company Ltd and the Chalet des Anglais Company Ltd with Christopher Cox, Tony Firth and Jeremy Lever as directors and trustees. The first Board meetings of the companies and the Trust were held on 29 November 1970, to allow the rest of the process to go ahead.[17] Roger Mynors transferred the shares in the British companies to the trustees on 25 March 1971,[18] and the French sale of the Chalet to the *Société Civile* was completed on 19 May, at a sale price of 65,000 francs, or £5,000.[19]

The trustees' first and major challenge, inevitably, was finance and it would remain so for a long time. The cost of setting up the Trust had been less than expected but was still a significant sum: in addition to buying the Chalet for £5,000 there were fees of £741 to pay in France and £310 in England.[20] There was the need to reimburse Jeremy Lever, who had advanced the Trust the £5,000 purchase price and also paid the French legal fees, and who was to bail out the Trust with advances several times over the next few years, as did Christopher Cox.[21] Additionally the trustees had become responsible for insurance and French property taxes. Knowing this they had widened Tony Firth's 1967 appeal to include all those who had been at the Chalet;[10] the response was strong but even so the trustees were obliged to restrain all expenditure, for example by trimming the insurance to an absolute minimum.[22] Considering how large these costs were in today's terms, one can only admire the commitment of these first trustees to ensuring the Chalet's continued existence. Roger Mynors expressed himself horrified by how much work and expense was needed and how it would fall on the three of them. He did, however, sound an appropriate note of hope: 'I know there is a blessing on it and hope future generations yet unknown will be able to profit from it.'[23]

The challenges were not limited to finance. There was work to do to prepare for the future: the old track to the rear of the Chalet needed widening to accommodate a jeep.[22] Christopher Cox was concerned about raising sufficient funds to continue making repairs to doors and shutters, with an eye to the rest of the structure when it became practicable.[24] He also wanted a replacement for Louis Broisat but in fact this was never to be a possibility.

These problems were hardly helped when the 1971 opening party found that the Chalet had been broken into by an intruder forcing the door of the petit salon. Virtually all the kitchenware and tableware had been stolen, along with blankets and quilts and a number of boots. However, the Chalet des Anglais fared better than Solange Boucher-Véret and her family at the Chalet du Rocher, who lost a number of antique items. It was widely thought that this theft was committed by a member of the family of the chief of police: the Bouchers subsequently discovered some of their belongings in an antique shop owned by that family.[25]

Donations to the appeal contained a number of covenants spread over ten years. In the early years these generated an annual income of between £1,000 and £2,000 and provided the main support.[26] The trustees' dedication to prudent management is reflected in the accounts, which show that in most years they generated a small surplus to protect against years when costs were heavy. This meant that their reserves rarely rose above £5,000, a small sum considering the risks in maintaining an historic building on the side of a mountain.[26] This situation persisted through the decade to 1980 when the covenants ran out, and then throughout most of the succeeding decade although reduced maintenance in the 1980s allowed the reserves to grow a little. However, any real improvement in the Trust's position had to wait for a future appeal.

As it happened, the challenge of bringing back Balliol solved itself. In June 1970 Tony Firth had written to Christopher Cox, to say a 'nice Balliol don called Kenny wants to use the Chalet from 9–20/9 for a highly philosophical reading party and I've said yes, provided he himself comes in advance for 2 days, to learn the ropes. I know you've always favoured reviving the Balliol connection, so I assume you'll approve.'[27] What had happened at Balliol was that Anthony Kenny, a Philosophy tutor and a keen mountain man who had cut his teeth in the Apennines, Alps and Dolomites while studying at the English College in Rome,[28] had been approached by two of his students, John Hare and Tony Klouda. They had heard of the pre-war parties and wanted to know why Balliol was no longer involved.[29] Both today are inclined to disclaim being prime movers in the return of Balliol but Tony Kenny is in no doubt that their approach was the stimulus.[30,31]

The only don remaining at Balliol with any experience of the Chalet – and that limited to a 1956 holiday – was Maurice Keen, who had recommended the approach to Firth and Cox. On their advice Tony Kenny asked permission from Roger Mynors, which he duly obtained.

By the time of Tony Kenny's request the parties for 1970 had already been set and there was the challenge of finding time for Balliol in seasons limited to the summer vacation and by local services which closed down in late summer. In those days the Chalet was opened by the middle of July and closed in the first week in September. Christopher Cox had come to expect the first month of the season, shared between two groups, and he was to continue this practice until he died. Tony Firth, by contrast, continued to run single Univ groups, although people came and went during the party. The year 1970 posed no problem because Tony Kenny had asked for the second week in September but there were future years to consider. In fact, Balliol parties would continue to be limited to the end of the season until 1977 when they came to alternate with Univ; it may be no coincidence that Tony Kenny was elected to the Trust Board in 1976.

Tony Kenny's first party ran from 9 to 19 September 1970 and half the party consisted of senior members, including the parents of both John Hare and Tony Klouda. Richard Hare, who held the chair of Moral Philosophy at Corpus Christi College, brought experience of UK reading parties.[32] Tony Klouda's father Antonin had been Private Secretary to the Czech Foreign Minister Jan Masaryk and had emigrated after the latter's death in 1948 (whether by suicide or murder is still debated).[31] The Klouda family brought with them a Land Rover, which was invaluable on the mountain. One member of the party, J. L. H. Thomas, had been studying in Heidelberg and at his suggestion Tony Kenny invited the philosophers Ernst Tugendhat and Lorenz Krüger from there.[33] Tugendhat proved to be a skilled chef, a factor which may have contributed to his regular appearance at the Chalet during the 1970s, although those who shopped for him found him demanding.[34] Senior philosophers invited in later seasons included the Americans Donald Davidson and Alvin Plantinga, both keen mountaineers.[35]

The Balliol party found services tenuous at the tail end of the season; the TMB was running only twice a day, the *téléphérique* from Les Houches to Bellevue closed down on 13 September and the Col de Voza chairlift to the Prarion had already closed. The party was aided by the Kloudas' Land Rover and the Hottegindres were helpful as always. The party's first attempt at Tête Rousse succumbed to snow and poor visibility with part of their route covered by recent avalanche but despite these challenges the party managed this ascent at a second attempt and with the aid of the vehicle also made excursions to the Aiguilles Rouges and to Mont Joly.

The Balliol party was always intended to undertake serious philosophical discussion and with the presence of four senior philosophers it could hardly do otherwise. Tony Kenny suggested that they study Wittgenstein's *On Certainty*, the German guests being keen to make contact with analytical philosophers and to learn the Oxford view of Wittgenstein, then more popular in the UK than Germany.[29] The evening's discussions were minuted for future reference, beginning a series of what were called 'protocols' after a practice J. L. H. Thomas had encountered in Heidelberg.[33] This practice would persist for Balliol parties for the next twenty years.[29] It is a mark of the calibre of the party that of the six undergraduate members five went on to distinguished careers in Philosophy, the sole exception being Tony Klouda, who was destined for an international career in Medicine.

Involvement by Tony Kenny and Balliol now allowed the trustees to explore the money left by Sligger for the support of the Chalet. However, the Balliol Trust Deed stated that the fund was intended only to support undergraduates for travel abroad or to other reading parties. There was no provision for supporting maintenance. The trustees decided they would have to consider imposing a rent on visitors of £1 per week, which would bring in around £50 a year, although they argued about the effect on undergraduates' willingness to go to the Chalet.[36] As it was, an undergraduate rent was finally agreed and has persisted virtually unbroken since then.

Tony Kenny ran a similar party in 1971 and then in 1972 enlarged it by adding a colleague in Ancient Philosophy, Jonathan Barnes from Oriel College, who would subsequently join him at Balliol. Both brought their wives, Nancy and Jennifer, and the Kennys' two sons, Robert and Charles, and the Barnes' two daughters, Catherine and Camilla (Fig. 63) also attended. They were to retain this partnership, with their families, through most of the years up to 1990, when Tony Kenny moved to take up the Wardenship of Rhodes House, although when Tony Kenny became Master of Balliol in 1978 Jonathan Barnes took over the duty of the Philosophy parties and Tony Kenny also encouraged other tutors to take an interest.[34] The combination of families gave the Balliol parties a domestic atmosphere that was radically different from those of their bachelor don colleagues at the other colleges, something which they exploited consciously; when the party was reading the children had lessons.[34,37] Nancy Kenny and Jennifer Barnes took over the kitchen with the aim of introducing undergraduate cooks to the practicalities of catering.[34] The Balliol parties' walking pattern also varied from that of the other colleges: walks were voluntary but were usually day-long and went further afield than the other colleges did; this was aided by Tony Kenny's previous mountain experience.

Being dedicated to the study of Philosophy, the Balliol parties tended to be smaller than those of the other colleges: in the years up to changes in the season in 1982 the number of junior members was rarely above ten and more usually around five or six. The daily pattern was similar to that of the other colleges, although modified for discussion. Breakfast was at eight and cleared for reading at nine. The morning was spent in study and followed by a simple lunch of soup, bread and cheese and some discussion could take place in the afternoon. An ample dinner was the main event, after which the day's seminar was held, at which some members presented papers they had prepared and others took notes to be typed up as the protocol on their return home. The day ended with a celebratory drink: the protocols frequently end, 'At 10.15 wine was taken', and the drinking could be extensive.[38]

This was the first time in the reading parties that study had concentrated on a set text. An idea of the serious intent of these parties and their deep discussion may be gained from the choices for individual years. For example, those for the first five years of the Kenny–Barnes parties were:[39]

1972: Aristotle: *De Anima*
1973: Aristotle: the *Eudemian Ethics*
1974: St Thomas Aquinas
1975: Aristotle: the *Politics*
1976: Donald Davidson: *Language, Mind and Epistemology*

It might be wondered if these parties were suitable for children but Catherine Barnes, who went there first when she was about eight, remembers them as 'the best holiday you could imagine'.[40] For children there was first the excitement of the twenty-four-hour journey: the boat train and the ferry, the journey to Paris and then the overnight train journey to Le Fayet, waking up to see the mountains. This was followed by the TMB to Col de Voza and the walk up to the Prarion Hotel, where the reward was always a glass of lemonade. The undergraduates, too, were welcoming and involved the children in their tasks as well as Chalet games. The children even sat in on the evening discussions: Catherine recalls that they may not have understood the drift of the conversation but could enjoy it because it was obviously witty, although they were usually sent to bed before the talk ended.[40] The children had the loft to themselves at night, complete with spiders and sometimes mice, and were given a chamber pot to prevent them from having to climb down to the toilet during the night. They also took part in the walks, even demanding ones like Pointe Inférieure.

In 1970 an event occurred which would certainly have appealed to Christopher Cox's sense of tradition: his party was visited by Noémie Martin, widow of the Chalet's first *gardien*, Anselme, who had died in 1914. She bought with her two of her daughters who had been members of the Chalet staff in the 1920s, Berthe Martin and Julia Broisat, together with her grandson Jacques, his wife Mimi and their two children, Brigitte and Fabrice, and another great-grandson, Thierry Broisat, grandson of Julia (Fig. 61). At the age of ninety-five Noémie Martin was still a strong woman: the Martin family home was at Mont Paccard on the track to Saint Gervais, nearly 600 metres below the Chalet, and in annotating the photograph of them for the diary Christopher was careful to point out that the party had travelled on foot.

During this decade Christopher Cox consolidated his policy of inviting senior colleagues or other guests to the parties. Herbert Nicholas continued to visit until 1978 and was joined by physicist Arthur Cooke, who was there each year from 1974 until 1983 apart from 1976 when he was elected Warden of New College. The lawyer Harvey McGregor was a frequent visitor after becoming a New College tutor in 1973. Retired Registrar of the University Sir Folliott Sandford came for four years and French Tutor Merlin Thomas was in the habit of dropping in on the way to his summer retreat in Sicily. When the mother of brothers Charles Sherlock (Chalet 1973 & 1975) and John

Sherlock (Chalet 1974–5) was widowed in 1975 Christopher paid for her to stay at the Prarion Hotel so that she could join the party.[41] A surprising visitor, perhaps, in view of Christopher's agnosticism, was the Roman Catholic priest Barnabas Sandeman, who said Mass daily in his bedroom.[42] In fact Sandeman had been a student of Christopher's at New College. He had moved on to Ampleforth and Christopher was reintroduced to him by Allen Warren during a visit to Allen at York University.[43] It may well have appealed to Christopher's sense of Sligger's tradition that he could accommodate a member of the Catholic clergy, possibly as his version of the Abbé Klein.

Members found that these senior visitors mixed well with the group in the same way that Christopher did, though there was a feeling that Herbert Nicholas was more inclined to stand on a don's dignity.[44] Christopher was prone to pricking any such tendency: when during the toilet replacement in 1978 Herbert complained that the noise was preventing work Christopher roundly told him that a new toilet was more important than 'yet another' American history.[45] A later tussle in the kitchen over Herbert's feeling that a cracked serving dish was unhygienic resulted in the dish smashing on the floor: the silence that followed was broken by Christopher saying in a shocked voice, 'Herbert, you've broken Sligger's plate!'[46]

Another feature of the Cox parties was involvement of the Warden. In the case of William Hayter little encouragement may have been needed: Hayter had been a chaletite in the 1920s before a successful diplomatic career and had paid a visit during the last pre-war party of 1938. In 1976 Hayter was succeeded by Arthur Cooke, who was to prove a strong supporter of the Chalet parties, joining the Trust Board in 1976 and continuing until 1983 shortly before he retired. New College has retained a strong association between the Chalet and successive Wardens through Harvey McGregor (Warden 1985 to 1996), Alan Ryan (1996 to 2009) and the present Warden, Miles Young, one of Christopher's party members in 1975 and 1976.

The Cox parties continued to take the month of July in two groups with junior leaders. John Emmerson moved on, as did Allen Warren (although he reappeared regularly as a visitor) but leaders such as Andrew Whiffin, Norman Vance, Edward Forman, Ian Bradley and Robert Chambers continued to support Christopher with the selection of members and direction of the party. There was general appreciation that these leaders tried to put together representative groups from the undergraduate years.[47,48] As the seasons had expanded the junior managers were now assisted by a 'bursar', responsible for the French expenses and expected to account in detail at the end of the party.[41] This job could be demanding; John Sherlock's accounts for two parties in 1975 ran to six closely typed pages and involved several hundred pounds.[49] As well as the party's living costs and charges to the members there were sums to be handed on to other colleges for items such as laundry in the village and a buy-on of groceries and wine by incoming parties. The latter were not always met with complete agreement: Christopher Cox left negotiation with Tony Firth to John Sherlock and then commended him for the skill with which he had managed it.[50] Today the parties take a simplified approach: gas is the only item subject to buy-on and each party manages its own resources. Nonetheless, today all colleges use a bursar, principally for apportioning the costs of shopping.

Christopher Cox also involved the New College chaplains in the leadership of his parties: John Muddiman (1973–5) and Christopher Dent (1976–7), and later Jeremy Sheehy (1985–9). Jeremy Sheehy's replacement as chaplain was Stephen Tucker, who had been a member of Christopher's parties as a graduate from 1973 and who on return to New College would lead parties for another fifteen years. Christopher Dent remembers being approached by Christopher to assist the party in partnership with the junior fellows, with the opportunity to learn the ropes in the first year and take on the party the following year. He recalls that the Chalet was in rather poor shape, leaking windows and damp being a problem, although fine weather transformed the experience.[42]

Interaction between Christopher's personality and the Chalet became more intense as the years progressed. Members report that his recall of who had done what and what happened to them was extraordinary and that he was eager for them to appreciate the link between the 1970s and the 1930s; to some he seemed to be trying to recreate a past almost as if it were a form of therapy.[44,51] As John Hudson (Chalet 1976–7) puts it, 'For New College, Sir C was the Chalet and the Chalet was Sir C.'[47] The flamboyance of his Bermuda shirts also increased, as did competition among the party to sport the most outlandish tie at dinner.[48]

Andrew Whiffin (Chalet 1971–2) said that Christopher had charisma.[52] It is illustrative of the close friendships which Christopher inspired that when Andrew moved on to his first teaching position he felt able to submit a spoof school report on Christopher.[53] Anyone familiar with Christopher's letters will recognise the truth of comments that the layout of his essays left much to be desired, as bits were scrawled in corners, making the argument difficult to follow; this was softened by the assertion that they were full of facts and useful information. Satire is also represented by the assessment that 'he is coming out of his shell these days', having previously been silent and mouse-like. Andrew's report ends with the hope that Christopher will use the vacation sensibly, an obvious reference to the Chalet.

An innovation which New College introduced was the Chalet Cookery Book. This begins with an introduction explaining how students were required to take over duties which in the past had been provided by servants. The opening recipe for chicken casserole is by Charles Sherlock (Chalet 1973) and the lawyer Harvey McGregor added *boeuf des avocats*. The book has been added to by successive generations and provides a valuable source of inspiration to novice cooks; John Muddiman (Chalet 1973–5) made custard from basic ingredients and 'The Rev Muddiman's Custard' has remained an option for parties since, as David Loughman (Chalet 1975) found, and is certainly more palatable than the inappropriately named *crème anglaise* available locally.[54] A notable New College dish introduced in 1975 by Arda and Gül Denkel from Turkey was *imam bayildi*, an Ottoman meal based on stuffed peppers which although popular to the point of becoming traditional was found to make a heavy drain on the stock of olive oil and so increased the party's costs.[1,55]

Andrew Orange (Chalet 1974–5) remembers that dinner cooking could be highly competitive and that washing up was a communal event, usually with singing (Fig. 66); this was helped by the quantity of wine at dinner.[48] Culinary competition resulted in inventive choices: for Andrew Whiffin (Chalet 1971–2) new experiences such as globe artichokes were a highlight.[52] Glen Plant (Chalet 1977) had been impressed by a meal of *haricots verts* in garlic in Saint Gervais and was disappointed when he could not buy sufficient beans to introduce the party to the dish.[56]

The Univ and New College parties otherwise followed the pattens they had established in the late 1960s. Tony Hope (Chalet 1970 & 1973) remembers the enjoyable mix of quiet study and Chalet games, especially tennis, and felt it was a perfect balance of work and play.[57]

The New College parties continued to provide 'vivid splashes of the Edwardian and Victorian chaps ... doing strenuous hill walking in ordinary clothes combined with serious reading, clever conversation and the sort of refined gossip that Oxford perfects'.[44] The parties led by Tony Firth and Jeremy Lever (Fig. 64) maintained the combination of study and strenuous days out on the hillside with, of course, the traditional lunch in Annecy, despite Jeremy Lever being inclined to take a dim view of this departure from Chalet routine.[58]

For some the experience of the Alps and all the business of mountain railways and chairlifts only added to their appreciation; for others the proximity of Mont Blanc served as a test of stamina, even those with no previous Alpine experience.[46] There were no Univ ascents of Mont Blanc during this time and Tony Kenny's approach was to introduce students to the Tête Rousse climb, noting that most aspirations to go higher did not survive the sense of perspective which this gave.[37] However, as we have seen, New College managed three successful ascents in the mid-1970s: Edward Forman, David Loughman and Clive Norton in 1975, followed by Stephen Adcock, John Hudson and Gareth Williams in 1976 and Glen Plant and two others in 1977. Christopher Cox took to calling them *'les Petits Montblanquois'*.[54]

Although the view remained that the Chalet was not a base for climbers, experienced mountaineers were not excluded and could take advantage of the Chalet's location. One with a taste for solo expeditions was New College's James Bradby (Chalet 1970–73) (Fig. 68), who liked to use his vacations for European hiking and cultural trips.[59] Each summer during his time at Oxford he spent around two weeks at the Chalet, though he admits that his interest in mountains meant that he only partially followed any reading programme. One day in 1972, having seen in the Chalet diaries the accounts of previous ascents of Mont Blanc, he left the Chalet at 4.15 a.m. and reached the summit at 2.15 p.m. by the usual route through Tête Rousse and the Goûter refuge, returning at speed so that he could join New College's dinner at the hotel. This was the first ascent by any chaletite since 1962. Two weeks later he achieved a night ascent of the Hörnli Ridge on the Matterhorn and on his journey back to Geneva felt it would be fitting to visit the Chalet; he recalls the warm welcome and good meals provided by Tony Firth and Jeremy Lever.[59]

The following year James' record was even more impressive. On an August afternoon walk to Col de Tricot he decided to climb the

Arête de Tricot, a classic route for climbers.[59] He reached this at 2 a.m. After a couple of hours' rest in a bivouac in the snow he continued into a night ascent over the Aiguille de Bionnassay to reach the Goûter again. He describes the Aiguille at dawn as 'a spectacular traverse' and chaletites who have studied the knife-edge of the Aiguille from the hotel will have no difficulty believing this. A further outing after the New College party was more eventful: on an attempt on a hot day to traverse from the Dômes de Miage to the Goûter he ran out of water and, descending a rock gully to get down to the Miage glacier, lost his rucksack, which contained his money, passport and spare clothes, over a ledge. Starting to get visual and auditory hallucinations he was obliged to abandon his attempt and descend to a stream where water allowed him to recover. Unfortunately a friend he intended to meet at Bellevue had not arrived, so, with only the clothes he stood up in, he had to prevail once again on the hospitality of Tony Firth at the Chalet. Here he spent a couple of days recovering and then returned for the rucksack. Going out at 1 a.m. equipped with a rope, he located the rucksack but had wisely told Max Hottegindre of his plan, who had said he would call out the mountain rescue if James was not back by 2.30 p.m. Short of time, James was obliged to hide the heavy rucksack and dash back without it to Bellevue to telephone Max to say that he was safe. The rucksack was finally retrieved the following day, on the journey to the airport.[59]

James' exploits, not surprisingly, have achieved a place both in Chalet folklore and in the memory of the Hottegindre family. Max, who had good cause to know what chaletites could get up to, was probably seriously concerned but the incident brought them closer together; Max afterwards called James 'M. Mont Blanc' and offered him a ski holiday in return for tutoring his third son, Yves.[55]

Christopher Cox, as expected, was careful to record these exploits in the diary but did so in slightly muted tones; in the case of the Mont Blanc ascent he made it clear that this was suitable for 'only those with climbing expertise', underlining this in red for emphasis. He made later diary entries about serious climbs in red ink to illustrate the care needed on these excursions, which were outside his traditional experience of the reading parties.

It should be recalled that even the walks normally undertaken by parties were open to risk. Several of the higher walks in particular contain turns from which a fall could be serious and glaciers are not always fit to be crossed in walking boots. Balliol's Paul Flather (Chalet 1985) became transfixed by the early morning view from the Tête Rousse glacier and, having lingered too long, found himself sliding towards the precipice when he set off again.[60] Attempting to arrest himself with fingernails in the ice, he began to doubt that he would survive when he saw a member of the party at the refuge, who was training for the priesthood, fall to his knees in prayer. Whether this was a factor or not, Paul's salvation appeared in the form of a climber with crampons who halted his slide. Appraised of the story back at the Chalet that evening Tony Kenny merely said, 'Aren't you on cooking duties tonight?'[60]

One risk which thankfully seems to have receded in recent years is that of snake bite: Mark Slaney (Chalet 1978–9) suffered the bite of a mountain adder while collecting wood.[61] Gareth Williams remembers running to the hotel for antiserum and being treated to a hair-raising race back on Yves' motorbike, only for the haste to be dissipated in a debate about who among the inexperienced students was to do the injection, none of them wanting to give it into the patient's buttock.[62,63] Eventually Nigel Beard (Chalet 1978–9), as a biochemist and therefore the closest thing to a medic, injected the leg; the administration proved to be timely.[63] Among other animal risks, only the local farmers' guard dogs can appear threatening at times. The *sangliers*, the wild boar who inhabit the mountain, are nocturnal, reclusive and rarely seen, although they can be dangerous if disturbed, especially when guarding their young. Otherwise the *marmotte*, the symbol of the Haute-Savoie, is a rare sighting, as are the *chamois* at higher levels. On high walks there may be an occasional glimpse of the larger *bouquetin*, or mountain ibex, an impressive but placid creature.

Travel methods began to diversify during this time. Some students had cars and driving out was generally cheaper than train and could be useful for essential supplies or building material, while also providing an enjoyable journey across France. Some brave chaletites managed to hitch-hike.[64] Flying to Geneva became a new option.[65] However, the traditional overnight train journey was still used by many, requiring the two-hour walk up from Saint Gervais without the help formerly provided by Louis Broisat in bringing up luggage.[54,66] The journey could take over twenty-four hours, door to door, and did not always go to plan; some had to walk up in the dark, or even through the night, arriving for breakfast.[44,46] Tim Haggis (Chalet

1972) decided to camp out on the ascent and arrived to the welcome smell of porridge.[65] The party leaders provided guidance on travel but Christopher Cox, having a taste for the intricacies of railway time-tables, liked to involve himself in members' plans. Christopher Dent recalls that, as he was travelling from Germany, Christopher worked out a complicated itinerary with a night in the very basic Hôtel Ter-minus in Le Fayet.[42]

The household arrangements did not differ greatly from those of the previous decade. Cooking was on camping stoves with bottled gas. A makeshift shower was installed in the Turkish bath using a tank and hosepipe, and the system, although updated, remains the indoor facility today. Jugs need to be filled from the kitchen water heater and the luxury of the wash depends on how many jugs members have the patience to fill. Jeremy Lever, however, still tended to use the Chalet's ancient hip bath on the lawn.[67] Paraffin lamps were intro-duced to supplement candles and reduce fire risk. Sleeping bags were beginning to make an appearance but some parties – especially the New College ones, who would be the last to abandon the practice – still used bed linen and also table linen. This was the cause of some tension between party leaders: there was now no laundry service from Louis Broisat's family and laundry had to go to Saint Gervais. The Trust records began to contain exchanges over failure to collect laundry, or failure to arrange payment.[68] Shopping still required long trips to Saint Gervais but Max and Simone, supportive as ever, pro-vided milk and eggs from the hotel. Indeed, the period is marked by increasing calls on the hotel for assistance: it is difficult to avoid the feeling that without the Hottegindres the parties could simply have driven themselves into the ground.

Friendship with the Boucher family also grew during this period. Solange Boucher-Véret was forced to give up visiting the Chalet du Rocher due to advancing age but her elder son Hugues continued to use it and in 1981 was finally able to purchase it.[69] It was thought that Dennis Poore's wife had blocked any sale because she regarded the chalet as an asset, even though she and her husband had stopped using it. The sale was said to be precipitated when Hugues answered the phone in Utrecht one day to hear Christopher saying, 'She's dead. You'd better move quickly.'[70] Hugues Boucher and his wife Nelleriek used their chalet regularly each summer with their children Knud, Lila, Frank and Ernst (Fig. 69) and a warm welcome to chaletites was always available at 'the other chalet'. (Lila once told me that one attraction of her youthful summers was the large number of young men next door!)[69] Hugues undertook extensive renovation of his chalet but always with authenticity, of which Christopher approved. When Hugues and his sons restored the front wall (for which he had taken brick-laying lessons in Holland) Christopher offered to lay the first stone. As they had already built a section they suggested that he baptise it when finished, which he duly did with a bottle of red wine.[69] In tribute the family called it 'Cox Corner' and Lila made a slate plaque, which remains there, with an inscription in memory, in her words, of 'the most wonderful, lovable friend of the whole family'.[69] Chaletites are very familiar with Cox Corner: with the Bouchers' permission Chalet parties use the path past the Chalet du Rocher as a shorter route from the Prarion than Sligger's old rear track to the Chalet des Anglais.

It is a mark of the friendship with the Hottegindre family, and especially the place the Chalet held in the affections of Christopher Cox, that when Christopher celebrated his seventy-fifth birthday in New College in November 1974, rather than doing so with family or friends, he chose to invite Max and Simone to Oxford to take part in a celebration of the Chalet and its friendships.[71] This event turned into an extended weekend reception in their honour (Figs 70 & 71). They were met on Friday at Heathrow airport by Christopher Cox and Nancy Kenny and taken to the Kennys' home in Cumnor where Jonathan and Jennifer Barnes joined them for dinner, after which they visited David Cox at Univ (David had recently been President of the Alpine Club of Great Britain). On Saturday they toured New College and saw the view of Oxford from its tower. After coffee with the Warden William Hayter they were received by Vice-Chancellor Sir John Habakkuk and then saw a degree ceremony in the Sheldonian Theatre. Lunch at Univ with Tony Firth and some of his chaletites was followed by an afternoon break at Cumnor before dinner in the Founder's Library at New College with fifty chaletites and afterwards a large reception. On Sunday they met the Dean of Christ Church and were given lunch by Frank and Patrick Lepper with some of the chaletites of Frank's parties. Charles and Helen Stanley-Baker accompanied them back to the airport. It says much for Christopher's regard for them that he was prepared to bury the celebration of a significant birthday in their visit to Oxford.

In Christopher's speech at the dinner – in which he admitted disarmingly that he had to speak from notes to keep to the point – he said that he was among those who had long wished for Max and Simone to visit England and that the fact that they had been prepared to leave the hotel to do so was a mark of the great friendship between the Chalet and the family.[72] He gave the Hottegindres messages from those who could not be there and paid tribute to those who had kept the Chalet going, including Louis Broisat, 'amusing, lovable and loyal old rogue'. In proposing the toast to Max and Simone he said, *'chaque génération de chaletites devient sensible au charme et à la grâce de vous, Madame, et de Max, et chaque génération apprend de nouveau les réalités de votre amitié solide et fidèle'* ('each generation of chaletites becomes aware of the charm and grace of you, Madame, and of Max, and each generation learns anew the reality of your strong and faithful friendship'). It was a sentiment that could have been expressed by any chaletite present and indeed by any since.

In her letter of thanks after the visit Simone wrote, *'C'est à la fois un Conte de Fées, et beaucoup mieux parce qu'un Conte de Fées puisque c'est une réalité: réalité exprimant tant d'amitié et de délicatesses'* ('It's both a fairy tale, and much better because a fairy tale as a reality: a reality expressing so much friendship and delicacy').[71]

It was sad, therefore, that the following year Tony Firth's association with the Chalet ended when he left Oxford to take up the Vice-Wardenship of Goldsmith's College, London.[73] Those who knew him well had noticed that his usual urbanity was failing and that he could easily become irritable.[74] At that time History was becoming more research-dependent and a pastoral don like Tony had less place. It may also be that he faced problems in his personal life and he very probably had become disenchanted with teaching the History syllabus. On the first night of the 1976 party he asked Rajiva Wijesinha (Chalet 1973–4 & 1976) to stay back after dinner and over a drink explained that he had decided to leave Univ.[67] Rajiva suspected that a key factor may have been that at the age of forty Tony could no longer regard himself as sharing the undergraduate generation. Sensing the end of an era, the party decided to give him a farewell dinner which they felt should be at the Chalet itself in commemoration of his commitment to the reading parties.[67] Tony's departure brought to an end his association with twenty-two years' parties, apart from brief visits he made to Christopher Cox's party in 1978 and to later Univ parties. However, he remained a trustee until 1989.

Tony Firth's departure left the Univ parties in the hands of Jeremy Lever, David Burgess having moved on to London and no other Univ Fellow being available. However, a few years later Jeremy introduced two Univ colleagues, Iain McLean, a Fellow in Politics, and Bill Sykes, the new chaplain. There were changes in Balliol parties, too; Tony Kenny was elected Master of Balliol in 1978 and felt that in this position he should take a larger number and wider spread of Balliol students.[35] Jonathan Barnes continued the Balliol parties dedicated to Philosophy. Members recalled from these parties that Jennifer Barnes was a good cook and got them all involved in the cooking and supplies.[75] Individuals were allocated titles according to their jobs: Matthew Taylor (Chalet 1983–5 & 1987) recalls being appointed Mr Tilley Lamp and confounding the party's scepticism by proving competent.[76] The parties tended to relax on the final evening with after-dinner performance turns varying from talented to bizarre.[76] One such was licking *crème de menthe* off another chaletite's stomach as a forfeit.[75]

A further change in the Balliol parties took place in 1978. Carol Clark, the college's tutor in French and the first woman fellow of any of the men's colleges, put together a party of modern languages students with the support of Ray Ockenden from Wadham College.[77] Ray Ockenden brought with him experience of reading parties in Cornwall, having in the early 1970s revived parties which Wadham had run in the 1930s.[78] Both he and Carol were accompanied by their sons, continuing the family tradition established by Tony Kenny and Jonathan Barnes. They also adhered to the practice of studying as a group but widened the scope, concentrating on European Romantic authors; members were expected to give brief presentations and Chris Reading recalls that this was an opportunity to extend reading into unfamiliar areas.[77] Carol Clark would run a similar party in 1986 but her main contribution to the parties came a decade later in a twenty-year partnership which lasted through retirement and up to her death.

The trustees' main challenge was the fabric, for which they were now solely responsible. There was now no Louis Broisat for maintenance and little had been done since 1971. New advice was needed and they approached a local mason, Claude Pognan, the son of Louis' sister Lea who had been a maid at the Chalet in the 1920s. When M. Pognan visited to survey the Chalet he brought with him his sister Francine Duffoug and her daughter Annick. His report came as a relief to the trustees; the Chalet was essentially sound.[79] He recommended improving drainage by reducing the ground level around the kitchen and installing underground drainage pipes, repairing the wood of the porches and the roofs, replacing the flashing around the chimneys and repainting the steel cladding on the roof. The only pressing problem was leaking through holes in the lead flooring of the balcony, which had led to rot in the underlying boards and in some beams.

As trustees have found since, matters do not always move quickly on the mountain and it can be difficult to induce craftsmen to start work. The balcony would ideally have been repaired in 1975 but the craftsman M. Pognan had recommended dragged his feet. On the recommendation of Max Hottegindre they engaged instead the local carpenter in Bionnassay, Rémy Parcevaux (Fig. 65), working with a M. Magliocco to provide new zinc cladding for the floor.[80] This work was completed in 1976.

All should now have been under control but new problems were found on opening up in 1977.[80] The kitchen water supply failed, the toilet floor was found to have serious wet rot and smoke was leaking from the salon chimney into the first floor and loft. Anthony Nowlan chipped away old mortar from the chimneys and attempted a temporary repair and Claude Pognan was called in again to advise. M. Magliocco came to replumb the kitchen and Jeremy Lever took advantage of his presence to obtain a quote for the first gas-fired water heater for the kitchen.[68] Until then water was boiled on the stove, which proved wasteful in gas. The water heater proved to be a great benefit but lasted only two years before it had to be replaced: no one had appreciated that unless completely emptied of water it would fracture due to expansion of ice during the winter (it has to be said that this has been a recurring problem, reflecting the difficulty in completely emptying the tortuous piping).[81]

This was the background to Edward Forman's plan for a 1978 works party, to which the trustees had added re-painting the roof.[6] Max advised on the use of ladders and Stephen Adcock's skill in rope work helped, as the painting was done on belays from the ridge (Fig. 72); Mark Slaney remembers that the lower parts had to be painted with hot bitumen while hanging upside down from the ladder.[61] While this work progressed Anthony Nowlan stripped out and refitted the old toilet and all the flooring (Fig. 73), work which was aided by the pleasing if surprising discovery that French plumbing used British Imperial sizes.[45] For good measure later Balliol and Univ parties dug drainage trenches around the perimeter and installed permeable 'Leuco-Drain' piping to take rainwater away from the building.

Catching the general mood of enthusiasm, Christopher Cox decided to open up the store at the back of the Chalet, which had not been in use for years. This revealed it to be almost completely full of empty wine and spirits bottles, an excess which he was inclined to attribute solely to the habits of Balliol and Univ parties.[45]

The kitchen took a step towards modernity in 1979 when Harvey McGregor offered the purchase of a gas-fired fridge.[82] On his visits to the Chalet he had been in the habit of preparing cold cucumber soup and lemon mousse (both of which he entered in the Chalet Cookery Book), which had to be chilled in the stream for want of anything better.[55] The trustees were quick to see the benefits and accepted gladly. The following two seasons were less positive: the next opening party found sewage seeping through the ground around the disused ground-floor toilet and contractors had to be brought in to install a new *fosse septique*, a cesspit of multiple chambers.[83] Concern over problems with the *fosse* and difficulties in getting repairs have prompted parties since to burn all toilet paper as a matter of policy. In 1981 the frame of the loft skylight was also found to be broken and the loft suffering from water penetration.[84] The trustees were far from being out of the wood.

Throughout this period there is a sense of underlying anxiety in communications passing among the trustees. This is hardly surprising, as they had become responsible for a large building in an isolated spot on a mountain and, unlike today when many people have some acquaintance with DIY, their level of skill was limited. It is easy to see how Edward Forman's proposals were seized on with relief. Christopher Cox had been right when he perceived that support from the Hottegindres would be vital. He was keen that Claude Pognan should be retained for annual advice but sadly the mason succumbed to cancer and died in 1979. He had steadfastly refused any payment on the basis that those at the Chalet were friends of the family.

The mood of anxiety is reflected in the trustees' response to the visit of Gilbert Blanc from the Commune to renew the boundary markers on the Chalet's land. The trustees had assumed that the ground between the two streams separating the two chalets was theirs but M. Blanc confirmed that it belonged to the Commune and understandably dismissed the trustees' historical claim to this land as 'Mesopotamia' as an irrelevance.[85] Worse, he floated the rumour that this land might be the site of a new *téléski*. A call to Roger Mynors confirmed that the Chalet had no title to this land but the threat of an invasion between the two chalets put the trustees, especially an appalled Christopher Cox, into a flurry of activity to establish the facts.[86] Such rumours often arise in French local planning and Jeremy Lever, with his greater understanding of international law, was able to prevent the dust being raised further by insisting that legal opinion should be taken only if the suggestion became a reality.[87] In fact, calm study of the map and topography would have shown the trustees that the land there offered no suitable site for any ski run that could be served by such a lift. A new ski lift was later installed on the south side of the jeep track, well away from both chalets.

A more concrete anxiety occurred in 1978 when the company running the TMB mooted closure, aggravated by the summer closure of the chairlift from Col de Voza to the Prarion.[88] This was a traditional approach to the Chalet and Christopher Cox mobilised his New College connections in its support. Sir Patrick Reilly had moved into banking but raised the issue with his successor in Paris, Sir Nicholas Henderson.[89] The ambassador knew the Rothschild family, who owned the TMB company, and when lunching with them pressed the case for the TMB, commenting in his diary, perhaps drily, that its continuation was 'said by Patrick Reilly and Jeremy Lever to be essential to the maintenance of the famous Sligger Urquhart chalet'.[90] This was hardly the most pressing item on his agenda; Anglo–French relations had been strained for some years, most recently over fishing rights. Contact was established with the local TMB manager, who confirmed that the company needed to reduce costs and the proposal was to reduce the service rather than abandon it.[91] In the event, the TMB service did reduce in frequency and the chairlift closed for the summers.

In retrospect it is difficult to see why this issue caused concern because a *télécabine* had been running from Les Houches to the hotel since the early 1970s, as Jeremy Lever admitted.[92] This offered a more convenient means of getting onto the mountain, followed by a downhill walk to the Chalet. Further, Simone Hottegindre could obtain concessionary tickets and the approach was described in the parties' guidance notes, though only as a fall-back from the TMB.[93] Perhaps their view was dominated by the long tradition of access from Saint Gervais. In the event, by 1982 Jeremy Lever was noting that the TMB had been little used since the summer closure of the *télésiège* and that the *télécabine* had become the standard approach to the Chalet.[94] Quite apart from offering an easy downhill walk it has the advantage of introducing travellers to the Prarion Hotel at the start of their visit. However, there is a complication for first-time chaletites, namely that when the Boucher chalet appears below them in the trees they tend to assume that they have arrived.[95]

An event that might have caused more ripples in the Chalet's community, especially in view of its intimate environment, was the admission of women to the exclusively male undergraduate colleges in 1979. In fact this innovation appears almost to have passed without notice as far as the reading parties were concerned. For one thing, women had been regular guests, even of the bachelor-led New College and Univ parties, and the Balliol parties had a family atmosphere, as we have seen. Caroline Kay, one of two female members who joined the New College party in 1980, commented that their presence seemed completely unremarkable.[96] In fact any lack of turbulence was almost certainly due to the fact that by the time it happened this event was old news. Many colleges had been pressing for mixed admissions for most of the 1970s.[97] The University, having initially acknowledged concerns among the women's colleges over competition, eventually approved an experimental admission of women to five of the men's colleges in 1974. When this came up for review the University proposed a voluntary ballot for the other men's colleges to compete for mixed admissions. This was promptly overridden by those colleges which did not win a place in the ballot and all but two went ahead and admitted their first women students in Michaelmas term 1979.[98] Further, by the time women students were invited to the Chalet they had completed their first year and any novelty on either side had no doubt worn off. The proportion of women chaletites rose steadily over the next few years, in line with their increasing presence in the colleges.

In 1979 Jeremy Lever brought chaplain Bill Sykes and Iain McLean (Fig. 74) into the Univ parties and Iain subsequently introduced his wife Jo. Iain, a keen walker, remembers that his first two years were dedicated to trying to climb Mont Blanc, succeeding at the second attempt, and that only four days later the same group climbed the Gran Paradiso in Italy (4,061 m).[99] He also took part in efforts to clear the track to the rear of the Chalet, as it had become overgrown. With better French than Bill Sykes, he developed good relations with the Hottegindres and reintroduced the Italian circuit walk, doing it with Jeremy Lever, who he found 'slow but relentless'.[99] Unusually among party leaders, he was also skilled in the croissant run to Saint Gervais. Iain's involvement came to an end when he left for a professorial chair at Warwick University but he retained his love of the Alps, frequently calling in at the Chalet when in the area.

Bill Sykes would lead parties for the next sixteen years. As chaplain he was well placed to select and invite Univ members and, a man of gentle and calm strength with a natural good humour, he fostered a spirit of camaraderie in groups from a diverse cross-section of the college.[100,101] Felix Mayr-Harting (Chalet 1989–90) recalls that he made the environment feel free while exerting gentle control and a sense of order.[102] Andy Baker (Chalet 1986) recalls leaving Bill's room at Univ bemused that he had been offered a place but after his visit came to regard the Chalet as one of the ways that Univ made its members welcome.[103]

Having served in the Gurkha Rifles during National Service, Bill Sykes had a lasting love for Nepal and its people and was a strong walker.[104] He introduced to the Univ parties the principle that they walk as a group, alternating walking days with reading ones (many experienced hill-walkers like the efficiency of this). Walks tended to be day-long, with an early start in the crisp morning air. Back at the Chalet there would be plenty of Chalet tennis and the croissant run became a staple item, as it did for the other colleges during this period. While morning reading was taken seriously the evenings were light-hearted, with a tendency over dinner to choose a theme for the worst puns members could come up with.[102] Members noted how Bill could always join in the fun without losing his dignity.

As always Christopher Cox was inclined to fret about the changes. Having initially been impressed with both Iain and Bill, he began to wonder if they needed support from more senior colleagues at Univ or whether they were sufficiently skilled in such mysteries as closing for the season, and he shared his concerns with Tony Firth, who remained the Univ trustee.[105,106] Both Bill Sykes and Iain McLean in fact showed their mettle as party leaders and Christopher's feelings may have been no more than those of an elderly man who must have known that with failing health at the age of eighty-two his own influence would soon come to an end.

It is a mark of his dedication that Christopher found it very difficult to let the Chalet go. By 1981 he recognised that the walk between the Chalet and the hotel was beyond him and he accepted the suggestion of his friends Hugh and Yvonne Dinwiddy that the next year he should stay at the hotel with them and keep an eye on the Chalet party from there.[107] Christopher himself would have been quick to see the parallels with Sligger's final years. Sadly it was not to be because he became too ill to travel before the 1982 season began. Warden Arthur Cooke went out to the Chalet for the start of the season but was obliged to return to Oxford when he heard the news that Christopher had died on 6 July. It was a moment of great sadness in the history of the Chalet, as the anonymous diarist of New College Second Party recognised in writing the single entry, 'We did most of the usual things but we did none of them without thinking of how much more we should have enjoyed them in the presence of Christopher Cox. So we record emptiness.'

The death of Christopher Cox brought to an end a chapter in the Chalet's history. He was the last representative of those who could speak from personal experience of Sligger and while he had by no means tried to anchor the Chalet's practice in Sligger's time, his view of Chalet tradition had been so strong that without him it was inevitable that life at the Chalet would change, at least for members of New College.

Tributes to Christopher Cox were many and fulsome and it is testimony to the importance he attached to the Chalet that it figured prominently. In a memorial address his friend Herbert Hart said that the Chalet had been the chief focus of his later years: 'he worked long and successfully with others to secure for this cherished institution a sound financial and physical basis, and had gently fostered the re-interpretation of its traditions, so that mixed reading parties in the Long Vacations became firmly established in the life of three Colleges'.[108] Nelleriek Boucher wrote to Arthur Cooke to say that he 'gave us and our children a lasting love'.[109] For Stephen Tucker, who knew him well from nearly ten years' parties, 'he was himself a living contact with an historical culture which was eccentric, humane, at the centre of political affairs yet humorously detached as well'.[55] From a personal point of view I number myself among those who can regret not having shared the Chalet with him.

The trustees naturally wanted a suitable memorial to be placed in the Chalet. The possibilities discussed included a fruit bowl or a photograph of him in his characteristic position on the south-west porch.[110,111] Finally, a pencil portrait was installed at the Chalet alongside the portraits of Sligger and Strachan-Davidson.

The death of Christopher Cox presented New College with a problem, so close had been his identification with the parties. His practice of working through junior lieutenants like Allen Warren and Edward Forman had ensured that no colleague had been fully prepared for taking over the senior role. Warden Arthur Cooke wrote to Tony Kenny to say there was need to find a new trustee – no tutorial fellow of New College had been engaged in the parties except George Forrest (Fig. 75), who had been invited by Christopher in 1980 and had spent a week there that year and in 1981.[113] Stephen Tucker had greater experience of the Chalet but had left New College for a parish in Hove. Harvey McGregor, although a frequent visitor, had not run parties, so George Forrest was elected to the Board. This gave New College two representatives, the Warden and George Forrest, so the trustees took the opportunity to expand the Balliol presence by inviting Jonathan Barnes onto the Board to join Tony Kenny.

George Forrest was a Classics Tutor and may have been recommended by Christopher Cox but the two men were very different.[55] Christopher was a liberal imperialist, George a Marxist and atheist. However, he had shown an interest in the Chalet which would have appealed to Christopher when in 1980 he conducted an excavation of the ruin of Sligger's chapel behind the Chalet. By this time the woodshed/stable had collapsed and was good only for firewood. George tickled Christopher by claiming his excavation had found evidence that Hannibal and his elephants had passed that way in their invasion of Italy.[55]

George Forrest took a democratic approach to the parties, widening the selection process; sign-up sheets were posted in the Common Rooms and selection made from them.[55] He abandoned the New College claim on the first month of the season, allowing an equal rotation of colleges throughout the summer, and the Chalet moved to a pattern in which each college had two parties of around ten days each. He continued the New College pattern of morning reading and free choice of activity thereafter but under his leadership dress at

the Chalet became much less formal.[55,113] He also oversaw the introduction of sleeping bags for the New College parties, which eased
some of the tensions over managing the laundry. George may have
been behind an attempt to sell Sligger's Della Robbia reliefs from the
chapel, which were now housed in the Chalet.

In one respect George would not have appealed at all to Sligger:
he had a taste for heavy smoking and drinking and when he later
introduced his colleague and friend Noel Worswick (Fig. 75) it was
said that they would see the reading morning set up and then repair
to the hotel for an alcoholic breakfast.[43] There were those who felt
George to be less in sympathy with undergraduates but Rob Poynton
(Chalet 1983–4) found that he had no difficulty in treating undergraduates as friends and after his Chalet trips Rob took to dropping into
George's rooms at New College: visits were usually accompanied by
a drink, often 'half a pint of lukewarm Martini'.[114] George Forrest
would remain the engaged New College fellow and trustee for nearly
ten years. When Arthur Cooke retired in 1985 he was replaced as
Warden by Harvey McGregor, who also joined the Trust Board and
continued to be a visitor to the Chalet but did not lead parties.

Another change which George made was to replace the junior
fellows who assisted the parties with undergraduate or graduate students. This policy had mixed results, as George followed Christopher's
policy of giving them their head in managing the party. Niggles over
handover continued and in 1985 Jeremy Lever was moved to warn
that the New College approach needed more engagement from the
trustee if equipment was not to be lost or broken and if diary entries
were to be considered appropriate.[115,116]

Just how effective some of the New College junior managers
could be is illustrated by a later contribution. Since the loss of Louis
Broisat and his mule in the 1960s delivery of food in the necessary
amount could be problematic: Lila Boucher recalls that in the late
1960s Max Hottegindre had difficulty getting his jeep close to the
chalets and stopped at the nearby turning for La Charme and blew
his horn so that both chalets could send out runners to collect the
stores.[69] Further, as Les Houches became the chalets' main source of
supplies it was necessary to transport goods from the hotel or the *télécabine*. As we have seen, parties had become expert at manhandling
barrels of wine down the hill without letting them roll down to Saint
Gervais but bulk orders of groceries were less manoeuvrable.

Christie Bolton, manager of the 1992 party, saw the need and back home in Ireland her father Mike constructed a mountain trolley with the aid of her twelve-year-old brother Eric.[117] Having been a military engineer Mike Bolton was familiar with using what came to hand and the trolley was based on two Honda 50 motorcycle wheels, ideal for irregular ground. The frame was of light but strong tubular steel and the base and walls were steel mesh. There was a long steel handle which could be used as a yoke by two chaletites and – vital for moving heavy loads on steep inclines – brakes on both wheels controlled from the handle. The trolley was delivered by car by Noel Worswick, and George Forrest named it 'Christelle' in tribute to Christie's inspiration.[118] 'Christelle' served faithfully for many years, bringing down such items as new stoves and mattresses as well as groceries, until a much later redevelopment of the rear track made vehicle deliveries to the back door possible.

An example of how the Chalet could attract interest is provided by an unexpected visit from a Paris professor of International Studies in 1985. Roger Lhombreaud had been a research student at Merton College in the 1950s and his attention was caught when he read in a French magazine that on the Prarion there was a chalet owned by the University. He and his wife holidayed regularly in Saint Gervais and so in August took the opportunity to investigate. When they found Tony Kenny's party playing cricket they decided not to intrude but Roger sent a letter the next day to say he was mystified how Oxford students came to be there.[119] The next party, Jeremy Lever's, invited them to tea a week later and presumably satisfied some of the Professor's curiosity. In another visit in 1986 the Lhombreauds entertained the Univ party to drinks and ice cream at the hotel and left them with some press cuttings from *Le Monde* they thought might be of interest, one of them relating to real tennis. What Roger Lhombreaud doesn't appear to have shared with them was that he had been a teenage Resistance fighter and had also written the biography of the Victorian poet Arthur Symons.[120] Sligger would surely have applauded this contact.

By the late 1980s the wood of the Chalet had endured both the summer heat and winter frosts of nearly eighty years and not surprisingly had suffered. There were also repeated challenges with the water supply and the *fosse septique*, and the exterior rendering was wearing badly, as was the wood cladding to the front which bore the

brunt of the Alpine sun.[116] Many window frames and shutters had
warped and were poorly fitting, the roof needed repainting and most
of the gutters were failing. Internally the kitchen floor and walls
needed renovating and the trustees were concerned about the state
of the flooring throughout. The chimney functioned erratically and
a lot of the furniture was damaged.[116]

The residue from the 1970s appeal had brought in around £1,000
a year but insurance and French property taxes accounted for around
two thirds of this and covenants were running out.[121] After dealing
with other costs such as laundry, breakages and a new stove there was
little left for even the most essential work. It was clear to the trustees
that another appeal would be needed and the Board decided that it
would be appropriate to base this on the approaching 1991 centenary
of Sligger's first reading party.[122]

In the meantime the most pressing issues had to be addressed.
The cost of employing craftsmen in the mountain environment has
always been high and after the example of 1978 the trustees hoped that
savings could be made by using volunteers. In 1986 Jonathan Barnes
raised a party of volunteers and with the support of Philosophy colleague Jim Hankinson he relaid some of the kitchen floor and made
repairs to the first-floor shutters.[123] They also investigated cracks in
the rendering on the rear stone wall and concluded that the stucco
needed replacement; Jonathan Barnes proposed a volunteer working
party for the first month of the 1987 season with the aim of replacing
the rendering and also part of the ground-floor wood cladding.[123]

Anyone embarking on a large DIY project knows that they rarely
go as smoothly or quickly as envisaged. The 1987 works party (Fig.
80) was no different but was also unlucky with unforeseen events.[124]
For example a Lada 4x4 vehicle hired for support suffered successively a ruptured fuel pipe, a flat battery and the collapse of part
of its steering; these vehicular failures are bad under normal conditions but much worse on a mountain. The first cement mixer to
be delivered was an electric model and had to be replaced; Matthew
Taylor (Chalet 1983–5 & 1987) recalls manhandling its successor up
the overgrown rear track to the Chalet, part of which had been lost
in a landslide.[125] Regular work was impeded by rain throughout the
month and slowed by journeys for more materials when it turned out
that the suppliers' original estimates were inadequate.[124] The chimney
was found to be leaking into the upstairs rooms and the group had

to manage without proper heating. Five days in, the toilet drainage blocked; an earth closet was constructed on the hillside using one of Sligger's cane chairs with the seat cut out, giving it a fine mountain view, as Jonathan Barnes noted.[124] Matthew Taylor occupied it one night during a storm and felt he might have been in a production of Wagner's *Die Walküre*.[125]

As parties through the decades have found, events can move very slowly on the mountain. It was three days before scaffolding and sufficient materials had reached the Chalet to allow a start and, as most supplies had to be dropped either at the Boucher chalet or at the bottom of the rear track, considerable time was spent on the exhausting work of moving them by hand.[124] Jonathan Barnes estimated that by the end of the month they had transported around 16 tons of material in this way.

Stripping the old rendering proved arduous and slow. Some fell away easily but hard chiselling by hand was required for the rest.[124] When there was no rain the sun was hot and they found that a few hours' work was all that was possible without a rest. Work also had to be suspended each time the scaffolding was moved to a new position. They were helped by the fact that successive workers arrived in relays while others retired home to recuperate; Jonathan Barnes was adept at declaring a rest day when he judged that the party was nearing its limit. It took eleven days to remove all the old rendering while some prepared the wooden walls for replacing the cladding.

The process of new rendering proved to be little better. A false start was rectified when their supplier, Gérard Marthelet, pointed out that the ratios for the mix had been misunderstood but even so the work remained hard and proceeded slowly.[126] M. Marthelet, who became a regular visitor and, one suspects, also counsellor out of sympathy for what these British academic amateurs had taken on, advised that the rendering should be protected with a sealing coat of Roquenduit. Jonathan Barnes was inclined to despair of completing the work in time but M. Marthelet produced the solution: an air-compressed mortar sprayer for a hire of £200.[124] It was a pity that the one which arrived broke down two days later, and M. Marthelet had to be called in again. The device eventually allowed the group to complete the rendering and top seal, three weeks after the work had begun. The cladding was also completed by the end of the month, despite also involving unforeseen challenges.

Moving heavy materials and performing arduous manual work combined with little heating, primitive toilet facilities and frequent journeys for supplies on challenging mountain roads inevitably took their toll on the party's energy. The group also found that the mortar irritated their skin badly. The daily journal which Jonathan Barnes made of their progress speaks of fatigue, aching muscles, showering that could be painful and evenings in the salon 'in stupefied exhaustion'.[124] His daughter Catherine, who had recently graduated, took on the cooking and recalls that it seemed to rain almost all the time and that tempers became frayed.[127] Under these conditions setbacks were particularly hard to bear; one of Jonathan's entries reads: 'A depressing day: the more we do, the more we discover to do.'[124] One afternoon he dispatched two chaletites in the Lada to shop in Saint Gervais and to refill the wine barrel. Well into the return journey they realised that they had forgotten to pick up the barrel: Charles Garland (Chalet 1984–7) reports that it was only the thought of arriving back at the party without the wine that made a three-point turn possible on the jeep track.[126]

After Jonathan Barnes' party had surrendered the Chalet to Tony Kenny's party, Gérard Marthelet moved in to repair the chimney and toilet drain. The following year another Barnes works party again had their challenges: this time the kitchen drain collapsed and needed to be replaced and, in a way that is depressingly familiar to party leaders since, they found that many of their tools had been lost during the previous year's parties.[124] However, they were able to complete the wood cladding on the front and west ground-floor walls and to dig out the foundations and repoint and seal them. Their plan to repaint the roof was defeated only by the late delivery of the bitumen paint.

The achievement has to be admired: these doughty volunteers left the Chalet in much better condition and thirty years on the rendering shows little sign of deterioration. They also saved the Trust a large sum: when he saw what was being tackled Gérard Marthelet estimated that the rendering alone would have cost 200,000 francs if done by a professional.[124] This was equivalent to around £20,000 then.

The 1987 works had cost £14,000 in total and the appeal was not yet in existence. To cover this the Trust secured interest-free loans of £2,500 from the three colleges, and also from All Souls College due to Jeremy Lever's fellowship there, topped up by a personal loan from

Jeremy.[122,128] The outstanding work was estimated at between £30,000 and £40,000 and the trustees also wanted to establish an endowment which would allow a regular programme of maintenance to go forward; this would mean doubling the Trust's annual income. The target for the appeal was therefore set at £100,000.[122]

The response was excellent, with more than two hundred old chaletites contributing. However, the majority of donations, as in the previous appeal, were in the form of covenants, some of them for ten years. The total projected income was nearly £60,000, of which two thirds had been received by 1990.[129] This was well below the target and set against this were outstanding bills for the *fosse septique* and chimney replacements, as well as repayment of loans, so that by 1991 there was a surplus of only £21,000.[130] Much of this was eaten up by unavoidable costs over the next ten years and the aim of regular maintenance had necessarily to be curtailed. To help, the rent requested from each party had been increased to £30 a week and the Trust was further helped when New College and Univ agreed to convert their loans into gifts.[129,131,132] Despite this it would take until 2000 for the trustees to achieve their aim of doubling the annual income from the endowment.[133]

After the 1987 season an event of great sadness hit the Chalet community. Max and Simone Hottegindre had been running the Hôtel du Prarion for thirty-five years when they decided to retire to the family home in Saint Gervais, though they still wanted to stay in contact with Chalet parties.[134] In 1982 they had invited their third son, Yves, back from California to help and he became the new *patron*. In January 1988 the couple were motoring in the valley with two of their granddaughters when the car hit roadworks that were obscured by snow and overturned, killing Max and one of the girls, Sophie-Marine.[135] This was the sad loss at the young age of sixty-six of a man who had loyally supported Chalet parties throughout all their needs even though he never had any obligation to the Chalet or its leaders. The trustees were very conscious of his help and in 1986 had approached the Hebdomadal Council of the University to ask if he could be awarded an honorary degree; unfortunately the Council had taken the view that his support did not represent the academic contribution for which the degree was intended.[123]

The accident was a hard event for a couple who had worked long and steadily at developing the Hôtel du Prarion and had intended to enjoy their retirement together. Simone returned to the hotel, where as 'Madame' she has retained a keen interest in the Chalet and its students and proved an informative and stimulating conversation companion. As parties since then have found, Yves Hottegindre has been as loyal a support as his father, and has borne out Christopher Cox's belief that the hotel is essential to the survival of the parties. Yves has often regarded the *crises*, large or small, which can afflict parties with a quiet tolerance and amusement, a characteristic which many have said was also part of his father's personality. As the hotel has remained a focus for the family, successive party leaders have had the pleasure of knowing the other members, Yves' brothers Georges, Pierre and Olivier, and sister Claudine and their offspring, in what has become a large extended family. Not for nothing have Chalet leaders been able to speak since Christopher's time of '*La Grande Amitié*', the great friendship between the Hottegindre family and the Chalet des Anglais.

The following year the Chalet suffered its own tragedy when a Univ member had a fatal fall. Andrew Stillwell had entered Univ in 1986 and had distinguished himself as captain of the hockey and squash teams, also rowing and playing tennis and lacrosse.[136] A popular member of college and of the chapel choir, he had an enthusiasm for life that his peers found infectious. He was already a skilled climber and proved to be an active member of Jeremy Lever's August party. On 1 September Andy was descending from Pointe Inférieure above Col de Tricot when he slipped in a couloir and suffered a serious head injury.[137] The mountain rescue service lifted him off the mountain in a commendably short time and he was later transferred to Geneva for intensive care.

Andy Stillwell never recovered consciousness, dying in Geneva on 9 September. Jeremy Lever recorded in a retrospective note in the diary the great grief of the party at his loss. The following year Andy's parents joined the Univ party and walked to Col de Tricot, where they scattered flowers from some Andy had planted at home: this could have been a sombre occasion but those there felt that it was invested with a *joie de vivre* typical of Andy's personality.[102] In his memory his friends raised money for a new boat for the Univ boat house.[138] He is also commemorated by a plaque in the antechapel at Univ and his photograph hangs in the Chalet.

This tragedy was a reminder of the ever-present dangers of the mountain environment. In his report to the trustees Jeremy Lever emphasised that even the most skilled walker or climber is at risk of accident.[137] There have been many such accidents over the decades at the Chalet and thankfully most have been mild but this was one event where an accident operated to deprive a fine young man of his future.

Jeremy Lever also wrote to resign from the Trust, emphasising as he did so that the decision had been taken before the season began but that he felt it had become progressively more difficult for him to put together parties from Univ and that Bill Sykes was much better placed to do this.[139] He included a plea that all trustees should be fully engaged in the parties and in management and maintenance, pointing out that a disproportionate responsibility was being laid on Jonathan Barnes. He invited his New College colleagues – albeit highly respectfully – to review their practice, in all probability an allusion to reliance on junior managers and its variable results.

In fact this was a time of significant change, both within the Trust and in the leadership of the parties. Of those who had founded the Trust and retained control since, Christopher Cox had died, Tony Firth had resigned and Jeremy Lever had asked to leave but in fact agreed to stay on for a couple of years until Univ found a replacement. At New College Arthur Cooke had retired as Warden and was replaced by Harvey McGregor. David Burgess and Iain McLean, who had never been trustees, had moved on, Jonathan Barnes was about to leave for a post in Geneva and Jim Hankinson was moving to the United States. Ian Rumfitt (Chalet 1984–91 & 1994), who had supported Jonathan both as undergraduate and graduate (in doing so confirming his own vocation to academic Philosophy), was also moving on.[140] In 1990 Tony Kenny went to Rhodes House to take up the Wardenship and introduced a single Rhodes House party to the season but would give up the Trust Board in 1994.

The only trustees remaining who had served any time were Harvey McGregor, who was now Warden of New College and whose visits to the Chalet in recent years had been limited to a few days, George Forrest, whose continuing commitment to the Chalet would be dogged by poor health, and Bill Sykes. The next few years would see an influx of new leaders who would be fully engaged in both the reading parties and in the management of the Trust.

At the same time, the trustees were still in the position where finance remained a serious concern. It has to be said that without the generosity of past chaletites and the willingness of the colleges to support the Trust, it is difficult to see how the Chalet could have survived this period; at times survival must have seemed tenuous at best. In view of this it is perhaps surprising that the trustees declined requests from people who wanted to rent the Chalet and did not pursue the approach from a television company who wanted to film there.[131] The pattern of the 1991 appeal had proved similar to that of the previous one in generating a slow if steady income and since 1971 the financial management of the Chalet had been driven by recurrent crises in which, after the immediate need had been met, the momentum of maintaining the Chalet was lost. When Jeremy Lever wrote to resign from the Trust he warned of the need to sustain a regular programme of maintenance.[139] As we shall see, this advice went largely unheeded for ten years and resulted in a far greater effort being required in the future.

The Trust was now established thanks to the efforts of the first trustees and had successfully provided two decades of reading parties but the entire period had been dominated by financial concerns and crises in the fabric. In retrospect it is easy to see that the time had arrived when the Trust needed stability and long-term continuity of purpose. These would come in 1994 when the chairmanship was assumed by the seventy-year-old barrister and Warden of New College, Harvey McGregor, who, unlike any of his predecessors, would hold this position for the next twenty years.

CHAPTER SEVEN

RENEWAL: BUILDING THE MODERN APPROACH

WHEN UNIV CHALETITE ACER NETHERCOTT (Chalet 2002–9 and 2011–12) died in January 2013 friends from the university and sporting worlds combined to celebrate a man who in his thirty-five years had accomplished more than many do in an entire lifetime.[1] A prize-winning undergraduate in Philosophy who went on to a doctorate, he was at the same time a long-distance cyclist, an Ironman who raised funds for charity and a leading rowing cox who returned from the 2008 Olympic Games with a silver medal. He believed in living life to the full and was vocal about it. He was also one of the most passionate of chaletites.

Acer's commitment to the Chalet began with his first visit when he acted as the party's bursar.[2] This was followed by another seven visits as an undergraduate and then postgraduate researcher. No one who knew Acer could overlook the fact that he believed fervently that life was to be lived but at the Chalet his spiritual side emerged powerfully. He was a natural facilitator of parties, keen to impress on other members the significance of being there and to enhance the opportunities it offered. His contributions were unfailingly positive, pushing the party in what he perceived to be the right direction: it was natural to invite him back as an assistant leader after he completed his doctorate. The party leaders soon learned to appreciate the significance of his quiet approach and gentle, 'Could we have a word?' as a prelude to change for the better.

No sportsman as accomplished as Acer could have disregarded the chance of expending large amounts of energy on the Prarion. He made all the usual serious ascents, Tête Rousse and the Jonction especially, together with ice-cold plunges into Lac Blanc. He undertook the croissant run during each of his seven parties and in 2009 was put out that he failed to beat his 2002 record by twenty seconds, unwilling to accept the difference that seven years make. Once I unguardedly commented that croissants were welcome but that sometimes one longed for a *tarte au citron*: predictably, a sweating Acer appeared at breakfast the next morning with a backpack of croissants, lovingly cradling a *tarte au citron* to his chest. When in 2009 the Univ party laid on entertainment for a gathering of old members for the centenary of the New Chalet he showed unexpected talent as a performer of Monty Python sketches.

When late in 2009 Acer learned that he had a fatal disease his response was characteristic; it was something to be faced and fought. He took an aggressive approach to his treatment, seeking out specialists who he felt offered the best chances and accepting the risks he took in the process; many in his place might have felt defeated but this was never Acer's way. In 2010 he was hoping to join another party but surgery and chemotherapy precluded it. He may have suspected this would be the case when earlier in the year he summed up his motivation by quoting a passage from the French spiritual writer René Daumal that must have had profound resonance for a man who knew that he was at risk of losing his eyesight:[3]

> You cannot stay on the summit for ever; you have to come down again. So why bother in the first place? Just this: what is above knows what is below but what is below does not know what is above. One climbs, one sees; one descends, one sees no longer, but one has seen. There is an art of conducting oneself in the lower regions by the memory of what one saw higher up. When one can no longer see, one can at least still know.

Remission allowed Acer a full part in the 2011 party, including all the walks. Those who knew the severity of his condition recognised it as a valedictory move when he donated his Olympic Games shirt to the collection of climbing shirts held by the Tête Rousse refuge; it still hangs there. Later that year the tide turned against him but despite this he announced his intention of seeing the Chalet once again if possible. By this time his condition was only intermittently promising but his optimism never faltered: he wrote, 'Getting the most out of life, and knowing that you lived; that's what the Lac Blanc swim and the croissant run in the rain are for ...'[3]

By good fortune one of his Univ contemporaries, Laura McDiarmid, was available to support him and made a 2012 visit possible. It was obvious on his arrival that he was a desperately ill man and there could be no question of joining the other members in any exertion, though his smile on arrival told its own story. In these circumstances it was alarming to find that he was determined to undertake the croissant run one last time and he did so, leaving the Chalet at dawn and reappearing not for breakfast as usual but for that night's dinner. Typically, he made virtue of necessity and claimed a new record for the Chalet: the longest croissant run ever.[2]

No one can know what that last Chalet party cost in determination and endurance but on one of the final afternoons he sat on the lawn warming himself in the sun and radiating his enjoyment of the Chalet to everyone around him. It was the action of a man for whom appreciation of the moment transcended any consideration of disease and death and to those who knew his condition it was intensely moving. When his will was published University College discovered that he had left half his estate for the support of the Chalet. It was a last, practical, expression of the mantra with which his conversations about the Chalet always ended: 'I really love that place.' No party leader who knew Acer could ever doubt the effect the Chalet can have on people's lives.

¤

The last decade of the twentieth century was a time of change for the Trust and for the Chalet. Bachelor dons were now rare and had been replaced by married Fellows with families, whose personal life was based outside their college. In their summer vacations the Chalet had to compete with family commitments and in the circumstances it is impressive that there were still those for whom commitment to the Chalet was so strong that they were prepared to make it a regular summer fixture.

In contrast to these shifts in society and University life the trustees were resolved that the character of the Chalet would change as little as possible. Within just a few years a new team took over the Trust under Harvey McGregor's chairmanship and the resolution of the incoming trustees was sustained just as strongly as it had been by their predecessors.

Chalet trustees have always been concerned that leaders might not be found because of the nature of modern academic life but in fact renewal of the Trust's membership was achieved easily. For Balliol their chaplain, Douglas Dupree, and Adam Swift, a political philosopher, replaced Jonathan Barnes. Later the Balliol representation was expanded by Dominic O'Brien, an engineer. For New College their previous chaplain, Stephen Tucker, finally made it onto the Board after nearly twenty years' support for the Chalet and when George Forrest died the new Warden of New College, Alan Ryan (Fig. 91), joined the Board. For Univ Keith Dorrington, a medical physiologist, was recruited by Bill Sykes and then joined by Mark Newton, a physicist, when Bill stood down. Ngaire Woods, an expert in government who had been a junior fellow at New College before fellowships at both Univ and Rhodes House, replaced Tony Kenny and the Board moved steadily towards its modern configuration of three representatives from each college, assisted by one from Rhodes House for as long as their parties continued.

These changes produced the widest spectrum of expertise that management of the Chalet had ever enjoyed. Philosophy was still reflected in the membership but supplemented in equal numbers by Government, Law, Medicine, Physics and Engineering. This was a long way from the History and Classics of Sligger's era and, indeed, the early post-war period. This could only work to the Trust's benefit and that it is exactly how it proved.

This leadership also offered the possibility of new partnerships. At Balliol Douglas Dupree turned to Carol Clark (Fig. 95), who had led parties in 1978 and 1986. Carol was a small, feisty Scot with an impish sense of humour; their joint leadership is described as creating a 'hilarious' party atmosphere and would last for fourteen years.[4] The Balliol archivist Anna Sander became a strong supporter of their parties, taking charge of the kitchen for the parties led by Douglas and his successors Nicola Trott and Bruce Kinsey. At New College Alan Ryan invited Allen Warren back to help maintain New College interest, resulting in a productive partnership with Stephen Tucker; this was particularly valuable, as Harvey McGregor, although representing the college, had never led parties and would continue to be only an occasional visitor.[5]

New College had the advantage that their policy of using junior managers had generated a number of people who had moved on but were still willing to come back and support the reading parties (Fig. 91). In this way old members such as Matthew Armstrong (Chalet from 1991), Rupert Griffin (from 1997), Adam Fergus (from 2000) and Alex Dickens (from 2008) became regular supporters; this has been one of the benefits of the New College approach. Univ parties have benefited similarly despite retaining their emphasis on trustee-led groups. John McMillan, the college's junior research fellow in Ethics and a keen mountaineer, helped four parties in the early 2000s and added the ascent of Mont Blanc to his achievements before returning to his native New Zealand. Acer Nethercott (Fig. 97) followed him as an assistant leader and later Univ's trustee, Tom Smith, introduced his brother Ben, a paediatric surgeon. Tom and Ben climbed Mont Blanc together in 2006 and Ben continued to help out with parties after Tom's departure for a position in London.

Harvey McGregor brought to the chairmanship of the Board a lawyer's *savoir-faire* that previously had been supplied by Jeremy Lever. He was a man of marked urbanity which tended to hide his determination in pursuit of improvement. At the same time it did not obscure an egocentric streak which was part of his personal drive and which had kept him practising with no question of retirement. Unless forced to write he liked to transact all business on the phone and was disinclined to be put off; we once discussed Chalet business while I was in a toilet cubicle in Zurich airport. At times this could be frustrating, especially if one was occupied (I myself had a busy practice in the Oxford hospitals), but was part of his sustained effort to keep the Trust moving forward.

When I was elected to the Board in 1999, as the new member of the team I offered to take the minutes, feeling that no one should be expected to both chair a meeting and record it. Harvey instantly replied that he had been about to suggest it. This was an entirely typical response; eyebrows sometimes rose around the Board when Harvey asserted ownership of an idea to which members might have felt they had a claim. But this was simply part of his personal identification with the job with which the Board had entrusted him. In the same way he absorbed me into the new concept of a management secretary for the Board and it was an embarrassingly long time before I realised I was being groomed for the future. He was also loyal and supportive: over the years we worked together I made mistakes but he was never critical, merely accepting the fact and moving on.

Harvey worked from the approach that anything was possible and that in all matters of argument the opposition was presumed insane. When we had problems with the local farmer grazing his sheep around our water supply and causing people to become ill he wrote the Commune a letter which on the surface was urbanity itself but contained a threat in every paragraph. When the Trust received notice of a hefty fine because the French land taxes had not been paid Harvey travelled to France and treated the inspector to an extensive lunch, returning with a 100 per cent rebate. There are times in life when a Harvey McGregor is irreplaceable.

It was sometimes possible, when meeting under Harvey's chairmanship, to feel that his affability weakened his grasp of the agenda but this was to mistake his approach. He was never less than fully prepared for a meeting but allowed discussion to range freely. As a result the Board meetings took on a relaxed atmosphere like a meeting of friends (Fig. 96). However, when one surveys the minutes from 1994 onwards the forward momentum is unmistakable.

Advances in management would have counted for nothing if the reading parties had not been successful. In fact, over the last three decades the parties have run with remarkably few problems, largely adhering to the established practices of each college. Adam Swift maintained the Balliol tradition of group study, doing so in a relaxed atmosphere of communal participation in chores and in evening games such as Mafia.[6] He also followed the Balliol practice of involving his children; in 2013 his son Danny would reappear as a Univ chaletite. Douglas Dupree, as Balliol's chaplain, arranged parties which were ecumenical as to subject groupings but took as his model Bill Sykes' Univ practice of alternating reading and walking.[7] Having wide contacts within Balliol he chose a mix of undergraduates and graduates but also upheld the Balliol tradition of discussing a single book or small selection.[7] His colleague Carol Clark brought to the Balliol parties her excellent grasp of French, among her other qualities.

The Univ parties under Keith Dorrington and Mark Newton continued Bill Sykes' practice of alternating reading and walking days with the expectation that the party would walk together. It became standard practice to hire a vehicle to extend the scope of walks. A popular trip was to Lac Blanc on the north side of the valley. This involved driving to the far side of Chamonix and a cable car and chairlift to where a largely level walk across the escarpment leads to a glacial lake. Here Keith introduced to Univ parties the practice of nude bathing in water that often has a glacier extending into it even at the height of summer (Fig. 87). It has to be said that only occasional members of Univ parties, unlike Sligger's, have followed this example of disinhibition. Even so, Lac Blanc has proved to be a popular bathing site despite its freezing waters and there is usually keen competition among swimmers to endure the cold water long enough to swim to the central rocky island. Lac Blanc is a popular destination generally, as it has a good café, and French tourists eating their lunch on the surrounding rocks are often moved to give a round of applause to *les rosbifs* who, whether clothed or not, plunge into the icy water.

George Forrest maintained the New College pattern of free choice in activities. He also followed the example of Christopher Cox in leading both New College parties each year, with the support of Noel Worswick and Stephen Tucker. The diary photographs of this time show a clearly ailing man but, in a manner that was similar to that of Sligger and Christopher Cox before him, he found the Chalet hard to let go; a clinician who cared for him in his final year claimed that it was the determination to get there a last time that sustained him.[8] He managed to do so for the final time in 1997 with the aid of Noel driving him and with his wife Margaret to manage his medication. He died just after that party and a couple of years later Noel Worswick withdrew. He cited reasons of health but so strong had been the collaboration with George that it is difficult not to believe that this was also a factor in his decision.

The Rhodes House parties introduced a different element, consisting as they did of international graduate students whose recruitment to the University is the *raison d'être* of the Rhodes Trust. Tony Kenny continued to lead the parties, often with his wife Nancy, until he handed over to Ngaire Woods. The parties still had a set text or topic and these comprised items of international importance, as befitted the interests of the membership. Walks tended to the more adventurous and Tony Kenny noted a strongly competitive element among this group; some who were not lucky enough to be invited were resentful, while some who were but were unprepared for the rustic nature of the Chalet asked why the Warden had brought them to 'a Third World compound'.[9]

However, accounts in the diary reflect almost complete contentment among the reading parties. Many feel that their leaders were the key factor in bringing together a congenial group on the mountain.[10,11,12] Reading was appreciated for being protected time;[13] Alexander Dragonetti (Chalet 2006–7) says that reading in the salon felt 'like something out of a Jane Austen novel'.[14] Rotas for domestic tasks were embraced cheerfully and games such as table tennis proliferated, although the Prarion Hotel had better facilities than the Chalet's small and unstable dining table, at least until it was replaced with something equal to the task some years later (Fig. 99).[14,15] Evening games involving the whole group become common in the diary reports and at least one New College party put on a variety revue.[14,15]

One feature which has become notable is the standard of cuisine that proves possible from facilities which barely go beyond those of a Victorian kitchen. Sharing out cooking duties often reveals the competitive streak of the young and there is a drive to better the efforts of the previous evening's team. It is staggering what has been produced in these circumstances, such as full roast meals and cuisine from around the world. Home-made bread makes a frequent appearance and parties have identified valuable local sources, such as fresh goat's cheese at farms at La Charme and Bionnassay. Few members today experience what Sligger's students regarded as spartan fare.

Rupert Griffin went further during his visits to the New College parties. Preparing a banquet for around twenty people with Calor gas stoves that never, because of the altitude, got as hot as needed, he found that *crème brûlée* could be created with the aid of an antique blowtorch; he also brought specialised kit such as piping tools from home.[10] Another move was to establish relations with a *crêperie* in Les Houches where its more extensive kitchen facilities allowed him to prepare delights such as salmon mousse to transport to the Chalet.[10]

It is inevitable in view of the timing of reading parties that some chaletites receive the results of their degree examination while they are at the Chalet. This experience becomes shared by the whole party, who are ready with congratulation or consolation as circumstances demand. Thankfully, for party leaders in particular, congratulation has tended to predominate and often stimulates an enhanced level of catering and entertainment. Being on the Prarion while waiting for this news can be stressful for some but for others provides a welcome distraction.

A very enjoyable feature of these years was the welcome at the Chalet du Rocher, where Hugues and Nelleriek Boucher traditionally offered tea and a tour of their chalet. Owing to Hugues Boucher's insistence on authentic restoration this retains many of the original features of David Urquhart's 1868 design, including the Turkish bath and Turkish arcading. It was a sad loss to the reading parties and the party leaders when Nelleriek Boucher died in 2016 but Hugues and the rest of his family continue to use the chalet and the friendship endures.

The Prarion Hotel has also proved a continuing presence in the parties' enjoyment of the mountain, with practical support or amused tolerance from Yves Hottegindre as the occasion indicates, together with the interest of his mother Simone in young people especially. Drinks at the hotel (still known as the '*Pavillon*' or '*Pav*' to New College members) feature at the end of most walking days; sometimes the evening cooking team have to be encouraged to drink up and get down to the Chalet to start work. All parties now sustain the tradition of a final evening's dinner at the hotel, often consisting of shared cheese fondue with its ability to stimulate conversation. As Christopher Cox predicted in the 1950s, it is difficult to see how parties could succeed so well without these associations.

My own introduction to the Chalet came in 1996 and while my story is only one example of how the Chalet interacts with us it does provide an illustrative viewpoint. Keith Dorrington, on hearing that I had become interested in hill walking, invited me to assist him and I confess that I approached this with some anxiety, never having enjoyed anything like camping. I recall that when we drove past a hotel near Chamonix I thought that it would provide a fall-back if the Chalet proved unbearable. I need not have worried: as for so many chaletites before me, my first ascent in the *télécabine* to the view of Mont Blanc, together with introduction to Yves Hottegindre and his family at the Prarion Hotel and my first sight of the Chalet itself were sufficient to dispel any fears and the effects have not worn off after twenty-five years.

Keith Dorrington had put together a particularly happy group for 1996's first Univ party (the second, which closed the season, was led by Mark Newton), including several medical students and members of the chapel choir with whom I had much in common. I also found the Univ model of alternating study days and outings to be congenial and surprised myself with how much ascent proved bearable at this altitude. However, the most powerful experience was simply the conversation, both while out walking on the slopes and also back at the Chalet, especially over dinner, a practice on which Keith Dorrington puts particular emphasis.[16] When I returned to Univ in the autumn I had a new vision of the relationship between tutor and student and I knew by then I was not alone in finding this to be one of the best effects of the Chalet.

In 1996 we took over from Douglas Dupree, who was leading his first party. Douglas had been unfortunate with the weather, having been rained in for most of his stay, an eventuality which most leaders rightly fear. He had also had the problem that Carol Clark had become sick and had to move into the Prarion Hotel. After this poor introduction to Chalet life he freely admitted that the fact the party had stayed owed much to just a few positive individuals who kept up the spirits of the others. We, on the other hand, had perfect weather for ten days, which greatly enhanced the pleasures of the walks.

Like others before me, I rolled up my sleeves for some DIY, which included replacing a leaking toilet cistern; like many, I had been delighted to find the Chalet equipped with a flush toilet.[16] At the plumbers' merchant in the valley I found that sign language works when one hasn't acquired the necessary vocabulary (a *chasse d'eau*) and I returned to the Chalet with the cistern borne in a bear-hug. Installation went smoothly and Keith Dorrington was kind enough to report to the trustees that the Chalet had found an enthusiastic new leader. We began to prepare 1997 together; Keith planned to make one of his ascents of Mont Blanc and aimed to use Univ First Party with Mark to acclimatise and then join me for Second Party after his ascent. However, mountains have a way of interfering with human plans. The night before I was due to leave the UK he telephoned to say he had returned to Oxford in view of the altitude effects of a successful ascent of the mountain. I was on my own.

The advance party of myself, my elder daughter Marina and one of our medical students had arranged beds at a youth hostel for our first night but we discovered on arrival that the person I had dealt with had left the company and my reservation would not be honoured. The fact that I had printed confirmation was met with a characteristic Gallic shrug; the hostel was simply full. They did, however, suggest another hostel, in Chamonix, where we arrived to discover a parade in progress and the hostel difficult to locate. The traffic diversions proved tedious to cope with and, finally, as we passed the rear of the Richemond Hotel for the third time, my patience ran out and I told my companions I was booking us in. The elderly patron M. Sarraz could not have been more welcoming; the hotel, although small by Chamonix standards, had been built in 1913 in the heyday of the expansion of Chamonix of which Sligger so strongly disapproved, and had remained in the hands of his family and retained many original features. I didn't know at that time it had also been the local Gestapo headquarters during the war. Throwing open the shutters the next morning to a stunning sunlit view of Mont Blanc remains one of my best memories. Since then Keith Dorrington and I have frequently used the Richemond for our arrival and departure, and M. Sarraz became a valued acquaintance until his death in 2017 at the age of ninety-seven. The hotel is now in the hands of his son Bruno and daughter Claire.

My 1997 guidebook on mountain craft had told me of the dangers which the environment can pose. In the event, we had no avalanches or landslides and my party proved positive, congenial and successful. However, one warning in my book was that the unexpected cannot be prepared for. This had already happened with Keith's departure for Oxford but more was to come. On a Sunday evening late in our stay we were relaxing after dinner following a day's outing to Col de Tricot. For an Anglican equivalent to Sligger's services at the Chalet I had offered those interested the chance to read the Compline service in candlelight in the dining room before going to bed, but just before the service the door opened and a stranger with backpack walked in, announcing that he had arrived early for his college's party the next day.

In view of what ensued I should name neither the individual nor the college. Having had a problematic journey which had lasted thirty-two hours our guest had arrived late in the valley and had walked up to the Chalet in the dark, never having undertaken the Saint Gervais walk before. He was plainly exhausted but was insistent that we were expecting his college the next morning, when I was just as clear we had a couple of days to run before handing over to a different college. His assertion that his party's notes confirmed his view was not at all encouraging: I had a full Chalet and incorrect scheduling of another party would not be the easiest of challenges to surmount. When the notes were produced it emerged that this was a simple confusion: he had arrived a month early.

This discovery was the culminating exhaustion of a long journey and he was put to bed in a room which was vacant because its occupants were at the Goûter refuge that night in an attempt on Mont Blanc. In the meantime, after a tiring walking day and dinner wine, my party fell apart in hysterics. One member joked that our newcomer could do the croissant run, with the advantage of having a month in which to get back. We did the Compline service, although not surprisingly this wasn't easy with laughter from the non-participants echoing through the Chalet; there was no eye contact around the table. That night as I lay down to sleep I could feel the building still quivering with giggling.

Before bed I had telephoned Keith in Oxford to let him know what had happened. Word came back from his college the next morning that our visitor was indeed a bona fide undergraduate and that I was to show him the door when he was awake. This was clearly too harsh a treatment of one of our own kind in a foreign land and when he woke I discovered that his Chalet party was meant to be the start of a month's European travel with a friend, which was now in jeopardy. So I was relieved when my party agreed that he should join us and I am glad to say that a couple of days later the incoming trustee took the same view.

In fact we had gained a committed and enthusiastic chaletite who was a good cook and a strong hill-walker. One of our exchanges will bear repeating. Out on the mountainside the next day he expressed surprise that Univ parties mixed reading and walking, having been under the impression that they merely settled in and drank for ten days. I could only be honest and reply that this was precisely what everyone thought his college did. By such interactions are items of Chalet folklore demolished.

In a later year my elder daughter Marina decided to revive the walk to Mont Joly.[16] John McMillan thought the party could do it all on foot and a group of five went down to Saint Gervais and across the Bon Nant valley to climb to the peak (2,525 m) through the village of Saint-Nicolas-de-Véroce. The peak of Mont Joly (Fig. 86) is reached by a final scramble and provides a magnificent panorama which includes the whole of the west face of Mont Blanc and its surrounding ridges. This was a seventeen-hour excursion on foot and on the way back the party stopped for dinner at the auberge in Bionnassay. The *patron*, finding Marina spoke French well and hearing what they had done, asked if he could take them up to the Prarion Hotel in his jeep.[16] She declined on the grounds that after completing so much on foot they should finish that way. As they left the others who had not understood the conversation were not entirely pleased with this decision on their behalf when they found out. The Mont Joly ascent has figured regularly in Univ parties since, although car transfer to and from Saint Nicolas makes it less exhausting. I was able to maintain the Chalet's tradition for family attendance when my younger daughter Claire joined parties. Both daughters became committed chaletites and so too did their fiancés, Charles and Ashley, in later years.

The different opinions held by the reading parties of each other's colleges are worth noting. Traditionally, each college tends to see the others as too serious, too lax or too rigid. Invariably, each college regards the others as holding the record for consumption of wine. Naturally, these views come from individuals who maintain that their alma mater has the optimum approach! In fact, while over the years the practice of the colleges has tended to converge, each still retains elements of its traditional format and each continues to be successful: there is more than one route to a successful reading party and, one might justifiably say, '*Vive la différence*'.

One feature that the parties maintain is to give members a sense of the history in which they participate. Copies of the diaries back to 1891 are available to study and each party adds its own entry in whatever style appears appropriate at the time. Readings from Cyril Bailey's *Memoir* of Sligger, and especially from *The Perfect Chalet-ite*, are undertaken, for example over dinner; while this is part of the history of the Chalet it might be asked what relevance this period piece has to modern Chalet life. Univ's Master Sir Ivor Crewe commented: 'What always struck me was that Sligger felt the need to set rules and expectations to a group of young men sharing a similar social and educational background, most of them already accustomed to collective living at school. Today's Chaletites are far more diverse in background – a United Nations of women as well as men, graduates as well as undergraduates. What they have in common is the College as an academic community, which is deepened and enriched by the experience of living together in mildly rudimentary conditions. The leaders provide some gentle guidance on how this might be best be done, and no more is needed to be a good Chaletite.'[17]

While the reading parties have been generally successful, they are always at the mercy of circumstance. In 2006 Alan Ryan's party was hit by a particularly intense combination of events. Last-minute cancellations were compounded by a security scare in British airports which prevented the travel of all but nine members and left the party with neither manager nor bursar. Worse still, all nine were new to the Chalet with little idea how it worked and they were rained in for almost all their time. This experience was aggravated by the fact that the *télécabine* was out of action and all the parties that season had to resort to taking the TMB to Col de Voza and walking.

Years before this a Univ party under Bill Sykes had a more dramatic escapade. The party was walking to the Jonction on Montagne de la Côte, the initial stage of the first ascent of Mont Blanc by Balmat and Paccard in 1786. This steep ridge is one of the buttresses on the north side of Mont Blanc and, although the walk to the point where the Taconnaz and Bossons glaciers divide around the ridge (hence 'La Jonction') does not go as high as (for example) the Tête Rousse walk, it is a demanding walk at a gradient which rarely eases. Today this requires a chairlift from Les Montquarts on the outskirts of Chamonix into the forest which clothes the lower part of the ridge. Then comes a steep zig-zag walk through the trees until the path emerges over the ice-fall of the Bossons glacier, one of the area's most spectacular viewpoints. Shortly after this there is a welcome café at the Chalet des Pyramides, where those who want to avoid the rest of the climb may enjoy a *croûte savoyarde* and a glass of wine while studying the glorious view. Above the café the path ascends over rocky slopes for another 1,000 metres until the ridge ends above the ice field from which the two glaciers separate (Fig. 85). This had become a traditional outing for Bill Sykes' parties and the scene at the top amply repays the effort of getting there.

What happened to the 1994 party was that Bill and two others had decided to cry off the complete ascent and were descending from the café when a sudden rockfall in front of them swept the path away. Cut off on the ridge, they could only return to the café and wait for the rest of the group to come down from the top. The mountain rescue helicopter came out to survey the scene and advised them that they had to climb back into the exposed rocky zone, cross the ridge and descend by a tenuous path along the side of the Taconnaz glacier. They succeeded but recorded that this was a path to be taken only *in extremis*. The demanding descent delayed their return and the group were faced with the walk up to the Chalet from Les Houches, hardly a welcome end to a day like that.

This reminder of the unpredictability of mountains appears to have significantly dented Bill Sykes' engagement with the Chalet and he never led another party for Univ, although he did return later as a guest. In recent years there has been a further collapse of part of the ridge below the Chalet des Pyramides, which is now reached by exposed wooden steps.

Otherwise, the main challenge parties are likely to experience is the weather. Mountain conditions can change rapidly and even at the height of summer the temperature at altitude can fall dramatically: occasionally a party may wake to find a dusting of snow on the lawn. Rain can come in quickly and it is always necessary to carry waterproofs and additional layers, especially if the destination is somewhere high like Tête Rousse. Rain can be a serious challenge if it settles in for a spell, and cabin fever becomes common. On the other hand, a certain amount of rain is welcome because the Chalet is dependent on drainage from the water meadow below the Prarion for its water supply. In recent hot summers no party has been obliged to close up for lack of water but some have come near this. Overnight rain is preferred, of course, but if this is heavy it tends to block the stream filter with silt: going up the stream to clear it on a cold, wet morning is one of the Chalet's least welcome tasks.

The Chalet's altitude is such that it can find itself in thick cloud, especially early in the day before the sun comes over Mont Blanc. More strikingly, cloud inversion may leave the Chalet in bright sun while a silver-white layer fills the valley so densely that it suggests it could be walked on.

Alpine storms are characteristically short but fierce. One advantage of the Chalet's position is that storms which come in from the west over Aravis can be appreciated as they approach (Fig. 90). Experienced from inside the Chalet they can be romantic, with rain pounding on the steel roof while lightning flashes and thunder rolls round the peaks. It is a different matter if out on the mountain because lightning can strike frighteningly close and taking cover is essential. Gareth Williams (Chalet 1976 & 1978–9) remembers being on the summit of Brévent when an Alpine storm came in rapidly.[18] The group's hair stood on end and fence posts began to hum with electric charge: rapid descent is mandatory in such conditions.

On the other hand, days on the west side of Mont Blanc can be clear and warm, sometimes to excess because the sun is fierce at altitude, and parties need good sun protection. A particularly attractive feature of such a day is the way the light changes as the sun goes down. From the terrace of the hotel the west side of Mont Blanc can be seen to pass through a succession of different colours, an event that often interrupts the final evening's dinner at the hotel when keen photographers flood out onto the terrace. A most memorable view from the Chalet is sunset over Aravis, which likewise goes through rapidly changing moods. Some will argue the greater attraction of the dawn light coming around Mont Blanc when seen from the peak of the Prarion: this is an experience which is likely to be recommended by fewer chaletites than seeing the sunset, for understandable reasons.

The success of the modern parties does not obscure the fact that the trustees still had a large building to care for which was expensive to maintain and sorely in need of maintenance. There were also unexpected crises: in 1994 George Forrest's opening party discovered the theft of the fine Scandinavian wood-burning stove which had been installed by Jonathan Barnes in the salon only five years before. A French replacement was found at 'half the cost'. The Trust was still not in a position to pay for much professional work and, although the leaders and members like Rupert Griffin, who installed a new floor in the toilet,[10] had done what repairs they could, there were concerns about the structure of the building itself, including the possibility of ground movement. For all that, the trustees were determined to retain the historical atmosphere; an approach in 1994 which offered inexpensive electrification was rejected on grounds not of cost but of authenticity.[19] A further appeal was considered but the colleges were engaged in major campaigns of their own and it was felt better to avoid any competition and hold out until the approaching centenary of the New Chalet in 2006–9.[20]

It is not surprising therefore that when the trustees were approached in 1995 through Keith Dorrington with a proposal of shared ownership and risk they felt obliged to consider it seriously.[21] A livery company had proposed that the Chalet be used as a winter ski base with the Trust retaining summer use for reading parties. The walls would have needed extensive insulation and electricity would have been required. The trustees had invited an evaluation from an architect in Saint Gervais [22] but he turned out to be slow to respond, so in 1997 Keith Dorrington, in view of his premature return to Oxford, asked me to chase up the architect myself. I located his office but found a sign announcing that he was at lunch. This was presumably a lunch of traditionally French proportions because he had still not returned by the time I was obliged to leave or risk missing the late afternoon cable car back onto the Prarion.

That evening my party fell to discussing the proposal and I was surprised by the strength of feeling against it, even among those who were at the Chalet for the first time. The comment 'this place is a retreat', a view I did not expect to come from a modern undergraduate, summed up the prevailing attitude. Although not then a trustee, I wrote to the Board that night to report the discussion, commenting as I did so that at the time of the fire in 1906 Sligger had commented that 'the Chalet' was an institution, not a building, and that an institution was based on its character rather than its accommodation.

In fact there were more serious concerns on the Prarion itself. Yves Hottegindre advised that the Chalet had no viable water supply in the winter and that evacuation in the event of an emergency would be nearly impossible. Hugues Boucher was adamant that if the proposal went ahead he would withdraw the privilege of access across his land. The trustees were obliged to concur and the project died. At times in the Chalet's story there have been points where it could easily have been lost. What might have come from this proposal – which had been made with the best intention – cannot be known but it might have resulted in the loss of the Chalet's character. This episode amply illustrates the weight of responsibility on the trustees for an historic building under conditions which are costly and always will be.

By 2001 it had become clear that action was needed to prevent further deterioration of the fabric. Jeremy Lever's warnings of the 1990s had largely been disregarded apart from ad hoc DIY and the succeeding decade had been marked by increasing anxiety but little action. As a result the problems of 1990 had increased and new ones had arisen. Gradual erosion of the hillside had raised the ground level around the north wall and the kitchen had become damp, causing its interior rendering to fragment. Cracks had appeared in the stonework above the ground floor, increasing concerns about possible ground movement. Floors were subsiding across the Chalet and because of this the staircase had separated from the internal wall. The home-made sink unit had become rotten with fungi and constituted a health risk. The external storeroom at the rear had not been in use for decades and the ground-floor toilet had been unusable since the Second World War.

Worse, the Chalet's security was being breached with increasing regularity: trustees opening up at the start of the season or visiting during the ski season became accustomed to finding that the building had been broken into and used as a bivouac. It could be a hair-raising experience, I can confirm, checking over a shuttered building with the aid only of a torch and a walking pole while not knowing if an occupant might be encountered. This use of the Chalet was surprising, as the Prarion Hotel is only a short distance away and is required by law to keep a ground-floor door unlocked for those who need shelter at night. Nothing was taken from the Chalet during this time but the risk of theft or damage was clear, especially if intruders started a fire.

It was time to invoke professional help, so Univ agreed to make its surveyor, Richard Pye, available and he visited that summer. His highly detailed report might have been thought daunting had not his overall advice been that nothing unmanageable had been found.[23] That said, his five-year rolling programme of renovation was costed at £116,000, which provided for the work to be done by a team from Oxford who would stay at the Prarion Hotel. There were additional costs for work of local contractors, such as clearance of the rear track, which had become overgrown again, for vehicle access.

The first year's programme was clearly urgent and Harvey McGregor advised the Board that it could fund one year's work from its capital but no more.[24] An appeal to past chaletites seemed untimely in view of development campaigns in progress in the three colleges, so it was decided to appeal once again to the colleges themselves in the hope that they would each contribute £5,000 per annum for five years.[24] The Board was gratified by prompt agreement from the colleges and this support enabled a programme of restoration that would have been unthinkable to previous generations.

Rhodes House was also approached and the governing body took the opportunity to review its involvement. Its trustee, Ngaire Woods, had become heavily engaged in national work and had not been able to run a party since 1998. She felt ready to resign from the Trust but with no apparent successor; Tony Kenny had come back to lead a party in 1999 but none from Rhodes House had occurred since. With a request for a donation in the face of uncertain participation, Rhodes House decided it was time to withdraw from the Trust.[25]

At Univ the governing body, in confirming its support, invited the trustees to consider widening access to the Chalet. The Univ trustees therefore ended the system of personal invitation and moved to advertising the parties and inviting applications, a system which has worked consistently well since.

In 2002 Richard Pye put together a team of Oxford craftsmen and the Board allowed them the last two weeks of the season, provided that all the preparatory work could be achieved in time. To facilitate this Univ and Balliol agreed to run only one party each. In later years, when the works team started in late June before parties began, Univ usually followed the works team with a single party, feeling that it would be unfair to disadvantage the other colleges while Univ's Works Department was responsible for the programme.

The 2002 programme cost £20,000 and concentrated on the security of the building itself.[26] The rear track was cleared by M. Marsura with a mechanical digger. He also excavated a trench around the perimeter of the Chalet and delivered materials for the Univ party to build a new French drain around the building: this self-help provided a degree of economy. The trustees also found a firm in Sallanches, Kauder, who would install modern fire extinguishers and service them annually. The works team added fire escape ladders and smoke detectors.

The work included rendering and painting the kitchen and scullery walls and investigating rotten areas of the floors.[26] Authentic materials, in particular the mélèze timber, were sourced through David Cardwell, who ran a firm based in Les Houches and had been identified by Richard Pye as a contact for future work. The team's main task for this first season was to restore the doors and shutters and to stabilise the balcony rail. The efficacy of this work was immediately obvious. As the works team could not be expected to close up the Chalet for the winter, Dominic O'Brien and I agreed to fly back to do this, and, having allowed two days for this task, we found that the work had made everything so easy that we completed it on the first morning. We repaired to the Prarion Hotel for a celebratory two-day holiday in the company of Dominic's partner, Lisa.

When it became known that extensive work was planned there was understandable concern among those who had come to love the Chalet's character. Rupert Griffin, who was dedicated to the use of traditional methods, wrote to me to express his anxiety that the building should not change.[27] Similar feelings are commonly expressed by many chaletites. Rupert had been at the Chalet when the works team had arrived and so had an idea of what was planned. I could therefore be completely reassuring that the principle shared by the Board was that the Chalet would retain its traditional character as far as possible. There would, however, have to be limited compromises dictated by the need to cater for parties: the kitchen in particular was well below any acceptable standard for food safety.

Rupert Griffin's closely reasoned letter showed his intimate experience of the Chalet's operating conditions and made several pertinent suggestions which were incorporated into future plans, such as raising the lower ledge of the kitchen window so that the windows could be opened above the sink unit.[27] He pointed out that the Chalet had a number of disused horse-hair mattresses which he could use in his own work on upholstery. In addition, on hearing that the Board had decided to abandon Tilley lamps in favour of butane lanterns, he offered to service the remaining lamps and find good homes for them. The Board was pleased to be able to approve both gifts in recognition of Rupert's commitment.[25]

After the restoration had begun the Board experienced an unexpected hiccough. That season the first New College party was led by Alan Ryan before his departure for California on sabbatical leave, leaving the second party in the hands of Stephen Tucker and junior managers. In September 2002 two junior members submitted to New College a highly critical report on safety at the Chalet.[28] They also felt that the Chalet was under-used (although numbers had been normal in both New College parties), and reported an erroneous perception that only those destined for a first-class degree were invited. The Chalet was claimed to be alienating, suffocated by tradition and an elitist atmosphere.[28] It is not clear to what extent this view was dictated by their own experiences: judging from the Chalet diary the parties seem to have proceeded normally.

The programme of work had been freely discussed at the Chalet that summer and the report included items which were in any case planned or had been carried out by the time it reached New College. However, the report suggested that the Chalet was an accident in waiting and recommended that party leaders be trained in first aid and that a mountain vehicle be stationed at the Chalet at all times for

74

75

74 New leaders: Bill Sykes (left) and Iain McLean (centre) in 1979. **75** New leaders: George Forrest (left) and Noel Worswick in 1992.

76

77

76 Chalet art: pen and ink sketch by Jason Chen, 2003. Reproduced by kind permission of Dr Jason Chen. **77** Chalet art: pen and ink sketch of the salon by Dr Jason Chen, 2003. Reproduced by kind permission of Dr Jason Chen.

78

79

78 The Chalet as it first appears through the trees to the modern arrival from the télécabine Les Houches. **79** Tony Kenny (far left) with a Balliol party at Tête Rousse with, on his left, Camilla, Jennifer and Jonathan Barnes.

80

81

80 Jonathan Barnes (far left) with Jim Hankinson behind him and members of the heroic 1987 works party. **81** Col de Tricot: a favourite destination, Pointe Inférieure to the left, Mont Vorassay to the right.

82

83

82 Above the clouds: on the ascent to Tête Rousse. **83** The Prarion (centre) seen from Tête Rousse, the Aiguille de Varens to the right, the Aravis ridge in the background.

84 Resting on the ascent to the Jonction. **85** *'La Jonction'* of the Taconnaz and Bossons glaciers.

86

87

86 Mont Joly from the Prarion: a fine, if long, day's outing. **87** Braving the icy water at Lac Blanc.

88

89

88 At the spectacular icefall of the Argentière glacier. **89** After a day's walking: drinks at the 'Pav'.

90

91

90 A characteristic night storm over Aravis. **91** Alan Ryan (sitting, centre) with a New College party in 2003. Future trustee Will Poole is on his left and assistants Adam Fergus on his right, Rupert Griffin (standing rear far left) and Matthew Armstrong (standing far right).

92

93

92 Morning reading in the salon. **93** Afternoon reading on the lawn.

94

95

94 Hugues (rear right) and Nelleriek Boucher (rear left) join a Chalet dinner in 2002. **95** Incoming Balliol leaders join Univ at their dinner at the hotel in 2008: Carol Clark (front right), Douglas Dupree (second from left), Anna Sander (fourth from left), with Stephen Golding (second from right) and Keith Dorrington (third from left).

96

97

98

96 The Trust Board in 2010: (standing, from left) Stephen Tucker, Keith Dorrington, Dominic O'Brien, Will Poole; (seated, from left) Stephen Golding, Harvey McGregor, Douglas Dupree (Alan Ryan and Adam Swift absent). **97** Acer Nethercott donates his Olympic Games shirt to the collection at the Tête Rousse refuge, 2011. **98** Allen Warren (right) and Roy Wallington on the summit of the Prarion with the Aravis ridge in the background.

99

100

99 The magnum opus of Michel Parcevaux (far left), the new dining table, arrives. Reproduced by kind permission of Dr Keith Dorrington. **100** The refitted kitchen, 2015.

101

102

101 Friends at the Hôtel du Prarion: (from left) Yves Hottegindre, Simone Orset-Hottegindre, Stephen Golding, Sabrina Planquart, Keith Dorrington. **102** The 2009 centenary celebration: the Univ party with the past chaletites assembled by Lord Butler (seated, fourth from right) and Lady Butler (seated, far left).

103

104

103 The 2009 centenary celebration: New College's Chalet dinner (Will Poole in centre). **104** A characteristic sunset over Aravis.

105

106

105 Epilogue: Sir Ivor Crewe celebrates the wedding of James Grice and Jen Thum on the Chalet lawn in 2015. **106** Chalet art: watercolour by Lady Butler. Reproduced by kind permission of Lady Butler.

emergencies. This latter idea was dismissed by the Board; the mountain tracks are unsuitable for any but experienced drivers and the Chalet's emergency evacuation was and would remain the excellent mountain rescue service in Chamonix.[26] There was also much that the trustees had no difficulty in addressing because most of the safety items were already in hand.

At this time Alan Ryan was the only member of New College's governing body who could speak with recent personal experience of the Chalet and he was in the United States. The New College officers naturally felt that they could not ignore apparently genuine concerns about safety and they recommended that a Health and Safety inspection be made.[29] They also questioned whether they could allow college members to go to the Chalet until this was resolved. From the United States Alan Ryan replied robustly that if New College prevented students from going to the Chalet he would invite members as his personal guests.[29] In the event it did not come to this and the 2003 season was to proceed as normal.

Another factor which taxed New College was uncertainty over where liability lay between themselves and the Trust.[30] This was approached sensitively, given that the Chalet was owned by a company in France. Harvey McGregor naturally took the view that, as a leading barrister and recognised expert in damages, not to mention being chairman of the Trust and a previous Warden of New College, he had an authoritative point of view. The outcome was that the Board accepted the inspection on the grounds that New College's concerns would be addressed.

By this time I had become *de facto* manager of the renovation programme and when the inspector contacted me it was a relief to hear that he intended to assess the Chalet in the context of its environment. In fact when the trustees received the report there was no significant action to take apart from improving fire evacuation notices; having occupied nearly a year with much concern but little positive outcome, the issue was now dead.[31] An endearing feature of the inspector's report was his comment on evidence of mice and suggestion that traps should be set. Unlike the inspector, presumably a city-dweller, the trustees were perfectly aware that the Chalet offered winter accommodation to the local field mice and would do so no matter how many traps were set (although summer incursions are unwelcome and usually dealt with chemically).

An opening party can be an interesting experience, especially if the previous year's closing party failed to store soft furnishings off the floor (all need to be hung from ceilings or over high furniture) or inadvertently left out consumables to help the mice through the winter. My daughter Claire recalls that one member, in attempting to pour away a bottle of cooking oil which had been left open during the winter, came upon an obstruction and squeezed the bottle so hard that a drowned mouse was projected into orbit across the lawn.[32]

Works visits continued annually until 2007 and by then the Chalet was in a very different state. The restoration included the external porches and support to the balcony, the shower room, a protective rail around the loft hatchway, new gutters and replacement of the loft skylight which had leaked repeatedly. A new system with built-in filtration was created for water from the stream. Raising the floorboards on the ground floor showed that the mélèze beams of 1909 had been laid directly on the ground and had rotted through: replacements were laid on concrete bearers protected with bitumen. Pleasingly, almost all the 1909 floorboards were healthy and could be reused. Restoration of the rear lobby allowed the staircase to be secured once more. The petit salon, which had become a damp storeroom, came back into use as a practical day room and spare bedroom. A notable addition was to refit the ground-floor toilet. The original intention had been to make this a tool store but Keith Dorrington insisted that parties would be helped by a second WC. This work was done in 2007, a mere fifty-five years after the need was first noted. In keeping with the Oxbridge way of commemorating developments, this toilet has earned the title of 'The Dorrington Room', at least among Univ parties.

Throughout this work the Board was determined to retain the atmosphere of the Chalet save in two cases, both of them unavoidable. When the workmen dealt with the storeroom outside the kitchen they found that the wooden bearers on which the roof had been cast had rotted away and when the roof was removed the walls fell in. The walls had not been keyed into the Chalet wall as might have been expected if the store was original and it was thought that it might have been added at the same time as the chapel, as they appeared to share a standard of workmanship. A timber-built replacement was the only option. However, this work carried particular significance; the store was essential to Chalet tennis and the roof had to be of the same dimensions, height and pitch if the game was to continue unchanged. That was because a skilful player could hit the ball so low onto the roof that their opponent could not see where it would fall, making it harder to reach it before it hit the ground. These requirements were not difficult to achieve, although the addition of groins in the metal cladding has added a new dimension to the game.

The kitchen was the other main departure from the 1909 configuration, as it needed to conform to modern standards for catering, which meant replacing the wooden surfaces with stainless steel. In a rolling programme over the next few years free-standing sink units and side tables were obtained from a local plumber's merchant, Brossette in Sallanches, although a nod to tradition was made by keeping the tables and asking Philippe Chatellard, the local craftsman in stainless steel, to fit them with steel surfaces. M. Chatellard also constructed steel shelving for kitchen equipment.

An item which caused some heart-searching was Sligger's 1909 kitchen dresser: a hundred years of damp and the depredations of mice had made its base so distasteful that only bottled or tinned food could reasonably be stored in it. At length it was decided to sacrifice the base but to preserve the upper part, where Sligger's inter-war staff had inscribed their names. This was fixed to the wall as a rack for equipment and spices.

Work on the kitchen continued after the works parties: in 2013 the trustees invested in a large cooking range similar to those in mountain refuges. This replaced the two small camping stoves which usually survived only a few years in the mountain environment. The kitchen finally achieved its modern configuration in 2015 (Fig. 100) with the installation by M. Chatellard of a steel mesh larder cupboard across one wall of the scullery, replacing the decommissioned fridges which had previously been used to protect food from mice.

The trustees' aim had been to bring the Chalet to a state which could be maintained with less effort and cost. However, there are unexpected risks with any building of this age. In 2009 the New College party found that sewage was backing up due to collapse in one of the chambers of the *fosse septique* and M. Marsura was brought in once more. Under newly introduced regulations the *mairie* came to inspect the new installation the following year; the Chalet satisfactorily passed inspection but the inspector advised that it should no longer discharge kitchen drainage into the open stream. A tank for the separation of grease had to be installed in the kitchen outflow and connected to the new *fosse septique*.

Even before this later work the Board had to address the mounting cost of the repairs. By the end of the 2007 season the Trust had spent £104,000 and had been obliged to provide nearly £30,000 from its reserve over and above the support received from the colleges.[33] It was clear that further income was needed to support the development. Since 1971 the Trust had relied on donations from previous chaletites and the colleges and the trustees decided that it was time to attempt to put the Trust's finances on a secure footing which might obviate these appeals. The Board decided that there should be a further appeal to old chaletites, taking advantage of the imminent centenary of the New Chalet in 2009.[34] The objectives were to restore the amount spent on the works and to put the Trust in a position where its income could meet foreseeable expenses without further appeals. It was also felt desirable to be able to offer bursaries to students who would otherwise be unable to go to the Chalet. The target was set at £350,000.[35]

Each of the colleges agreed to support the Board's initiative to appeal but Balliol decided to take a different approach. The college was just about to launch a new development campaign and was understandably wary of anything that might compete. After discussion with Harvey McGregor the college agreed to donate each year from its general fund a sum equivalent to the interest the Trust might have received if a full-scale appeal for the Chalet had gone ahead at Balliol.[36] This was estimated at £4,000 a year with review at five years.

The chairman and other trustees threw their weight behind the appeal to New College and Univ members. In the appeal brochure Harvey McGregor wrote: 'The Chalet is a unique establishment, both socially and physically. Where else in our educational world would you find a place high up in beautiful mountains to which students have been repairing for summer reading parties since the end of the century before last? ... The Chalet is old, with a long history and needs not only to be maintained but to be brought up to modern standards while keeping it essentially simple. ... There is still much to be done if the Chalet is to survive through another century ... The Chalet must go on; it is far too precious to lose.'[35] Harvey also threw himself into personal appeals to colleagues in the Law and raised a significant contribution to the total.

For Univ Lord Butler wrote: 'I was lucky enough to be invited to the Chalet when I was an undergraduate. Among my memories of my very happy time at Univ, this is among the happiest and most vivid. I find that the same is true of my contemporaries who shared that experience. When I returned to Univ as Master nearly forty years later, one of the aspects I looked forward to most keenly was a return to the Chalet. I have taken part in three house parties as Master and I have found the experience is as unchanging as the surrounding mountains. I have also rejoiced to see that it has a similarly profound effect on the students of today as it has done for the last hundred years. It is worth preserving.'[35]

He was supported by Bill Sykes, who wrote: 'During my time at Univ hundreds of undergraduates and graduates have been to the Chalet and have been overwhelmed by the beauty of the French Alps and the Mont Blanc massif. We evolved, over the years, a strategy for reading one day and walking the next and many Chaletites have recorded that their time at the Chalet has been a high spot of their lives. A major enjoyment has been living at the Chalet, a noble building that has remained relatively unchanged over a hundred years. We intend to keep it so.'[35]

Many old chaletites responded to the 2009 appeal and by the following year gifts had exceeded £120,000.[37] Because many were made as pledges over several years, the income continued to rise, reaching nearly £154,000 by 2014.[38] This was less than the trustees had hoped for but was sufficient to put the Trust for the first time in its history in a position where the interest from its capital was sufficient for regular maintenance and where careful management would allow the capital to grow towards the self-reliance the trustees were seeking. Later, in 2015, the Trust would be helped by a major legacy of 260,500 Australian dollars from the will of Christopher Cox's lieutenant of the late 1960s, John Emmerson.[39] On return to his native Australia John had gone on to be a successful barrister and he had never forgotten the efforts of Christopher Cox and the others to establish the Trust. In his will he recalled his time at the Chalet and with a lawyer's skill for allowing for all eventualities, indicated that the gift depended on whether 'there is any such Trust'.[40]

Success in the early stages of the appeal gave the trustees the confidence to plan further than originally envisaged. In 2006 Harvey McGregor took the opportunity of a visit to review the provision of furniture for parties which had become larger than before. Over the next few years nearly £8,000 was spent on new bedsteads and dining chairs and a third sofa for the salon as well as restoration of the existing sofas in the salon and petit salon.[41] New soft furnishings for these were provided by Harvey at his own expense.[41] The prize item was a robust new dining table, designed to seat twenty comfortably. This was made in Bionnassay by Michel Parcevaux, son of Rémy Parcevaux who had repaired the balcony in 1977. Michel Parcevaux was delighted to renew the family connection with the Chalet; the table was the largest single item he had ever made and its delivery on a trailer and insertion through the front window was a memorable event (Fig. 99). It is only honest to report that a few minutes after his departure the table was in use for table tennis, for which it is eminently suitable. The old extending dining table, memorable for the characteristic noted by Jean Elrington in 1952 that its middle legs regularly fell off, went back to his workshop for restoration as a round table for the petit salon.

Harvey had become concerned that he did not have documentation of the ownership of the Chalet and used his 2006 visit to explore this with the *mairie* and the Commune. From the time of his arrival I became his batman and driver and the experience proved rather wearing. The work had to be done during the day and it was blisteringly hot in the valley. Because no work can ever be done with French officialdom in the middle of the day, he treated me to lunch in the sun in the main square of Bonneville and insisted on buying a bottle of full-bodied claret. I was certainly not at my best after this and as we waited in the stifling Commune office that afternoon Harvey went pale and leaned against the wall, apparently asleep. He had me wondering if I would have to explain to the Board how I hadn't taken better care of the eighty-year-old chairman but as soon as our appointment was called he was back on form and firmly in charge in impeccable French.

The Trust's improved position allowed the employment of more local labour when the Oxford works parties ended. For many years the Chalet's front door had been fragmenting as its panels were breaking down. Sadly, Michel Parcevaux, who had been such a promising find, had died from a winter chest infection but David Cardwell contracted a joiner, Jean-Luc Gobbo, who installed in the existing deep frame a double door, glazed on the inner door to let light into the salon and with an outer solid door for security. Work to replace the front guttering was undertaken by Laurent Guffond, the local roofing specialist, ending water penetration into the salon which happened regularly during heavy rain.

In the century since 1909 the larches around the Chalet had grown up and obscured the west view across the valley to the ridges of Aravis and the Aiguille de Varens. This was disappointing and there was a feeling on the Board that it should be corrected. This had its challenges, as the mélèze timber is protected and can be managed only by the Commune. Initial enquiries resulted in the *forestiers* clearing deciduous growth on the Chalet's own land in 2013 but the larches had to wait their turn as part of the local forestry programme. This became the personal project of Mark Byford, elected to the Board that year as a New College trustee in place of Stephen Tucker, and the wish to accomplish this was so strong that Allen Warren was able to run a successful New College appeal for the purpose.[42] This did so well that while waiting for the Commune's programme the Trust was able to employ Jean-Luc Gobbo to build a substantial wood rack, the final replacement for Sligger's woodshed which had been lost in the 1960s.[43]

None of this ambitious programme would have been possible without the generous support of the colleges and gifts from past chaletites. It also relied heavily for success on the Board's policy of a rolling programme over more than a decade as gifts came in and income from the Trust's capital increased. It could have been very tempting to have spent heavily in a shorter time. However, the Board's policy ensured that at the end of the programme the Chalet was in a state fit for purpose and its future could be viewed with confidence. This is not to say that future needs can be avoided in an historic building that has to survive the extremes of Alpine winters and summers: for example, French drains need regular replacement and at the time of writing it cannot be long before the steel roof will need replacing.

Quite apart from the need to maintain the building, the work involved in running parties should not be underestimated, nor should the risks. Injury and serious illness can be dealt with by the Chamonix mountain rescue service; despite trauma being their main objective the service also provides care for medical problems occurring in the mountains.[44] The Chalet keeps a medicine chest for simple problems but sometimes has to call on local primary care. Even in the days of modern walking boots, blisters can destroy the pleasure of a day out on the hill; being medical I have offered an evening foot clinic since I began to take parties. No matter how much care is taken or advice given there are the inevitable small challenges from the Chalet's environment: sprained ankles, cut fingers, deep wood splinters, the occasional case of dehydration or sunstroke.

To this can be added the challenges of catering for up to twenty people in a building which has more in common with a Victorian farmhouse that any modern facility. Elements can fail on the stove or overenthusiastic students may break the controls. The water supply fails regularly if a storm brings silt down the stream. Gas-fuelled water heaters and fridges do not survive well through Alpine winters and they become temperamental; in these circumstances the engineering background of a Keith Dorrington or Dominic O'Brien becomes invaluable. A regular finding on opening has been that the tubing of the water heater has been split by winter freezing no matter how assiduous the closing party has been in emptying it. This has resulted in a new heater always being kept in reserve. In the last few years Univ's most recent trustee, Jack Matthews, pointed out that the split tended to occur at the same spot: an investigation by Keith Dorrington located a small and well-hidden drainage screw that appeared to be to blame. Our lack of knowledge of this is testimony to the complexity of operating manuals, especially in a language which is not one's own; advice was presumably buried in the operating manual somewhere.

These minor but unexpected problems are an irritation under good conditions; if the party is challenged by cold or by being rained in – a condition not at all welcome to the energetic young – they can easily appear more significant than they are. In the circumstances one wonders how leaders dedicated to providing a rewarding and productive stay maintain their equilibrium, either with their students or with each other. The fact is that the community spirit at the Chalet rarely falters and if one goes through a bad day occasionally, a good one usually follows. The parties benefit from the fact that they can call on the Hottegindre family's expertise, as well as friendly support from the Boucher family at the neighbouring Chalet du Rocher. It is debatable to what extent the post-war parties could have survived alone: committed and indeed passionate about the Chalet as the trustees are, academics are not always the most experienced in the requirements of *la vie champêtre*.

Sligger's chaletites had the advantage of servants, cook, laundress, caretaker and porter. The modern chaletite has a very different experience. Although some drive out or travel by train, flying to Geneva is now the norm and a very efficient bus service direct to Les Houches from the airport has replaced walking across the city to take the local and very slow stopping train. The long walk up from Saint Gervais with luggage or the TMB to Col de Voza and a shorter walk are no more, except for the very hardy; the *télécabine* from Les Houches to the Prarion Hotel is more enjoyable transport when carrying a full backpack. Today's chaletites have to carry everything they need: sleeping bag, books, sometimes a laptop computer, clothes for a wide range of conditions including torrential rain, sun hat, screen and glasses, and a torch – essential in a building with no electricity.

At the Chalet jobs are shared out: cooking, washing up, burning the day's rubbish (including toilet paper for fear of clogging the *fosse septique*), chopping wood for the stove. There may be some DIY. The season's opening party has the addition of reassembling the water supply, reinstalling the water heater, persuading the gas fridges to take light and also cleaning everything, moveable and immoveable: the season's closing party has all these jobs in reverse. Yves Hottegindre usually delivers each party its grocery order by jeep but top-up shopping is always needed: the *télécabine* provides easy access to supermarkets in Les Houches (or at least easy by mountain walking standards) but some still brave an afternoon walk down to Saint Gervais. All this would be strange to Sligger but one wonders if he would still see the community as adhering to his principles.

One thing Sligger could not have predicted was the Chalet being linked to the outside world by mobile phones. These ubiquitous items have not altered the reading parties even though this might have been feared. For Will Poole, who joined the Board when Alan Ryan stood down in 2009 but who came with previous experience as an undergraduate, the attraction was that the communal life with its cooking, reading, walking and conversation took place in an unimpeded atmosphere that was slipping away elsewhere.[45] In fact, many chaletites turn their phone off except when needed, in deference to the Chalet's atmosphere. Mobile network cover in the mountains has improved steadily throughout this period and carrying a phone is of course valuable in case of difficulty or accident.

As in so many aspects of modern life, it is now difficult to contemplate being in the mountains without the ability to communicate with the outside world. Laptop computers (charging by courtesy of the Prarion Hotel) have added a new dimension to reading and work. Univ's Master Sir Ivor Crewe, who on joining the college became a committed chaletite in succession to his daughter Deborah (Chalet 1992) and son Daniel (Chalet 1999), was able to set up a bedroom office in which essential college business could be tackled before breakfast. He says: 'I was always assigned the luxurious upper west room with its wide view of the Aravis mountains, magnificent in the pink-then-orange glow of dusk. I generally rose early to sit at the table and attend to urgent college business. The scraping of chair on bare floorboard was usually enough to wake Stephen [Golding], whose room was directly below, who then padded down to the kitchen to make a pot of tea. I believe I was the first to go online at the Chalet. There was no wi-fi network of course – Sligger would have spun in his grave at the thought of installing a router – so chaletites would walk up to the Hôtel du Prarion and use its precarious connectivity. But by trial and error I discovered that if I balanced my iPhone on the window ledge I could sometimes connect to "G3" and use the iPhone as a "hot spot" for my laptop. Of course, charging up either was another challenge altogether. On such slender threads did the welfare of the College hang.'[46]

Chalet games persist, although the advance of vegetation has necessarily ended Chalet golf. Chalet tennis remains popular and so does cricket, modern parties remaining conscious of the instruction in *The Perfect Chalet-ite* that the shutters are to be closed: repairs are difficult to achieve in the mountain and can be disproportionately demanding of time. Recent generations have introduced volleyball and Michel Parcevaux' dining table – his magnum opus – serves enthusiasts of table tennis. Sometimes members bring a musical instrument such as a guitar and add a new element to the party.

The croissant run has become a staple item of modern parties, with everyone who does it eager to inscribe a record ascent time in the diary. It would be invidious to attempt to name an overall winner, especially as the records are not exactly standardised, but my feeling after twenty-five years of non-participant observation is that anything under sixty minutes is honourable and anything approaching forty evidence of high athletic prowess. It should also be remembered that the croissant run, like the parties themselves, is subject to mountain conditions: in 1985 Paul Flather of Balliol found himself battling with torrential rain, mud and the risk of sliding down to Saint Gervais. He decided to bow to circumstance and returned to his bed with no loss in his standing.[47] What is more constant is the welcome given at breakfast by the rest of the party to those sweating chaletites who arrive with freshly baked croissants to supplement the porridge and preserves.

The centenary of the 1909 Chalet occurred while the restoration programme was proceeding and was appropriately marked by each of the colleges. Balliol hosted a centenary lunch in Oxford and their archivist Anna Sander produced an exhibition. New College staged three fundraising events in Oxford supported by an exhibition prepared by their archivist Jennifer Thorp, and in France the college held celebratory dinners at the Chalet (Fig. 103) and, in the spirit of Christopher Cox, at the Prarion Hotel. Univ opened the summer season at the Chalet to old members and around thirty came to stay at the Prarion Hotel during the Univ parties, joining the party in activities which included a celebratory dinner. Many members came as a result of the initiative of Lord Butler, who put together a large group of his contemporaries (Fig. 102). Undergraduate members noted that while the older guests were perhaps not so active on the mountainside, they suffered no comparison when it came to enjoying the Chalet and its entertainment. Lila Boucher presented the Chalet with a poem of friendship she had written, inscribed on a piece of her mother's artwork, and Univ rounded off the centenary year with a weekend event in the autumn, assisted by Anna Sander's exhibition. At the Univ dinner Lord Butler spoke memorably about his visits to the Chalet and the contribution of the parties to college life, and paid tribute to the party leaders who down the years had ensured Univ's participation. The celebration ended on Sunday morning with a thanksgiving service led by Bill Sykes.

A ripple in what should have been a time of great celebration came in 2011 when the student newspaper *Cherwell* published an article criticising Balliol for its policy of selecting parties, in essence accusing Douglas Dupree, who was Dean, of handpicking students with whom he wanted a summer holiday.[48] The Junior Common Room at Balliol had passed a motion condemning the college's subsidy of what was perceived to be favouritism. The *Cherwell* article ended with the statement that the trustees were not available for comment; this was interpreted as journalese for no effort having been made as none was ever discovered. This was a pity, as the trustees certainly would have wanted to have counter the statement that the Chalet existed to provide a holiday.

It was rather unfair that Douglas Dupree was the target of the *Cherwell* article in view of the fact that he was moving to Florida. However, the article did illuminate the traditional means by which tutors put together parties who they felt would benefit, which did not sit easily with modern views on equality of opportunity. This is supported by those who were not invited to the Chalet.[49] As we have seen, Univ had changed its practice at the request of the college when confirming its support for the restoration programme. Today admission to the Chalet from all three colleges is by application and subsequent selection; not all applicants may secure a place but there is equal opportunity.

Both the *Cherwell* incident and the New College Health and Safety affair in 2002 can be regarded as examples of how the Chalet stirs strong emotions, especially if imperfectly understood from outside. From this point of view it has been fortunate to rest in the hands of an independent Trust, which allows a comfortable distance between its management and that of the colleges and the University. Both these issues were driven by what appeared to be laudable motives but which could easily have disadvantaged the colleges. In New College this was prevented but in Balliol it actually happened; the incoming trustee, Nicola Trott, felt that it was better to abandon the 2011 season while the issue was explored, which meant that Balliol members lost their access for a year.[50] Either of these reports or an intervention like them could have led to the permanent withdrawal of a college, which would have been tragic for the members of that college. The Trust and the Chalet would survive such an eventuality; Jeremy Lever was wise enough not to specify the constituent colleges when he devised the Trust settlement.[51] The trustees' responsibility is to maintain the Chalet for members of the University of Oxford and withdrawal of a college would simply require the Trust to open itself to other colleges to satisfy its charitable objective.

It is a sad coda to this period of achievement that Harvey McGregor died in 2015 at the age of ninety. The trustees were about to hold a celebration of his twenty years in the chair when an acute illness intervened, greatly to his disappointment, as he was looking forward to what would also have been a commemoration of the way the Trust had matured under his leadership. When he tried to call me from his hospital bed it became painfully clear that he was already past being able to hold a conversation, but I was impressed that even then the Chalet was at the front of his mind.

In the five decades of its existence the Chalet Trust has succeeded in its *raison d'être*, namely the provision of summer reading parties for members of the University, as begun by Sligger in 1891. The fact that that it has done so in the face of so many challenges is testament to the commitment of those who have led it and those who have supported it. Most parties now run smoothly despite the fact that conditions on the mountain can never be totally predictable. A forty-year battle with finance and an ageing building has not prevented the Trust from achieving a mature configuration, nor has it prevented the Chalet from being fit for purpose and easier to maintain than ever before. Whatever challenges have to be faced in the future – and it would be an unusual future which did not contain challenges where the Chalet des Anglais is concerned – both the Chalet and the Trust are well placed to face them.

WHAT HAS IT MEANT?

I STAND ON THE BALCONY, the early morning air striking through the tracksuit. Below me the overnight mist is clearing from the vegetation and a few early insects are at work in the wild lupins, the alleged descendants of Mrs Urquhart's nineteenth-century seedlings. Across the valley the morning sun is painting the tips of Aravis in shades of breath-taking pastel. A different world, it seems, from the High Street in Oxford, and yet this is College too.

Sligger, visionary that he was in starting all this, was phlegmatic when the Chalet burned down in 1906, taking the view that the Chalet was an institution, not a building that could be destroyed by fire. And this institution still works its pervasive magic. Even sitting in an Oxford college in the cool light of autumn, the memories of a successful Chalet party come flooding back: the camaraderie of life in primitive surroundings, of unexpected successes in the kitchen, of the sheer joy of the process of simply living, surrounded by some of the best scenery in the world, of the evening laughter around the fire, of members of the party being reduced to varying stages of undress in the lounge at the Prarion Hotel after being caught in an Alpine storm, and of the hotel terrace doing duty as college bar after a hard day's walking on the mountain. The library is here, in the gentle rustle of morning reading, and chapel, too, in Compline in the candlelit calm of an Alpine night. And above all, conversation, and lots of it; life, the universe, and everything. Yes, College is here, and with it the essence of everything that makes College life valuable.

Gratitude inevitably goes to those students who took charge of domestic business and lightened the load on a novice leader, and to the Hottegindres at the Prarion Hotel for much support and encouragement; principally, though, to the party members for sharing their lives and for providing memories which will be lifelong. Sligger's vision remains alive and well on the slopes of Mont Blanc.

(From the author's report to University College of the 1997 party)[1]

⌗

The lifetime of the reading parties has seen profound changes in the circumstances of both students and tutors. The unmarried don living in college in close proximity with students has become a rarity. Now party leaders are likely to have a life outside the college and to be raising a family while developing their careers. In that sense Tony Firth and Christopher Cox were unrepresentative post-war leaders and Tony Kenny and Jonathan Barnes examples of how dons' lives were changing. What is remarkable is that despite the conflicting pressures there have been those who were still prepared to add the Chalet to their working life.

Academic employment has also changed significantly since Sligger's time. University staff are now subject to evaluation in which research dominates and teaching is of secondary importance. This is true even of collegiate universities like Oxford and Cambridge; tutors may still have rooms surrounded by those of their students but today these serve largely as offices and teaching rooms because the tutor's research and personal life are likely to lie outside college. The academic environment has moved progressively away from the concept of students and tutors sharing a communal life in the way that Sligger knew and which fuelled his reading parties.

So does it matter that Sligger's vision – or a version of it – survives today on the Prarion? When he began his parties in 1891 the vacation reading party was a ubiquitous practice into which the Chalet fitted comfortably. Now with few exceptions the others have gone. For Sligger the Chalet was a means of providing insight into European culture. Today students have greater opportunity for travel, having access to grants to extend their studies. Moreover, the University itself is now a more international environment; students are likely to number different nationalities among their friends. It can be asked whether ten days' reading in an isolated cabin on a French mountain can compete with the opportunities available now and whether the Chalet has outlived its usefulness. And yet the Chalet has not only survived but thrives; places are regularly oversubscribed and some applicants have to be disappointed. So what are the explanations for this survival and popularity?

During the preparation of this history a number of chaletites responded to a questionnaire seeking answers to these questions.

Replies were invited in alumni circulars and questionnaires were also offered to past chaletites attending college events. Of 106 questionnaires offered, 79 were returned: this is a high response rate for educational survey by questionnaire and almost certainly reflects the affection in which the Chalet is held.[2]

Respondents represent every decade of the post-war parties between 1952 and 2009. Most were able to look back at their time at the Chalet from the perspective of life and career. Asked to identify their abiding memory, one in three chaletites gave being a member of the Chalet's community as the leading feature. This was closely followed in almost equal numbers by appreciation of the value of private study, of group discussion, of the enjoyment of the walks, and of the beauty of the locality.

The strength with which these feelings are held is reflected in the language used in the replies. The common term is 'camaraderie' but others like 'unique', 'a privilege', 'an academic ideal', 'height of college experience', 'a highlight', 'unforgettable' and 'abiding memory' are typical of the warmth which spills out of the replies. Some go further: 'the most impactful educational experience of my life' is one such.[3] New College Warden Miles Young (Chalet 1975–6) would say to anyone going on a party that it was likely to be the best experience of their life.[4] Some found it hard to be selective: 'The personal experiences are too many to choose one. The Chalet changed me and gave me so many memories that I cannot communicate in one thought. To mention one would do the others a disservice.'[5]

That chaletites should be sensitive to a feeling of community at the Chalet is unsurprising in view of the fact that they came from a collegiate university in which the college community is indispensable. On the other hand, this might mean that they would be inclined to take this aspect of Chalet life for granted. As it is, even when compared to life in an Oxford college the Chalet does offer a more closely knit environment. The rustic conditions at the Chalet probably contribute here, despite what the popular perception might be of living conditions in historic Oxford colleges.

As might be expected, Balliol members who attended the Philosophy parties between 1970 and 1995 express strong appreciation of group discussion. However, this is not limited to Balliol but is distributed across the other colleges. Once again, Oxford students may be regarded as having been primed by their experiences in small group tutorials but this does not adequately explain why it remains a powerful memory decades after the event. Similar feelings are expressed on the value of private study, even though preparation of the weekly essay in term might be thought sufficient private study to satisfy anyone. One reason may be that deep reading is best appreciated when it is voluntary: if so the Chalet can be fairly said to contribute to an approach which sees learning as a personal journey, a rationale which would be regarded by an educationist as a high-level approach to learning.[6]

Matthew Taylor (Chalet 1983–5 & 1987) sums this up: 'I think it would be something to do with the difference between term-time experience of Oxford (intense and frenetic, driven by the rush to master reading for a weekly essay) and a more measured way of engaging with study. It felt less "drop dead" serious than weekly tutorials, and therefore you could engage with it in a slightly more reflective way (often in the company of some pretty renowned specialists), while leavening it with the pleasure of being among the mountains in good company.'[7]

While mountain walking may be expected to be popular among the fit young, it is surprising that this is listed as a leading feature by only one in five respondents. Some chaletites indeed report that the Chalet was their introduction to mountain walking and that this became a lifelong interest but it is notable that this aspect of Chalet life has to jostle with the academic aspects for precedence in chaletites' priorities. We are back here to the words Evelyn Waugh put into the mouth of Charles Ryder's father: why should Alpine scenery be conducive to education?

The trustees have long believed that the locality is key to the reading parties' long survival. It is undeniable that the setting is inspiring. As we have seen, there can be a tendency to regard the party as a holiday in a desirable location, especially among those who have not been there; chaletites themselves are better informed that the party, while incorporating some relaxation, would not fall within the conventional definition of a holiday. Even so, the attractions of the locality are borne out by the enthusiasm among chaletites for repeat visits and the number of old members who visit if they are holidaying locally.

In fact, the mountain environment may not be as significant as we have thought. In the early 1970s Ray Ockenden (Chalet 1978) revived reading parties which Wadham College had run in the 1930s, using a coastal house in Cornwall which has also been used by Professor Matthew Leigh of St Anne's College.[8,9] The Wadham parties run along very similar lines to those at the Chalet des Anglais and have persisted, being taken on in succession by Peter Thonemann. It is notable that the reasons both Ray Ockenden and Peter Thonemann give for the popularity and survival of their parties correspond closely to what Chalet trustees also say: tutor–student interactions, shared life, study achievement and camaraderie. It appears, therefore, that although the Chalet des Anglais can boast the incomparable setting of the French Alps, survival of the reading parties may more closely reflect what happens within the Chalet itself.

The mountain environment may, perhaps, contribute at a deeper level. In her moving account of a year with the Chamonix mountain rescue service, the historian Anne Sauvy contrasts movement in modern life towards a materialistic and selfish existence with the effort, discomfort and deprivation that face anyone drawn to mountain life.[10] She concludes that mountains provide a new perspective because they possess a dimension lacking elsewhere in life. As the Indian mountaineer Hari Pal Singh Ahluwalia expressed it, the person who climbs a mountain becomes conscious of his or her smallness and loneliness in the universe and the physical act has a kinship with an inward spiritual journey.[11] Not surprisingly, those who climbed Mont Blanc from the Chalet list this as one of their leading memories.

Although many chaletites mention games like Chalet tennis in their reminiscences, these appear to be of secondary importance. A stronger element which emerges is the sense of being part of history. This is closely related to studying the Chalet diaries since 1891 and is no doubt enhanced by the importance attached to history by Christopher Cox and other leaders.

When chaletites are asked whether the Chalet was important during their time at university one theme emerges above all: the Chalet's role in friendships, either in making new ones or in consolidating existing ones. The majority also report that friendships made at the Chalet are generally lifelong. This is closely related to the sense of community that exists among chaletites as described by Mark Savage (Chalet 1969–75) in a speech at a recent Chalet celebration. Mark commented that when one goes on a trip with a group of unfamiliar people they could be entirely disparate. Attendees at a Chalet event, by contrast, knew that they would meet like-minded people whatever their age or generation.

A remarkable finding is that one in six chaletites report that their reading party was significant in a decision about their future. This is strongest among those who went into teaching, several of whom report using approaches learned at the Chalet. It also appears in some form throughout many answers, such as exploring their subject in greater detail, in-depth discussion, or simply from having the time to reflect on their future. One quote is typical: 'I think that the busy way life is lived today leaves little time for critical thought and reflection. The Chalet allowed me to catch up on my academic reading, reflect on my own learning, plan for the future, and have substantive conversations with peers and tutors about academic subjects.'[3]

Supporters of the University of Oxford would argue that a fundamental element of its approach is that the student is master of his or her own destiny, college teaching being intended to promote self-exploration and self-knowledge. If this is true, or remains at least partly true under the pressures of modern academic life, we can ask why students come to the point of considering their future while in a wooden hut halfway up a mountain where life holds the distractions of strenuous outings, tenuous plumbing and the need to produce that night's dinner. Or is it that uniting in these challenges has a formative influence which goes beyond the needs of the moment? Reading the warmth in which the replies are couched, one can only regret that all the Edwardian reading parties did not survive; they may have made a significant contribution to students' development. To quote one recent chaletite of four seasons: 'The Chalet was a very important experience in my undergraduate time. Whilst studying you fall into a narrow world where your study can become the only thing you think about, the only thing which is important, and your perspective can be narrowed to the belief that it is the only thing which matters. The Chalet offers a beautiful, challenging, funny educational experience which opens up your eyes and mind and gives a totally different perspective to life and community which is uplifting whilst giving you personal challenges, be it physical or mental. Perspective can be a very powerful thing.'[5]

One of the most striking features from these replies is that the spectrum of views remains similar among chaletites from all six decades of the post-war reading parties. The Chalet's impact appears unaltered through years of social change and evolving approaches to education. More striking still is that these replies concur with how Sligger's chaletites reported their experience. One can only conclude that the Chalet offers values which have not been altered by changes in educational or social policy.

Another quality which chaletites report with warmth is the ability to engage with dons in an equal and non-hierarchical way as a form of democratic levelling.[12,13] For some this has resulted in lifelong friendship. A college tutor might argue that this approach is intended in college tutorials but chaletites' responses suggest that in Oxford the effect is not as strong as when experienced at the Chalet. If so, it may reflect the way in which Oxford colleges and their communities have been obliged to change under the force of modern educational policies.

The small group tutorial practised in colleges is essentially Socratic in approach, as Jowett's Hellenism would have recognised. It is a practice which assumes that mutual trust between tutor and student will be based on close contact and understanding between both.[14] The views of chaletites appear to support the case for maintaining such interaction, whatever the challenges to it might be.

This is not the place to debate in detail the pressures on higher education institutions and demand for greater relevance to the needs of society, nor of the changes consequent on restriction in public funding.[15] Especially relevant for Oxford colleges has been increasing competition between universities and a shift away from direct funding of colleges.[16] In this environment it is questioned whether individual or small group tuition is an efficient use of resources. However, tutorials remain popular among students and to preserve these and other aspects of college life colleges have responded with efforts to increase independent income.[17,18] In view of the increasing distance between tutor and student resulting from demands on tutors to meet academic targets, some colleges have employed junior research fellows to bridge the gap, similar to how New College has used them in its reading parties.[18] Despite these efforts the principle of living and learning together is becoming rarer.[19] This is in distinct contrast to the warmth with which chaletites appreciate living and studying together at the Chalet, which indicates that something of value is at risk of being lost.

In 1934 when Jimmy Palmer paid tribute to Sligger's success

with students he said, 'A rich common life is a great achievement.'[20] Responses from today's chaletites show that this remains true despite all the changes in education since then. New College's junior leader Ian Bradley (Chalet 1969–72 & 1974) was in no doubt about this aspect when he wrote in the *Times Higher Education Supplement*: 'Yet however much composition and style has changed since Urquhart's day, the value of reading parties remains the same. They bring students and teachers together in relaxed and informal surroundings with the result, quite apart from academic benefits, that both parties see each other as human beings rather than simply as stereotypes, as is all too easy in the pressures of the university term.'[21]

This concept of bringing student and tutor together informally is today open to question and in modern universities staff would perceive risks in anything resembling fraternisation. According to *The History of the University of Oxford*, in the early 1960s there was no perceived role for reading parties; it states that 'some tutors made well-intentioned but faintly archaic attempts at organising vacation reading parties' but that these did not last very long.[22] (This was when Christopher Cox was campaigning for the Chalet and the remark may have particular reference: this section was authored by President of Corpus Christi College Sir Keith Thomas, who was studying Modern History at Balliol when the post-war parties were beginning.) The Franks Commission enquiry into the role of the University in higher education was told by the Student Council Committee that it saw the role of the don as being limited to instructing the mind. The National Union of Students told the Commission that there was 'a lack of will on both sides' for close contact between tutors and students.[22] The evidence from chaletites runs counter to this and suggests that these views may be short-sighted about the potential benefits.

Insight into these issues also comes from the United States, where colleges are usually only residential but where over recent years moves have been made to introduce a shared collegiate life similar to Oxford and Cambridge. Robert O'Hara, writing from experience at Harvard and a residential college in North Carolina, points to the value of faculty accommodation and social interaction on campus, and of tutors' perceptions of students as individuals rather than classes.[23,24] He argues that colleges should see campus housing and life as part of their academic, not their business, function.[25] These themes are reinforced by Richard J. Light, who analysed the views

of 400 Harvard undergraduates.[26] Light's students report the value
of working in small teams, of shared activities outside study and of
diversity in promoting learning and behavioural changes. This argues
for shared college life in what O'Hara terms a 'Community of Learning'. Mark Ryan's view from experience at Yale is of a heightened
sense of community in which students educate each other in their
journey towards the concept of identity and self, which he sees as the
primary function of the college years.[27] What is shared by all these
observations is that students exposed to equality, bonds of friendship
and shared diversity find that dormant interests and new enthusiasms
are wakened, a formative process in which personal and intellectual
development go hand in hand.

These principles would have been familiar to Sligger and his contemporaries. John Henry Newman, in analysing university life, wrote
that 'the conversation of all is a series of lectures to each, and they
gain for themselves new ideas and views, fresh matter of thought,
and distinct principles for judging and acting, day by day'.[28] The tutor
who is closely engaged with his or her students at a personal level is
an important facilitator in this process. Sligger embodied this concept
in his reading parties and did his utmost to nurture it. The responses
of chaletites up to the present day only reinforce the view that, whatever the challenges or risks, shared collegiate life has an added value
that is worth striving for and preserving in whatever way today's university environment will allow.*

So powerful is chaletites' experience that inevitably there are some
who found themselves out of sympathy with it: these comments are
made rarely in questionnaire returns but appear in other correspondence, although they are not numerous. Tony Kenny estimates that as
many as one in ten of his parties might have felt this way.[29] This has
to be seen in the context that it was possible for members of Balliol
to equate their Philosophy parties with their college work, which
may overestimate the incidence of this response. However, there
have certainly been some for whom the Chalet proved too strong
in character or who found their leaders difficult to tolerate: tutors
like Christopher Cox, who tried strenuously to immerse members

---

*At this point one might also recall that Arthur Hugh Clough, who contributed to
the early concept of reading parties, wrote the line: 'Say not the struggle naught
availeth.'

in the Chalet's traditions, might well not appeal to all tastes. Generally, though, negative reactions are uncommon and most members appreciate the engagement of leaders who are seen to have 'radiated a huge amount of fondness for the Chalet building, the Chalet experience, the surrounding area of beauty and the local people'.[5] Overall it appears understood that leaders are dedicated to students taking full advantage of the Chalet and are genuinely caring of their welfare.[3]

Turning to the leaders' responses to the parties, they also report the outstanding feature to be close interaction with students. It is natural that those who were college chaplains – Christopher Dent,[30] David Burgess,[31] Bill Sykes,[32] Douglas Dupree[33] and Stephen Tucker[34] – would see the Chalet as an extension of their ministry but the feeling is universal among the others. Several emphasise the importance of the Chalet providing a different forum from college. Once again, one could question whether such interaction ought to be part of a college tutor's normal armamentarium but several point to the Chalet's atmosphere and schedule – or lack of it – as being especially contributory: a 'unique forum' in Jack Matthews' view.[35] Adam Swift feels it made a 'huge difference' in relationships, both personally and intellectually,[36] and David Burgess agrees that it allowed greater understanding of the students as well as generating lifelong friendships.[31]

The value of reducing distance between tutor and student is especially appreciated by those who have also been head of their college. For Tony Kenny the advantages came from academic contact that was unencumbered by other demands.[29] More recently Miles Young also picks out the benefits of having unstructured time together.[4] For Balliol's Senior Tutor, Nicola Trott, this community aspect is key: '… each party is different, and builds, almost instantaneously, its own little society. Lots of individual personalities flourish and find a ground there, but we all gather as one fellowship around the *salle à manger* at meal times.'[37] These feelings are so strongly held among leaders that one wonders if there is a case for reintroducing the facility to colleges: after he began leading parties Douglas Dupree started to provide informal lunches for his chaletites back at Balliol.[33] Responses of tutors, like those of students, suggest that the benefits of close interaction should not be abandoned thoughtlessly, whatever the pressures to do so.

As might be expected, leaders like Stephen Tucker and Allen Warren who came under the influence of Christopher Cox say that the parties offer insight into the individual's place in the flow of history. This view is also borne out by chaletites' comments.[34,38] Allen Warren sees participation in a reading party as widening the student's view of the cultural significance of their education and, for the tutor, as having a place in a rationale which sets teaching in the context of all the student's career.[38]

As many chaletites have found, the reading party is an opportunity to extend skills. Increasing one's prowess in cooking without modern aids is an obvious example. Today's students are more independent than their predecessors but such is the nature of modern life that for many things like chopping firewood are new and some learn for the first time how to lay and maintain a wood fire. Some report a more fundamental effect: Mark Slaney (Chalet 1978–9), looking back over a career as a hospital consultant, sees life at the Chalet as emblematic of the striving for achievement which is part of a university degree and a successful career thereafter.[39]

It is testimony to the pressures which have built up in Oxford that the Chalet should be regarded as productive for academic work. The fact is that both chaletites and their leaders find the Chalet a suitable environment for catching up on the previous term's work, or preparing for the next, planning a project or drafting a paper. As one commented, 'It provided a tranquil environment where I could read without any distractions and enabled me to crystallise my thoughts.'[40] The arrival of laptop computers (charging courtesy of the Prarion Hotel) has merely extended this facility: a dissertation may now be completed or a thesis polished in the peace of the mountains.

In the same way that the occasional student may find their leaders difficult to tolerate, those leaders do not always have a smooth ride from chaletites. Occasionally a member can be demanding or disruptive, perhaps taking the view that they are in a hotel provided by their tutors, or – a mercifully rare occurrence in this leader's experience – simply set out to destabilise the party for reasons of their own. Close proximity to each other can be enjoyable and productive but sometimes also wearing. Although getting to know each other better is usually a positive experience, neither students nor leaders are obliged to like what they find. For all that, when asked whether they would recommend leading a party to a colleague, several leaders say that the wish to mix closely with students is the *sine qua non*.

The dedication of the leaders has to be viewed in the light of the significant demands of the role. Before the season there is the selection of applicants, arrangement of finances, organising groceries and supplies and ensuring that members are fully advised on the needs and precautions for their visit. At the Chalet there are the challenges that can arise in an isolated rustic building: failing water supplies, dubious plumbing and drainage and whatever else the mountain environment may throw at the party. There is always the risk of an emergency in remote conditions. The fact that busy academics are prepared not only to take it on but to persevere with it is a tribute to the attractions of the parties, certainly, but also to the character of those leaders.

Sometimes leaders' best efforts can be defeated by circumstance. For example, Keith Dorrington once offered to lead the party down to the village of Servoz *en route* to a day at Lac Vert. This makes an enjoyable descent from the Chalet but ideally requires transport on to the lake. We agreed that I would go down by *télécabine* and meet them with the minibus at the car park on the outskirts of Servoz. When I arrived at the village I stopped for coffee at the café in the centre, as one would in France especially. At this point I had a distress call from one of the party: half the group had become separated and were lost on the mountainside. So, feeling a little like Rommel in the desert, I spread my map over the table, ordered another coffee and settled down to finding out where they were and guiding them down. It became clear that they would approach the village from the opposite direction from that of their colleagues and I had a decision to make: should I stay and provide a focal point for the two groups, or abandon the strays and take the van out to the car park for the others? I decided to sit tight on the basis that if the lost group arrived first I could drive them out to meet the others. Regrettably, Keith's mobile phone failed to make contact on the mountain so I couldn't let him know of these plans.

I had another decision to make when the café began to fill up for lunch. I had no news either of the strays or the main group. It had also started to rain very heavily. Not wishing to appear rude to the café owners, I decided to order lunch and wait further. Unfortunately both groups arrived simultaneously from opposite directions just as my meal was served, so Keith, having been denied a dry pick-up and having trudged through heavy rain from the outskirts of the village, found me dry and comfortable and tucking into a *croûte savoyarde* and glass of wine under a protective awning. He was understand-ably enraged. However, the Chalet's attractions put such days into perspective, and so we keep turning up each year and friendly part-nerships survive.

As we have seen, the life of tutors has changed since Sligger's time and an ever-present anxiety is whether there will be anyone pre-pared to take on the parties in the future; the role is only ever likely to appeal to a minority. Any tutor who accepts leadership of a party today finds this in competition with their academic work and proba-bly also the demands of family life. It is more demanding still when the leader is based outside college, as has been the case for New Col-lege's Stephen Tucker, Allen Warren and Mark Byford. Academics now move posts with greater frequency and a keen leader such as Univ's Tom Smith can be lost when a new position takes them away from Oxford. That said, when vacancies have arisen there has always been someone prepared to accept the challenge and the future can be viewed with optimism. Changes may be needed, as they have been since 1891, but the fundamentals on which the Chalet's popularity is based are likely to endure. As Will Poole expresses it, these values may be at risk of loss generally but they don't have to be lost every-where.[41] Bruce Kinsey takes a similar view: 'I had even heard of the Chalet before I arrived as Chaplain of Balliol, and it did not disappoint when I finally got there. We often talk about community, friendship, and the value of the Oxford experience, but so often the pressure and drive of term and hubbub of college life means there is little time to talk, reflect, relax and read and be the sort of academy we struggle to be. The Chalet offers those times and opportunities, which is why it touches the soul of those who get there.'[42]

Another aspect which helps to explain the affection with which the Chalet is viewed is that it is associated with aspects of living which are not commonly experienced elsewhere. The atmosphere is unique and many chaletites tie their memories to a particular feature: the smell of wood smoke in the salon, late afternoon sunlight slanting through the windows, candlelit dinners, or the smell of morning dew in the undergrowth, for example. Such memory tags are simple but powerful: for Keith Dorrington life at the Chalet is indelibly associated with 'reading in the solitude of my room while wrapped in a blanket and seated in a wicker chair that creaks with every movement'.[43]

Certainly for those who lead parties the Chalet appears to be its own reward. Tony Kenny, writing to support the 2009 appeal, said, 'With the aid of my wife, over the years, I took or attended twenty-five parties … Our guests at these parties – with very few exceptions – delighted in the unique mixture of physical and intellectual excitement in the clear Alpine air surrounded by the glory of the great peaks. Certainly in our own minds those chalet weeks stand out as some of the finest experiences of our lives.'[44] For Tom Smith's brother Ben, who has combined support for Univ parties with the demands of being a hospital consultant, the vision is important; he sees it as a unique opportunity to adapt the Chalet's relevance to today's generation while remaining true to its founding principles, with the outcome of encouraging resourcefulness, collaboration and aspiration to contribute to personal development.[45] It is a pertinent comment that leaders like Will Poole, Mark Byford and Jack Matthews started out as junior members and were inspired to come back as leaders.

It is also a fact that the Chalet proves popular among the heads of colleges, such as Lord and Lady Butler, who were keen to renew their undergraduate experience of the Chalet when Lord Butler became Master of Univ. Other chaletites who came back in the same way have been New College's William Hayter and Harvey McGregor and its current Warden, Miles Young. The Chalet has also appealed to Tony Kenny at Balliol, Alan Ryan at New College and Ivor Crewe at Univ, for whom it was a new experience. That all of them were prepared to add the summer reading party, and in some cases trusteeship, to positions which were already highly demanding is further testimony to the Chalet's impact.

The mountain environment should not be dismissed as a motivating factor. Asked how he would recommend leading a party to a junior fellow, Alan Ryan suggested showing them the view from the hotel (Fig. 57) and he was right: on a fine afternoon this is an unforgettable scene.[46] The Chalet's circumstances, the locality, scenery, the people, even the walk down to it, emerge powerfully from chaletites' reminiscences. Although conditions at the Chalet can be trying, especially in bad weather, the memories which persist are those of clear air, inspiring views and calm sunlit afternoons in quiet study or conversation. Reading the accounts, it is difficult not to feel that through everything the Chalet still retains an echo of the summer house-party atmosphere of Sligger's time.

For myself, I was fortunate to be invited by Keith Dorrington to become involved at a time when I was ready for a new challenge. I did not know when I took up that invitation what the effect would be. The relationship with members of Univ that was born out of that peculiar environment changed my view of what a collegiate university represents. I came to see how the interaction between tutor and student which the college system invites is challenged in Oxford but survives in pure form out on the mountain. It gave me a new understanding of what it meant to be involved in the development of young people, and twenty-five parties later its appeal and effect remain just as strong.

It is worth reiterating that the reading parties have been fortunate in the support they have received from two generations of the Hottegindre family at the Prarion Hotel and from the Boucher family at the neighbouring chalet. It is impossible to say whether the parties would have survived without this but party leaders have known that when difficulties have come – and difficulties on the mountain can be real – they have not been alone in facing them. These conditions have fuelled strong and enduring friendship on both sides: *La Grande Amitié*, as Christopher Cox celebrated it and as it has been known since.

So those of us who currently have the stewardship of this remarkable institution have good cause to understand Sligger and what drove him to persevere with his summer parties on the slopes of Mont Blanc. In doing so we ensure our part in their story while by the same token he and the Chalet become part of ours. The reading parties preserve his tradition despite all the changes they have been through and today they continue to grow organically. Well into its second century the Chalet des Anglais still works its magic on those who go there and its contribution to the lives of students at the University of Oxford, as required by the Trust's objectives, shows no sign of abating.

There is no better example of the regard in which the Chalet is held than the decision of Jen Thum and James Grice to celebrate their marriage there in 2015. An Anglo-American alliance, this was formally celebrated in Central Park in New York but a matching event was needed for European and college friends. James and Jen, having been chaletites and loved the Chalet's environment, decided that the event must be there. This was no small undertaking, either for them or for us: American members of the family naturally wanted to travel over for it and accommodation had to be found locally for a large number of guests.

The Chalet was in the hands of Univ Second Party under the leadership of Keith Dorrington and myself and a day was set aside for the ceremony. The guest list of more than sixty included a large number of previous chaletites whom we were glad to welcome back as well as many who had never been there, some of whom had never before trodden the slopes of a mountain. The delighted exclamations of newcomers as they emerged through the bushes and had their first sight of the Chalet were heart-warming, if familiar to those of us who are old-timers.

Caterers took over the kitchen and dining room, apparently unconstrained by what must have been for them unusually primitive conditions. Rooms were set aside for guests to change and the Chalet resonated to American accents exclaiming things like, 'Can you believe they're not allowed to put the toilet paper down the toilet?!' Sligger came from an era when women dressed formally, even in Alpine conditions, and *The Perfect Chalet-ite* made stipulations on standards of dress but even he cannot have foreseen a large number in wedding outfits contributing to what must surely have been the best-dressed group ever to have assembled at the Chalet.

Jen and James had written a form of service which was conducted on the lawn by Univ's Master, Sir Ivor Crewe (Fig. 105). Our Boucher neighbours from the Chalet du Rocher were appropriately represented by Hugues and Nelleriek's son Frank and his family and after the ceremony everyone repaired to the Chalet for a champagne reception and splendid wedding breakfast. Following the guests' departure for a dance in Chamonix, Univ Second Party subsided into its normal routine; the day had included no reading or walking but even so felt that it had upheld the best traditions of the Chalet and had been one of which Sligger could only have approved.

And so this present history of the Chalet des Anglais ends with an event which is also a beginning for two young people, as has been the case in different ways for so many of those for whom it has been a memorable episode in their lives. Even well into its second century this remarkable institution remains capable of offering something new and valuable to those of us lucky enough to be part of it. *Pace* Evelyn Waugh and his feelings about Sligger, Alpine scenery has indeed proved conducive to education but where the Chalet des Anglais is concerned there has been much, much more to it than that. And long, long may it continue.

APPENDIX ONE

THE PERFECT CHALET-ITE

This text is reproduced from the private printing by Francis Urquhart of 1934. It was also reproduced in *Francis Fortescue Urquhart: A Memoir* by Cyril Bailey, published by Macmillan and Co Ltd in 1936. Macmillan sold the copyright and it has not been possible to trace the current owner. If this becomes known the information will be included in a future edition.

I.   1.- He gives a week's notice before he arrives, at least. And says what train he is coming by. And he does not change his plans at the last moment.
     2.- He brings out one pair of boots, or at least of strong shoes capable of having nails put into them. He brings out flannels and a sweater for cold weather.
     3.- He is prepared, if asked, to bring out golf-balls or other such small things.

II. 1.- If he has registered luggage by Calais or Boulogne to S. Gervais he sees it through the Customs at Calais or Boulogne.
     2.- When he arrives at S. Gervais-les-Bains-Le Fayet, if he is a new arrival, he gives up his luggage and bulletin to the porter of the Hotel du Mont Blanc.
     3.- He comes up to the Village of S. Gervais by cogwheel train (T.M.B.) or motor-bus as the case may be. At the Village, if he is a perfect man, as well as a perfect Chalet-ite, he is sure to be met.
     4.- If, by some accident, he should not be met he leaves his belongings at the Hotel du Mont Blanc (they will come up later with his luggage by mule cart) and walks up, asking his way to the Châlet des Mélèzes, or Châlet des Anglais.
     5.- He will not be too impatient with the height he has to walk up, nor with the flies.

6.- He will be glad to arrive at the Chalet.

> N.B.- Even very imperfect Chalet-ites have been known to fulfil II. 6.

> N.B. 2.- It is possible to go by T.M.B. to the Col de Voza from which there is an easy walk to the Chalet. A newcomer should ask the way at the Col de Voza to the Pavillon du Prarion, and there ask the way to the Châlet des Mélèzes. Experienced Chalet-ites can take the T.M.B. to Motivon Station.

III. AT THE CHALET

1.- The P.C.-ite will not burn down the Chalet. He will even be extra careful not to do so. Reading in bed with the candle on the pillow may be dangerous.

2.- The P.C.-ite will have *immense consideration** for the feelings of the servants and of the people generally. He will call them 'Monsieur' or 'Madame' and take off his hat even to men. He will say 'Bon jour' or 'Bon soir' to complete strangers, etc.

> N.B.- The manners of the people used to be very good, but owing to the invasion (*v. sub.*) they have got gradually worse – and are bad. Out on the mountain and some way from the Village these courtesies are still observed.

> * The Perfect Chalet-ite, as he is a very intelligent and thoughtful young man, will realize that when a number of young men are gathered together, especially in a rather out-of-way place, there is a great danger of their getting slack and indifferent in many of the little observances of social life, and that it is important to react against this and keep up a certain standard: for instance, he will wear a coat at luncheon and, as a symbol of respect for the others, he will wear a tie at dinner, he will be decent even in hot weather, he will not make too much noise when going to bed, remembering that the servants go to bed early and that the house is very 'transparent' to sound. A party keeps together on better terms and gets through more work if its members practise self-restraint in these small but important things.

3.- The P.C.-ite will remember that the staff is small and will be prepared to help the maid in all kinds of small ways, keeping his room tidy, keeping his bath towel clean by not leaving it on the floor, not being too particular about clean plates for every course.

4.- The P.C.-ite will not bump his head on the staircase more than once.

5.- The P.C.-ite will try to keep the sitting-room tidy by not leaving coats, etc., lying about – he will try to keep it clean by sweeping out gravel, etc., he will wipe his shoes at the door. He will try to prevent its looking like a cricket pavilion.

N.B.- Kitchen tennis is apt to make shoes very gritty.

6.- *In the Bath*. The P.C.-ite will not leave the soap in the brass bowl. He will see that the inside door of the bath is shut when he turns on the shower. He will do the first part of his drying before he comes out of the wet part of the bath, so as not to make too much of a mess in the dry part.

The traditional, and correct, form of washing is not to make a soapy mess in the big bowl, but to mix hot and cold water *there*, to throw some of it over the body, with the brass bowl, and then to soap. Clean water can then be thrown over the body. Thus the body is washed in clean and not in dirty water.

7.- The plu-Perfect Chalet-ite has a cold shower every morning.

8.- When there is a fire in the sitting-room the P.C.-ite won't expect the staff to look after it, but will light it, get wood from the 'bucher' himself, etc.

IV. WORK, GAMES, ETC.

The P.C.-ite will be careful not to talk too much during worktime. It can be very annoying to other people and yet the victims don't like to protest.

1.- Work should, if possible, start by 9.

2.- A break in the middle of the morning is generally taken by the P.C.-ite about 11. And he will distribute or consume a limited amount of chocolate.

3.- The P.C.-ite will normally work between tea and dinner – but in very hot weather he will sometimes go out then and read earlier.

4.- The P.C.-ite will frequently declare that a run down to the Village with the post and a walk up with the incoming post is an excellent form of exercise. He will almost as frequently practise this exercise. Another P.C.-ite will accompany him.

N.B.- Post at S. G. in about 12. Post out about 5.

5.- All ball-games played on the lawn, such as hockey, cricket, etc., will remind the P.C.-ite of the danger of breaking windows and the great inconvenience of broken windows. The P.C.-ite will shut the shutters. The P.C-ite when playing Chalet golf will be particularly careful about windows – especially when approaching the 6th hole from down the bank. Even a careless drive, at the 2nd or 9th hole may be disastrous.

6.- After dinner the P.C.-ite will enjoy a reasonable mixture of talk and work. He will, perhaps, occasionally play cards, knowing that if they are played constantly they become the habit of a group and break up the party. 'Card playing', he will say with perhaps some sententiousness, 'is the enemy both of conversation and of reading.'

7.- The P.C.-ite will sometimes have very good talks at the Chalet.

V. ON THE MOUNTAIN

1.- The P.C.-ite will very soon learn the names of the various mountains within view – if there is any one to tell him! He will learn the names of characteristic places and chalets on the mountain – e.g. Lachat, La Charme, Polypody rocks, the Col, etc. He will be familiar with the different peaks on Mt. Blanc and he will discover as many faces as he can in the Aravis ridge after sunset.

2.- He will be properly contemptuous of Chamonix.

3.- When out for long walks the P.C.-ite will aim at the following virtues:

(a) Start as early as possible – the only limit is the temper of the less P.C.-ites.

(b) Keep the party together.

(c) Keep his eyes open and *see*. The plu-P.C.-ite will be able to find his way back from any long walk.

4.- He will not take liberties with the mountains unless he knows them very well, *e.g.* he will not walk on slippery grass slopes without nails in his shoes.

5.- He will never roll stones down hill-sides even when he thinks the stone is bound to stop within sight.

6.- On the lower slopes where the ground is *cultivated* the

P.C.-ite will not make short cuts across fields even if the crops have been taken in. This refers particularly to the Valleys and to slopes near Villages – *e.g.* going down to S. Gervais. It does not, of course, apply to pastures.

VI. The P.C.-ite will be good-tempered and good-natured – always ready to help – not grumbling too much even in bad weather – ready to enjoy a walk (not too long!) in cloud and rain – open to the influences of the mountain – 'la paix de la grande nature' – ready at times for some thought and meditation.

LAST.- The P.C.-ite will never forget to write his name in the book before leaving.

NOTE

During the 40 years that reading parties have gone on at the Chalet, gratitude is due to its Guardian Angels especially for two things:

A. During all that time there has never been the least scandal, trouble or worry with any of the people of the country, servants or others. The many Chalet-ites (there must have been over 300) have always behaved excellently and have, I believe, a good reputation in the country. My sister tells me she has heard them called 'les beaux jeunes hommes de M. Urquhart' – that also is a reputation! But I think they have a reputation for being ἀγαθοί (1) as well.

B. There has never been any accident on walks or climbs from the Chalet.

The P.C.-ite doesn't '*climb*' much. The Chalet is not a good centre. Climbing takes up time and money, etc. But many Chalet-ites have learnt to love the mountains and a number have taken their first steps in climbing from the Chalet and become good climbers later on. The P.C.-ite is chiefly a *walker* in the Alps.

(1) I suppose scholars will say that 'ἀγαθος' does not mean 'good' – but I don't see why it shouldn't.- F. F. U.

Some books recommended to Perfect and less Perfect
Chalet-ites:

> Doughty's *Wanderings in Arabia*, or *Arabia Deserta*.
> Whymper's *Scrambles in the Alps* – probably still the best
> introduction to Alpine books.
> Stephen Hewett's *Letters from the Front*.
> It is worth reading an ancient *Quarterly Review* article
> "Pedestrianism in the Alps" (or in Switzerland) which will be
> found in the volume of Forbes' Alpine articles.

HISTORY

The original Chalet was built in 1864. It was much smaller
than the present one. The ground plan was about as big as the
present ground plan without dining-room or kitchen. It had
only two storeys. No balcony. It was gradually increased by
adding rooms on ground floor.

'The Chalet' has had two periods.

I.   From its building to 1879. Something about this period can
     be found in Miss Robinson's *Life of David Urquhart* and in
     Mrs. Bishop's *Life of Mrs. Urquhart*.
II. 1891–to the present time.
     In the *interval* the Chalet was only occasionally occupied
     – and the large garden, which stretched right away to the
     'Oxus' below the other Chalet, went wild. The lupins which
     were quite few in the garden spread everywhere.
     In 1891 – The first reading party occurred.
     1892, the year of the 'Catastrophe de S. Gervais' – no one
     was at the Chalet.
     1893 – Reading parties began and have continued ever since,
     except during the War.
     1906 – September – the old Chalet was burnt down.
     1908 – The new Chalet built.
     1909 – Finished and occupied.
     During 1907, 1908 and July 1909, the usual parties lived at the
     other Chalet.
     The 'Invasion'.- The first signs of the invasion of the

Mountain by the outer world was the building of the little
inn on the Col – some time in the 80's.

Other stages in the Invasion are: the railway coming to S.
Gervais-le-Fayet, the cog-wheel railway coming up to the
Col de Voza and the building of the Hotel there.

The immense increase of hotels and villas, in and around S.
Gervais.

The '*Other Chalet*'.- Officially 'Chalet du Rocher', built by
Major Poore, a friend of my father's in 1868. The plans,
building, etc., were looked after by my father.

The Poore family frequently came out in the 70's, but they
ceased coming regularly in the 80's. Wynford Phillips bought
it as a wedding present for his wife. Mrs. Phillips (who
became Lady St. David's), came out fairly often with her
two sons. Both were killed in the War and Lady St. David's
died and Lord St. D. sold the house back for a small sum to
the Poores.

The Poore family have made themselves into a limited
liability Company, 'Poores Ltd.' The eldest son of the late
Major Poore is Gen. Poore – known a number of years
ago as a cricketer, R. M. Poore. One of the daughters is the
Duchess of Hamilton. I have frequently tried to get her sons
to come out, but without success.

The house is sometimes let. The Rev. M. R. Ridley has taken
it once or twice – but it is nearly always shut up.

The corrugated iron roof is the result of the closing of
the slate quarries on the Mountain. Louis Broisat, when
the ugliness of the roof was remarked upon, made the
historic reply, 'Il ne faut pas faire attention à la beauté sur la
montagne.'

SOME WALKS ON OR NEAR THE PRARION

Mainly for New Arrivals

The Col de la Forclaz, between the Prarion and the Tête Noire. Leave by the back gate, down the grass slope and beyond, keeping to the right of the stream till you come to a broad path, almost level, from left to right.

TWO ROUTES

A.　Follow the path towards the right – it will soon become overgrown and turn into rather a rough track but it will take you to the Forclaz. This path was started in 1914 but never finished.

B.　A prettier route. Take a little path which leads obliquely off from A. to the left, keeping round the mountain, but below A. It will lead you to the bottom of the pretty Forclaz Valley and then up to the Col.

FROM THE FORCLAZ

A.　*Up to Tête Noire.-* Worth doing. There is a clearing at the top and a good view. The top of Mt. Blanc is visible and even the Prarion looks impressive.

B.　*Up Prarion.-* From top of pass keeping to the right. There is a slight path, often vanishing. You must keep to the ridge as much as possible, avoiding the practically impenetrable 'vorace' bushes on the right. These make a direct route to the Chalet impossible, or nearly so. It is shorter to go up to the top and down again. A good scramble.

N.B.- On a cloudy and wet day this makes a good scramble the other way. Up to top of Prarion first – then along ridge towards Tête Noire, then down the Arrête, keeping to the right there is a track.

C.　*Round the N. side of Prarion to the Col.*

N.B.- 'The Col' always means the Prarion Col just to the N. of the Pavillon.

Owing to the way in which the slaty rocks of the Prarion slope on the N. side it is impossible – at least *very* troublesome – to go round at more or less the same level. From Forclaz go past the

Old Cross and follow the path to the right a good way down till it comes out of the trees. There you will find raspberry bushes and springs and a path going round the mountain upwards to the left. This will bring you above the Col de Voza.

Or you can work up a shallow green valley to the right, after a bit, which gets steeper and has bushes, but it will bring you straight up to the Col. A path at first – then only a track.

D. TO SERVOZ

Either (*a*) From top of Forclaz take a path leading away to left through the woods. Almost level for some way. Then it comes to a clearing and you must *turn sharp to right and down*. The path zigzags through fields – keep to the right and you will reach a group of chalets with a little Chapel. Pass that and make for a very obvious square white house, *not* a chalet. It is a school and a good landmark. Keep below it and you will find a path leading down a little valley, through woods to a saw mill and the *high road*. Follow this to the left for about half a mile (?) to Servoz Station where you take the road over the bridge to Servoz.

Or (*b*) Go down through the Forclaz pass, past the Old Cross, and follow the path to the *right* – down through the woods till you come into the open, down a bit further near some chalets, then double back to the left and keep right on till you reach the houses and the school described in (*a*).

La Charme, the simplest little walk on a cloud day.

Pass the 'other Chalet', keep straight on, pass the 'La Chat' Chalet, keep on more or less level till the next little chalet ('L'Abbaye'). It is only a 'byre', only cows – no one lives there. There you will find a broad path leading up to the left. Follow it, past a wooden Cross, to La Charme, a big chalet at the end of the mountain, with a hideous corrugated iron roof. From there you can either go up to the top just above it and so home along the top plateau of Prarion, (1) or you can follow a path on the E. side of Prarion which will bring you to the 10th hole.

N.B.- From L'Abbaye there are three paths:

    (a) Just described, going *up*.

    (b) A path zigzagging *down*, which is a way to Motivon Station.

    (c) A little path practically *level* at first, it leads *slowly* down and round. If you follow it round it brings you to some deserted chalets underneath some big slabs of rock, then to woods, through which a little path, almost level, leads you to the end of the mountain and the railway. On the other side of the railway is a sort of terrace of rock good for flowers, jutting out towards Contamines – a pleasant spot. You can come home by crossing the railway again and taking a path which leads up to La Charme (*v. sup.*).

(1) On a really thick cloud day it is possible, with a little ingenuity, to lose one's way (a bit) on this return journey and so make the walk more interesting.

FLOOR PLAN OF THE NEW CHALET OF 1909

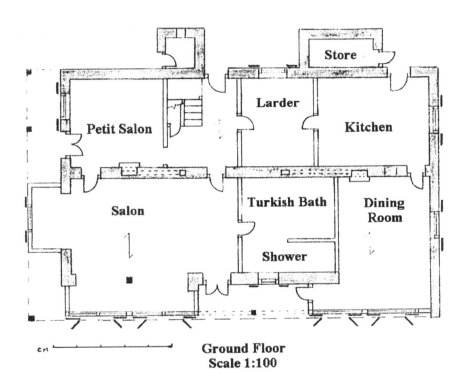

Ground Floor
Scale 1:100

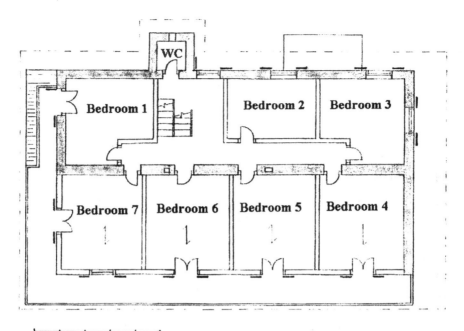

First Floor
Scale 1:100

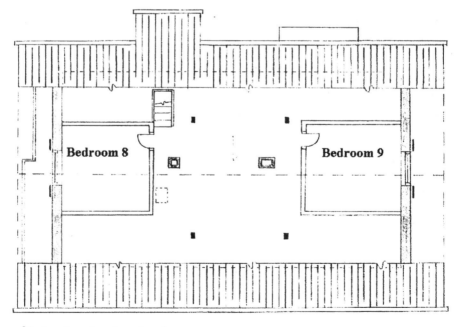

Attic Floor
Scale 1:100

THE CHALET TRUST

Members of the Chalet Trust

1971–1982	Sir Christopher Cox (New College)
1971–1994	Sir Jeremy Lever (All Souls)
1971–1989	Tony Firth (Univ)
1976–1994	Sir Anthony Kenny (Balliol)
1976–1985	Arthur Cooke (New College)
1982–1995	Prof Jonathan Barnes (Balliol)
1982–1997	Prof George Forrest (New College)
1985–2015	Harvey McGregor, QC (New College)
1987–2002	Prof R. Jim Hankinson (Balliol)
1988–1995	Rev Bill Sykes (Univ)
1992 to date	Dr Keith Dorrington (Univ)
1992–2013	Rev Stephen Tucker (New College)
1993–2002	Prof Ngaire Woods (Rhodes House)
1995–2009	Dr Mark Newton (Univ)
1995–2012	Prof Adam Swift (Balliol)
1995–2010	Rev Douglas Dupree (Balliol)
1996–2009	Prof Alan Ryan (New College)
1996–1999	Noel Worswick (New College)
1999 to date	Dr Stephen Golding (Univ)
1999 to date	Prof Dominic O'Brien (Balliol)
2009 to date	Dr William Poole (New College)
2009–2017	Dr Tom Smith (Univ)
2010 to date	Prof Nicola Trott (Balliol)
2013 to date	Dr Mark Byford (New College)
2015 to date	Rev Bruce Kinsey (Balliol)
2017 to date	Dr Jack Matthews (Univ)

Chairmen of the Board of the Chalet Trust

1972–1981   Sir Christopher Cox
1982–1985   Sir Jeremy Lever
1986–1988   Tony Firth
1989   Sir Jeremy Lever
1990   Sir Anthony Kenny
1991   Sir Jeremy Lever
1992   Sir Anthony Kenny
1993   Prof Jonathan Barnes
1994–2015   Harvey McGregor, QC
2015 to date Dr Stephen Golding

Honorary Trustees of the Chalet Trust

Prof R. Jim Hankinson
Rev Bill Sykes (deceased)
Noel Worswick (deceased)

CONTRIBUTORS

Francis Urquhart presented the researcher with a challenge when he instructed Cyril Bailey that after completion of the posthumous *Memoir* all his personal papers and diaries should be destroyed and letters either returned to their authors or destroyed. So I thank the following for having contributed memories and other material. The list is believed to be complete at the time of writing: any inadvertent omission will be corrected in a future edition.

Dr Stephen Adcock
Prof Lincoln Allison
David Anderson
Ros Anderson
Rev Thomas Athill
Andrew Baker
Thomas Baldwin
Catherine Barnes
Prof Jonathan Barnes
Dr Peter Barnes
Dr Christopher and Valerie Bateman
Robert and Paddy Bateman
Prof Melissa Bateson
Nigel Beard
Mark Blythe
Mike Bolton
Ernst Boucher
Frank Boucher
Hugues and Nelleriek Boucher
Dr Lila Boucher
Philippe Boucher

James Bradby
Rev Dr Ian Bradley
Rev Prebendary David Burgess
Lord and Lady Butler of Brockwell
The Very Rev Father Leo Chamberlain
Penny Clement
Terence Coghlan, QC
Martin Conder
Dr Tom Cotton
Daniel Crewe
Prof Sir Ivor Crewe
David Critchley
Thomas Cullen
David Dannreuther
Jon Davies
Hugh Davies-Jones
Rev Canon Christopher Dent
Bruce Dinwiddy, CMG
Dr Keith Dorrington
Alexander Dragonetti

Francine Duffoug
Rev Canon Douglas Dupree
Melanie Eddis
Rt Hon Sir David Edward
Jean Elrington
Dr Simon Esmonde Cleary
Alun Evans
Dr Nick Evans
David Fanthorpe
Dr Adam Fergus
Prof Christopher Fielding
Dr William
    Twistleton-Wykeham-Fiennes
Dr Steb Fisher
Dr Paul Flather
Dr Edward Forman
David Foster
John Fox
Robin Fox
Charles Garland
Kevin Garnett, QC
Philip Gawith
Dr Stuart Golodetz
Peggotty Graham
Drs James Grice and Jen Thum
Rupert Griffin
Rev Tim Haggis
Prof Robert James Hankinson
Prof John Hare
Benjamin Hargreaves
Nicholas Hearn
Prof Tony Hope
Yves Hottegindre
Graham Hoyland
John Hudson
Robert Jordan
Max Jourdier
Andrew Joy
Dr Edward Joy

Caroline Kay
Sir Anthony and Lady Kenny
Rev Bruce Kinsey
David Kirk
Dr Anthony Klouda
Prof David Langslow
Prof Matthew Leigh
Anthea Lepper
Patrick Lepper
Sir Jeremy Lever, QC
Colin Liddell
Christopher Long
Heather Long
Dr David Loughman
David Mack
His Excellency Robert
    McDonagh
David McDonald
Dr Harvey McGregor, QC
Prof Iain McLean
Douglas McNeil
Angus McPhail
Dr Christie Marr
Fabrice Martin
Dr Patrick Martin
Dr Jack Matthews
Barney Mayhew
Felix Mayr-Harting
Sir David Miers
Prof Marcus Miller
Toby Miller
Dr Leslie Mitchell
Joseph Monk
Claire Morris
David Morris
Hugo Morriss
Dr Oswyn Murray
Dr Acer Nethercott
Sir Tim Noble

Sydney Norris
John Norton
Anthony Nowlan
Christopher Oastler
Dr Ray Ockenden
Reggie Oliver
Andrew Orange
Mme Simone
  Orset-Hottegindre
Anthony Parsons
Hephzi Pemberton
Prof Glen Plant
Dr William Poole
Roger Potter
Robert Poynton
Andrew Primrose
Kit Prins
Robin Raw
Christopher Reading
Jonathan Rée
Sir Bernard Rix
Philip Robbins
Stephen Roberts
Dr Claus-Joerg Ruetsch
Prof Ian Rumfitt
Prof Alan Ryan
David Sacks
Dr Michael Samuel
Mark Savage
Nicholas Schlee
Geoff Sharpe
Sir Nigel Sheinwald
John Sherlock
Dr Mark Slaney

Dr Ben Smith
Roger Smith
Dr Tom Smith
Dr Marina Golding Smitherman
Eric Southworth
Mark Studer
Pireeni Sundaralingam
Prof Adam Swift
Rev Bill Sykes
Matthew Taylor
Mr J. L. H. Thomas
Dr Peter Thonemann
Andrew Thornhill, QC
Dr Nicola Trott
Rev Stephen Tucker
Prof Christopher Tyerman
John Vernor Miles
Michael Walker
David Walton
Lt Andrew and Dr Jessica Ward
Dr Allen Warren
Dom Weinberg
Jeremy Welch
Sir Peter Westmacott
Andrew Whiffin
Helen Whittow
Michael Wigan
Prof Rajiva Wijesinha
Gareth Williams
Owain Williams
Dr Heng Wong
Prof John Woodhead-Galloway
Ian Woodward
Miles Young

NOTES

Prologue: A Journey

1   Waugh, E. (2000). *Brideshead Revisited*. Penguin Books, London, p. 62.

Chapter 1. The Fruits of Eccentricity

1   Bishop, M. C. (1897). *Memoir of Mrs Urquhart*. Kegan Paul, Trench, Trübner and Co, London, p. 205.

2   Taylor, M. 'Urquhart, David (1805–1877)'. *Oxford Dictionary of National Biography*, Oxford University Press, 2004. oxforddnb.com/view/article/28017, accessed 24.9.2012.

3   Hopkirk, P. (1990). *The Great Game: On Secret Service in High Asia*. John Murray, London, pp. 153–61.

4   Briggs, A. (1958). 'David Urquhart and the West Riding Foreign Affairs Committees'. *The Bradford Antiquary*, 39, 1–11.

5   Robinson, G. (1920). *David Urquhart: Victorian Knight Errant*. Blackwell, Oxford, p. 135.

6   Urquhart, D. (1850). 'The Bath', in *The Pillars of Hercules; or, a narrative of travels in Spain and Morocco in 1848*. Richard Bentley, London, Vol 2, Chapter 8, pp. 33–88.

7   *Manual of the Turkish Bath. Heat a mode of cure and a source of strength for men and animals, from the writings of Mr Urquhart*, ed. Sir John Fife. John Churchill and Sons, London, 1865.

8   Shifrin, M. (2015). *Victorian Turkish Baths*. Historic England, Swindon, pp. 30–37.

9   Ibid., p. 34.

10 Ibid., p. 64–9.

11 Ibid., p. 84.

12 Bishop, p. 2.

13 Shifrin, p. 239.

14 'The Death of William Urquhart, or, Karl Marx loved a good gossip'. www.victorianturkishbath.org/3TOPICS/AtoZArts/BabySF.htm, accessed 4.1.2014.

15 Shifrin, p. 298.

16 Bishop, p. 193.

17 Ibid., p. 203.

18 Rowlinson, J. S. (1998). '"Our Common Room in Geneva" and the early exploration of the Alps of Savoy'. *Notes Rec. Royal Society of London*, 52, 221–35.

19 Ring, J. (2000). *How the English Made the Alps*. John Murray, London, pp. 20–22.

20 Ibid., pp. 31–5.

21 Swinglehurst, E. (1982). *Cook's Tours: The Story of Popular Travel*. Blandford Press, Poole, p. 37.

22 Bishop, p. 206.

23 Wills, A. (1860). *'The Eagle's Nest' in the Valley of Sixt; a summer home among the Alps*. Longman, Green and Roberts, London.

24 Cook, E. (1968). *The Life of John Ruskin*. Ardent Media, London, pp. 62–4.

25 Bishop, p. 208.

26 Robinson, p. 206.

27 Bishop, p. 219.

28 Bailey, C. (1936). *Francis Fortescue Urquhart: A Memoir*. Macmillan and Co Ltd, London, p. 65.

29 Shifrin, p. 76.

30 Bailey, p. 190.

31 Jones, D. L. 'Philipps, John Wynford, 1st Viscount St Davids, 13th Baronet, of Picton Castle, (1860–1938)'. *Dictionary of Welsh Biography*, 2008. biography.wales/article/s6-PHIL-WYN-1860, accessed 1.8.2019.

32 Institut Géographique National Carte de Randonnée No 3531ET: St-Gervais-les-Bains, Massif du Mont Blanc.

33 Oxford, Balliol College, Papers of David Urquhart, I.L.3. Letter from David Urquhart to Robert Poore, dated 20 June (year unknown).

34 Bailey, p. 127.

35 Oxford, Balliol College, Papers of David Urquhart, I.L.3. Letter from David Urquhart to Robert Poore, dated October 1868.

36 Bishop, pp. 331–4.

37 Ibid., p. 244.

38 Ibid., p. 272.

39 Ibid., p. 341.

40 Ibid., p. 356.

41 Bailey, p. 11.

42 HM Courts and Tribunals Service: Will of Harriet Angelina Urquhart, dated 13 December 1877.

43 Goldstein, E. 'Tyrrell, William George, Baron Tyrrell (1866–1947)'. *Oxford Dictionary of National Biography*, Oxford University Press, 2004. doi.org/10.1093/ref:odnb/36608, accessed 24.9.2012.

44 Drumm, W. (1991). *The Old Palace: A History of the Oxford University Catholic Chaplaincy*. Veritas Publications, Dublin, p. 24.

45   Ibid., p. 33.

46   Bailey, p. 27.

47   Faber, G. (1957). *Jowett: A Portrait with Background*. Faber and Faber, London, pp. 186–9.

48   Clough, A. H. (1849). *The Bothie of Toper-na-fuosich: a long-vacation pastoral*. John Bartlett, Cambridge, MA.

49   Bailey, p. 25.

50   Fletcher, F. (1937). *After Many Days: A Schoolmaster's Memories*. Robert Hale and Co, London, p. 63.

51   Bailey, p. 26.

52   Powell, A. (2001). *To Keep the Ball Rolling: The Memoirs of Anthony Powell*. University of Chicago Press, Chicago, p. 81.

53   Oxford, Balliol College, Chalet papers, I.1.3.1.7. Letter from David Urquhart junior to Francis Urquhart, dated 11 July 1893.

54   Oxford, New College Archives: PA/Cox 2/13/4/337. Letter from Francis Urquhart to Christopher Cox, dated 29 April 1934.

55   'Obituary: Gerard Craig Sellar', *Spectator*, 30 November 1929, p. 815.

56   Oxford, Balliol College, Papers of Cyril Bailey, 1/1. Unpublished autobiography by Cyril Bailey.

57   Bailey, C. (1938). 'The Treasures of the Humble'. *The Alpine Journal*, 50, p. 193.

58   Granville-Barker, H. 'Trench, (Frederic) Herbert (1865–1923)'. *Oxford Dictionary of National Biography*, Oxford University Press, 2004. doi.org/10.1093/ref:odnb/36551, accessed 6.8.2019.

59   Personal communication, Robin Fox.

60   Oxford, Balliol College, Papers of Cyril Bailey, 5/26. Letter from Cyril Bailey to his mother, dated 5 September (year unknown).

Chapter 2. The Reading Parties

1   Oxford, Balliol College, Papers of Cyril Bailey, 1/1. Unpublished autobiography by Cyril Bailey.

2   Oxford, Balliol College, Papers of Cyril Bailey, 5/22. Letter from Cyril Bailey to his mother, dated 2 June 1912.

3   Oxford, Balliol College, Papers of Cyril Bailey, 5/22. Letter from Gemma Bailey to Mrs Bailey, dated 3 June 1912.

4   Durier, C. (1892). 'La Catastrophe de Saint-Gervais-Les-Bains, Juillet 1892'. *Le Tour du Monde*, 64, 417–32.

5   Mathews, C. E. (1900). *The Annals of Mont Blanc*. L. C. Page and Co, Boston, p. 241.

6   Studdert-Kennedy, G. 'Palmer, Edwin James (1869–1954)'. *Oxford Dictionary of National Biography*, Oxford University Press, 2004. doi.org/10.1093/ref:odnb/38837, accessed 3.11.2016.

7   Oxford, Balliol College, Papers of Cyril Bailey, 5/25. Letter from Cyril Bailey to his mother, dated 1 August 1897.

8   Oxford, Balliol College, Chalet papers, 245/4. Letter from S. Llewellyn to J. Jones, dated 3 November 1997.

9   Oxford, Balliol College, Chalet papers, I.1.3.1.7. Letter from David Urquhart junior to Francis Urquhart, dated 11 July 1893.

10   Record of Martin family births and deaths: kindly supplied by M. Fabrice Martin.

11   Huxley, J. (1970). *Memories*. George Allen and Unwin, London, p. 63.

12   Knatchbull-Hugessen, H. (1949). *Diplomat in Peace and War*. John Murray, London, p. 9.

13   Bailey, C. (1936). *Francis Fortescue Urquhart: A Memoir*. Macmillan and Co Ltd, London, p. 75.

14   Taylor, A. J. P. (1983). *A Personal History*. Hamish Hamilton, London, p. 71.

15   Cadogan, E. (1961). *Before the Deluge: Memories and Reflections, 1880–1914*. John Murray, London, p. 92.

16   Wright, A. (1996). *Foreign Country: The Life of L. P. Hartley*. Andre Deutsch, London, p. 65.

17   Boothby, R. (1977), in *My Oxford*, ed. Ann Thwaite. Robson Books, London, p. 28.

18   Bailey, p. 69.

19   Forbes, J. (1850). *A Physician's Holiday*. John Murray, London, 2nd ed., p. 19.

20   Mollier, C. and Gallay, J-P. (2002). *Au Pays du Mont-Blanc*. Éditions Gallay-Mollier, Chamonix, Sallanches, p. 72.

21   Whymper, E. (1896). *Chamonix and the Range of Mont Blanc*. John Murray, London.

22   Whymper, E. (1910). *Chamonix and the Range of Mont Blanc*. John Murray, London, 2nd ed.

23   Galzin, S. (1986). 'Les Anglais en Savoie'. *L'Histoire en Savoie*, 82, 14.

24   Ring, J. (2000). *How the English Made the Alps*. John Murray, London, p. 54.

25   Ibid., p. 45.

26   Wills, A. (1860). 'The Eagle's Nest' in the Valley of Sixt; a summer home among the Alps. Longman, Green and Roberts, London, p. 103.

27   Baedeker, K. (1907). *Switzerland and the adjacent portions of Italy, Savoy and Tyrol: Handbook for travellers*. Karl Baedeker, Leipzig, London and New York, p. 310.

28   Bailey, p. 189.

29   Oxford, Balliol College, Chalet papers, I.1.4. Deed of sale of the Chalet des Mélèzes from David Urquhart to Francis Urquhart, dated 10 July 1896.

30   Bailey, p. 18.

31   Oxford, Balliol College, Chalet papers, Misc 245/18. Copy of Will of Chichester Fortescue.

32   Crocker, W. (1981). *Travelling Back*. Macmillan, London, p. 33.

33   Drumm, W. (1991). *The Old Palace: A History of the Oxford University Catholic Chaplaincy*. Veritas Publications, Dublin, p. 46.

34   Ibid., pp. 59–60, 93.

35   HM Courts and Tribunals Service: Will of Francis Fortescue Urquhart, dated 19 August 1934. probatesearch.service.gov.uk.

36   Bailey, p. 95.

37   Oxford, Balliol College, Chalet papers, I.1.5. Letter from Humphrey Paul to Francis Urquhart, dated 18 September 1906

38   Kenny, A. (1997). *A Life in Oxford*. John Murray, London, p. 58.

39   Bailey, p. 65.

40   Jones, D. L. 'Philipps, John Wynford, 1st Viscount St Davids, 13th Baronet, of Picton Castle, (1860–1938)'. *Dictionary of Welsh Biography*, 2008. biography.wales/article/s6-PHIL-WYN-1860, accessed 1.8.2019.

41   Oxford, Balliol College, Chalet papers, I.1.3.5.4. Agreement between M. Besia and Francis Urquhart for work on the Chalet, dated 1907.

42   Oxford, Balliol College, Chalet papers, I.1.3.5.5. Agreement between J. A. Bouchard and Francis Urquhart for work on the Chalet, dated 1907.

43   Oxford, Balliol College, Chalet papers, I.1.3.2. Bills and receipts from M. Besia and J. A. Bouchard, dated variously.

44   Bailey, pp. 67–8.

45   Oxford, Balliol College, Chalet papers, I.1.8, I.1.9. Deed of sale of the Chalet de Mont Forchet from Miss Alice le Geyl to Francis Urquhart, dated 28 August 1913, with receipt.

46   Oxford, Balliol College, Chalet papers, I.1.3.5. Bill from Épicerie to Miss le Geyl and Francis Urquhart, dated 4 December 1908.

47   Oxford, Balliol College, Chalet papers, I.1.11. Bill from Alphonse Bouchard to 'M. Eurguard', dated 22 August 1920.

48   Birkenhead, Lord (1969). *The Life of Viscount Monckton of Brenchley*. Weidenfeld and Nicolson, London, p. 43.

49   Oxford, Bodleian Library. Letter from Harold Macmillan to Francis Urquhart, dated 27 July (presumed 1921). MS Macmillan dep c. 452, fol. 181.

Chapter 3. Education and Relationships

1   Thorpe, D. R. (2011). *Supermac*. Pimlico, London, pp 24–8.

2   Ibid., p. 33.

3   Oxford, Bodleian Library. Letter from Harold Macmillan to Francis Urquhart, dated 25 December 1913. MS Macmillan dep c. 452, fol. 28.

4   Thorpe, p. 40–41.

5   Horne, A. (1988). *Macmillan 1894–1956*. Macmillan, London, p. 23.

6   Oxford, Bodleian Library. Letter from Harold Macmillan to Francis Urquhart, dated 10 December 1912. MS Macmillan dep c. 452, fol. 5.

7　Oxford, Bodleian Library. Letter from Harold Macmillan to Francis Urquhart, dated April 1913. MS Macmillan dep c. 452, fols 13 & 14.

8　Thorpe, p. 39.

9　Oxford, Bodleian Library. Letter from Harold Macmillan to Francis Urquhart, undated. MS Macmillan dep c. 452, fol. 14.

10　Oxford, Bodleian Library. Letter from Harold Macmillan to his mother, undated. MS Macmillan dep c. 4526, fol. 241.

11　Oxford, Balliol College, Photograph albums of Francis Urquhart, Vol 6.

12　Oxford, Bodleian Library. Letter from Harold Macmillan to Francis Urquhart, 4 August 1913. MS Macmillan dep c. 452, fol. 16.

13　Horne, p. 27.

14　Oxford, Bodleian Library. Letter from Harold Macmillan to Francis Urquhart, undated. MS Macmillan dep c. 452, fol. 52.

15　Thorpe, p. 44.

16　Oxford, Bodleian Library. Note of Harold Macmillan to Francis Urquhart from RMS *Empress of France*, undated. MS Macmillan dep c. 452, fol. 161.

17　Elmhirst, W. (1969). *A Freshman's Diary 1911–1912*. Blackwell, Oxford.

18　Boase, T. S. R. (1934). Quoted in Bailey, C. (1936). *Francis Fortescue Urquhart: A Memoir*. Macmillan and Co Ltd, London, p. 42.

19　Massey, R. (1977), in *My Oxford*, ed. Ann Thwaite. Robson Books, London, p. 43.

20　Bailey, C. (1936). *Francis Fortescue Urquhart: A Memoir*. Macmillan and Co Ltd, London, p. 52.

21　Oxford, Balliol College, Chalet papers, Misc 245/43. Letter from Philip Mason to John Jones, dated 19 July 1997.

22　Annan, N. (1990). *Our Age: Portrait of a Generation*. Weidenfeld and Nicolson, London, p. 19.

23　Personal communication: Dr Allen Warren quoting A. J. P. Taylor.

24　Jones, L. E. (1956). *An Edwardian Youth*. Macmillan and Co Ltd, London, pp. 32–4.

25　Pryce-Jones, D. (1983). *Cyril Connolly: Journal and Memoir*. Collins, London, p. 83.

26　Mason, P. (1978). *A Shaft of Sunlight: Memories of a Varied Life*. Andre Deutsch, London, p. 58.

27　Clifford, P. R. (1994). *An Ecumenical Pilgrimage*. West Ham Central Mission, London, p. 30.

28　Bailey, p. 28.

29　Crocker, W. (1981). *Travelling Back*. Macmillan, London, p. 33.

30　Oxford, Balliol College, Chalet papers, Misc 245/43. Letter from Herbert Scheftel to John Jones, dated 29 July 1997.

31　Oxford, Balliol College, Chalet papers, Misc 245/43. Letter from Percy Wykes to John Jones, dated 11 August 1997.

32   Boothby, R. (1977), in *My Oxford*, ed. Ann Thwaite. Robson Books, London, p. 28.

33   Grimond, J. (1977), in ibid., p. 111.

34   Oxford, Balliol College, Chalet papers, Misc 245/19. Letter from Lord Hailsham to John Jones, dated 29 July 1997.

35   Clark, K. (1974). *Another Part of the Wood: A Self-portrait*. John Murray, London, p. 95.

36   Fisher, C. (1995). *Cyril Connolly*. St Martin's Press, New York, p. 57.

37   Lees-Milne, J. (1980). *Harold Nicolson: A Biography*. Chatto and Windus, London, p. 21.

38   Berlin, I. (1981). *Personal Impressions*. Hogarth Press, London, p. 93.

39   Radic, T. (ed.) (2004). *Race Against Time: The Diaries of F. S. Kelly*. National Library of Australia, Canberra.

40   Quennell, P. (1973). 'A Kingdom of Cockayne', in *Evelyn Waugh and his World*, ed. D. Pryce-Jones. Weidenfeld and Nicolson, London, p. 37.

41   Connon, B. (1991). *Beverley Nichols: A Life*. Constable, London, p. 82.

42   Oxford, Balliol College, Chalet papers, Misc 245/43. Letter from Walter Crocker to John Jones, dated 29 July 1997.

43   Mitchell, L. (2009). *Maurice Bowra: A Life*. Oxford University Press, Oxford, p. 133.

44   Ibid., p. 58.

45   Ibid., p. 161.

46   Personal communication: Dr Leslie Mitchell.

47   Bowra, M. (1966). *Memories 1898–1939*. Weidenfeld and Nicolson, London, p. 120.

48   Betjeman, J. (1977). *Summoned by Bells*. John Murray, London, p. 104.

49   Grimond, J. (1979). *Memoirs*. Heinemann, London, p. 57.

50   Snow, P. (1999). 'Decadent Decade?' *Oxford Today*, Michaelmas 1999. Wiley-Blackwell, Oxford.

51   Carpenter, H. (1990). *The Brideshead Generation*. Houghton Mifflin Company, Boston, p. 90.

52   Jones, J. (1997). *Balliol College: A History*. Oxford University Press, Oxford, 2nd ed., p. 261.

53   Braham, T. (2004). *When the Alps Cast Their Spell*. Neil Wilson Publishing, Glasgow, p. 30.

54   Forsey, E. (1990). *A Life on the Fringe*. Oxford University Press, Toronto, p. 39.

55   Hart-Davis, R. (1986). *The Lyttelton Hart-Davis Letters*, Vols 3 & 4. John Murray, London, p. 198.

56   Powell, A. (1983). *To Keep the Ball Rolling: The Memoirs of Anthony Powell* (rev. ed.). University of Chicago Press, Chicago, p. 81.

57   Hart-Davis, p. 196.

58   Carpenter, pp. 84–7.

59 Mosley, C. (ed.) (2010). *The Letters of Nancy Mitford and Evelyn Waugh*. Penguin Books, London, p. 357.

60 Waugh, E. (2005). *Two Lives*. Continuum, London, p. 298.

61 Huxley, J. (1970). *Memories*. George Allen and Unwin, London, p. 64.

62 Hastings, M. (2010). *Finest Years: Churchill as Warlord 1940–45*. HarperPress, London, p. 92.

63 Annan, p. 43.

64 Dowling, L. (1994). *Hellenism and Homosexuality in Victorian Oxford*. Cornell University Press, Ithaca, pp. 64–6.

65 Ibid., p. 72.

66 Ibid., p. 32.

67 Ibid., p. 86.

68 Rees, G. (1972). *A Chapter of Accidents*. Chatto and Windus, London, p. 62.

69 Ibid., p. 91–4.

70 Betjeman, J. (1977), in *My Oxford*, ed. Ann Thwaite. Robson Books, London, p. 65.

71 MacNeice, L. (1982). *The Strings are False: An Unfinished Autobiography*. Faber and Faber, London.

72 Quennell, P. (1976). *The Marble Foot: An Autobiography, 1905–1938*. Collins, London, p. 123.

73 Blakiston, N. (ed.) (1975). *A Romantic Friendship*. Constable, London.

74 Lewis, J. (1997). *Cyril Connolly: A Life*. Jonathan Cape, London, p. 92.

75 Pryce-Jones, D. (1983). *Cyril Connolly: Journal and Memoir*. Collins, London, p. 60.

76 Fisher, p. 65.

77 Pryce-Jones. *Cyril Connolly*, pp. 68–9.

78 Oxford, Bodleian Library. Letter from Harold Macmillan to Francis Urquhart, dated 23 June 1916. MS Macmillan dep c. 452, fol. 120.

79 Oxford, Bodleian Library. Letter from Harold Macmillan to Francis Urquhart, dated 11 September 1916. MS Macmillan dep c. 452, fol. 116.

80 Oxford, Bodleian Library. Letter from Harold Macmillan to Francis Urquhart, dated 19 October 1916. MS Macmillan dep c. 452, fol. 124.

81 Oxford, Bodleian Library. Letter from Harold Macmillan to Francis Urquhart, dated 11 February (year not stated). MS Macmillan dep c. 452, fol. 143.

82 Oxford, Bodleian Library. Letter from Harold Macmillan to Francis Urquhart, dated 29 September (year not stated). MS Macmillan dep c. 452, fol. 159.

83 Oxford, Bodleian Library. Letter from Harold Macmillan to Francis Urquhart, dated 27 July (year not stated). MS Macmillan dep c. 452, fol. 181.

84 Oxford, Bodleian Library. Letter from Harold Macmillan to Francis Urquhart, dated 30 March 1931. MS Macmillan dep c. 452, fol. 231.

85   Oxford, Bodleian Library. Letter from Harold Macmillan to Francis Urquhart, dated 12 September (year not stated). MS Macmillan dep c. 452, fol. 192.

86   Oxford, Bodleian Library. Letter from Harold Macmillan to Francis Urquhart, dated 2 August 1931. MS Macmillan dep c. 452, fol. 227.

87   Lees-Milne, p. 30.

88   Rose, N. (2006). *Harold Nicolson*. Pimlico, London, p. 24.

89   Bailey, p. 101.

90   Jenkins, R. (1986). *Asquith*. Collins, London, p. 23.

91   Bonham Carter, M. and Pottle, M. (eds) (1996). *Lantern Slides: The Diaries and Letters of Violet Bonham Carter 1904–1914*. Weidenfeld and Nicolson, London, p. 107.

92   Jenkins, p. 265.

93   Ibid., p. 262.

94   Pryce-Jones. *Cyril Connolly*, p. 80.

95   Malik, H. S. (1972). *A Little Work, a Little Play*. Bookwise (India) PVT Ltd, New Delhi, p. 56.

96   Ibid., pp. 65–7.

97   Hillier, B. (1988). *Young Betjeman*. John Murray, London, p. 170.

98   Knatchbull-Hugessen, H. (1949). *Diplomat in Peace and War*. John Murray, London, p. 9.

99   Williams, R. (1957). *Gaslight and Shadow: The World of Napoleon III*. Greenwood Press, Connecticut, p. 298.

100   Lukitz, L. 'Bell, Gertrude Margaret Lowthian (1868–1926)'. *Oxford Dictionary of National Biography*, Oxford University Press, 2004. www.oxforddnb.com/view/article/30686, accessed 22.9.2012.

101   George Boyce, D. 'Casement, Roger David (1864–1916)'. *Oxford Dictionary of National Biography*, Oxford University Press, 2004. www.oxforddnb.com/view/article/32320, accessed 14.10.2011.

102   Newcastle University: Gertrude Bell Archive; gertrudebell.ncl.ac.uk/letters.php. Letter from Gertrude Bell to her stepmother, dated 18 August 1900.

103   Newcastle University: Gertrude Bell Archive; gertrudebell.ncl.ac.uk/letters.php. Letter from Gertrude Bell to her stepmother, dated January 1900.

104   Newcastle University: Gertrude Bell Archive; gertrudebell.ncl.ac.uk/letters.php. Letter from Gertrude Bell to her father, dated 21 August 1900.

105   Newcastle University: Gertrude Bell Archive; gertrudebell.ncl.ac.uk/letters.php. Letter from Gertrude Bell to her stepmother, dated 21 August 1904.

106   Hale, K. (ed.) (1998). *Friends and Apostles: The Correspondence of Rupert Brooke and James Strachey, 1905–1914*. Yale University Press, New Haven, p. 275.

107   Elliott, I. (1953). *Balliol College Register*. Oxford University Press, Oxford, p. 150.

108   Macmillan, H. (1966). *Winds of Change*. Macmillan and Co Ltd, London, p. 96.

109   Hassall, C. (1964). *Rupert Brooke: A Biography*. Faber and Faber, London, p. 510.

110 Jones, N. (2014). *Rupert Brooke: Life, Death and Myth*. Head of Zeus, London, p. 374.

111 Ibid., p. 27.

112 Golding, S. and Gillman, P. (2017). 'George Mallory and Francis Urquhart: An Academic Friendship'. *The Alpine Journal 2017*, The Alpine Club, pp. 231–8.

113 Gillman, P. and Gillman, L. (2000). *The Wildest Dream: The Biography of George Mallory*. The Mountaineers Books, Seattle, p. 98.

114 Ibid., p 76.

115 Balliol College Record, Balliol College October 1955. Obituary of Frank Fletcher.

116 Robertson, D. (1969). *George Mallory*. Faber and Faber, London, p. 71.

117 Pye, D. (1927). *George Leigh Mallory: A Memoir*. Republished 2002: Orchid Press, Bangkok, p. 68.

118 Foster, A. J. 'O'Malley, Sir Owen St Clair (1887–1974)'. *Oxford Dictionary of National Biography*, Oxford University Press, 2004. doi.org/10.1093/ref:odnb/64927, accessed 30.1.2020.

119 Bailey, p. 82.

Chapter 4. Between the Wars

1 Urquhart, F. F. (1918). Introduction to *A Scholar's Letters from the Front*. Longmans, Green and Co, London, pp. vii–xvii.

2 Hewett, S. H. (1918, posth). *A Scholar's Letters from the Front*. Longmans, Green and Co, London.

3 Bailey, C. (1936). *Francis Fortescue Urquhart: A Memoir*. Macmillan and Co Ltd, London, p. 52.

4 Ibid., p. 51.

5 Jones, J. (1997). *Balliol College: A History*. Oxford University Press, Oxford, 2nd ed., p. 247.

6 *Balliol College War Memorial Book, 1914–1919*. Printed by Robert Maclehose and Co Ltd, University Press, Glasgow, Vol 2, p. 260.

7 Goldstein, E. 'Tyrrell, William George, Baron Tyrrell (1866–1947)'. *Oxford Dictionary of National Biography*, Oxford University Press, 2004. doi.org/10.1093/ref:odnb/36608, accessed 23.1.2016.

8 Jones, D. L. 'Philipps, John Wynford, 1st Viscount St Davids, 13th Baronet, of Picton Castle, (1860–1938)'. *Dictionary of Welsh Biography*, 2008. biography.wales/article/s6-PHIL-WYN-1860, accessed 1.8.2019.

9 Bailey, p. 190.

10 Jones, J., p. 258.

11 Stewart, J. I. M. (1977), in *My Oxford*, ed. Ann Thwaite. Robson Books, London, p. 83.

12 Wilson, A. (1977), in ibid., p. 92.

13 Annan, N. (1990). *Our Age: Portrait of a Generation*. Weidenfeld and Nicolson, London, p. 47.

14 Pryce-Jones, D. (1983). *Cyril Connolly: Journal and Memoir*. Collins, London, p. 60.

15 Ollard, R. (ed.) (2003). *The Diaries of A. L. Rowse*. Allen Lane, London, p. 112.

16 David Ion Dannreuther: letter to the author of 20 September 2019.

17 David Ion Dannreuther: letter to the author of 12 September 2019.

18 David Ion Dannreuther: letter to the author of 26 September 2019.

19 Lewis, G. (1997). *Lord Hailsham: A Life*. Jonathan Cape, London, p. 41.

20 Hailsham, Lord (1990). *A Sparrow's Flight: Memoirs*. Collins, London, pp. 58–60.

21 Ibid., p. 54.

22 Wright, A. (1996). *Foreign Country: The Life of L. P. Hartley*. Andre Deutsch, London, p. 65.

23 Forsey, E. (1990). *A Life on the Fringe*. Oxford University Press, Toronto, p. 39.

24 Bailey, p. 127.

25 Broisat family papers, kindly supplied by Mme Francine Duffoug.

26 Oxford, Balliol College, Chalet papers, I.1.17.9. Letter from Francis Urquhart to Roger Mynors, dated 28 July 1927.

27 Personal communication: Dr Lila Boucher.

28 Oxford, Balliol College, Chalet papers, I.1.30. Letter from Francis Urquhart to Roger Mynors, dated 15 August (presumed 1933).

29 Jones, J., p. 264.

30 National Archive: catalogue of papers of Robert Montagu Poore and brothers. discovery.nationalarchives.gov.uk/details/r/85719366-7da1-49c8-a5a1-2fa5016b3ef3, accessed 6.5.2020.

31 Grandjacques, G. (2011). 'Le pavillon de Bellevue'. *En Coutère: revue du Club Histoire et Traditions Locales*. MJC, Saint Gervais, 32, 7–11.

32 Oxford, Balliol College, Chalet papers, I.1.4. Deed of sale of the Chalet des Mélèzes from David Urquhart to Francis Urquhart, dated 10 July 1896.

33 Personal communication: Mme Simone Orset-Hottegindre.

34 Orset-Hottegindre, S. (2011). 'Le Prarion'. *En Coutère: revue du Club Histoire et Traditions Locales*. MJC, Saint Gervais, 32, 12–18.

35 Delachat, C. (2009). *Léon Orset: Un Guide d'Autrefois*. Les Héritiers du Mont-Blanc, pp. 85–91.

36 Ibid., pp. 68–79.

37 Bailey, p. 189.

38 Clan Urquhart, at: www.scotsconnection.com/clan_crests/urquhart.htm, accessed 6.5.2020.

39 Bailey, p. 84.

40 Oxford, Balliol College, Chalet papers, I.1.18. Letter from Francis Urquhart to Roger Mynors, dated 11 July 1929.

41 Oxford, Balliol College, Chalet papers, I.1.20. Transcript of French will of Francis Urquhart, made 13 September 1929.

42 Oxford, Balliol College, Chalet papers, Misc 245/43. Letter from Richard Southern to John Jones, dated 21 May 1997.

43 Oxford, New College Archives: PA/Cox 2/13/4/18. Letter from Francis Urquhart to Christopher Cox, dated 3 February 1932.

44 Hart, H. L. A. (1982). Sir Christopher Cox. New College Record 1982, p. 10.

45 Oxford, New College Archives: PA/Cox 2/3/8/288. Letter from Tom Boase to 'Richard', dated 22 August 1932.

46 Oxford, New College Archives: PA/Cox 2/13/4/319. Letter from Francis Urquhart to Christopher Cox, dated 29 August 1932.

47 Oxford, New College Archives: PA/Cox 2/13/4/320. Letter from Francis Urquhart to Christopher Cox, dated 11 September 1932.

48 Oxford, New College Archives: PA/Cox 2/13/4/322. Letter from Francis Urquhart to Christopher Cox, dated 24 March 1933.

49 Oxford, New College Archives: PA/Cox 2/13/4/323. Letter from Francis Urquhart to Christopher Cox, dated 18 April 1933.

50 Oxford, New College Archives: PA/Cox 2/13/4/332. Letter from Francis Urquhart to Christopher Cox, dated 16 September 1933.

51 Oxford, New College Archives: PA/Cox 2/13/4/325. Letter from Francis Urquhart to Christopher Cox, dated 19 July 1933.

52 Oxford, New College Archives: PA/Cox 2/13/4/327. Letter from Francis Urquhart to Christopher Cox, dated 6 August 1933.

53 Oxford, New College Archives: PA/Cox 8/2/1/unnumbered. Letter from Roger Mynors to Christopher Cox, dated 4 April 1934.

54 Oxford, New College Archives: PA/Cox 2/13/4/337. Letter from Francis Urquhart to Christopher Cox, dated 29 April 1934.

55 Oxford, Balliol College, Chalet papers, MPB/88/6. Correspondence between Francis Urquhart and Morrell, Peel and Gamble, Solicitors, and M. Cordier, Avocat, dated 12 July 1934.

56 Oxford, Balliol College, Chalet papers, I.1.30. Letter from Francis Urquhart to Roger Mynors, dated 15 August 1934.

57 Oxford, Balliol College, Chalet papers, I.1.27. Letter from J. Vulliez to Francis Urquhart, dated 29 August 1934.

58 Oxford, Balliol College, Chalet papers, II.2.3. Letter from Christopher Cox to Roger Mynors, dated 22 September 1934.

59 Personal communication: Mme Simone Orset-Hottegindre.

60 Bailey, pp. 151–2.

61 Oxford, Balliol College, Chalet papers, II.1.1.16. Letter from Gabriel Perroud to Harriet Urquhart, dated 29 September 1934.

62 Oxford, Balliol College, Chalet papers, II.1.1. Memorial notice in *Le Petit Dauphinois*, unnamed.

63 Mathew, T. (1934). 'Francis Urquhart: A Great Oxford Don'. *The Argus* (Melbourne, Victoria), Saturday 1 December 1934, p. 6.

64 Oxford, New College Archives: PA/Cox 8/2/2/unnumbered. Letter from Humphrey Sumner to Christopher Cox, dated 30 December 1935.

65 Perrin, J. (2012). 'John Hoyland: The Missing Dates', in *The Climbing Essays*. Neil Wilson Publishing, Dumfries, pp. 117–24.

66 Smythe, T. (2013). *My Father, Frank: Unresting Spirit of Everest*. Bâton Wicks, Sheffield, pp. 199–200.

67 Hoyland, J. S. (1934). *John Doncaster Hoyland*. Printed for private circulation: Bodleian Library, Oxford.

68 Evershed and Brodie, M. (rev.). 'Somervell, Donald Bradley, Baron Somervell of Harrow (1889–1960)'. *Oxford Dictionary of National Biography*, Oxford University Press, 2004. doi.org/10.1093/ref:odnb/36189, accessed 9.3.2017.

69 *Balliol College Register 1900–1950*. Oxford University Press, Oxford, 1953.

70 Smythe, F. S. (1934). 'The Accident on the S. Face of Mont Blanc'. *Alpine Journal*, 46:249, pp. 415–19.

71 Hoyland, G. (2013). *Last Hours on Everest*. Collins, London, p. 163.

72 Mitchell, L. (1995). A. D. M. Cox. University College Record, October 1995, pp. 25–9.

73 Oxford, Balliol College, Chalet papers, II.2.5.1. Letter from Christopher Cox to Roger Mynors, dated 22 September (year not stated).

74 Oxford, Balliol College, Chalet papers, II.2.5.10. Letter from Christopher Cox to Roger Mynors, dated 22 September 1935.

75 Oxford, New College Archives: PA/Cox 1/2/5/295. Letter from General Robert Montagu Poore to Christopher Cox, dated 17 October 1934.

76 HM Courts and Tribunals Service: Will of Francis Fortescue Urquhart, dated 19 August 1934. probatesearch.service.gov.uk.

77 Oxford, Balliol College, Chalet papers, Misc 80/10. Letter from Roger Mynors to Sir Henry Pelham, dated 20 December 1936.

78 Oxford, New College Archives: PA/Cox 2/10/1/2. Letter from Roger Mynors to Christopher Cox, dated 6 October 1935.

79 Oxford, New College Archives: PA/Cox 2/10/1/3. Letter from Roger Mynors to Christopher Cox, dated 4 September 1936.

80 Oxford, Balliol College, Chalet papers, II.2.18.2. Letter from Christopher Cox to Humphrey Sumner, dated 9 October 1938.

81 Oxford, Balliol College, Chalet papers, II.2.12.2. Letter from Christopher Cox to Roger Mynors, dated 26 September 1937.

82 Oxford, Balliol College, Chalet papers, II.2.5.10. Letter from Christopher Cox to Roger Mynors, dated 26 September 1935.

83 Oxford, Balliol College, Chalet papers, II.2.12.1. Letter from Christopher Cox to Roger Mynors, dated 10 September 1937.

84 Oxford, New College Archives: PA/Cox 2/10/1/4. Letter from Roger Mynors to Christopher Cox, dated 4 September 1935.

85 Oxford, New College Archives: PA/Cox 2/10/8/317. Letter from Richard Pares to Christopher Cox, undated.

86 Personal communication: Mme Simone Orset-Hottegindre.

87 Oxford, Balliol College, Chalet papers, II.2.9.2. Letter from Louis Broisat to Roger Mynors, dated 10 June 1936.

88 Oxford, New College Archives: PA/Cox 2/10/1/11. Letter from Roger Mynors to Christopher Cox, dated 2 January 1936.

89 Oxford, Balliol College, Chalet papers, II.2.13. Letter from Louis Broisat to Roger Mynors, dated 30 September 1936.

90 Oxford, New College Archives: SC/C1/10/1/1. Letter from Frank Lepper to Aidan White, postmarked 28 July 1938.

91 Oxford, New College Archives: SC/C1/10/1/2. Letter from Frank Lepper to Aidan White, postmarked 4 August 1938.

92 Oxford, New College Archives: SC/C1/10/1/3. Letter from Aidan White to his father, Horace White, 1 September 1938.

93 Oxford, New College Archives: SC/C1/10/1/4. Letter from to Aidan White to his father, postmarked 7 September 1938.

94 Oxford, New College Archives: SC/C1/10/3/5. Handwritten note by Aidan White on copy of *The Times* obituary of David Cox of 4 January 1994.

95 Oxford, New College Archives: SC/C1/10/1/6. Letter from Christopher Cox to Aidan White, dated 19 September 1938.

96 Hansard Report, House of Commons Debate 21 February 1956. api.parliament.uk/historic-hansard/commons/1956/feb/21/industrial-wages, accessed 9.2.2020.

97 Oxford, Balliol College, Chalet papers, II.2.17.2. Letter from Louis Broisat to Roger Mynors, dated 4 January 1939.

Interlude: Sligger and the Chalet in Fiction

1 Ahluwalia, H. P. S. (2003). *Everest: Reflections from the Top*, ed. Christine Gee, Garry Weare and Margaret Gee. Rider, London.

2 Golding S. J. (2021). *That Other Summit: A Story of Man, Mind and Mountain*. Amazon, UK.

3 Bede, C. (1982). *The Adventures of Mr Verdant Green*. Oxford University Press, Oxford (first published in three parts, 1853, 1854 and 1857).

4 Coke, D. F. T. (1906). *The Comedy of Age*. Chapman and Hall, London.

5 Beerbohm, M. (1911). *Zuleika Dobson, or, an Oxford Love Story*. Heinemann, London.

6 Mackenzie, C. (1913). *Sinister Street*. Macdonald and Co, London.

7 Green, M. (1976). *Children of the Sun: A Narrative of 'Decadence' in England after 1918*. Basic Books, New York, p. 188.

8 Gentleman, F. (2018). *The Reading Party*. Muswell Press, London.

9 Sadleir, M. T. H. (1915). *Hyssop: A Novel*. Constable and Co Ltd, London.

10 Sadleir, M. T. H. (1940). *Fanny by Gaslight*. Constable and Co Ltd, London.

11 Pater, W. (1892). *Emerald Uthwart*. Published in *The New Review*, June and July 1892, printed privately for the King's School, Canterbury, 1905.

12 Bowra, M. (1966). *Memories 1898–1939*. Weidenfeld and Nicolson, London, p. 119.

13 Donoghue, D. (1995). *Walter Pater: Lover of Strange Souls*. Alfred A. Knopf, New York, p. 59.

14 Ibid., p. 99.

15 Housman, A. E. (1896). *A Shropshire Lad*. Kegan Paul, Trench, Trübner and Co, London.

16 Dougill, J. (1998). *Oxford in English Literature: The Making, and Undoing, of 'The English Athens'*. University of Michigan Press, Ann Arbor, p. 113.

17 Powell, A. (1983). *To Keep the Ball Rolling: The Memoirs of Anthony Powell* (rev. ed.). University of Chicago Press, Chicago, p 81.

18 Powell, A. (1951). *A Question of Upbringing*. Heinemann, London.

19 Nichols, B. (1922). *Patchwork*. Henry Holt and Co, London.

20 Connon, B. (1991). *Beverley Nichols: A Life*. Constable, London, p. 74.

21 Ibid., p. 83.

22 Waugh, E. (2000). *Brideshead Revisited*. Penguin Books, London.

23 Sykes, C. (1977). *Evelyn Waugh: A Biography*. Penguin Books, London, p. 345.

24 Byrne, P. (2009). *Mad World: Evelyn Waugh and the Secrets of Brideshead*. HarperPress, London, p. 238.

25 *The Scarlet Woman: An Ecclesiastical Melodrama*. Silent film produced privately by Terence Greenidge and Evelyn Waugh in 1924, in DVD transcription from the collection of the late Professor Charles Linck, and kindly supplied by Pamela Cattabiani, Texas A&M University.

26 Linck, C. E. (1969). 'Waugh-Greenidge Film – *The Scarlet Woman*'. *Evelyn Waugh Newsletter*, 3:2. The Evelyn Waugh Society. Available from: leicester. contentdm.oclc.org/digital/collection/p16445coll12/search.

27 Waugh, E. (1964). *A Little Learning*. Chapman and Hall, London, p. 209.

28 Mulvagh, J. (2009). *Madresfield: The Real Brideshead*. ISIS, Oxford, p. 321.

29 Byrne, pp. 62, 151.

30 David, H. (1997). *On Queer Street: A Social History of British Homosexuality, 1895–1995*. HarperCollins, London, p. 15.

31 Sykes, p. 88.

32 Whitemore, H. (1997). *A Letter of Resignation*. Amber Lane Press, Oxford.

33 Thorpe, D. R. (2011). *Supermac*. Pimlico, London, p. 540.

34 Ibid., p 93.

35 Hopkins, G. (1921). *A City in the Foreground*. E. P. Dutton and Co, New York.

36 Inscription by Francis Urquhart in a copy at the Chalet of *The Weather*

Calendar, or a Record of the Weather for every day of the Year, collected and arranged by Mrs Henry Head, Oxford University Press, 1917.

37   Brookfield, A. (2013). 'Lost and Found', in *Oxford's Loudest Laughter*, ed. R. Wijesinha. International Book House, Kurunegala.

38   Oliver, R. (2005). 'The Babe of the Abyss', in *The Complete Symphonies of Adolf Hitler and Other Strange Stories*. Tartarus Press, Leyburn.

39   Personal communication: Reggie Oliver.

40   Personal communication: identity withheld on request.

41   Attallah, N. (2018). No Longer with Us: Encounters with Naim Attallah. Quartet Books, London, pp. 12–13.

42   Villa La Pietra: lapietra.nyu.edu/, accessed 1.5.2020.

43   David, pp. 3–7.

44   Personal communication: Dr Lexie Elliott.

Chapter 5. Renaissance

1   Oxford, Balliol College, Chalet papers, III.1.1. Letter from Meredith Starr to Roger Mynors, dated 20 July 1945.

2   Boulton, J. T. and Robertson, A. (eds) (1985). *The Letters of D. H. Lawrence, Vol 3: October 1916 to June 1921*. Cambridge University Press, Cambridge, pp. 158, 163.

3   'Roland Meredith Starr (aka Hubert Close)'. www.meherbabatravels.com/his-close-ones/men/meredith-starr/, accessed 25.2.2016.

4   Monbaron, S. (1999). *Subud: The Coming Age of New Reality*. Simar Enterprises, Oregon, p. 511.

5   Rodogno, D. (transl. Belton, A.) (2006). *Fascism's European Empire: Italian Occupation during the Second World War*. Cambridge University Press, Cambridge, pp. 361, 395.

6   Personal communication: Mme Francine Duffoug.

7   Personal communication: Mme Simone Orset-Hottegindre.

8   Personal communication: M. Jean Sarraz-Bournet.

9   Cerri, A. 'The Battle of Glieres'. worldatwar.net/article/glieres/index.html, accessed 29.2.2020.

10   Nisbet, R. G. M.. 'Mynors, Sir Roger Aubrey Baskerville (1903–1989)'. *Oxford Dictionary of National Biography*, Oxford University Press, 2004. doi.org/10.1093/ref:odnb/39814, accessed 25.1.2016.

11   Winterbottom, M. (1993). 'Roger Aubrey Baskerville Mynors, 1903–1989'. *Proceedings of the British Academy*, 80, 371–401.

12   Hayter, A. (ed.) (1996). *A Wise Woman: A Memoir of Lavinia Mynors*. Erskine Press, Banham, p. 71.

13   Ibid., p. 290.

14   Oxford, Balliol College, Chalet papers, III.1.5. Letter from R. D. Poore to the Master of Balliol College, dated 26 June 1947.

15 Oxford, Balliol College, Chalet papers, III.1.2.1. Letter from Comte R. de Rohan Chabot to Roger Mynors, dated 30 March 1946.

16 Personal communication: Dr Allen Warren.

17 Oxford, Balliol College, Chalet papers, III.1.6. Letter from F. A. Lepper to Roger Mynors, dated 29 September 1947.

18 Oxford, Balliol College, Chalet papers, III.1.9. Letter from K. C. Lawson to Roger Mynors, dated 13 February 1952.

19 Hayter, p. 105.

20 University College Record 1956. Giles Alington. University College, Oxford, Vol 3, pp. 3–8.

21 Personal communication: Sir David Edward.

22 Personal communication: Sir Jeremy Lever.

23 Oxford, New College Archives: SC/C1/1/2. The Chalet: notes for an Appeal, unnamed, 1967.

24 University College Record 1998. Mr E. S. R. Dammann. University College, Oxford, pp. 131–2.

25 Personal communication: Jean Elrington.

26 Personal communication: John Fox.

27 Personal communication: Roger Smith.

28 Personal communication: Michael Walker.

29 Orset-Hottegindre, S. (2011). 'Le Prarion'. *En Coutère: revue du Club Histoire et Traditions Locales*. MJC, Saint Gervais, 32, 12–18.

30 Personal communication: Dr Lila Boucher.

31 Personal communication: Yves Hottegindre.

32 Oxford, New College Archives: PA/Cox 2/9/2. Letter from Christopher Cox to Frank Lepper, dated 14 November 1945.

33 Whitehead, C. (2003). 'Sir Christopher Cox: An Imperial Patrician of a Different Kind', in *Colonial Educators: The British Indian and Colonial and Education Service 1858–1983*. I. B. Tauris, London, p. 188.

34 Oxford, New College Archives: PA/Cox 8/2/3/unnumbered. Letter from Christopher Cox to Frank Lepper, dated 5 November 1958.

35 Oxford, Balliol College, Chalet papers, III.1.11. Letter from Frank Lepper to Roger Mynors, dated 31 August 1954.

36 Oxford, New College Archives: PA/Cox 8/4/3. Automobile Association Chalet notebook compiled by Jean Elrington and Elizabeth Lepper, also containing correspondence between Frank Lepper and Roger Mynors.

37 Oxford, Balliol College, Chalet papers, III.1.10.2. Letter from Rosemary Ince to Roger Mynors, dated 25 August 1954.

38 Hayter, p. 113.

39 Tyerman, C. J. 'Keen, Maurice Hugh (1933–2012)'. *Oxford Dictionary of National Biography*, Oxford University Press, 2016. doi.org/10.1093/ref:odnb/105559, accessed 16.2.2016.

40 Sedley, S. 'Bingham, Thomas Henry [Tom], Baron Bingham of Cornhill (1933–2010)', *Oxford Dictionary of National Biography*, Oxford University Press, 2014; doi.org/10.1093/ref:odnb/102527, accessed 18.2.2016.

41 Oxford, New College Archives: PA/Cox 8/2/3/unnumbered. Letter from Christopher Cox to Frank Lepper, dated 14 August 1956.

42 Roberts, S. C. (1922). *The Story of Dr Johnson: Being an Introduction to Boswell's Life.* Cambridge University Press, Cambridge, p. 128.

43 Escott, B. E. (2010). *The Heroines of SOE: Britain's Secret Women in France.* The History Press, Stroud, pp. 59–63.

44 Oxford, Balliol College, Chalet papers, III.1.23. Letter from Hugh Keen to Roger Mynors, dated 18 August (year not stated).

45 Cormeau, Y. 'Starr, George Reginald [*alias* Hilaire] (1904–1980)'. *Oxford Dictionary of National Biography*, Oxford University Press, 2004. doi.org/10.1093/ref:odnb/31715, accessed 22.2.2016.

46 Personal communication: Dr Leslie Mitchell.

47 Personal communication: Robert Bateman.

48 Personal communication: George (Rev Fr Leo) Chamberlain.

49 Personal communication: Sir David Miers.

50 Personal communication: Roger Potter.

51 Personal communication: identity withheld on request.

52 Personal communication: Sydney Norris.

53 Personal communication: Mark Savage.

54 Personal communication: Kevin Garnett, QC.

55 Personal communication: Rev Thomas Athill.

56 Personal communication: identity withheld on request.

57 Personal communication: Prof Rajiva Wijesinha.

58 Personal communication: Thomas Cullen.

59 Personal communication: Hugh Davies Jones.

60 University College Record 2002. Mr Anthony Edward Firth. University College, Oxford, pp. 11–14.

61 Personal communication: Sarah Lowry.

62 Personal communication: Rev Dr Ian Bradley.

63 Personal communication: Robin Raw.

64 Oxford, Balliol College, Chalet papers, III.1.18. Letter from Miles Tuely to Roger Mynors, dated 4 September 1962.

65 Oxford, Balliol College, Chalet papers, III.1.15.3. Letter from Christopher Bateman to Roger Mynors, undated.

66 Personal communication: Penny Stanley-Baker.

67 Oxford, Balliol College, Chalet papers, III.1.13.1. Letter from John Buxton to Roger Mynors, dated 31 August 1958.

68 Oxford, Balliol College, Chalet papers, III.1.15.1. Letter from John Buxton to Roger Mynors, dated 16 September 1959.

69   Oxford, New College Archives: PA/Cox 8/2/3/unnumbered. Letter from Christopher Cox to Frank Lepper, dated 20 August 1958.

70   Oxford, New College Archives: PA/Cox 8/2/3/unnumbered. Letter from Christopher Cox to Frank Lepper, dated 4 September 1959.

71   Oxford, Balliol College, Chalet papers, III.1.16. Letter from Christopher Cox to Roger Mynors, dated 27 March 1960.

72   Whitehead, C. (2003). 'Margaret Read: Social Anthropologist Turned Colonial Educator', in *Colonial Educators: The British Indian and Colonial and Education Service 1858–1983*. I. B. Tauris, London, p. 227.

73   Oxford, New College Archives: PA/Cox 8/2/3/unnumbered. Letter from Christopher Cox to Frank Lepper, dated 20 August 1963.

74   'Harold Salvesen: obituary'. *Glasgow Herald*, 2 February 1970.

75   Personal communication: Rev Christopher Dent.

76   Personal communication: Caroline Dalton.

77   Personal communication: Andrew Thornhill, QC.

78   Personal communication: Max Jourdier and Bruce Dinwiddy.

79   Oxford, New College Archives: PA/Cox 8/2/1/unnumbered. Letter from Christopher Cox to John Emmerson, dated 28 August 1970.

80   Personal communication: Prof John Woodhead-Galloway.

81   Lacey, N. (2004). *A Life of H. L. A. Hart*. Oxford University Press, Oxford, p. 108.

82   Oxford, New College Archives: PA/Cox 6/3/unnumbered. Typescript of address given at memorial service for Christopher Cox by Prof Herbert Hart.

83   Personal communication: Miles Young.

84   Personal communication: identity withheld by request.

85   Warren, A. (1982). 'C.W.M.C as *Patron*'. New College Record, New College, Oxford, pp. 17–19.

86   Personal communication: David Fanthorpe.

87   Personal communication: Rev Stephen Tucker.

88   Personal communication: identity withheld on request.

89   Personal communication: Andrew Orange.

90   Whitehead, C. (2003). 'Freda Gwilliam: The "Great Aunt" of British Colonial Education', in *Colonial Educators: The British Indian and Colonial and Education Service 1858–1983*. I. B. Tauris, London, p. 244.

91   Oxford, New College Archives: PA/Cox 8/1/2/unnumbered. Letter from William Hayter to Christopher Cox, dated 10 August (1970 by implication).

92   Oxford, New College Archives: PA/Cox 8/2/3/unnumbered. Letter from Christopher Cox to Frank Lepper, dated 16 August 1969.

93   Oxford, New College Archives: PA/Cox 6/2/3. Letter from Tony Firth to Arthur Cooke, dated 7 July 1982.

94   Oxford, New College Archives: PA/Cox 8/2/3/unnumbered. Letter from Christopher Cox to Frank Lepper, dated 4 August 1966.

95 Oxford, New College Archives: PA/Cox 8/2/3/unnumbered. Letter from Christopher Cox to Frank Lepper, dated 5 August (year not stated).

96 Personal communication: identity withheld on request.

97 Personal communication: Prof Lincoln Allison.

98 'Lever, Sir Jeremy (Frederick)'. *Who's Who*, 2007. Oxford University Press, Oxford, © A & C Black. doi.org/10.1093/ww/9780199540884.013.U24360, accessed 22.5.2020.

99 Oxford, New College Archives: SC/C1/3/1. Letter from Patrick Reilly to Christopher Cox, dated 5 September 1966.

100 Oxford, New College Archives: PA/Cox 8/2/3/unnumbered. Letter from Christopher Cox to Frank Lepper, dated 9 February 1967.

101 Oxford, Balliol College, Chalet papers, III.1.20. Letter from Tony Firth to Roger Mynors, dated 2 October 1967.

102 Oxford, New College Archives: SC/C1/3/1. Letter from Christopher Cox to Patrick Reilly, dated 18 December 1967.

103 Oxford, New College Archives: SC/C1/1/2/unnumbered. Letter from Harold Macmillan to Christopher Cox, dated 9 May 1968.

104 Oxford, Balliol College, Chalet papers, III.1.21. Letter from Tony Firth to Roger Mynors, dated 10 July 1973.

105 Oxford, New College Archives: SC/C1/3/1. Letter from Christopher Cox to Patrick Reilly, dated 18 December 1967.

Chapter 6. The New Order

1   Personal communication: Dr Edward Forman.

2   Personal communication: Miles Young.

3   Personal communication: identity withheld on request.

4   Personal communication: Anthony Nowlan.

5   Report to the Chalet Trustees dated 11 April 1978, kindly supplied by Dr Edward Forman.

6   Oxford, Papers of the Chalet Trust. Minutes of the Chalet Trust meeting of 29 April 1978.

7   Oxford, Papers of the Chalet Trust. 1978 Working Party Report and Accounts, 22 July 1978.

8   Oxford, New College Archives: SC/C1/2/3. Letter from Anthony Kenny to Jeremy Lever, dated 15 September 1978.

9   Oxford, Papers of the Chalet Trust. Letter from Edward Forman to Arthur Cooke, dated 5 April 1982.

10 Oxford, New College Archives: SC/C1/1/2. The Chalet: notes for an Appeal, unnamed, 1967.

11 Oxford, New College Archives: SC/C1/3/2. Letter from Christopher Cox to Patrick Reilly, dated 18 December 1967.

12 Personal communication: Sir Jeremy Lever.

13 Oxford, Papers of the Chalet Trust. Legal Opinion of P. M. F. Horsfield, Lincoln's Inn, to Jeremy Lever dated 4 December 1969.

14 Oxford, Papers of the Chalet Trust. Letter from the Department of Education and Science to Macfarlanes solicitors, dated 11 August 1969.

15 Oxford, Papers of the Chalet Trust. Letter from Macfarlanes solicitors to Jeremy Lever, dated 15 March 1971.

16 Oxford, Papers of the Chalet Trust. Letter from Macfarlanes solicitors to Christopher Cox, dated 23 December 1970.

17 Oxford, Papers of the Chalet Trust. Minutes of the Board meetings of the Chalet des Anglais Co Ltd and the Chalet des Mélèzes Co Ltd on 29 November 1970.

18 Oxford, Papers of the Chalet Trust. Charitable Settlement between Roger Mynors and the Chalet trustees, dated 25 March 1971.

19 Oxford, New College Archives: SC/C1/1/8. Letter from Christopher Cox to Jeremy Lever, dated 5 July 1971.

20 Oxford, Papers of the Chalet Trust. Schedule of fees and disbursements, 1971.

21 Oxford, Papers of the Chalet Trust. Letter from Tony Firth to Christopher Cox, dated 27 July 1971.

22 Oxford, New College Archives: SC/C1/1/8. Letter from Christopher Cox to Henry Dumas of Willis, Faber and Dumas, Ltd, dated 9 December 1971.

23 Oxford, New College Archives: SC/C1/2/11. Letter from Roger Mynors to Tony Firth, dated 26 March 1971.

24 Oxford, New College Archives: PA/Cox 8/2/1/unnumbered. Letter from Christopher Cox to Tony Firth, dated 29 August 1970.

25 Personal communication: Mme Nelleriek Boucher-Verloop.

26 Oxford, Papers of the Chalet Trust. Annual Accounts, 1971–1980.

27 Oxford, New College Archives: PA/Cox 8/2/1/unnumbered. Letter from Tony Firth to Christopher Cox, dated 2 June (presumed 1970).

28 Kenny, A. (2018). *Brief Encounters: Notes from a Philosopher's Diary*. Society for Promoting Christian Knowledge, London, p. 19.

29 Kenny, A. (1997). *A Life in Oxford*. John Murray, London, pp. 60–63.

30 Personal communication: Prof John Hare.

31 Personal communication: Dr Anthony Klouda.

32 Kenny. *Brief Encounters*, p. 84.

33 Personal communication: Mr J. L. H. Thomas.

34 Kenny, *Brief Encounters*, p. 109.

35 Kenny, A. (2007). 'Reminiscences of the Chalet des Anglais', in Balliol College Annual Record, Balliol College, 2007.

36 Oxford, New College Archives: PA/Cox 8/2/1/unnumbered. Letter from Tony Firth to Christopher Cox, dated 10 July 1971.

37 Personal communication: Sir Anthony Kenny.

38 Personal communication: Sir Nigel Sheinwald.

39 Oxford, Balliol College, Chalet papers, Misc 40/12. Protocols of reading parties from 1970–1976.

40 Personal communication: Catherine Barnes.

41 Personal communication: John Sherlock.

42 Personal communication: Rev Christopher Dent.

43 Personal communication: Dr Allen Warren.

44 Personal communication: identity withheld on request.

45 Personal communication: Anthony Nowlan.

46 Personal communication: David Fanthorpe.

47 Personal communication: John Hudson.

48 Personal communication: Andrew Orange.

49 Accounts for New College parties of 1975: kindly supplied by John Sherlock.

50 Letter from Sir Christopher Cox to John Sherlock, dated 21 September 1975: kindly supplied by John Sherlock.

51 Personal communication: identity withheld on request.

52 Personal communication: Andrew Whiffin.

53 Spoof school report on Sir Christopher Cox by Andrew Whiffin: kindly supplied by Dr Edward Forman.

54 Personal communication: Dr David Loughman.

55 Personal communication: Rev Stephen Tucker.

56 Personal communication: Prof Glen Plant.

57 Personal communication: Prof Tony Hope.

58 Personal communication: Dr Leslie Mitchell.

59 Personal communication: James Bradby.

60 Personal communication: Dr Paul Flather

61 Personal communication: Dr Mark Slaney.

62 Gareth Williams, from an oral history session at University College on 9 September 2018.

63 Nigel Beard, from an oral history session at University College on 9 September 2018.

64 Personal communication: Nicholas Hearn.

65 Personal communication: Rev Tim Haggis.

66 Personal communication: Sir Peter Westmacott.

67 Personal communication: Prof Rajiva Wijesinha.

68 Oxford, New College Archives: SC/C1/2/3. Letter from Anthony Kenny to Christopher Cox, dated 23 August 1977.

69 Personal communication: Dr Lila Boucher.

70 Personal communication: Ernst Boucher.

71 The Chalet Trust: report inserted into the diary entry for 1974.

72 Script of speech by Sir Christopher Cox, kindly supplied by Prof Jonathan Barnes.

73 University College Record, 2002. Mr Anthony Edward Firth, obituary, p. 11.

74　Personal communication: Robert Bateman.

75　Personal communication: Toby Miller.

76　Personal communication: Matthew Taylor.

77　Personal communication: Christopher Reading.

78　Personal communication: Dr Ray Ockenden.

79　Oxford, New College Archives: SC/C1/2/3. Notes by Sir Christopher Cox of survey conducted by M. Claude Pognan, dated 27 July 1974.

80　Oxford, New College Archives: SC/C1/2/3. Report by Dr Edward Forman on the state of the Chalet in 1977.

81　Oxford, New College Archives: SC/C1/2/10. Letter from Arthur Cooke to Anthony Kenny, dated 14 July 1981.

82　Oxford, New College Archives: SC/C1/2/3. Memorandum of Sir Christopher Cox, dated 30 May 1979.

83　Oxford, New College Archives: SC/C1/2/4. Letter from Arthur Cooke to Tony Firth, dated 29 July 1980.

84　Oxford, New College Archives: SC/C1/2/10. Letter from Iain McLean to Tony Firth, dated 25 March 1981.

85　Oxford, New College Archives: SC/C1/1/3. Letter from Tony Firth to Christopher Cox, dated 30 July 1974.

86　Oxford, New College Archives: SC/C1/1/3. Letter from Christopher Cox to Tony Firth, dated 9 August 1974.

87　Oxford, New College Archives: SC/C1/1/3. Letter from Tony Firth to Christopher Cox, dated 20 August 1974.

88　Oxford, New College Archives: SC/C1/2/3. Letter from Sir Patrick Reilly to the mayor of Saint Gervais, dated 10 October 1978.

89　Oxford, New College Archives: SC/C1/2/3. Letter from Sir Nicholas Henderson to Sir Patrick Reilly, dated 1 November 1978.

90　Henderson, N. (2000). *Mandarin: The Diaries of Nicholas Henderson*. Phoenix Press, London, p. 227.

91　Oxford, New College Archives: SC/C1/2/3. Letter from Sir Patrick Reilly to Sir Nicholas Henderson, dated 24 November 1978.

92　Oxford, New College Archives: SC/C1/2/3. Letter from Jeremy Lever to Christopher Cox, dated 6 November 1978.

93　Chalet party notes for 1975. Kindly supplied by John Sherlock.

94　Oxford, New College Archives: SC/C1/2/9. Letter from Sir Jeremy Lever to Sir Patrick Reilly, dated 17 December 1982.

95　Personal communication: Ashley Morris.

96　Caroline Kay, from an oral history session at University College on 9 September 2018.

97　Brock, M. (1994). 'The University since 1970', in *The History of the University of Oxford, Vol VIII: The Twentieth Century*. Clarendon Press, Oxford, pp. 746–9.

98 Darwall-Smith, R. (2008). *A History of University College, Oxford*. Oxford University Press, Oxford, p, 514.

99 Personal communication: Prof Iain McLean.

100 Personal communication: Douglas McNeil.

101 Personal communication: Jon Davies.

102 Personal communication: Felix Mayr-Harting.

103 Personal communication: Andrew Baker.

104 Mitchell, L. (2015). Memorial address for Rev William Sykes. University College Record, Oxford, pp. 62–5.

105 Oxford, New College Archives: SC/C1/2/4. Letter from Christopher Cox to Jeremy Lever, dated 6 January 1980.

106 Oxford, New College Archives: SC/C1/2/9. Letter from Christopher Cox to Tony Firth, dated 15 October 1981.

107 Oxford, New College Archives: PA/Cox 6/13. Letter from Bernard de Bunsen to Arthur Cooke, dated 22 July 1982.

108 Oxford, New College Archives: PA/Cox 6/3/unnumbered. Typescript of address given at memorial service for Christopher Cox by Prof Herbert Hart.

109 Oxford, New College Archives: PA/Cox 6/2/28. Letter from Nelleriek Boucher to Arthur Cooke, dated 20 July 1982.

110 Oxford, papers of the Chalet Trust. Minutes of the Board meeting of 20 November 1982.

111 Oxford, New College Archives: PA/Cox 6/2/125. Letter from Iain McGilchrist to Arthur Cooke, dated 8 September 1982.

112 Oxford, New College Archives: PA/Cox 6/2/26. Letter from Arthur Cooke to Anthony Kenny, dated 19 July 1982.

113 Personal communication: Prof Melissa Bateson.

114 Personal communication: Robert Poynton.

115 Oxford, New College Archives: SC/C1/2/11. Letter from Jonathan Barnes to George Forrest, undated.

116 Oxford, New College Archives: SC/C1/2/11. Report from Jeremy Lever to Chalet trustees, dated 7 September 1985.

117 Personal communication: Mike Bolton.

118 Personal communication: Dr Christie Marr.

119 Oxford, papers of the Chalet Trust. Letters and attachments of Prof Roger Lhombreaud inserted into the 1985 diary entry.

120 'Les Français Libres, de juin 1940 à juillet 1943: Roger Lhombreaud.' www. francaislibres.net/liste/fiche.php?index=81520, accessed 26.9.2019.

121 Oxford, papers of the Chalet Trust. Annual Accounts, 1976–1985.

122 Oxford, papers of the Chalet Trust. Minutes of the Board meeting of 21 March 1987.

123 Oxford, papers of the Chalet Trust. Minutes of the Board meeting of 13 December 1986.

124 Unpublished journal of 1987 and 1988 working parties. Kindly supplied by Prof Jonathan Barnes.

125 Personal communication: Matthew Taylor.

126 Personal communication: Charles Garland.

127 Personal communication: Catherine Barnes.

128 Oxford, papers of the Chalet Trust. Minutes of the Board meeting of 10 October 1987.

129 Oxford, papers of the Chalet Trust. Minutes of the Board meeting of 15 December 1990.

130 Oxford, papers of the Chalet Trust. Annual Accounts for 1991.

131 Oxford, papers of the Chalet Trust. Minutes of the Board meeting of 10 October 1988.

132 Oxford, papers of the Chalet Trust. Minutes of the Board meeting of 14 December 1991.

133 Oxford, papers of the Chalet Trust. Annual Accounts for 2001.

134 Oxford, New College Archives: SC/C1/2/4. Letter from Arthur Cooke to Tony Firth, dated 11 July 1982.

135 Personal communication: Mme Simone Orset-Hottegindre.

136 University College Record, 1990. Mr A. M. Stilwell, obituary, p. 114.

137 Oxford, papers of the Chalet Trust. Report of Jeremy Lever to the Board, dated 21 September 1989.

138 University College Record, 1991, frontispiece.

139 Oxford, papers of the Chalet Trust. Letter from Jeremy Lever to the Board, dated 21 September 1989.

140 Personal communication: Prof Ian Rumfitt.

Chapter 7. Renewal

1 University College Record, 2013. Acer Gary Nethercott, pp. 202–5.

2 University College Record, 2013. The Chalet, pp. 71–3.

3 Personal communication: Dr Acer Nethercott.

4 Personal communication: Hephzi Pemberton.

5 Personal communication: Dr Allen Warren.

6 Personal communication: Dom Weinberg.

7 Personal communication: Dr Nicola Trott.

8 Personal communication: identity withheld on request.

9 Personal communication: Sir Anthony Kenny.

10 Personal communication: Rupert Griffin.

11 Personal communication: Dr Edward Joy.

12 Personal communication: Heather Long.

13 Personal communication: Dr Peter Barnes.

14 Personal communication: Alexander Dragonetti.

15 Personal communication: Dr Stuart Golodetz.

16 Personal communication: Dr Marina Golding Smitherman.

17 Personal communication: Sir Ivor Crewe.

18 Personal communication: Gareth Williams.

19 Oxford, papers of the Chalet Trust. Minutes of the Board meeting of 22 October 1994.

20 Oxford, papers of the Chalet Trust. Minutes of the Board meeting of 25 October 1997.

21 Oxford, papers of the Chalet Trust. Minutes of the Board meeting of 10 October 1995.

22 Oxford, papers of the Chalet Trust. Minutes of the Board meeting of 14 September 1996.

23 Oxford, papers of the Chalet Trust. Inspection Report of Mr Richard Pye, dated 1 September 2001.

24 Oxford, papers of the Chalet Trust. Minutes of the Board meeting of 10 November 2001.

25 Oxford, papers of the Chalet Trust. Minutes of the Board meeting of 10 May 2003.

26 Oxford, papers of the Chalet Trust. Minutes of the Board meeting of 16 November 2002.

27 Oxford, papers of the Chalet Trust. Letter from Rupert Griffin to Stephen Golding, dated 26 July 2002.

28 Oxford, New College Archives: SC/C1/6/2. Report to New College, dated September 2002.

29 Oxford, papers of the Chalet Trust. Letter from the Acting Warden of New College to Harvey McGregor, dated 22 May 2003.

30 Oxford, papers of the Chalet Trust. Letter from the Acting Warden of New College to Harvey McGregor, dated 2 June 2003.

31 Oxford, papers of the Chalet Trust. Risk Assessment prepared by Kelly Associates, July 2003.

32 Personal communication: Claire Morris.

33 Oxford, papers of the Chalet Trust. Works programme costs summary, 2002–2007.

34 Oxford, papers of the Chalet Trust. Minutes of the Board meeting of 6 May 2006.

35 Oxford, papers of the Chalet Trust. Appeal brochure, 2008.

36 Oxford, papers of the Chalet Trust. Minutes of the Board meeting of 21 May 2009.

37 Oxford, papers of the Chalet Trust. Annual Accounts for 2010.

38 Oxford, papers of the Chalet Trust. Annual Accounts for 2014.

39 Oxford, papers of the Chalet Trust. Annual Accounts for 2015.

40 Oxford, papers of the Chalet Trust. Letter from David Emmerson to Stephen Golding, dated 1 May 2015.

41 Oxford, papers of the Chalet Trust. Minutes of the Board meeting of 28 October 2006.

42 Oxford, papers of the Chalet Trust. Minutes of the Board meeting of 7 May 2016.

43 Oxford, papers of the Chalet Trust. Minutes of the Board meeting of 29 October 2016.

44 Sauvy, A. (2005). *Mountain Rescue: Chamonix-Mont Blanc*. Bâton Wicks, London, p. 62.

45 Personal communication: Dr William Poole.

46 Personal communication: Sir Ivor Crewe.

47 Personal communication: Dr Paul Flather.

48 Kinder, A. 'Outrage over students "handpicked" for chalet'. *Cherwell*, 21 May 2011. cherwell.org/2011/05/21/outrage-over-students-handpicked-for-chalet/, accessed 23.5.2011.

49 Personal communication: identity withheld on request.

50 Oxford, papers of the Chalet Trust. Minutes of the Board meeting of 21 May 2011.

51 Oxford, Papers of the Chalet Trust. Charitable Settlement between Roger Mynors and the Chalet trustees, dated 25 March 1971.

Epilogue: What Has It Meant?

1 University College Record, 1998. The Chalet, p. 36.

2 Simpson, M. A. (1984). 'How to … Design and Use a Questionnaire in Evaluation and Educational Research'. *Medical Teacher*, 6, 122–7.

3 Personal communication: Dr Marina Smitherman (questionnaire return).

4 Personal communication: Miles Young (interview on 1.2.2019).

5 Personal communication: Claire Morris (questionnaire return).

6 Saljo, R. (1979). 'Learning in the Learner's Perspective'. Reports from the Institute of Education, University of Gothenburg, No 76.

7 Personal communication: Matthew Taylor (questionnaire return).

8 Personal communication: Dr Ray Ockenden and Dr Peter Thonemann (interview on 13.3.2018).

9 Personal communication: Prof Matthew Leigh.

10 Sauvy, A. (2005). *Mountain Rescue: Chamonix-Mont Blanc*. Bâton Wicks, London, pp. 8–9.

11 Ahluwalia, H. P. S. (2003). *Everest: Reflections from the Top*, ed. Christine Gee, Garry Weare and Margaret Gee. Rider, London, p 3.

12 Personal communication: Dr William Twistleton-Wykeham-Fiennes (interview on 22.11.2019).

13 Personal communication: Barney Mayhew (interview on 27.2.2020).

14 Brown, C. M. and Gunderman, R. B. (2020). 'The Socratic Method'. *Academic Radiology*, 27, 1173–4.

15 Tapper, T. and Palfreyman, D. (2000). *Oxford and the Decline of the Collegiate Tradition*. Woburn Press, London, p. vii.

16 Ibid., pp. 167–8.

17 Ibid., p. 177.

18 Ibid., p. 15.

19 Ibid., p. 70.

20 Bailey, C. (1936). *Francis Fortescue Urquhart: A Memoir*. Macmillan and Co Ltd, London, pp. 151–2.

21 Bradley, I. (1974). 'Silent Upon a Peak'. *Times Higher Education Supplement*, August 23 1974, No 149.

22 Thomas, K. (1994). 'College Life, 1945–1970', in *The History of the University of Oxford, Vol VIII: The Twentieth Century*. Clarendon Press, Oxford, p. 200.

23 O'Hara, R. J. (2009). 'How to Build a Residential College'. collegiateway.org/howto, accessed 6.12.2010.

24 O'Hara, R. J. (2009). 'Objections to the Residential College Model'. collegiateway.org/objections/, accessed 6.12.2010.

25 O'Hara, R. J. (2009). 'Four Foundations for the Renewal of University Life'. collegiateway.org/foundations, accessed 6.12.2010.

26 Light, R. J. (2001). *Making the Most of College: Students Speak Their Minds*. Harvard University Press, Cambridge, MA, pp. 75, 98, 173.

27 Ryan, M. B. (2001). *A Collegiate Way of Living*. Jonathan Edwards College, Yale University, New Haven.

28 Newman, J. H. (1873). *The Idea of a University: Defined and Illustrated*. Basil Montagu Pickering, London, pp. vi, 9.

29 Personal communication: Sir Anthony Kenny (questionnaire return).

30 Personal communication: Rev Christopher Dent (questionnaire return).

31 Personal communication: Rev David Burgess.

32 Personal communication: Rev Bill Sykes.

33 Personal communication: Hephzi Nicol (telephone interview on 21.3.2015).

34 Personal communication: Rev Stephen Tucker (questionnaire return).

35 Personal communication: Dr Jack Matthews (questionnaire return).

36 Personal communication: Prof Adam Swift (questionnaire return).

37 Personal communication: Dr Nicola Trott.

38 Personal communication: Dr Allen Warren (interview on 21.6.2016).

39 Personal communication: Dr Mark Slaney.

40 Personal communication: Dr Heng Wong.

41 Personal communication: Dr Will Poole (questionnaire return).

42 Personal communication: Rev Bruce Kinsey.

43 Personal communication: Dr Keith Dorrington.

44 Kenny, A. (2008). Oxford, papers of the Chalet Trust. Appeal brochure, 2008.

45 Personal communication: Ben Smith (questionnaire return).

46 Personal communication: Prof Alan Ryan (questionnaire return).

SOURCES AND SELECT BIBLIOGRAPHY

Sources

The principal documentary sources are *The Chalet Book* (the reading parties' diaries from 1891 to the present day), Francis Urquhart's annotated photograph albums and Cyril Bailey's *Francis Fortescue Urquhart: A Memoir* of 1936. I have drawn extensively on these but to avoid tedious repetition have not referenced them in the text except for particular points or quotations. Archival material is also drawn from the papers of the Chalet, of Cyril Bailey and of Francis Urquhart held by Balliol College and of Christopher Cox held by New College. Papers of the Chalet Trust are held by the Trust and copies of key documents are also lodged in the Archives of Balliol College, New College and University College.

Relevant biographies and autobiographies are referenced in the text. Biographies of many chaletites are in the *Oxford Dictionary of National Biography* and further information is in the Registers published by their colleges.

All the images featuring in the plate sections are from *The Chalet Book*, Francis Urquhart's annotated photograph albums or the author's own collection, unless where noted in the caption. Images of artwork come from those works given to the Chalet by the artists.

Select bibliography

Annan, N. (1999). *The Dons: Mentors, Eccentrics and Geniuses*. HarperCollins, London.

Baedeker, K. (1907). *Switzerland and the adjacent portions of Italy, Savoy and Tyrol: Handbook for travellers*. Karl Baedeker, Leipzig, London and New York.

Bailey, C. (1936). *Francis Fortescue Urquhart: A Memoir*. Macmillan and Co Ltd, London.

Betjeman, J. (1979). *An Oxford University Chest*. Oxford University Press, Oxford.

Bewes, D. (2013). *Slow Train to Switzerland*. Nicholas Brealey Publishing, London and Boston.

Bishop, M. C. (1897). *Memoir of Mrs Urquhart*. Kegan Paul, Trench, Trübner and Co, London.

Braham, T. (2004). *When the Alps Cast Their Spell*. Neil Wilson Publishing, Glasgow.

Carpenter, H. (1990). *The Brideshead Generation*. Houghton Mifflin Company, Boston.

Deslandes, P. R. (2005). *Oxbridge Men: British Masculinity and the Undergraduate Experience, 1850–1920*. Indiana University Press, Bloomington and Indianapolis.

Dougill, J. (1998). *Oxford in English Literature: The Making, and Undoing, of 'The English Athens'*. University of Michigan Press, Ann Arbor.

Dowling, L. (1994). *Hellenism and Homosexuality in Victorian Oxford*. Cornell University Press, Ithaca.

Elmhirst, W. (1969). *A Freshman's Diary 1911–1912*. Blackwell, Oxford.

Hailsham, Lord (1990). *A Sparrow's Flight: Memoirs*. Collins, London.

Hewett, S. H. (1918, posth). *A Scholar's Letters from the Front*. Longmans, Green and Co, London.

Jones, J. (1997). *Balliol College: A History*. Oxford University Press, Oxford, 2nd ed.

Kenny, A. (1991). *Mountains: An Anthology*. John Murray, London.

Kenny, A. (1997). *A Life in Oxford*. John Murray, London.

Kenny, A. (2018). *Brief Encounters: Notes from a Philosopher's Diary*. Society for Promoting Christian Knowledge, London.

Klein, F. (1915). *Diary of a French Army Chaplain*. Translated from *La guerre vue d'une ambulance* by M. Harriet M. Capes. Andrew Melrose, London.

Mathews, C. E. (1900). *The Annals of Mont Blanc*. L. C. Page and Co, Boston.

Proctor, M. R. (1977). *The English University Novel*. Arno Press, New York.

Pryce-Jones, D. (ed.) (1973). *Evelyn Waugh and his World*. Weidenfeld and Nicolson, London.

Pryce-Jones, D. (1983). *Cyril Connolly: Journal and Memoir*. Collins, London.

Ring, J. (2000). *How the English Made the Alps*. John Murray, London.

Robinson, G. (1920). *David Urquhart: Victorian Knight Errant*. Blackwell, Oxford.

Sauvy, A. (2005). *Mountain Rescue: Chamonix-Mont Blanc*. Bâton Wicks, London.

Shifrin, M. (2015). *Victorian Turkish Baths*. Historic England, Swindon.

Snow, P. (1991). *Oxford Observed: Town and Gown*. John Murray, London.

Tapper, T. and Palfreyman, D. (2000). *Oxford and the Decline of the Collegiate Tradition*. Woburn Press, London.

Thwaite, A. (ed.) (1977). *My Oxford*. Robson Books, London.

Whymper, E. (1896). *Chamonix and the Range of Mont Blanc*. John Murray, London.

INDEX

'Aiguilles', 'Cols' and 'Monts' are indexed respectively under A, C and M.
Detailed coverage of a topic is entered in **bold**.
The single initial 'M' after a name signifies 'Monsieur' rather than a given name.
University colleges entered are Oxford colleges unless stated otherwise.